# Talking History

"Together, the contributors to this excellent book trace the evolution of the IHR's seminars across a hundred years, describe and evoke the 'seminar culture' that has always been so vivid and vital part of its purpose and mission, and candidly recognize the challenges that such a 'seminar culture' faces today. This is a very timely and very important work."

**—David Cannadine, President of the British Academy (2017–21) and Director of the Institute of Historical Research, University of London (1998–2003)**

"All historians, no matter what their career stage or area of research, will be enriched and stimulated by reading a volume that shows how historical topics arise and shift alongside the composition of the profession, its political and economic contexts and social conventions. The authors offer a distinctive perspective on both history and historiography. Historians have to start from their own times: *Talking History* helps us understand the past of our field; it offers inspiration and hope for the future."

**—Ludmilla Jordanova, Emeritus Professor of History and Visual Culture at Durham University, UK. Author of *History in Practice* (3rd edition, 2019)**

# Talking History

Seminar Culture at the Institute of Historical Research, 1921–2021

Edited by David Manning

Available to purchase in print or download
for free at https://uolpress.co.uk

First published 2024 by
University of London Press
Senate House, Malet St, London WC1E 7HU

© authors, 2024

The right of the authors to be identified as authors of this Work has been asserted by them in accordance with sections 77 and 78 of the Copyright, Designs and Patents Act 1988.

This book is published under a Creative Commons Attribution-NonCommercial-NoDerivatives 4.0 International (CC BY-NC-ND 4.0) license.

Please note that third-party material reproduced here may not be published under the same license as the rest of this book. If you would like to reuse any third-party material not covered by the book's Creative Commons license, you will need to obtain permission from the copyright holder.

A CIP catalogue record for this book is
available from The British Library.

ISBN 978-1-914477-61-4 (hardback)
ISBN 978-1-915249-04-3 (paperback)
ISBN 978-1-915249-07-4 (.epub)
ISBN 978-1-915249-05-0 (.pdf)
ISBN 978-1-914477-62-1 (.html)

DOI https://doi.org/10.14296/lbja4300

Cover image: Dame Lillian Penson's Seminar [on British foreign policy in the later nineteenth century], June 1957, Dame Lillian is seated on the far left; © Professor Walter L. Arnstein. Institute of Historical Research, Wohl Library: IHR/10/2/2. Reproduced by kind permission of the Institute of Historical Research's Wohl Library and Professor Walter L. Arnstein's family.

Cover design for the University of London Press by Nicky Borowiec.
Book design by Nigel French.
Text set by Westchester Publishing Services in
Meta Serif Pro, designed by Paul D. Hunt.

*For our colleagues, friends and loved ones at
the Institute of Historical Research, past, present and future.*

# Contents

| | |
|---|---|
| *List of figures* | ix |
| *Notes on contributors* | xi |
| *Acknowledgements* | xv |
| *Notes and list of abbreviations* | xvii |
| Introduction<br>*David Manning* | 1 |
| **1.** A history of the history seminar: the 'active life' of historiography at the Institute of Historical Research<br>*David Manning* | 11 |
| **2.** The Italy 1200–1700 Seminar<br>*Trevor Dean and Kate Lowe* | 43 |
| **3.** The Economic and Social History of the Early Modern World Seminar<br>*David Ormrod* | 63 |
| **4.** The British History in the Seventeenth Century Seminar<br>*Jason Peacey* | 91 |
| **5.** The British History in the Long Eighteenth Century Seminar<br>*Penelope J. Corfield* | 115 |
| **6.** The Low Countries History Seminar<br>*Ulrich Tiedau* | 135 |
| **7.** The Modern French History Seminar<br>*Pamela Pilbeam with David Manning* | 157 |
| **8.** The Imperial and World History Seminar<br>*Sarah Stockwell* | 175 |
| **9.** The Postgraduate Seminar in Theory and Method (1986–2008)<br>*Rohan McWilliam* | 201 |
| **10.** The Women's History Seminar<br>*Kelly Boyd* | 223 |

viii CONTENTS

**11.** The IHR's seminar culture: past, present and future –
a round-table discussion 243
*David Bates, Alice Prochaska, Tim Hitchcock, Kate Wilcox,*
*Ellen Smith and Rachel Bynoth, and Claire Langhamer*

*Afterword* 267
*Natalie Thomlinson*
*Index* 271

# List of figures*

**Figure 0.1** The IHR Common Room, *c*.2000.                                  5

**Figure 0.2** Dame Lillian Penson's Seminar [on British foreign
   policy in the later nineteenth century], June 1957.                         5

**Figure 1.1** Blueprint of proposed temporary buildings for the
   'University of London Centre for Advanced Historical Studies'
   [the IHR] by Thompson & Walford Architects, undated
   [*c*.1921].                                                                  16

**Figure 1.2** The temporary building for the IHR on Malet St,
   London, 1926; creator unknown.                                              17

**Figure 1.3** The English History Room in the IHR, 1926; creator
   unknown.                                                                    17

**Figure 1.4** Senate House from the south-west.                               24

**Figure 1.5** a, b and c floor plans for the IHR in the new Senate
   House building, undated [*c*.1930]; creator unknown.                        25

**Figure 3.1** The Economic and Social History of the Early Modern
   World Seminar: chart of the Seminar's convenors, 1974–2020.                 66

**Figure 3.2** The Economic and Social History of the Early Modern
   World Seminar: graph of the Seminar's topics by period.                     67

**Figure 3.3** The Economic and Social History of the Early Modern
   World Seminar: graph of the Seminar's core themes (one):
   agriculture, industry and employment.                                       68

**Figure 3.4** The Economic and Social History of the Early Modern
   World Seminar: graph of the Seminar's core themes (two):
   overseas trade; finance; economic thought and policy.                       70

---

\* With special thanks to the Institute of Historical Research Wohl Library, the
Senate House Library Archives, the University of London and Professor Walter L.
Arnstein's family for kindly granting permission to reproduce the images which
appear in this publication.

**x    LIST OF FIGURES**

**Figure 3.5**  The Economic and Social History of the Early Modern World Seminar: graph of the Seminar's newer themes which experienced significant growth, only to decline in relative importance in the early twenty-first century.    73

**Figure 3.6**  The Economic and Social History of the Early Modern World Seminar: graph of the Seminar's papers by geographical area.    78

# Notes on contributors

**David Bates** is emeritus professor in medieval history at the University of East Anglia. He was director of the Institute of Historical Research (IHR) from 2003 to 2008. He first visited the IHR as a postgraduate student in the late 1960s and has remained in regular contact ever since.

**Kelly Boyd** is senior fellow at the Institute of Historical Research, University of London. Author of *Manliness and the British Story Paper: A Cultural History, 1855–1940* (2003), she also edited the two-volume *Encyclopaedia of Historians and Historical Writing* (1999) and co-edited, with Rohan McWilliam, *The Victorian Studies Reader* (2007). She is reviews editor and a member of the editorial board of *Cultural and Social History*. She is a long-time member and co-convenor of the IHR's Women's History Seminar.

**Rachel Bynoth** is lecturer in design (historical and critical studies) at Bath Spa University. She is an historian of eighteenth- and nineteenth-century social, political and cultural studies, specializing in emotions. She was co-convenor of the IHR's History Lab Seminar for two years, until August 2022.

**Penelope J. Corfield** is emeritus professor of history at Royal Holloway, University of London, and research fellow at Newcastle University. She was president of the British Society for Eighteenth-Century Studies (2008–12), and president of the International Society of the same name (2019–23). An enthusiast for research debates, she has long been active in London's seminar culture, and has, at different times, helped to organize the IHR's seminars in economic history, women's history, and the 'long' eighteenth century, defined broadly to embrace big themes.

**Trevor Dean** is emeritus professor of medieval history at the University of Roehampton. His expertise lies in the history of crime and criminal justice in late medieval Italy. He co-convened the Late Medieval and Early Modern Italy Seminar between 1996 and 2019.

**Tim Hitchcock** is professor emeritus of in digital history at the University of Sussex. He works on eighteenth-century London and digital history. He has co-convened the British History in the Long Eighteenth Century Seminar since 1993, and also helped establish the Postgraduate Seminar in Theory and Method and the Digital History Seminar.

xii NOTES ON CONTRIBUTORS

**Claire Langhamer** is director of the IHR and professor of modern history at the University of London. She is particularly interested in feeling, experience and ordinariness in twentieth-century Britain. She has published on children's writing, love and courtship, happiness, domesticity, emotional politics, emotion in the workplace, and women's leisure. She has a long-term commitment to using and developing the Mass Observation Archive and is a Mass Observation Trustee.

**Kate Lowe** is associate fellow of the Warburg Institute, University of London. She is an Italian Renaissance historian, and has worked on cardinals, nuns, conspiracies, links with Portugal, and sub-Saharan Africans in Renaissance Italy. She co-convened the Late Medieval and Early Modern Italy seminar at the IHR between 1996 and 2019.

**David Manning** is honorary fellow in history at the University of Leicester. His expertise pertains to the history of Christian thought and culture in Britain and the wider English-speaking world, *c.*1600–*c.*1800, and the history of historiography. He is an occasional member of the IHR's Religious History of Britain 1500–1800 Seminar.

**Rohan McWilliam** is professor of modern history at Anglia Ruskin University, Cambridge, and a former president of the British Association for Victorian Studies. He is an historian of British popular politics and popular culture. He founded the IHR's Postgraduate Seminar in Theory and Method in 1986 and ran it for its first year.

**David Ormrod** is emeritus professor of economic and cultural history at the University of Kent, research associate at the Centre for Financial History, Cambridge, and a fellow of the Academy of Social Sciences. He has written in the fields of early modern commercial and agrarian history and the history of art markets. He worked with museum curators and art historians while guest curator at the Museum of London and visiting fellow at the Institute of Historical Research.

**Jason Peacey** is professor of early modern British history at University College, London. His work focuses upon political culture, print and popular politics, in both domestic and wider European settings. He has been a regular attender of the Seventeenth Century British History seminar at the IHR since the early 1990s and has been one of its convenors since 2006.

**Pamela Pilbeam** is professor emeritus of French history at Royal Holloway, University of London. She has been a member of the IHR's Modern French

History Seminar since 1962, first as a PhD student to 1965, and as main convenor, 1974 to 2006. She held an IHR doctoral research fellowship (1964–5) and represented RHUL on the governing body of the IHR from the 1980s to 2006, serving on the IHR subcommittees which awarded postgraduate and research awards. Her past roles also include president of the Society for the Study of French History, Leverhulme emeritus fellow, Fulbright fellow, and founding editor of the Studies in Modern French History book series at Manchester University Press.

**Alice Prochaska** is a modern historian and archivist whose career has been spent mainly in administration. She worked as secretary and librarian at the IHR from 1984 to 1992, then subsequently as director of special collections at the British Library, university librarian at Yale University, and principal of Somerville College, Oxford. She has written on labour history in Britain, compiled guides to sources on US and Irish history, and these days is especially interested in the connections between identity and heritage. She also served on the government-appointed committee on the first National Curriculum in History (1989–90) and later joined two of the official Research Excellence Framework committees.

**Ellen Smith** is an early career researcher and currently teaching fellow in British social history at the University of Leicester. She is a historian of modern Britain and its empire, particularly colonial South Asia in the nineteenth and twentieth centuries. She has published on widowhood and commemoration in imperial contexts, and everyday life in India. She was coconvenor of the IHR's History Lab Seminar between 2020 and 2022 and, at time of writing, was an Arts and Humanities Research Council Midlands4Cities-funded PhD student at the University of Leicester.

**Sarah Stockwell** is professor of the history of empire and decolonisation at King's College, London. She has been a member of the Imperial and World History (formerly Imperial History) Seminar at the IHR since 1992, and a convenor of it for more than twenty years.

**Natalie Thomlinson** is associate professor of modern British cultural history at the University of Reading. She is an historian of feminism and gender in modern Britain, and her books include *Race and Ethnicity in the Women's Movement in England, 1968–93* (2016) and, with Florence Sutcliffe-Braithwaite, *Women and the Miners' Strike, 1984–5* (2023). She is one of the convenors for the IHR's Britain at Home and Abroad Seminar.

**Ulrich Tiedau** is professor of European history at the School of European Languages, Culture and Society (SELCS) of University College London. Since 2006 he is also coordinating editor of *Dutch Crossing: Journal of Low Countries Studies* and since 2011 co-convenor of the IHR's Low Countries History Seminar.

**Kate Wilcox** is library services manager at the Institute of Historical Research Library. She has worked at the IHR library since 2004.

# Acknowledgements

Each and every seminar series at the Institute of Historical Research is associated with a distinct sub-disciplinary field of enquiry and a particular group of people. Whilst interested parties share common ground, their contrasting points of reference and independent spirit make it all but impossible to capture a sense of collective value in a way that will be universally agreeable. Putting together such a unique book as this has involved some trial and error, but what we have achieved has been worth it. I am hugely grateful to all contributors for their insight, effort and patience, especially in putting up with my idiosyncrasies and a process that has been harder and longer than originally envisaged.

The labour of historiography takes time, but time waits for no one. Roger Mettam passed away before his prospective chapter could be realized and I am painfully aware that Roger's death will not have been the only loss suffered by the IHR's membership during the time that it has taken to produce this book. It is, however, in keeping with a study about historians as scholars and people that another would-be contributor, Anne Irfan, stepped away from the project to have a baby. Such experiences give us all pause for thought. I appreciated the generosity shown by both Roger and Anne and wish their respective families well.

The initial stages of this book were planned with the encouragement and assistance of Philip Carter and Julie Spraggon – thanks to both of you. It was a privilege to showcase the work of this book's contributors at the IHR's Centenary Festival at Senate House on 15 July 2022 – thanks to all who made that day so memorable.

I am honoured to have been able to work under the auspices of the Institute of Historical Research and the University of London Press. I wish to extend special thanks to Emma Gallon, Kate Wilcox, Michael Townsend, Zoë Karens and Tim le Goff; and, for much practical and moral support, I am indebted to Penelope Corfield, David Bates and Claire Langhamer.

# Notes and list of abbreviations

Comments regarding 'the seminar' will typically refer to the institution or culture of seminars, rather than a one-off meeting, whilst references to 'the Seminar' will stand as a shorthand for an aforementioned named seminar series. The life dates of scholars have been given when useful, although, judiciously, not in all cases. Other contextual details, including those relating to the personal archives of historians, are equally suggestive rather than exhaustive. For the sake of focus and readability what follows reflects a relatively simple, and at times oversimplified, appreciation of the evolution of the affiliate and constituent colleges, and now member institutions, of the University of London. A deeper awareness of the complex contingencies and fine-grain changes pertinent to understanding a range of issues touched upon by this book – the nomenclature and function of 'supervisors' and 'convenors' to mention just two – require more specialist investigations. The chapter titles, whilst perhaps a little inelegant when presented together here, reflect the current titles of the actual seminar series operating at the IHR.

## List of abbreviations

**IHR**    The Institute of Historical Research, University of London.

**KCL**    King's College (University of) London.

**LSE**    The London School of Economics and Political Science (University of London).

**QMUL**    Queen Mary University of London.

**REF**    The Research Excellence Framework (formerly the Research Assessment Exercise, or RAE).

**RHUL**    Royal Holloway, University of London.

**SAS**    School of Advanced Study, University of London.

**SOAS**    School of Oriental and African Studies, University of London.

**UCL**    University College (University of) London.

# Introduction

## David Manning*

Since its founding in 1921, the Institute of Historical Research has been the most formidable practitioner of the history seminar in the English-speaking world. The significance of this reality has yet to be fully grasped by either the Institute or its stakeholders. Part of the problem is that the life of the IHR's seminars has never been systematically recorded let alone evaluated. But then it is also the case that the venerable institution of *the history seminar* – a conceptual and linguistic abstraction of a complex, multifarious culture – is itself poorly understood. A history of the history seminar is something of a lacuna in not just the histories of historiography, scholarship and education but also the cultural memory of academia. Rectifying this is not easy. A marketized, instrumentalist culture now complicates an appreciation of both the function and value of the history seminar. The praxis of history seminars is changing in ways that are not unrelated to the existential upheavals in university life. Teaching seminars are adapting to 'engagement' and 'employability' agendas as well as a more streamlined approach to studying for assessment, whilst research seminars are suffering from a dearth of time in an historian's working day. It is an open question as to whether such transformations in seminar culture constitute the latest evolution of what historians do, or a more fundamental rupture in proceedings; but ambiguity in this moment is matched by a degree of silence about what is at stake. How can we defend the history seminar properly if we do not know what it is, and how can we understand what it is without an assessment of what it was?

Our book offers a timely intervention. It works with a paucity of sources and resources to cut through uncritical appeals to 'innovative practices' and 'the good old days' to tell a unique story and an imperfect, yet profound, history.

What follows is not the product of any orchestrated plan to commemorate or celebrate the centenary of the IHR with a study of its seminars. The idea for the book emerged in 2020 out of a serendipitous discussion between Penelope Corfield and myself on the history of historiography. This prompted me to reflect not just on the intergenerational nature of our conversation but on our contrasting experiences as members of the IHR. For whilst Penelope has been in the thick of things since the 1970s, my engagement has been very occasional, certainly marginal, and only since the late 2000s. Curiosity combined with a melancholic foreboding, prompted by the COVID-19 pandemic, to force a realization that the absence of a history of the IHR's seminars was lamentable, especially given that an increasing number of their prominent members were retired, or dead. More in hope than expectation, I started contacting past and present seminar convenors – most of whom I did not know personally – with a view to developing a volume of essays that would alleviate this lack in some way. In the midst of the COVID-19 'lockdowns', a project was born through the good will of would-be contributors and nothing more than written (in one case handwritten) correspondence. The initial momentum of my idea turned into a cooperative endeavour that was welcomed and supported by the IHR and the University of London Press. This formative period was destabilized by financial and political turmoil at the University of London's School of Advanced Study (SAS), of which the IHR has been a constituent part since 1994.[1] Restructuring precipitated losses and changes in personnel at Senate House and the IHR's operations were recast by its mission and strategy for the period 2020–2025. Such moves were part and parcel of ongoing challenges to the sustainability of researching and teaching in history and the humanities across the British university sector. This book emerges from these contexts to complement, rather than reflect, the IHR's ambitions for reflection and renewal.

Our project began with a set of guiding principles, but the actual work of preparing the book has involved negotiating and accepting certain realities that have come to determine the composition and condition of our text. The aim from the outset was to establish a critical, evidence-based history of some of the IHR's most long-lived seminar series, working primarily, although not exclusively, with those that started life in the 1920s, 30s and 40s. The feasibility of this design rested entirely on securing contributions from seminar convenors who could make up for the shortage of archival records by utilizing personal memories, papers and contacts to build up a body of hitherto unidentified sources from which to work. It was also necessary to find individuals who were willing and able to take responsibility for preparing and writing a chapter on behalf of the seminar that they were most closely associated with. Initial enthusiasm for the project did not always result in a firm commitment to produce a chapter. The practical challenges did not end there. Colleagues in post had to be willing to write an essay that would not necessarily help them meet their own key performance indicators for the next Research Excellence Framework (REF): the national audit of academic work that determines the allocation of public funding for research amongst British universities. Set against the internal politics of seminar series, it is not always straightforward for any one person to reflect a broader consensual view on how a particular seminar ought to be represented for posterity. And one prospective contributor – Roger Mettam (1939–2022) – sadly passed away before his chapter could be realized. Taken in the round, these points provide some context for how and why our text is the way that it is. The value of our book does not stand or fall on being representative of the IHR's seminars; but there are obvious gaps that would benefit from being filled at some point in the future.

Contributors have been in their element when working as subject specialists who can draw upon their lived experience as convenors and participants of seminars. Yet further research has involved them engaging with unfamiliar types of contemporary sources. This has been tricky. Crucially, though, our aim has never been to produce chapters that resemble specialist journal articles. What we have here will hopefully enhance public discussion, inform undergraduate and postgraduate learning, and inspire further scholarship. Each chapter shows critical intent, but the nature and scope of this endeavour reflects the primary sources available and the inclinations of authors. With a nod to both the individuality of authorial intention and the autonomy of each seminar series within the wider body of the IHR, the methodological design, structure and length of the chapters have not been standardized. And rather than appealing to university employees at 'different career stages', this book advances the work of scholars at different stages of life. Research and reminiscences intermingle as part of an organic open-ended conversation. There is insight and vulnerability in what follows.

Before introducing our chapters and some of their cross-cutting themes, I should say a little more about the IHR and its seminars, albeit with the caveat that a history of the Institute has yet to be written – notwithstanding an illuminating compendium of sources compiled by Debra Birch and Joyce Horn, *The History Laboratory: The Institute of Historical Research 1921–96* (1996), and the multi-authored blog series *From Jazz to Digital: Exploring the Student Contribution at the IHR, 1921–2021* (2021).

4    DAVID MANNING

The founding of the IHR was most certainly a 'landmark in British historiography'.[2] Established by the University of London on Malet Street in Bloomsbury during an era that coincided with the birth of modern postgraduate qualifications in Britain, the Institute quickly became the country's leading proponent of postgraduate study in history. Intriguingly, it was the teaching and learning activities of this enterprise that first gave expression to a fledgling seminar research culture between students and their teachers and amongst teachers themselves. In the first instance, seminars operated as a sort of dissertation supervision in the round, but gradually evolved to encompass other ambitions and activities. Seminar series were differentiated by the historical periods and themes that reflected the expertise of their convenors, who were typically academic staff at the University of London. Seminar groups met regularly, usually once a week or once a fortnight through term time, with some lasting no more than a year or two whilst others developed through several iterations to last for decades. From the very beginning the 'Institute came alive in the late afternoon': students and teachers met together in the Common Room for a cup of tea before participating in lively academic seminars (see Figures 0.1 and 0.2).[3] The form, content and function of these events have changed over the years. There was no simple shift to what might now be thought of as a traditional format of a fifty-minute paper followed by a similar length of time given over to question-led discussion. Nor was there a common linear path for seminars as they moved their emphasis away from postgraduate training towards the research undertaken by academics with a university position. A long view reveals a plurality and fluidity in format, membership and experience; yet the seminars have always been the beating heart of the IHR, and the people involved its lifeblood.

That said, the IHR has never been defined solely by its seminars. From its inception the Institute has had a national remit that has focused on at least three other core activities that reflect the work of the seminars whilst at the same time being somewhat separate from them. One, developing the historian's capacity to undertake research, especially by means of enhancing the IHR's library collections and more recently its digital online resources. Two, enabling historians from across Britain and around the world to connect and collaborate. Three, providing opportunities for historians to engage with representatives of other public institutions. In its own words the IHR is today, as it always has been, the UK's 'national centre for history, dedicated to supporting historians of all kinds'.[4]

Our book complicates and enriches this picture. My own offering presents a history of the history seminar within a political-polemical frame. Trevor Dean and Kate Lowe remarkably draw upon the reminiscences of

**Figure 0.1** The IHR Common Room, *c*.2000; © Kenneth Barr / University of London. Institute of Historical Research, Wohl Library: IHR/10/1/18. Reproduced by kind permission of the Institute of Historical Research's Wohl Library and the University of London.

**Figure 0.2** Dame Lillian Penson's Seminar [on British foreign policy in the later nineteenth century], June 1957. Dame Lillian is seated on the far left; © Professor Walter L. Arnstein. Institute of Historical Research, Wohl Library: IHR/10/2/2. Reproduced by kind permission of the Institute of Historical Research's Wohl Library and Professor Walter L. Arnstein's family.

forty-two people to illuminate the life of the Italy 1200–1700 Seminar and the influence of its founder, Nicolai Rubinstein. David Ormrod's exacting account of the Economic and Social History of the Early Modern World Seminar gives a unique perspective on the relationship between, and evolution of, its named sub-disciplinary fields of enquiry. The intellectual and personal loyalty engendered by the IHR's seminar culture is borne out in Jason Peacey's insightful study of the convenors, audiences and speakers of the British History in the Seventeenth Century Seminar. Penelope Corfield deftly explores the ecology of the British History in the Long Eighteenth Century Seminar, where historiographical developments have come from manifold labours of love that sustain intellectual rigour and friendly camaraderie. Ulrich Tiedau's carefully documented contribution shows how the Low Countries History Seminar was singularly formative in championing Dutch history in the English language. Pamela Pilbeam powerfully encapsulates that varied and enduring spirit of international collaboration at the heart of the IHR's seminar culture, which was been no more apparent than in the workings of the Modern French History Seminar. Sarah Stockwell's elegant reading of the life of the Imperial and World History Seminar establishes both an original study of the British academic world and a revisionist take on the emergence of postcolonial historiography. Rohan McWilliam's fascinating memoir on the Postgraduate Seminar in Theory and Method (1986–2008) recounts both a dramatic moment of reckoning for the IHR's commitment to postgraduate learning and period of methodological innovation. Kelly Boyd's absorbing study of the founding and running of the Women's History Seminar sheds new light on the relationships between feminist history, women's history, gender history and women historians. And a final round-table discussion with contributions from David Bates, Alice Prochaska, Tim Hitchcock, Kate Wilcox, Ellen Smith and Rachel Bynoth, and Claire Langhamer, provides an exceptional blend of sensitive and captivating comment on the past, present and future of seminar culture at the IHR. Natalie Thomlinson's thoughtful Afterword speaks to some of the resonances and silences in and between chapters, to some of the changes and continuities in the IHR's seminar culture.

Here a range of cross-cutting themes give way to stimuli for further study and research. The rise and fall of the IHR's modernist *raison d'être* takes on new meaning amidst a crisis in twenty-first-century meta-modernism. The IHR's seminar culture speaks to an original and significant history of British historiography in national and global contexts, from the early twentieth to the early twenty-first century. The seminars have been an extraordinary home to visitors and immigrants from abroad, servicing diverse national, international and transnational histories whilst also informing the making and breaking of colonial historiographies.

The seminars are a continuing wellspring of manifold experiences of learning that have contributed to the wider intellectual culture of London, Britain, Europe, North America and much of the English-speaking world. And the seminars bear witness to the enduring import of women historians. What constitutes 'research', 'teaching' and 'learning' in history must now be reassessed in light of the lives of historians, experienced both synchronically and diachronically. Historians can now be seen anew as both the subjects and objects of 'history'. Seeing ideas and phenomena associated with precarity, employment, inclusivity, professionalization, training, networking and public service evolve through contrasting iterations of meaning from one generation to the next is both interesting and challenging. The extent to which the IHR's historians have participated in the intellectual, political and cultural life of countries around the world puts to shame some of our present-day contrivances for identifying and evidencing the 'impact' of historical studies. Understanding the Institute's seminars as an academic resource that works in concert with the books and manuscripts at the British Library and other London-based archives is just as important as appreciating their position within the University of London. The interplay between oral–aural and reading–writing worlds is freshly appraised as essential to making historians and historiography. The labour of historians involves the head and the heart and gives way to histories of work, sociability and relationships, as well as eating, drinking and smoking. Historiography does not just have an intellectual history; it has a spatial, emotional, experiential and sensual history too. The way in which each generation of seminar participants has been both indebted to its forebears and yet also unaware of earlier precedents for some of the things it comes to be concerned with, or advocate for, is quite striking. Cultural memory is selective and fragile. In summary, the significance of the IHR's seminar culture is not derived from its foundational myth or its present-centred mission and strategy, but rather emerges from, and is sustained by, the ongoing learning practices of historians as *scholars and people*. What follows serves as a refreshingly novel and organic take on the perennial question *what is history?* and reinvigorates the relationship between academic historiography and more public forms of historical culture with a new sense of *embodied historiography*.[5]

Our book shows that the IHR's seminars have given rise to a complex long-lived culture that is neither monolithic nor static but rather a function of evolving, multifarious synergies between teaching, researching and learning, historiography and participation – intertextual, interpersonal, intergenerational and intercultural. The seminars form a local, national and international hub for scholars and scholarship in ways that are intellectually and socially nourishing. The seminars are vital enablers of high-quality research in a way not dissimilar to critical editing and peer review but with the added zest of embodied interaction. The seminars constitute a living tradition, stimulating and incorporating dynamic change over time to contribute not just to the development of historiography but intellectual life more generally, often in conversation with major political events and cultural phenomena.

Albert Pollard (1869–1948) – the IHR's original visionary, co-founder and first director – once mused that the essential purpose of the IHR and, by implication, its seminars, was:

> to create a corporate tradition of historical technique which shall not be dissipated ... by the conclusion of any particular task, the disappearance of individuals, or the dispersal of equipment, but shall have, like Solomon's House in ... [Francis Bacon's] *New Atlantis*, fellows, novices and apprentices, 'that the succession do not fail'.[6]

Such ideals may seem outmoded in the 2020s; however, they also serve as a reminder that learning is not without a sense of devotion, or even romance. To deny how scholars feel about their seminar culture would be to ignore its liminal position between professional and personal worlds; and as the former negotiates inclusion, so the latter negotiates tribalism. But more than this, Pollard's words challenge us to re-affirm the historian's craft.

History matters because historiography matters, and historiography matters because academic historians themselves matter. We must do more to make academic historians and their scholarship reflect our multicultural and intercultural society, but by carefully renewing academic practice without just reacting obsequiously and uncritically to public wants. Writing in 2015, David Lowenthal alerted us to how many public factions now struggle to 'tolerate an alien past' but instead domesticate history by 'imputing present-day aims and deeds to earlier times', either 'praising them for echoing their own precepts or damning them for failing to conform to them'.[7] With some caveats and qualifications, academic historians do not attest to how the world ought to have been. Rather, they continue, by their method, to understand and evaluate the complexities, varieties, nuances and contradictions of past people – with profound implications for appreciating how and why the present is the way that it is. In this endeavour historians now have a vital role to play in redefining the public nexus between research and education, in keeping with a sense of civic learning that the IHR helped to inaugurate. It is with this in mind, I look at our chapters and argue that the critical undogmatic traditions of the IHR's seminar culture must continue, *that the succession do not fail*.

## Notes

\* A preliminary version of this introduction was delivered to the IHR's Centenary Festival at Senate House in July 2022. Thanks to Penelope Corfield and David Bates for providing feedback on the draft text. I alone am responsible for any remaining shortcomings.

1. 'About us', School of Advanced Study, University of London: https://www.sas.ac.uk/about-us-6 [accessed 2 Nov. 2022].

2. G. Parsloe, 'Recollections of the Institute, 1922–43', *Bulletin of the Institute of Historical Research*, xliv (1971), 270–83, at p. 276.

3. Parsloe, 'Recollections', 270.

4. Institute of Historical Research, University of London: https://www.history.ac.uk [accessed 2 Nov. 2022].

5. Cf. H. Carr and S. Lipscomb (ed.), *What Is History, Now? How the Past and Present Speak to Each Other* (London, 2021); and, D. Bloxham, *Why History? A History* (Oxford, 2020).

6. A. F. Pollard, *Factors in Modern History*, third edition (London, 1932), p. 312. Cf. *Francis Bacon: The Major Works*, ed. B. Vickers (Oxford, 2002), p. 480 and p. 487. Cf. 1 Chron. XXVIII:10–13.

7. D. Lowenthall, *The Past Is a Foreign Country: Revisited* (Cambridge, 2015), pp. 585–610, at p. 595.

# References

## Published sources

'About us', School of Advanced Study, University of London: https://www.sas.ac.uk/about-us-6 [accessed 2 Nov. 2022].

Bloxham, D., *Why History? A History* (Oxford, 2020).

Carr, H., and Lipscomb, S. (ed.), *What Is History, Now? How the Past and Present Speak to Each Other* (London, 2021).

*Francis Bacon: The Major Works*, ed. B. Vickers (Oxford, 2002).

Institute of Historical Research, University of London: https://www.history.ac.uk [accessed 2 Nov. 2022].

Lowenthall, D., *The Past Is a Foreign Country: Revisited* (Cambridge, 2015).

Parsloe, G., 'Recollections of the Institute, 1922–43', *Bulletin of the Institute of Historical Research*, xliv (1971), 270–83.

Pollard, A. F., *Factors in Modern History*, third edition (London, 1932).

Chapter 1

# A history of the history seminar: the 'active life' of historiography at the Institute of Historical Research

## David Manning*

This chapter is very much an essay, and one of synthesis at that. It serves as an exploratory history of the history seminar with a particular focus on the Institute of Historical Research (IHR). But this opening conversation is not without fresh insight and comes with the added frisson of heading a book that uniquely situates the IHR's seminars within an historiographical culture that considers the work of historians as both scholars and people.

This last point leads to something of a provocation: a call to re-appraise the capacity of historical scholarship to service the public good. Independent, uncompromising research in history is becoming less practicable amidst claims that it lacks 'real world' application and is still practised by an unrepresentative elite. Select voices within higher education have suggested that the teaching seminar in history is an exclusory, outmoded form of learning. These points appear to be implicitly grounded upon two inter-related presuppositions. One, historiography – when left to its own devices – is somehow solely a function of the contemplative life. Two, historiography – especially when working under the auspices of publicly funded institutions – must be governed by external forces to ensure that it produces tangible, measurable benefits to society. Yet this essay affirms that the history seminar was not and is not some listless feature of the contemplative life but rather a manifestation of the 'active life' in ways evocative of the *vita activa* considered in Hannah Arendt's *The*

*Human Condition* (1958). For when the history seminar advances dialogues and polylogues in historiography, it not only engenders intellectual interaction between people in the moment but elicits an interpenetration of the other and the familiar, a past and present humanity. Such processes of participation resonate with those acts of disclosure and self-disclosure that Arendt saw as vital to citizenship, to the pluralism of political freedom in *the real world*.[1] For the history seminar to be of sincere public service it must be liberated from the category mistakes of its detractors (and some of its advocates), as well as the conformist means and materialistic ends they prescribe and enforce.

Such a suggestion is proffered here less as an argument *per se* and more as a stimulus for thinking through some of the implications of the rest of this essay, which comprises four thematically constructed and chronologically sequenced discussions that are *not* representative of a series of distinct phases in the life of the history seminar but *do* shine a flickering light on some of its distinctive characteristics as they change over time.

## Modernist historiography and Christian heritage

The history seminar emerged as a *method of learning* in English universities at the turn of the twentieth century. Momentum was created by re-casting the theory and practice of what had become a feature of American and German and tertiary education, originating with the contrasting experiments of the history library seminar hosted at the University of Königsberg (1832) and the history discussion group (1825–31) at the Berlin home of Leopold von Ranke (1795–1886).[2]

Changes to the English curriculum were formative.[3] The nineteenth century saw the Bachelor of Arts transformed from a multidisciplinary academic apprenticeship to a programme of study for just one subject. The University of Oxford established its single honours degree in history in 1872; Cambridge followed suit three years later; Owens College Manchester – which became the University of Manchester in 1904 – by 1882; and University College London by 1896.[4] Subject specialization went hand-in-hand with a certain sense of professionalization whereby historiography shaped a new strand of pedagogy. In contrast to the catechetical form of tutorial teaching which prepared students for exams, select historians developed schemes of learning in their own area of expertise. Professors shared their scholarship with students and introduced them to the practical methods of primary source analysis – an early expression of the fabled art of 'research-led' teaching that gave rise to the history special subject. A move that also reflected a threefold modernist mission to

A HISTORY OF THE HISTORY SEMINAR    13

supersede whiggish historiography, champion historical enquiry as an empirical science, and set about discovering the truths of the past.

Learned sociability was given a new lease of life at Balliol College, Oxford, in 1882 when the visiting scholar and alumnus of Harvard University Samuel Brearley (d. 1886) enlightened his peers and teachers in the ways of German-American seminar culture. The stimulus was enough to establish the Oxford Historical Seminar. Renamed two years later as the Stubbs Society in honour of William Stubbs (1825–1901), some-time regius professor of history and chaplain at Balliol, the seminar had history students deliver papers – often, although not exclusively, based upon the final-honours exam – with subsequent discussion overseen by a tutor.[5] Research mingled with machismo and naivety: assertions about national history, for example, were grounded in the political assumptions and moral codes of the young men who articulated them.

One counterbalance to these pursuits was to be found at Girton College, Cambridge. Here Ellen McArthur (1862–1927) reached first class in the history tripos of 1885 and thereafter established herself as the College's first designated teacher of history whilst undertaking postgraduate study under the direction of the historian and clergyman William Cunningham (1849–1919). McArthur not only tutored at Norwich House, a residence for women studying at the Cambridge Training College for Women Teachers (which later became Hughes Hall), but personally ran a hostel for women postgraduate students at Cambridge from 1896 to 1903.[6] These locales would have provided ample scope for academic discussion in ways suggestive of seminar culture. One of the College's first intake and a student of its principal, Elizabeth Hughes (1851–1925), later recalled, 'we paid visits to one another for a good-night chat' and in being 'quite untrammelled by having read any philosophical works, we brought fresh minds to the deepest problems'.[7] The extent to which McArthur's own lived experience operated at the intersections of teaching, postgraduate study and published scholarship also indicates a mode of 'research-led' teaching no less significant than that being advanced through the special subject. Indeed, McArthur's approach to scholarship ushered in a generation of leading women historians that included Lilian Knowles (née Tomn) (1870–1926), Caroline Skeel (1872–1951) and Eileen Power (1889–1940).[8]

At the same time as McArthur was innovating at Cambridge, Balliol alumnus and medievalist Thomas Tout (1855–1929) was developing the curriculum beyond the sphere of Oxbridge. As professor of history at Owens College, Tout's experiments in teaching helped to inaugurate a library seminar in history by 1895. Students gathered with their teacher to work with and amongst the books and documents they needed for their studies. They were then encouraged to enter into oral and written discourse on the subject of their own specialization. This 'hot house method' turned students into practising historians: 'of the forty-three students who graduated from Owens College in history between 1895 and 1904, eighteen published historical work'.[9]

These developments were part of a wider flourishing of seminar libraries, a phenomenon that was particularly evident at UCL.[10] Professors Flinders Petrie (1853–1942) and Ernest Gardner (1862–1939) founded seminar libraries for Egyptology (1882) and classical archaeology (1886), respectively; whilst, from 1898, the professor of German, Robert Priebsch PhD (1866–1935), enlivened his seminar teaching with practices imported from his time in Germany. In his 1904 inaugural lecture as professor of constitutional history, Albert Pollard (1869–1948) lamented that whilst 'English universities have maintained their hegemony of the national intellect; they certainly do not contribute so much to our intellectual prestige as German universities do to that of their Fatherland'.[11] These reflections were complicated. Pollard had graduated in 1891 with a first-class history degree from Jesus College, Oxford; but without an academic position he had spent a long time eking out a meagre living under the auspices of the *Dictionary of National Biography*. As much as this was worthy toil, it was some way from the intellectual heights of the kind of advanced study that led to being a Doctor of Philosophy. Pollard's old tutor, Reginald Poole (1857–1939), had been a student at Balliol and a tutee of Stubbs before gaining a PhD at Leipzig in 1882. Whilst a piecemeal experiment in postgraduate study was underway in England, for example with UCL's MA and DLitt (the latter awarded in recognition of published scholarship, but not as it is now a 'higher' doctorate above the PhD), it was still something of a coincidence that Pollard found himself a colleague of Priebsch before English universities started awarding PhDs.[12] At Oxford, Charles Firth (1857–1936) had battled, largely in vain, to implement Tout's innovations with a view to developing postgraduate study; but at UCL Pollard sensed an opportunity, declaring in 1904 that he had serious ambitions for a 'postgraduate school of Historical Research in London'.[13] Some practical impetus came by way of UCL's Evening School of History, which followed in the wake of the Historical Association (est. 1906) to give adult learners a degree with a view to them becoming teachers of history.[14] Here, Pollard and like-minded contemporaries found scope to participate in the seminar method. Such was the success of this venture that an increasing number of students showed a tendency to stay on for further study, albeit mainly on a part-time basis; by 1913–14 there were thirty-four postgraduate historians at UCL.[15] And, through 1919–20, momentum was re-established by the London Evening School of History with fifteen intercollegiate postgraduate seminars covering various aspects of historical studies.[16]

Founded a year before the BBC, the IHR was seen as uniquely resplendent in contributing to the national reconstruction after the Great War (see Figures 1.1, 1.2 and 1.3): a point made clear upon the formal opening of the Institute by historian and president of the Board of Education Herbert Fisher (1865–1940). Politics conspired with historiography to make the scientific pursuit of historical 'truth' the antidote to the evils of 'propaganda'. This quasi-hermeneutical ambition serviced a further goal to create a professional class to run the civic institutions of Britain and its empire as well as advance a new era of western internationalism.[17] Building upon the historiographical and pedagogical developments at UCL and the London Evening School of History, the IHR made a founding commitment to invite postgraduate students to 'come to the Institute to discuss their problems' and 'receive that oral guidance from which they are properly debarred in libraries' whilst having the archival material they need for their studies close at hand. The IHR's defining feature was therefore the history library seminar: a 'workshop for historical research', an 'historical laboratory', that was also a place where 'students and staff' of 'both sexes' and from 'all universities and all nations' could meet to pursue mutual interests in learning and history.[18] Pollard's Thursday-evening conferences were, however, the preserve of teaching staff: a non-teaching research seminar by another name that created a centripetal intellectual force in the IHR's early life (and then carried on in a more minor role for decades). In addition, there were eight seminar series for postgraduate learning in 1921–2, growing to sixteen by 1925–6.[19] Together these endeavours gave impetus to an emerging seminar culture that tacitly distinguished itself from earlier English, American and German examples by means of the vibrancy of its mixed-sex and international collaborations as well as the relative informality of its operations and its rich capacity for a sort of unity in diversity.

Modernist historiography may have been bound to explain the origins of the history seminar as part of its own foundational story, but the reality was surely more indeterminate. There were resonances between history seminars and select clubs, societies and salons in the early twentieth century – for example, the Bloomsbury Group's Thursday meetings – as well as in the nineteenth and eighteenth centuries. Older antecedents may be found in Humanist-Reformation discussions on history at sixteenth- and seventeenth-century universities, conventicles, seminaries, confraternities, academies and so on.[20] William Clark has shown how the activities of the late medieval *seminarium* (etymologically a 'seed-plot',

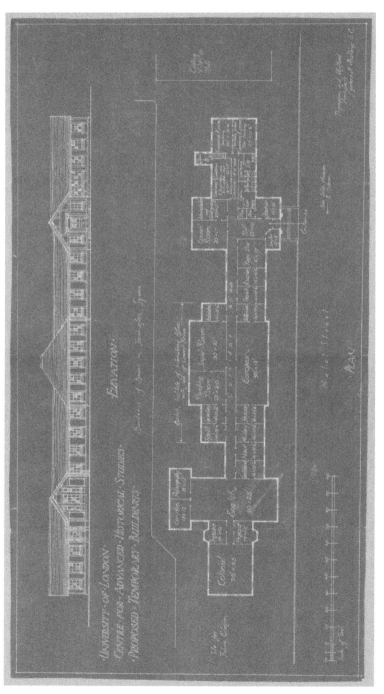

Figure 1.1 Blueprint of proposed temporary buildings for the 'University of London Centre for Advanced Historical Studies' [the IHR] by Thompson & Walford Architects, undated [c.1921], Institute of Historical Research, Wohl Library: IHR/11/1. Reproduced by kind permission of the Institute of Historical Research's Wohl Library.

**Figure 1.2** The temporary building for the IHR on Malet St, London, 1926; creator unknown. Institute of Historical Research, Wohl Library: IHR 10/1/2. Reproduced by kind permission of the Institute of Historical Research's Wohl Library.

**Figure 1.3** The English History Room in the IHR, 1926; creator unknown. Institute of Historical Research, Wohl Library: IHR 10/1/3 (i). Reproduced by kind permission of the Institute of Historical Research Wohl Library.

and by metaphorical extension a place of intellectual growth) and *convictorium* (meaning 'boarding school', but with connotations of communal eating and drinking) were carried over from secondary to tertiary education and joined together in the universities of Protestant Germany from the sixteenth century onwards. This move provided scope for academic conversation between men of differing social ranks whilst establishing quasi-autonomous institutions tasked with the bureaucratic rationalization of university curricula.[21] Incidentally, the narrower sense of a seminary being a discrete place of religious training appears to have stemmed from a renewal of clerical education initiated by the eighteenth canon of the Council of Trent (1545–63), with Catholic and then Protestant seminaries emerging thereafter.[22] Stretching further back to the fourteenth-century, Sisters and Brothers of the Common Life helps build a bridge to even older patterns of Christian and pagan heritage. St Clement of Alexandria's *Paedagogus* (*c*.194–202 CE) revealed the inner workings of the catechetical school of Alexandria. With Christ as the archetypal teacher, mortal pedagogues were simultaneously educators of and fellow learners with their students – notably male and female – and the distinction between school and church was non-existent.[23] Isocrates' academy at Athens preceded that of Plato by several years and advocated the practice of rhetoric amongst the broader principles of a liberal education. In his *Panegyricus* (*c*.380 BCE), Isocrates cognized history as a discipline of study, a branch of practical knowledge bound to *logos*, whilst *Panathenaicus* (*c*.342 BCE) represented mutually formative exchanges between teacher and students in a peripatetic prefiguring of the seminar.[24] As abstruse and ancient as the teachings of St Clement and Isocrates undoubtedly are, they were revived for late nineteenth- and early twentieth-century readers in English translation by the publishing series of the Ante-Nicene Christian Library (1884) and the Loeb Classical Library (1928 and 1929), respectively.

The IHR unwittingly defined itself just one letter away from the Christian *logos*, IHS. At least one early visitor to the Institute is known to have commented, however flippantly, that the Institute's monogram was a 'Jesuit device'.[25] Anecdotes aside, James Kirby has recently shown how the fifty years leading up to the foundation of the IHR saw a significant 'body of historical scholarship' exemplify 'the Church of England's confessional priorities'.[26] Historical enquiry could be initiated by scientific means, but the ends of historiography – the conversations, postgraduate dissertations, published articles and books which shaped an understanding of the past for an elite culture espoused by academics, teachers, civil servants, politicians, journalists and so on – struggled to escape, and tended to re-enforce, the paradigmatic ideologies, theologies and imaginings of the day. For all his empirical historicism, Pollard's Liberalism was guilty of valorizing 'the secular and sovereign nation state as the desirable terminus of an evolutionary historical process'.[27] If stereotypical modernist historiography laid claim to 'objective truth' with religious-like zeal then there were, of course, 'heretics'. John Fortescue's 1925 presidential address to the Royal Historical Society gently eschewed the idea of history as a science; championing, instead, the human imagination as a re-creative force of historical interpretation, before presenting historians as custodians of the honour, dignity and beauty of English prose.[28] Such ideas set up a curious dialectic between the *historian as interpreter* of past 'realities' and the *historian as mediator* between a tangible present and an intangible past, with the latter enabling a creative blurring between historical enquiry and normative cultures, ideological teleologies, literary traditions and prophetic stories. Pollard the man had shunned his family's Methodism only to adopt the credo of a rather impersonal moralist. By contrast, John Neale (1890–1975) – Pollard's protégé and later successor as seminar convenor – was no less demanding, but very much a Christian of an English nonconformist-Protestant strain. So, it was no simple coincidence that Neale would go on to supervise and run seminars for such Christian empiricists as Gordon Donaldson (PhD, 1938) and Patrick Collinson (PhD, 1957), who made their names in the historiography of the Scottish and English Reformations respectively.[29] The rigour of historicism proved a strangely irenic pursuit.

The IHR's early seminar culture was no bastion of secular modernist historiography. Rather it played host to diverse 'believers' and 'unbelievers' who found meaning in a communal learning process shaped by contingent forces in historiography, ideology and sociability.[30] Seminars were about empirical study, but this involved a suspension of disbelief in its ultimate purpose.

## Gendered and international learning

For much of the first half of the twentieth century, the history seminar was orientated around teaching and research as interdependent activities. This emphasis facilitated intellectual and social relations that both reinforced and reformed cultural norms in learning.

The IHR quickly established a reputation as the place of postgraduate study in history.[31] Yet no director of the IHR came to the post with a PhD until Michael Thompson in 1977. Such contrariness owed something to the time-lag of generational renewal, but it may also have reflected a gendered politics of learning. A symbiotic relationship between civic professions of political import and the professorial historiographer worked to galvanize a select group of relatively young men. Arnold Toynbee (1889–1975) was little more than thirty when he was elevated to a chair at King's College London in 1919; and by 1928 he had secured an ostensibly research-only professorship at the University of London so that he could also continue to work as director of studies at the Royal Institute of International Affairs (also known as Chatham House, est. 1920), a post he held from 1926 to 1955. Albert Pollard had only been thirty-three when he became a professor, but his 'higher calling' was to be found in creating and sustaining the IHR. Such men were Oxonians with no formal postgraduate training but nevertheless went on to play a significant role as seminar convenors and PhD supervisors. Their credentials as researchers and teachers were rather subsumed into authoritative roles of academic patronage and public service. The waning of the gentleman-scholar may have given way to the waxing of the male impresario professor.[32]

Such ambition was not, however, all consuming. With a national sense of higher education in its infancy, academic professionalism rarely equated to a full-time, career-long university position. (When Pollard started out, he did so as a part-time, underpaid professor who found inspiration and succour in public service, which in the case of the London Evening School worked at the interface between secondary and tertiary education.) Multiple careers, constructed either concurrently or sequentially, were not uncommon and satisfied a range of personal interests, financial needs and public duties, in times of war and peace. Whilst far from a social leveller, experiences of such plurality and precarity may have formed an underlying point of solidarity for up-and-coming historians of different backgrounds and nationalities, and of both sexes.

The University of London quickly established itself as home to the greatest number of full-time overseas students. Within this context, the IHR and its seminars served to reinvigorate both national and international histories by way of inter-cultural exchange. From the early 1920s onwards, there was healthy representation from the United States of America, Canada and Australia, as well as a growing number from Wales, Scotland and continental Europe. Whilst complicated by power dynamics arising from early twentieth-century attitudes to race, colonialism and internationalism, a small but not insignificant number of (mainly male) students of colour participated in the IHR's seminars to mutual benefit. In 1923–24, Tung-li Yuan (1895–1965) attended the preliminary course on sources and archives before returning to his native China where he would later become director of the National Library at Peiping, now Beijing (1942–49). That same year, Muhammad Shafik Ghorbal (1894–1961) attended Arnold

Toynbee's Near and Middle Eastern History Seminar.[33] In 1924–5, the IHR had a designated seminar on British India convened by Henry Dodwell (1879–1946) and this was attended by Bijan Raj Chatterji (1904–87) who subsequently became a pioneer in the study of Southeast Asian cultures. Such dynamics also operated in similar ways closer to home. Less than a decade after the Irish Civil War, the Ulsterman Theodore Moody (1907–84) and the Dubliner Robert Edwards (1909–88) gravitated to the IHR for doctoral study. Such a coming together was as cathartic as it was constructive. The Institute and its seminars instilled in Moody and Edwards such an appreciation of 'proper research training' and 'collaborative enterprise' that it inspired their role in the 'Irish Historiographical Revolution' of the 1930s.[34]

Women played a significant role in the development of history seminar culture.[35] By 1919–20, a fifth of the postgraduate seminars at the London Evening School were led by women, including: Lilian Knowles, who had achieved first class in the history tripos at Girton College, Cambridge, and a DLitt from Trinity College, Dublin,[36] before becoming reader in economic history at the LSE; Hilda Johnstone (1882–1961), who graduated MA from Manchester in 1906 and was reader in history at KCL, and also sister-in-law to Thomas Tout; and Eliza Jeffries Davis (1875–1943), who had begun her career as a teacher at Bedford High School, before graduating MA from UCL in 1913 and the taking up a post as lecturer on the sources of English history at the same institution. By 1928–9, six of the seventeen seminars at the IHR were convened by women: Eliza Davis, by then reader, had established herself as leader of the London History Seminar whilst her colleagues included Hilda Johnstone, by then professor, and the up-and-coming scholar Lillian Penson (1896–1963).[37] And, by 1930–31, 21 per cent of academics at London were women, compared to 11 per cent at Oxford and just 5 per cent at Cambridge.[38]

These women, and others like them, did not appear to suffer any straightforward reversal of opportunity as the history seminar was institutionalized at the IHR.[39] In 1921, Penson had become one of the first, and possibly the first, to be awarded a PhD in history by the University of London. She was appointed professor of modern history at Bedford College in 1930 and vice-chancellor of the University of London in 1948, the first woman to hold such a position anywhere in Britain; a damehood followed three years later. And throughout her illustrious career, Penson convened a seminar series on diplomatic history that ran from 1928 to 1963 (see Figure I.2). Davis never pursued doctoral study and published very little of her own work and yet became a formidable director of studies to PhD students. In 1923–4, she started supervising Norman

Brett-James (1879–1960), a graduate of Lincoln College, Oxford, whose doctoral research was worked around his day-job as a housemaster at the nonconformist Mill Hill School, London. Brett-James's labours resulted in the five-hundred-page *Growth of Stuart London* (1935) – still cited in the twenty-first century – wherein a preface made clear how the author was not only 'indebted' to 'Miss E. Jeffries Davis' for her 'advice and criticism' but to 'the London Seminar which she presides over'.[40] Surviving minutes from Davis's Seminar indicate her dynamic pedagogy. She would interject with comments about useful secondary and primary readings, historical details that were either probable or possible, queries about or answers to questions, as well as correcting discrepancies and errors.[41] The first outing of Pollard's Seminar in 1932–3 comprised six students, all women. Amongst their number, 'Miss Skinner' and 'Miss Stafford' together addressed 'Elizabethan finance & foreign policy ... [and] Anglo-Scottish relations at the end of the C16th', respectively; whilst 'Miss Puddifoot' queried the 'quantities of printed material surviving & not surviving', contrasting the Stationers Register with the Short Title Catalogue.[42] Caroline Robbins (1903–99), completed a PhD in history at Royal Holloway in 1926. Her attendance at the IHR's seminars not only informed her dissertation but her future approach to teaching at Bryn Mawr College, a women's liberal arts college in Pennsylvania, USA. According to Lois G. Schwoerer, Robbins conducted her graduate seminars through the 1930s, 40s and 50s 'with a great sense that she was training the next generation of historians'. It was said that she had an 'elliptical way of speaking, which required students to grasp her meaning' by reading works from set reading lists. 'Students' oral seminar reports received searching questions and sometimes sharp criticisms' and on at least one occasion 'reduced an apparently ill-prepared student to tears in a seminar'. Robbins 'did not approve of the feminist movement' but instead believed that women could succeed without major socio-political change if only they 'applied themselves seriously to their work'.[43] Whilst many pioneering women historians advanced the cause of feminism, not all escaped stereotypes of being either self-effacing or teaching-focused, or both, and some shunned feminism as a determining factor in their achievements.

## Research, politics and conviviality

A desire to free up academic discourse from the burden of pedagogy was in evidence at the IHR from its inception. Pollard's Thursday-evening conference set an early precedent, but this was a distinctly after-dinner affair which reflected a clubbable sensibility. The performative act of eating and drinking together may have symbolized a sense of community, if not an equity amongst members, and helped to initiate a transformation from day to night, from mundane toil to creative thought.[44] Befitting the occasion, the academic discussion, at least in the early years, was typically free flowing with 'no agenda, no programme, no opener for discussion'.[45] As delightful and constructive as this would have been for participants, no less significant were the experiments of Eileen Power, who 'turned her medieval history seminar for a time during the late 1920s and early 1930s into a research project' that drew in not just students but 'visiting foreign historians, as well as other academics from outside the LSE'.[46] Power's own scholarship went from strength to strength, and in 1938–9 she became the first woman to deliver the Ford Lectures at the University of Oxford.

Yet, for the most part, the history seminar at the IHR continued to work as a forum for teaching and learning. With the ability of hindsight, former students and junior staff had mixed feelings about this environment. From the vantage point of 1993, Joan Henderson (d. 2002) – schoolteacher, Tudor historian and *doyenne* of the IHR – recalled how Neale's Tudor History Seminar of 1948–9 was concerned with 'what his students had discovered in the past week' and how in the midst of discussion 'people were sent round the room to fetch printed Elizabethan records'; but then it was also the case that 'conversation afterwards was discouraged by one of the librarians of that time and the professors did not adjourn to discuss matters elsewhere over glasses of wine and beer'.[47] In his memoirs of 2006, the military historian Michael Howard (1922–2019) recounted how, as a lecturer at KCL in early 1950s, his 'Oxford superiority-complex withered in the face of such an array of talent – such *professionalism*' and yet he also grew weary of 'God Professors' and 'their obedient acolytes'.[48]

Through the mid-twentieth century, the history seminar outgrew its base function in undergraduate and postgraduate learning to establish itself as a multipurpose endeavour within a newly dynamic intellectual ecology.[49] In 1947–8, the IHR took up permanent residence in Senate House: an ostensibly new building, completed just a decade before, but with an art deco design which reflected a tragically outdated sense of 1930s optimism (see Figures 1.4 and 1.5). In that same year, the German-born émigré of Jewish heritage Gottfried Rudolph Otto Ehrenberg became a naturalized British citizen; and under his anglicized name, Geoffrey Elton (1921–94), established himself as an historian with a doctoral thesis on Thomas Cromwell, supervised by John Neale. In an emerging post-1945 paradigm, historical research and political ideology once again met at the IHR with a view to national and international reconstruction.

**Figure 1.4** Senate House from the south-west; © University of London. University of London Archives. Reproduced by kind permission of the Senate House Library and the University of London.

In 1953, Sir Lewis Namier (1888–1960) retired from his professorial chair at the University of Manchester to take up a leading role in the History of Parliament project, which had been re-launched in 1951 with financial and political backing from Churchill's government.[50] Namier was still at the height of his powers, but a bitter, cantankerous soul who had suffered prejudice all his life. Born Ludwik Bernstein, he was a Russian-Polish-Jewish émigré, who changed his name, and graduated from Balliol College, before becoming a naturalized British citizen in 1913. Whilst antisemitism was a determining factor in Namier being passed over for prestigious professorial appointments at Oxbridge and London, his final role offered an opportunity to imprint both a historiography and a national history with 'Namierism' – a prosopographical approach to political history, construed as a function of individual agency and self-interest. Whilst the IHR and its seminars constituted a multifaceted organization, irreducible to any single interest, the History of Parliament project drew upon the contrasting expertise of Namier and Neale and, in so doing, re-shaped their respective seminars in the pursuit of collaborative research beyond the confines of doctoral study. By 1956, Neale's Seminar had demonstrably altered from its pre-1950s state. As one member noted at the time: 'the seminar is a joint committee dedicated to research and evaluation'; for 'just as

A HISTORY OF THE HISTORY SEMINAR   25

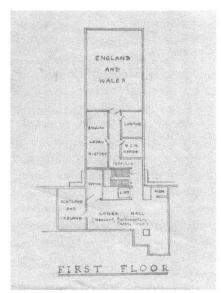

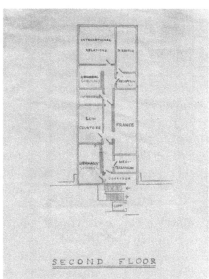

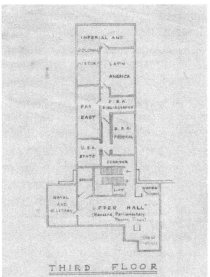

**Figure 1.5** a, b and c floor plans for the IHR in the new Senate House building, undated [c.1930]; creator unknown. Institute of Historical Research, Wohl Library: IHR/11/18. Reproduced by kind permission of Institute of Historical Research, Wohl Library.

its members before, at tea, take their problems and difficulties to discuss with Professor Neale [by this time also knighted], so it is the professor who will outline his latest work, binding the threads together with a wealth of illustration in a torrent of extempore analysis', and then 'it is he who stands on trial before the seminar, before the lynx-eyed Mr Gabriel with his colleagues ... Miss Henderson [etc.] ... lined up together on the right side of the table'.[51] In a similar vein, Namier's Seminar was 'nominally on British parliamentary history in the second half of the eighteenth century' but was 'in effect an extension of the work of the History of Parliament, and brought collaborators and students together'. Yet, Namier remained very much the leader for 'so marinated was he in the sources that ... he always seemed to be remembering history as personal experience'.[52]

At the other end of the political spectrum, Eric Hobsbawm (1917–2012) was coming of age. A British citizen by birth but a 'non-Jewish Jew' with parents of Polish and Austrian descent, Hobsbawm grew up in Vienna and spent time in Berlin before moving to England in 1933 – just after converting to Communism following his attendance at the last legal demonstration of the German Communist Party. As an undergraduate at King's College, Cambridge, Hobsbawm thrived, but his membership of the elite discussion group known as the 'Cambridge Apostles' was perhaps no less influential than his formal studies. After the Second World War, his Cambridge PhD dissertation, 'Fabianism and the Fabians, 1884–1914' (1950), was supervised by Michael Postan (1899–1981). Hobsbawm was a founding member of the Historians' Group of the Communist Party of Great Britain that typically met, either at Marx's House at Clerkenwell Green, or at Garibaldi's Italian restaurant off Farringdon Road, to engage in seminar discussion on historical problems. Between 1946 and 1956, the Group, which also counted E. P. Thompson (1924–93), Christopher Hill (1912–2003) and Dona Torr (1883–1957) amongst its members, was a major force in institutionalizing British Marxist historiography and galvanizing relations between like-minded students, teachers, academics and political thinkers, both nationally and internationally. Founding *Past and Present* (1952), and participating in an historical colloquium in Leningrad upon the invitation of the Soviet Academy of Sciences shortly after Stalin's death, were just two of their notable achievements.[53] Hobsbawm's political entanglements had a detrimental effect on his academic career: his rise to the rank of professor in 1970 was inordinately slow and he never secured a meaningful post at Cambridge despite trying; yet, he found a professional home at Birkbeck College in 1947 and there he remained. By the 1960s, Hobsbawm's teaching seminars were celebrated multisensory experiences. One of his students later recalled that he would often 'sit cross-legged on the top of the desk facing his students whilst we took turns at reading our most recent essays aloud to the group'; Hobsbawm would 'listen intently' and then provide 'comments', all whilst entertaining the various physical processes of preparing and smoking a pipe.[54] The IHR took a while to come round to having *Past and Present* on its bookshelves, and Hobsbawm did not make his debut as an IHR seminar co-convenor until 1965–66, pairing up with Oliver McGregor (1921–97, cr. Baron McGregor of Durris in 1978), professor of social institutions at Bedford College, to run the seminar on the 'social history of industrial society, with special reference to modern Britain'. But by the mid-1970s, this seminar was very much Hobsbawm's seminar; and, despite it being still predominately focused on doctoral research and learning, it bore testimony to how 'history unfolded in breadth and depth', marking for at least one student 'the pre-eminent intellectual experience' of their lives.[55] Around the same time, Hobsbawm also collaborated with George Haupt (1928–78), sometime director of Soviet and East European Studies at the École Pratique des Hautes Études, to establish at Paris a seminar series on social history in which papers would be designed to foster learned discussion but, significantly, 'with no expectation of publication'.[56]

Liberalism was not to be outdone at the IHR and found a champion in Conrad Russell (1937–2004) – son of the philosopher Bertrand Russell – who in 1958 graduated from Merton College, Oxford, and began, but did not complete, a doctorate under the supervision of Christopher Hill, before starting what would become a distinguished academic career as an historian of early Stuart England at Bedford College in 1960. At this time Russell's politics leaned towards Labour, but when in 1987 he was elevated to his hereditary peerage he sat on the Liberal benches – later taking on duties that aimed at reforming social security. At the IHR, Russell led the Tudor and Stuart Seminar from 1984 until his retirement in 2002, during which time he was professor of British history, first at UCL and then KCL. Members of the Seminar found Russell's intellectual enthusiasm 'contagious' and commended him for undertaking serious reading 'not merely for his own research but also for theirs'.[57] This feeling was mutual. The book that emerged from Russell's 1987–8 Ford Lectures, *The Fall of the British Monarchies 1637–1642* (1991), was dedicated 'to the members, past, present and future, of the Tudor and Stuart Seminar at the Institute of Historical Research', and in a telling preface Russell wrote of a 'special debt' to the Seminar for supplying 'some forty pairs of spectacles to pursue almost every problem' and 'usually, one of them has the right focus'.[58] Little wonder that this chain-smoking professor, feared and revered by his students, was a first amongst equals whose tenure as convenor of the Tudor and Stuart History Seminar is remembered nostalgically with much admiration.

Reflecting on the combined experiences of the Seminars associated with Namier, Hobsbawm and Russell, it seems that the IHR's seminar culture witnessed no strategic or uniform transformation from student-orientated to staff-orientated research. The extent to which the history seminar as an institution had expanded and diversified its remit to incorporate pedagogical, historiographical, professional, political and social interests was significant.[59] The PhD was still not an essential prerequisite for gaining either esteem as a scholar or an academic post at a university and seminars attracted a varied crowd of occasional visitors, including a smattering of amateurs drawn from the general public.[60] Notwithstanding social hierarchies, different approaches to research could converge upon mutual experiences in *learning*. That said, taken in the round, this environment was more blokeish: leading historiographers were 'men of affairs', and the overriding system was slow to respond to the calls for equality and inclusivity that emerged in the 1960s and 1970s.

The social component of this expanding history seminar culture appears to have been something of a given, although quite difficult to find documented. Formal seminar discourse was often followed by more informal discussions over dinner and drinks in a manner that combined the principles of good hospitality with a base desire to lubricate conversation with alcohol. Here, more candid and exploratory conversations could take place about what one *really* thought of the earlier proceedings. Finding someone of like mind could be just as important as finding someone to have a good argument with. Talk could easily drift between topics on historiography, teaching, administration, university gossip, politics, sport, music, art and even relationships – with all the pros and cons such discussions brought for making, breaking and segregating friendships. In the best traditions of pub culture, professors were to be found drinking and speaking freely amongst students, junior colleagues and others from outside academia. In the light of the #MeToo movement (est. 2006), however, it would be naive not to worry now about an unknown darker history of those who suffered harassment or assault in the aftermath of a seminar. More positively, though, seminar culture can lay claim to be a sensitive matchmaker. Those who shared a passion for research in the social environment of the seminar could find their interests affirmed and extended through interpersonal bonds of friendship and romantic love. Elfreda Skelton married her former supervisor, John Neale. Eileen Power married her former research assistant, Michael Postan. And Conrad Russell married his former student, Elizabeth Sanders. Elton and his future wife met as students at the IHR, and in later years,

> colleagues and pupils who enjoyed the hospitality which Geoffrey Elton and his wife, Sheila Lambert, herself a historian of distinction, dispensed liberally and frequently at their home in Cambridge saw him in his Anglo-Saxon mode, in turns the genial raconteur or sharp-tongued savager of fools and knaves, so far removed from the staid restraint of an earnest Teutonic.[61]

## Accountability and accessibility

Since the 1970s, but more noticeably since the 2000s, the multiplication, diversification and fragmentation of historiographical enquiry has become mixed up in battles over the hegemonic norms of teaching, learning and researching history. This has been further complicated by a revolution in the relationship between universities and the state, or rather universities and their 'stakeholders', especially in Britain.[62]

A resurgent instrumentalism has not just complicated empirical historiography but opened it up to the hermeneutical and methodological challenges of political historicism and popular historical culture.[63] The principles of academic historicism are being redefined in negotiation with various, sometimes conflicting, political, social and ethical imperatives. This process may be seen as an ongoing function of the discipline of history renewing itself. However, what does appear to be causing a more profound change is the extent to which university political culture has not only become unhinged from academe but is increasingly taking the lead in determining the nature and purpose of historiography as it is crafted and taught by historians on the payroll of universities.

The last part of this essay offers a more personal perspective, based upon sector-wide experiences of teaching and researching history in British universities since the late 2000s. That said, it reflects, however contentiously, a reality which, whilst not necessarily representative of experiences at Oxbridge and a handful of other select institutions, serves as a warning to what may happen to the IHR's seminar culture if it cannot be insulated from the vagaries of managerialist agendas that now overwhelm much of the university sector.

For many undergraduate and taught postgraduate programmes, the history teaching seminar has become subordinate to the contrivances of prescribed learning and assessment objectives. Here, educationalists have been instrumental in stealthily turning the seminar from a learning *method* to a mere *format*: a type of meeting which plays host to a 'range of activities that may take place when working with small groups of history students'.[64] Academic convention may once have assumed that such seminar 'activities' were in keeping with an established method of 'a gathering, preferably round a table, of a group with a presiding teacher in which individual students present views or even papers [on history] for guided discussion by the group'; but since the 2000s this has no longer been the case.[65] The trajectory from historiography to pedagogy that has traditionally given the history seminar its distinctive value has been eroded, even inverted, by the forces of managerialism, discombobulated by various competing demands of accountability and accessibility within a neoliberal paradigm. A marketized curriculum fetishizes what students want. Much of 'higher education' has become predicated upon maximizing degree outcomes in ways that foreground knowledge exchange to the detriment of both the principles of tertiary learning and their capacity to engender an intellectually heterogenous student body. The advance of modular degree programmes, the decline of end-of-year exams and the rationalization of timetables have also fundamentally changed the student experience. In reflecting these developments, a fair portion of the history seminar's autonomous historiographical discourse has been hollowed out so that it can be 'embedded' with homogenized activities that supposedly evidence 'engagement', 'inclusivity', 'employability', 'critical thinking skills', 'communication skills', 'technology-enhanced learning', 'citizenship', 'student satisfaction' and so on.[66] As a result, the history special subject – the cornerstone of history seminar culture writ large – is being turned into just a standard option module with no particular commitment to the seminar as the method of learning history: a point readily underscored by browsing the webpages detailing third-year modules for the BA in history at a range of institutions (including the University of Manchester, of all places).

Research postgraduate programmes are not in a dissimilar place. For the government-backed designs of Doctoral Training Programmes/Partnerships (DTPs) combine with the criteria of the Research Excellence Framework (REF) to establish an approach to research that can be unduly prescriptive in both its framing of historical projects and its insistence upon knowledge exchange. History PhD students are also increasingly being mandated to take time out from their studies to attend workshops on things such as media training and non-academic career skills. As well-meaning and pragmatic as this may be, such activities risk diluting the capacity of doctoral history students to undertake research, participate in seminars and become credible scholars.

If the historic fluidity between teaching, learning and research in the history seminar is being lost, then this does not bode well for the role of the history seminar as a method of scholarship. The university staff of today were the students of yesterday, so it only takes a few generational cycles for changes to be accepted without question. There are, however, other factors to contend with.

On a practical level, the job of a university academic is all but unrecognizable from what it was twenty or so years ago. Overworked staff ruthlessly prioritize their time, or else have it prioritized for them.

Collegiality can suffer under the weight of internal politics shaped by experiences of asymmetric power relationships, precarity and poor mental health. Now, the history research seminar is perhaps seen less as a necessity and more as a luxury, and one that few can afford. In a target-driven environment, it can be quite easy for staff to become habituated to the absence of seminar culture precisely because it rarely imparts immediate tangible benefits. If outright non-attendance does not scupper proceedings, then the practice of taking notes on laptops, tablets and smartphones provides cover for undertaking other more pressing bureaucratic tasks whilst 'listening' to someone speak; and in the case of webinars such infringements may be legion. Attempts to make seminars a more discernible feature of a 'professional' working day can be counterproductive. The advent of PowerPoint presentations may have led to something of a trend for presenting research findings in a lecture style rather than delivering a seminar paper with a proper, albeit developing, sense of argument. Facing a projector screen in a multipurpose room also means that seminar participants may just as likely line up in rows as sit collegiately around a table. The art of robust questioning and debating may be losing its lustre: partly because there is little consensus on what the terms of engagement are, or should be, and partly because it is harder to get a critical mass of expertise in a room to actually get a conversation going. The hermeneutics, methods and cultural norms of disciplinary rigour are getting confused or over-looked amidst a clamour for 'interdisciplinarity', which if taken seriously and followed to its logical conclusion spells the death of history as a discipline – and a prefiguring of this is already upon us with the decline of the standalone history department. There is less time and money for post-seminar sociability which in theory, although rarely in practice, can become something of a moral minefield. And what blended and online events gain in formal inclusivity they lose in excluding informal but vital discourse through the conviviality of meeting people face-to-face.

All is not lost. A recent job advert for a lectureship in history at UCL explicitly requested that the successful candidate should be willing and able to teach an undergraduate research seminar and participate in at least one of the IHR seminars. Yet, the nature and significance of this commitment will depend upon how the respective parties come to understand and value the history seminar. To avoid ambiguity, there must be a re-affirmation and re-invigoration of a protean seminar culture that acts as a custodian of the working needs of historians, considered properly as both means and ends, scholars and people.

## Afterword

In the third decade of the twenty-first century, calls to further democratize historical knowledge are being complicated by partisan attempts to shape and control it. A long-lived symbiotic relationship between academic historiography and political culture is becoming more transactional and asymmetrical. 'Public history' is no panacea. Despite its many virtues,[67] this approach to doing history is particularly vulnerable to commodification and may give licence to a reductive view that the study of history is principally about political access to and control of historical knowledge. But the difference between knowledge and understanding is not insignificant; and the leap to appreciating how and why and with what value academic historians work critically within a methodological, and hence disciplinary, framework to create intellectually credible claims about the past is no mean feat.

Whilst recourse to Arendt does not address the contemporary problems of access, representation and inclusion, her thesis on *action* helps to re-envisage the academic history seminar as a public good in and of itself. For a century, the IHR's seminars have served as a hive of industry enabling historians and their historiography to set agendas in teaching, learning and researching history whilst informing wider cultures. But what reading Arendt hopefully allows us to understand is that material outcomes are not the real issue here. For the history seminar is a living tradition that aggregates, incorporates or otherwise transforms discrete events into evolving processes that bind scholarship to people and people to scholarship. The history seminar makes historiography qua historiography a feature of the *real world*. In being free unto itself to write, read, listen and discuss, in both the manner it does and upon the subject that it does, the history seminar creates – to borrow a line from Arendt – that 'space of appearance ... where I appear to others as others appear to me'; and the beauty of this action is that it 'does not survive the actuality of the movement that brought it into being'.[68] Such practices, as they are freedoms, must be constantly re-enacted for them to live on. And it is essential that they do, for they engender *critical understanding*, the like of which is now needed more than ever.

## Notes

\* I am very grateful to Claire Langhamer, Peter Mandler, Robert Anderson, David Bates, Penelope Corfield and Andrew Campbell for valuable comments and corrections on earlier drafts of this chapter. I alone am responsible for any remaining shortcomings. I also wish to thank Michael Townsend and Zoë Karens for helping with various archive-related queries. My own experience of the IHR's seminar culture has been shaped by the generosity of Ken Fincham, Nicholas Tyacke and Elizabeth Evenden-Kenyon at the Religious History of Britain 1500–1800 Seminar. This chapter is written with love and gratitude to my brother and my parents.

1. H. Arendt, *The Human Condition* (Chicago, [1958] 2018), pp. 175–80, 192–206, 320–26. This essay also strikes up a conversation with M. Bentley, *Modernizing England's Past: English Historiography in the Age of Modernism, 1870–1970* (Cambridge, 2005), D. Cannadine, *Making History Now and Then: Discoveries, Controversies and Explorations* (Basingstoke, 2008), and J. Banner Jr, *Being a Historian: An Introduction to the Professional World of History* (Cambridge, 2012).

2. K. R. Eskildsen, 'Virtues of History: Exercises, Seminars, and the Emergence of the German Historical Discipline, 1830–1900', in *History of Universities: Volume XXXIV/1*, ed. K.-M. Chang and A. Rocke (Oxford, 2021), pp. 27–40 at p. 36. See also: O. Kruse, 'The Origins of Writing in the Disciplines: Traditions of Seminar Writing and the Humboldtian Ideal of the Research University', *Written Communication*, xxiii (2006), 331–52; and A. Grafton, 'In Clio's American Atelier', in *Social Knowledge in the Making*, ed. C. Camic et al. (Chicago, 2011), pp. 89–117.

3. For developments in Scotland, see: R. Anderson, 'University History Teaching and the Humboldtian Model in Scotland, 1858–1914', *History of Universities*, xxv (2010), pp. 138–84; and R. Anderson, 'The Development of History Teaching in the Scottish Universities, 1894–1939', *Journal of Scottish Historical Studies*, xxxii (2012), 50–73.

4. P. Slee, *Learning and a Liberal Education: The Study of Modern History in the Universities of Oxford, Cambridge, and Manchester, 1800–1914* (Manchester, 1986), pp. 56–152.

5. For an appreciation of the Stubbs Society in the 1960s, see: P. Brown, *Journeys of the Mind: A Life in History* (Princeton, 2023), pp. 227–31.

6. A. Erickson, 'Ellen Annette McArthur: Establishing a Presence in the Academy', in *Generations of Women Historians: Within and Beyond the Academy*, ed. H. Smith and M. Zook (Chem, 2018), pp. 25–48.

7. M. V. Hughes, *A London Girl of the Eighties* (London, 1936), p. 145; and for insights into conviviality see pp. 148–49. Cf. B. Smith, 'Gender and the Practices of Scientific History: The Seminar and Archival Research in the Nineteenth Century', *American Historical Review*, c (1995), 1150–76.

8. For more on the latter, see R. van de Wal, 'Dancing in the Kitchens of History: Eileen Power, 1889–1940' (unpublished PhD thesis, University of Groningen, 2022).

9. P. Slee, 'The Manchester School of History: Tout's Contribution to the Pedagogy of Academic History', in *Thomas Frederick Tout (1855–1929): Refashioning History for the Twentieth Century*, ed. J. Rosenthal and C. Barron (London, 2019), pp. 41–56 at p. 50.

10. H. H. Bellot, *University College London, 1826–1926* (London, 1929), pp. 420–21 and p. 406; M. Pendleton, 'A Place of Teaching and Research: University College London and the Origins of the Research University in Britain 1890–1914' (unpublished PhD thesis, University of London, 2001), pp. 169–80.

11. A. F. Pollard, 'The University of London and the Study of History' (1904), in A. F. Pollard, *Factors in Modern History* (New York, 1907), pp. 263–87 at p. 282.

12. Pendleton, 'A Place of Teaching and Research', pp. 131–4.

13. Pollard, 'The University of London', p. 276.

14. H. Butterfield, 'The History of the Historical Association', *History Today*, vi (1956), 63–4.

15. Pendleton, 'A Place of Teaching and Research', p. 173.

16. Pendleton, 'A Place of Teaching and Research', p. 205.

17. For context, see Bentley, *Modernizing England's Past*, pp. 70–91; T. G. Otte, *The Foreign Office Mind: The Making of British Foreign Policy, 1865–1914* (Cambridge, 2011), pp. 10–17; P. Satia, *Time's Monster: How History Makes History* (Cambridge, MA, 2020), pp. 1–11.

18. 'The Institute of Historical Research: The Building and Its Purpose' (1921), partially reproduced in D. Birch and J. Horn (comp.), *The History Laboratory: The Institute of Historical Research 1921–96* (London, 1996), pp. 13–15.

19. *Institute of Historical Research: First Annual Report, 1921–22* (London, 1923), pp. 8–9.

20. D. Manning, 'What Was Devotional Writing? Revisiting the Community at Little Gidding, 1626–33', in *People and Piety: Protestant Devotional Identities in Early Modern England*, ed. E. Clarke and R. Daniel (Manchester, 2020), pp. 25–42.

21. W. Clark, *Academic Charisma and the Origins of the Research University* (Chicago, 2006), pp. 141–82.

22. S. Ryan, 'Seminary Formation since the Council of Trent: A Historical Overview', in *Models of Priestly Formation: Assessing the Past, Reflecting on the Present, and Imagining the Future*, ed. D. Marmion, M. Mullaney and S. Ryan (Collegeville, MN, 2019), pp. 1–22.

23. Clement of Alexandria, *Paedagogus*, trans. W. Wilson, in *Ante-Nicene Christian Library: Translations of the Writings of the Fathers down to A.D. 325*, vol. IV, ed. A. Roberts and J. Donaldson (Edinburgh, 1884), pp. 113–348.

24. Isocrates, *Panathenaicus* (*c.*342 BCE), 200–272: trans. George Norlin, the Loeb Classical Library (1929); and Isocrates, *Panegyricus* (*c.*380 BCE), 9–10: trans. George Norlin, the Loeb Classical Library (1928). See also: W. L. Innerd, 'The Contribution of Isocrates to Western Educational Thought' (unpublished MA thesis, University of Durham, 1969), pp. 159–65.

25. G. Parsloe, 'Recollections of the Institute, 1922–43', *Bulletin of the Institute of Historical Research*, xliv (1971), 270–83 at p. 273.

26. J. Kirby, *Historians and the Church of England: Religion and Historical Scholarship, 1870–1920* (Oxford, 2016), pp. 221–2. See also: B. Young, 'History', in *Historicism and the Human Sciences in Victorian Britain*, ed. M. Bevir (Cambridge, 2017), pp. 154–85; and Bentley, *Modernizing England's Past*, pp. 45–69.

27. P. Cavill, 'A. F. Pollard', *Parliamentary History*, xl (2021), 45–58 at p. 48.

28. J. W. Fortescue, 'Presidential Address', *Transactions of the Royal Historical Society*, 4th ser. viii (1925), 1–13.

29. Later directors of the IHR, such as Geoffrey Dickens (1967–77) and Michael Thompson (1977–90), would also negotiate their academic work whilst sustaining a Christian faith. For details of Collinson's student days, see P. Collinson, *The History of a History Man: Or, the Twentieth Century Viewed from a Safe Distance. The Memoirs of Patrick Collinson* (Woodbridge, 2011), pp. 69–85.

30. Cf. Bentley, *Modernizing England's Past*, pp. 119–43 and 169–93.

31. I. Nicoll, 'A Statistical Profile of the London PhD in History 1921–90', *Oxford Review of Education*, xxii (1996), 273–94.

**32.** W. P. Webb, 'The Historical Seminar: Its Outer Shell and Its Inner Spirit', *The Mississippi Valley Historical Review*, xlii (1955), 3–23.

**33.** R. A. Hamed, 'Historiography in Egypt in the Twentieth Century', in *The Development of Social Science in Egypt: Economics, History, and Sociology*, ed. I. Handy (Cairo, 1995), pp. 18–40.

**34.** D. W. Hayton, 'The Laboratory for "Scientific History": T. W. Moody and R. D. Edwards at the Institute of Historical Research', *Irish Historical Studies*, xli (2017), 41–57 at pp. 56–7.

**35.** Cf. Laura Carter, 'Women Historians in the Twentieth Century', in *Precarious Professionals: Gender, Identities and Social Change in Modern Britain*, ed. Heidi Egginton and Zoë Thomas (London, 2021), pp. 263–85; 'Beyond Notability: Re-evaluating Women's Work in Archaeology, History, and Heritage in Britain, 1870–1950': https://beyondnotability.org [accessed 1 Aug. 2022]; J. Bourke, *Birkbeck: 200 Years of Radical Learning for Working People* (Oxford, 2022), pp. 174–203.

**36.** See S. Parkes, 'Steamboat Ladies (act. 1904–1907)', *Oxford Dictionary of National Biography* (online, 2007): https://doi.org/10.1093/ref:odnb/61643 [accessed 1 Dec. 2022].

**37.** For select minutes of the seminar series convened by Eliza Davis and Hilda Johnstone in the 1930s, see: Institute of Historical Research, Wohl Library: IHR/3/2/12, IHR/3/2/13, and IHR/3/2/16. See also: Institute of Historical Research, https://www.history.ac.uk/library/collections/provenance#davis-e-jeffries [accessed 1 Nov. 2022].

**38.** F. Perrone, 'University Teaching as a Profession for Women in Oxford, Cambridge, and London: 1870–1930' (unpublished DPhil thesis, University of Oxford, 1991), p. 57 and p. 328.

**39.** Cf. J. Thirsk, 'The History Women', in *Chattel, Servant, or Citizen: Women's Status in Church, State and Society*, ed. M. O'Dowd and S. Wichert (Belfast, 1995), pp. 1–11.

**40.** N. G. Brett-James, *Growth of Stuart London* (London, 1935), p. 9.

**41.** IHR/3/2/13 [no folio numbers], *passim*.

**42.** IHR/3/2/11 [no folio numbers]: 11 Oct. 1932.

**43.** L. G. Schwoerer, 'Caroline Robbins: An Anglo-American Historian', in *Generations of Women Historians: Within and Beyond the Academy*, ed. H. Smith and M. Zook (Chem, 2018), pp. 137–56 at pp. 152–53.

**44.** Birch and Horn, *The History Laboratory*, pp. 138–40.

**45.** Parsloe, 'Recollections of the Institute, 1922–43', p. 271.

**46.** M. Berg, *A Woman in History: Eileen Power, 1889–1940* (Cambridge, 1996), pp. 160–61.

**47.** J. Henderson, [untitled article?], *Past and Future* [the IHR magazine] (1993), reproduced in Birch and Horn, *The History Laboratory*, p. 131. For details on Joan Henderson, see: R. Strong, *Scenes and Apparitions: The Roy Strong Diaries 1988–2003* (London, 2016), pp. 185–6, p. 215, and pp. 409–10.

**48.** M. Howard, *Captain Professor: The Memoirs of Sir Michael Howard* (London, 2006), pp. 135–36 [italics indicate Howard's original emphasis].

**49.** A. T. Milne, 'Twenty-Five Years at the Institute, 1946–1971', *Bulletin of the Institute of Historical Research*, xliv (1971), 284–92; and C. Edwards, 'Recovering History Education's Forgotten Past: Diversity and Change in Professional Discourse in England, 1944–1962' (unpublished PhD thesis, University College London, 2016).

**50.** For context, see: D. W. Hayton, 'Colonel Wedgwood and the Historians', *Historical Research*, lxxxiv (2011), 328–55.

**51.** W. T. Jones, 'The Seminar Today', *The Pollardian* [Student Magazine] (UCL, 1956), 8–11, reproduced in Birch and Horn, comp., *The History Laboratory*, pp. 132–3.

52. D. W. Hayton, *Conservative Revolutionary: The Lives of Lewis Namier* (Manchester, 2019), p. 333 and p. 310. Cf. Bentley, *Modernizing England's Past*, pp. 194–218.

53. R. Evans, *Eric Hobsbawm: A Life in History* (Oxford, 2019), pp. 310–14.

54. Evans, *Eric Hobsbawm*, p. 422.

55. Evans, *Eric Hobsbawm*, p. 423.

56. Evans, *Eric Hobsbawm*, p. 500.

57. P. Croft, 'Conrad Russell', *Reviews in History*, no. 709a (2009): https://reviews.history.ac.uk/review/709a [accessed 1 Aug. 2022].

58. C. Russell, *The Fall of the British Monarchies 1637–1642* (Oxford, 1991), p. v and pp. ix–x.

59. Working from developments in 1940s America, the meaning of the term 'seminar' expanded to include any 'conference of specialists', see 'seminar, n.2.', *Oxford English Dictionary* online: www.oed.com/view/Entry/175679 [accessed 1 Aug. 2022].

60. P. Mandler, *History and National Life* (London, 2002), pp. 93–142.

61. T. Scott, 'Geoffrey Rudolph Elton (1921–1994)', *Renaissance Studies*, ix (1995), 344–6.

62. For context, see E. P. Thompson, ed., *Warwick University Ltd* (Nottingham, [1970] 2014); C. Russell, *Academic Freedom* (London, 1993); O. O'Neill, *A Question of Trust* (Cambridge, 2002); S. Collini, *Speaking of Universities* (London, 2017); P. Mandler, *The Crisis of the Meritocracy: Britain's Transition to Mass Education since the Second World War* (Oxford, 2020), pp. 72–122 and pp. 207–15; and S. Jones, *Universities Under Fire: Hostile Discourses and Integrity Deficits in Higher Education* (Basingstoke, 2022).

63. For context, see M. Foucault, *Society Must Be Defended: Lectures at the Collège de France, 1975–76*, trans. D. Macey (London, 2003), pp. 109–111, 172–212; J. Arnold et al., 'The Challenges of History', in *History after Hobsbawm: Writing the Past for the Twenty-First Century*, ed. J. Arnold et al. (Oxford, 2018), pp. 3–14; D. Bloxham, *Why History?* (Oxford, 2020), pp. 350–58; and H. Carr and S. Lipscomb, *What Is History, Now? How the Past and Present Speak to Each Other* (London, 2021), *passim*.

64. G. Preston, 'Seminars for Active Learning', *History in Higher Education: New Directions in Teaching and Learning*, ed. A. Booth and P. Hyland (Oxford, 1996), pp. 111–27 at p. 12. See also J. Davis and P. Salmon, '"Deep Learning" and the Large Seminar in History Teaching', in *The Practice of University History Teaching*, ed. A. Booth and P. Hyland (Manchester, 2000), pp. 125–36.

65. G. Elton, *The Practice of History* (Oxford, [1967] 2002), p. 151.

66. I say this advisedly with reference to what all these terms have come to connote in the British higher education sector since the 2010s. P. Scales, *An Introduction to Learning and Teaching in Higher Education: Supporting Fellowship* (London, 2017). Cf. S. Baumbach, 'To Be or Not to Be? Crisis and the Humanities in Germany', *The Changing Face of Higher Education: Is There an International Crisis in the Humanities?* ed. D. Ahlburg (Abingdon, 2019), pp. 83–100 at p. 92.

67. J. Champion, 'What Are Historians for?', *Historical Research*, lxxxi (2008), 167–88; and, L. Jordanova, 'Public History – A Provocation', a Talk at the first Public History Prize Workshop at the IHR (29 Oct. 2015): https://files.royalhistsoc.org/wp-content/uploads/2015/10/17210240/PHW-Jordanova-Provocation-29-Oct-15.pdf [accessed 1 Dec. 2022]. The IHR's Public History Seminar was founded in 2012 by Alix Green, John Tosh, Anna Maerker, Judy Faraday and Tim Boon.

68. Arendt, *The Human Condition*, pp. 198–9. Cf. S. Fox, 'Archival Intimacies: Empathy and Historical Practice in 2023', *Transactions of the Royal Historical Society* (2023), 1–25; and L. Stonebridge, *We Are Free to Change the World: Hannah Arendt's Lessons in Love and Disobedience* (London, 2024).

# References

## Archived sources

Institute of Historical Research, Wohl Library

IHR/3/2/11.
IHR/3/2/12.
IHR/3/2/13.
IHR/3/2/16.

## Published sources

Anderson, R., 'University History Teaching and the Humboldtian Model in Scotland, 1858–1914', *History of Universities*, xxv (2010), pp. 138–84.

Anderson, R., 'The Development of History Teaching in the Scottish Universities, 1894–1939', *Journal of Scottish Historical Studies*, xxxii (2012), 50–73.

Arendt, H., *The Human Condition*, second edition with new Foreword by D. Allen (Chicago, [1958] 2018).

Arnold, J. et al., 'The Challenges of History', in *History after Hobsbawm: Writing the Past for the Twenty-First Century*, ed. J. Arnold et al. (Oxford, 2018), pp. 3–14.

Banner Jr, J., *Being a Historian: An Introduction to the Professional World of History* (Cambridge, 2012).

Baumbach, S., 'To Be or Not to Be? Crisis and the Humanities in Germany', *The Changing Face of Higher Education: Is There an International Crisis in the Humanities?* ed. D. Ahlburg (Abingdon, 2019), pp. 83–100

Bellot, H. H., *University College London, 1826–1926* (London, 1929).

Bentley, M., *Modernizing England's Past: English Historiography in the Age of Modernism, 1870–1970* (Cambridge, 2005).

Berg, M. A., *A Woman in History: Eileen Power, 1889–1940* (Cambridge, 1996).

'Beyond Notability: Re-evaluating Women's Work in Archaeology, History, and Heritage in Britain, 1870–1950': https://beyondnotability .org [accessed 1 Aug. 2022].

Birch, D., and Horn, J. (comp.), *The History Laboratory: The Institute of Historical Research 1921–96* (London, 1996).

Bloxham, D., *Why History?* (Oxford, 2020).

Bourke, J., *Birkbeck: 200 Years of Radical Learning for Working People* (Oxford, 2022).

Brett-James, N. G., *Growth of Stuart London* (London, 1935).

Brown, P., *Journeys of the Mind: A Life in History* (Princeton, 2023).

Butterfield, H., 'The History of the Historical Association', *History Today*, vi (1956), 63–4.

Cannadine, D., *Making History Now and Then: Discoveries, Controversies and Explorations* (Basingstoke, 2008).

Carr, H., and Lipscomb, S., *What Is History, Now? How the Past and Present Speak to Each Other* (London, 2021).

Carter, L., 'Women Historians in the Twentieth Century', in *Precarious Professionals: Gender, Identities and Social Change in Modern Britain*, ed. H. Egginton and Z. Thomas (London, 2021), pp. 263–85.

Cavill, P., 'A. F. Pollard', *Parliamentary History*, xl (2021), 45–58.

Champion, J., 'What Are Historians for?', *Historical Research*, lxxxi (2008), 167–88.

Clark, W., *Academic Charisma and the Origins of the Research University* (Chicago, 2006).

Clement of Alexandria, *Paedagogus*, trans. W. Wilson, in *Ante-Nicene Christian Library: Translations of the Writings of the Fathers down to A.D. 325*, vol. IV, ed. A. Roberts and J. Donaldson (Edinburgh, 1884), pp. 113–348.

Collini, S., *Speaking of Universities* (London, 2017).

Collinson, P., *The History of a History Man: Or, the Twentieth Century Viewed from a Safe Distance. The Memoirs of Patrick Collinson* (Woodbridge, 2011).

Croft, P., 'Conrad Russell', *Reviews in History*, no. 709a (2009): https://reviews.history.ac.uk/review/709a [accessed 1 Aug. 2022].

Davis, J., and Salmon, P., '"Deep Learning" and the Large Seminar in History Teaching', in *The Practice of University History Teaching*, ed. A. Booth and P. Hyland (Manchester, 2000), pp. 125–36.

Elton, G., *The Practice of History* (Oxford, [1967] 2002).

Erickson, A., 'Ellen Annette McArthur: Establishing a Presence in the Academy', in *Generations of Women Historians: Within and Beyond the Academy*, ed. H. Smith and M. Zook (Chem, 2018), pp. 25–48.

Eskildsen, K. R., 'Virtues of History: Exercises, Seminars, and the Emergence of the German Historical Discipline, 1830–1900', in *History of Universities: Volume XXXIV/1*, ed. K.-M. Chang and A. Rocke (Oxford, 2021), pp. 27–40.

Evans, R., *Eric Hobsbawm: A Life in History* (Oxford, 2019).

Fortescue, J. W., 'Presidential Address', *Transactions of the Royal Historical Society*, 4th ser. viii (1925), 1–13.

Foucault, M., *Society Must Be Defended: Lectures at the Collège de France, 1975–76*, trans. D. Macey (London, 2003).

Fox, S., 'Archival Intimacies: Empath and Historical Practice in 2023', *Transactions of the Royal Historical Society* (2023), 1–25.

Grafton, A., 'In Clio's American Atelier', in *Social Knowledge in the Making*, ed. C. Camic et al. (Chicago, 2011), pp. 89–117.

Hamed, R. A., 'Historiography in Egypt in the Twentieth Century', in *The Development of Social Science in Egypt: Economics, History, and Sociology*, ed. I. Handy (Cairo, 1995), pp. 18–40.

Hayton, D. W., 'Colonel Wedgwood and the Historians', *Historical Research*, lxxxiv (2011), 328–55.

Hayton, D. W., 'The Laboratory for "Scientific History": T. W. Moody and R. D. Edwards at the Institute of Historical Research', *Irish Historical Studies*, xli (2017), 41–57.

Hayton, D. W., *Conservative Revolutionary: The Lives of Lewis Namier* (Manchester, 2019).

Howard, M., *Captain Professor: The Memoirs of Sir Michael Howard* (London, 2006).

Hughes, M. V., *A London Girl of the Eighties* (London, 1936).

*Institute of Historical Research: First Annual Report, 1921–22* (London, 1923).

Institute of Historical Research, Wohl Library: https://www.history.ac.uk/library/collections/provenance#davis-e-jeffries [accessed 1 Nov. 2022].

Isocrates, *Panegyricus* (*c*.380 BCE), trans. George Norlin, the Loeb Classical Library (Cambridge, MA, 1928).

Isocrates, *Panathenaicus* (*c*.342 BCE), trans. George Norlin, the Loeb Classical Library (Cambridge, MA, 1929).

Jones, S., *Universities Under Fire: Hostile Discourses and Integrity Deficits in Higher Education* (Basingstoke, 2022).

Jordanova, L., 'Public History – A Provocation', a Talk at the First Public History Prize Workshop at the IHR (29 Oct. 2015): https://files.royalhistsoc.org/wp-content/uploads/2015/10/17210240/PHW-Jordanova-Provocation-29-Oct-15.pdf [accessed 1 Dec. 2022].

Kirby, J., *Historians and the Church of England: Religion and Historical Scholarship, 1870–1920* (Oxford, 2016).

Kruse, O., 'The Origins of Writing in the Disciplines: Traditions of Seminar Writing and the Humboldtian Ideal of the Research University', *Written Communication*, xxiii (2006), 331–52.

Mandler, P., *History and National Life* (London, 2002).

Mandler, P., *The Crisis of the Meritocracy: Britain's Transition to Mass Education since the Second World War* (Oxford, 2020).

Manning, D., 'What Was Devotional Writing? Revisiting the Community at Little Gidding, 1626–33', in *People and Piety: Protestant Devotional Identities in Early Modern England*, ed. E. Clarke and R. Daniel (Manchester, 2020), pp. 25–42.

Milne, A. T., 'Twenty-Five Years at the Institute, 1946–1971', *Bulletin of the Institute of Historical Research*, xliv (1971), 284–92.

Nicoll, I., 'A Statistical Profile of the London PhD in History 1921–90', *Oxford Review of Education*, xxii (1996), 273–94.

O'Neill, O., *A Question of Trust* (Cambridge, 2002).

Otte, T. G., *The Foreign Office Mind: The Making of British Foreign Policy, 1865–1914* (Cambridge, 2011).

*Oxford English Dictionary*: www.oed.com/view/Entry/175679 [accessed 1 Aug. 2022].

Parkes, S., 'Steamboat Ladies (act. 1904–1907)', *Oxford Dictionary of National Biography* (online, 2007): https://doi.org/10.1093/ref:odnb /61643 [accessed 1 Dec. 2022].

Parsloe, G., 'Recollections of the Institute, 1922–43', *Bulletin of the Institute of Historical Research*, xliv (1971), 270–83.

Pollard, A. F., *Factors in Modern History* (New York, 1907).

Preston, G., 'Seminars for Active Learning', *History in Higher Education: New Directions in Teaching and Learning*, ed. A. Booth and P. Hyland (Oxford, 1996), pp. 111–27.

Russell, C., *The Fall of the British Monarchies 1637–1642* (Oxford, 1991).

Russell, C., *Academic Freedom* (London, 1993).

Ryan, S., 'Seminary Formation since the Council of Trent: A Historical Overview', in *Models of Priestly Formation: Assessing the Past, Reflecting on the Present, and Imagining the Future*, ed. D. Marmion, M. Mullaney and S. Ryan (Collegeville, MN, 2019), pp. 1–22.

Satia, P., *Time's Monster: How History Makes History* (Cambridge, MA, 2020).

Scales, P., *An Introduction to Learning and Teaching in Higher Education: Supporting Fellowship* (London, 2017).

Schwoerer, L. G., 'Caroline Robbins: An Anglo-American Historian', in *Generations of Women Historians: Within and Beyond the Academy*, ed. H. Smith and M. Zook (Chem, 2018), pp. 137–56.

Scott, T., 'Geoffrey Rudolph Elton (1921–1994)', *Renaissance Studies*, ix (1995), 344–6.

Slee, P., *Learning and a Liberal Education: The Study of Modern History in the Universities of Oxford, Cambridge, and Manchester, 1800–1914* (Manchester, 1986).

Slee, P., 'The Manchester School of History: Tout's Contribution to the Pedagogy of Academic History', in *Thomas Frederick Tout (1855–1929): Refashioning History for the Twentieth Century*, ed. J. Rosenthal and C. Barron (London, 2019), pp. 41–56.

Smith, B., 'Gender and the Practices of Scientific History: The Seminar and Archival Research in the Nineteenth Century', *American Historical Review*, c (1995), 1150–76.

Stonebridge, L., *We Are Free to Change the World: Hannah Arendt's Lessons in Love and Disobedience* (London, 2024).

Strong, R., *Scenes and Apparitions: The Roy Strong Diaries 1988–2003* (London, 2016).

Thirsk, J., 'The History Women', in *Chattel, Servant, or Citizen: Women's Status in Church, State and Society*, ed. M. O'Dowd and S. Wichert (Belfast, 1995), pp. 1–11.

Thompson, E. P. (ed.), *Warwick University Ltd* (Nottingham, [1970] 2014)

Webb, W. P., 'The Historical Seminar: Its Outer Shell and Its Inner Spirit', *The Mississippi Valley Historical Review*, xlii (1955), 3–23.

Young, B., 'History', in *Historicism and the Human Sciences in Victorian Britain*, ed. M. Bevir (Cambridge, 2017), pp. 154–85.


## Unpublished sources

Edwards, C., 'Recovering History Education's Forgotten Past: Diversity and Change in Professional Discourse in England, 1944–1962', PhD Thesis (University College London, 2016).

Innerd, W. L., 'The Contribution of Isocrates to Western Educational Thought', MA Thesis (University of Durham, 1969).

Pendleton, M., 'A Place of Teaching and Research: University College London and the Origins of the Research University in Britain 1890–1914', PhD Thesis (University of London, 2001).

Perrone, F., 'University Teaching as a Profession for Women in Oxford, Cambridge, and London: 1870–1930', DPhil Thesis (University of Oxford, 1991).

Wal, R. van de, 'Dancing in the Kitchens of History: Eileen Power, 1889–1940', PhD Thesis (University of Groningen, 2022).

Chapter 2

# The Italy 1200–1700 Seminar

**Trevor Dean and Kate Lowe**

One of the problems in researching medieval history lies in the sources – they are often incomplete or have inexplicable gaps. It was therefore a surprisingly familiar experience, when visiting the IHR archive, to find that the attendance registers for this Seminar, though starting in 1949, did not go beyond 2005, while the termly programmes began only in 1986 and were not always complete.[1] These gaps condition what we can say, but we shall also draw on the reminiscences of many of the Seminar attenders from its several phases, which cumulatively give a rounded and evaluative picture of the Seminar and how it was experienced and is recollected. This chapter is divided into two broad sections: in the first, we discuss who attended, who gave papers and the topics they addressed; in the second, we discuss issues of why people attended, how they benefitted and what value they put on the experience. We draw on three main sources: the attendance lists, the seminar programmes (both those in the IHR archive and others we have retained or retrieved),[2] and reminiscences from forty-two attenders.[3] Four sets of reminiscences have been taken from printed sources: Caroline Elam and Peter Denley in 1988 (both later gave further thoughts), Bill Kent in 2005, Camilla Russell in 2019 and Dale Kent in 2021.[4] Thirty reminiscences were collected for this essay during 2021, mainly by inviting known past attenders to write what they remembered about their experience of the Seminar. A few based responses on structured questions, but the great majority freely chose the direction and content of their comments. The final eight that do not fall into either category were generated in 2003–2010 by Kate Lowe collecting material for a study of Nicolai Rubinstein's intellectual formation.[5]

The Seminar was created by Nicolai Rubinstein in 1949 and was at first titled 'Italian Constitutional History', perhaps reflecting one of Rubinstein's major interests,[6] though it soon adopted the title 'Italian Medieval History', or 'Italian History'. Note the absence of the term 'Renaissance', which was not a defining construct for the Seminar. When Trevor Dean and Kate Lowe assumed the convenorship in 1996, they reformulated it as 'Late Medieval and Early Modern Italy', better to reflect their interests. Most recently, the title has been modified to 'Italy 1200–1700' under the convening of Serena Ferente, Catherine Keen, Patrick Lantschner, Stefan Bauer and Guido Rebecchini. Rubinstein (1911–2002) was born in Berlin. He began his university education at the Friedrich-Wilhelms-Universität, studying political economy, philosophy and history, and started a thesis on Italian fifteenth-century history. Expelled from Germany in 1933, he went to Italy to complete his studies in Florence with the Russian émigré medieval historian Nicola Ottokar (1884–1957). In 1939 he was forced by the racial laws to leave Italy for England. He lectured at Oxford and Southampton before being appointed to Westfield College, University of London, in 1945, where he stayed until his retirement in 1978. In the course of a long career, he wrote two crucial books on *The Government of Florence under the Medici, 1434 to 1494* (1966) and *The Palazzo Vecchio, 1298–1532: Government, Architecture, and Imagery in the Civic Palace of the Florentine Republic* (1995), edited several volumes of the *Letters of Lorenzo de' Medici*, and published dozens of academic articles, both on the history of medieval and Renaissance Florence and Tuscany, and on medieval and Renaissance political thought.

## Membership and content

Membership and attendance of the Seminar went through several distinct phases, which could be classified as early, middle and late Rubinstein, and post-Rubinstein. The four people who attended the very first meeting on 14 October 1949 were a mixed group, none of them studying Florence, which was central to Rubinstein's career, and only one of them even a member of the University of London. Daniel Waley (1921–2017) was still a PhD student at Cambridge, working on medieval Orvieto. He became a lecturer, at the LSE from 1952, and subsequently one of the major historians of non-Florentine communal Italy. He was the author of, among many works, the standard textbook, *The Italian City Republics*, now in its fifth edition.[7] Fanny MacRobert (1922–2000) was another Cambridge student, then recently married and living in London: her topic was German imperial towns in the fifteenth century.[8] She later became a schoolteacher. Dione Clementi (1914–2010), daughter of a former colonial governor, had worked

# THE ITALY 1200–1700 SEMINAR 45

at the wartime code-breaking centre at Bletchley Park and in 1949 was studying for her Oxford DPhil on twelfth-century Sicily; later she taught at Queen Mary College and published numerous studies of the political and constitutional histories of Sicily, southern Italy and England. Only the last member was actually studying for a London PhD, on the manuscripts of the Venetian cardinal Pietro Bembo: Daniel S. Duncan (d. 2002), who, despite not completing his PhD or publishing very much, did become head of department first at Birkbeck College, then (1966) at the University of Western Australia.[9] Both Waley and Duncan had served in the British army in Italy in the Second World War, and in both cases this inspired their choice of Italian history and literature as a career. The diffuse interests of this group are perhaps unsurprising: Rubinstein was not yet supervising doctoral students (his first was Rosemary Devonshire Jones, whose study of a Florentine diplomat and politician was completed in 1958).

Four attenders remained the average for the next decade, the maximum being eight. We should not be surprised at such numbers: students making it through to postgraduate study in Italian medieval history were few in the 1950s. In 1959–60, there were four members again: Waley, a permanent presence at the Seminar until the early 1960s; Alison Brown (Dyson in those days), then studying for her MA; 'Tilly' De La Mare (1932–2001), a Warburg PhD student of Florentine book producers; and the fourth was a former student at the Warburg whose PhD thesis had discussed a humanist treatise on 'famous men'. Brown went on to a successful career at Royal Holloway College, and her interests most closely paralleled those of Rubinstein: Florentine politics, the Medici and Renaissance political thought. De la Mare became assistant librarian at the Bodleian Library, Oxford (1964–88) and then a distinguished professor of palaeography at King's College London, with special interest in Florentine humanistic books and book collectors. In the intervening years, other Florentinists had come and gone, such as Louis Marks (1928–2010), who in later life went on to a more high-profile career as a screenwriter and drama producer for the BBC, drawing on his historical knowledge to set an episode of *Dr Who* in fifteenth-century Italy.

The content in these early years seems to have been determined by Rubinstein's own experience as a student in Berlin in the 1930s, attending seminars which 'focused on discussion of texts'. In his own valedictory, retrospective talk delivered in 1996, Rubinstein recalled that:

> Members of the Seminar did not read papers but collaborated on the discussion of texts – interpretation and philological criticism thereof. Members of the Seminar had to work quite hard ... It was customary for professors to choose for their seminar's subjects connected with

the work they themselves were doing. (Elam, contemporaneous notes on Nicolai's seminar paper).

Such content, however, did not fit the context of graduate studies in London: 'The Seminar was originally text-based, but this didn't work well: too few people and other members too busy to prepare' (Elam). So, about 1954, Rubinstein adopted the system of speakers giving papers.

In the early 1960s, the Seminar seems to have been close to expiring. In 1962–3 it ran only in the summer term with one attender (according to the register: that person does not recall this). The Seminar did not meet in 1963–4, as Rubinstein was at the Institute of Advanced Study, Princeton for the year. When it restarted in the autumn of 1964, the old core had disappeared (some only temporarily). This marked the start of a new phase. New members in the mid and late 1960s were PhD students, mostly supervised by Nicolai Rubinstein and with topics in Florentine history: studies of Florentine politicians, writers, preachers or art patronage. Diana Webb recalls that in the late 1960s, membership 'consisted of three married couples and me'. Two of these couples were Dale and Bill Kent,[10] and Bob and Jane Black. The third, as Jane Black recalls, was 'Ann and Christopher Fuller, who have long dropped out of the scene [and] were regular attenders, Ann working very productively on the church of Santo Spirito and its patrons, Christopher on Florentine preachers.' All of this group were studying fifteenth-century Florence, under the supervision of Rubinstein: political alignments 1427–34 (Dale Kent, PhD 1971), three elite families 1427–1530 (Bill Kent, 1971), a Florentine humanist and chancellor (Bob Black, 1974), political ideas in a work on 'civil life' (Jane Black, 1969); most of their theses were published as monographs. Indeed, prominent careers as Renaissance historians lay ahead for some of these: the Australian Kents became professors, first at La Trobe and later at California Riverside (Dale) and at Monash (Bill), and produced ground-breaking works on Florentine families, and on Cosimo and Lorenzo de' Medici; the Chicagoan Robert Black became professor at Leeds and wrote major new studies of Renaissance education. This group represented a significant shift in the Seminar's social profile: away from Oxbridge, towards the world. Numbers at the Seminar grew each year, from six in 1967–8 to eleven in 1969–70 and reaching twenty by 1974–5.

The content of the Seminar in this period was closely connected with the professor's own work, as Jane Black, who attended from 1967, recalled:

The emphasis was VERY Florentine, what with Nicolai's own preference and the overpowering presence of the Kents. The interchange was usually about particular fifteenth-century Florentine families ... The contributions consisted of people's last thesis chapter, not always riveting. Discussions were pretty technical ... Daniel Waley was a regular attender, sitting in a corner with unspoken impatience.

Such impatience arose from tension between the special status of Florentine history and a plethora of other historiographies in medieval Italy. Views from inside and outside Florence did not always coincide. Former students also recall frustration with the content: Jill Moore said that at first,

> the focus was overwhelmingly, stultifyingly, on a very short period of Florentine history, and as far as I could tell, I was the only person round the table working on a different period and a different area of Italy ... Nicolai was very much in charge (though kindly), and the Kents were clearly head prefects.

The dominance of Rubinstein's students continued into the 1970s, as recalled by Robertson: 'I have a memory that it was a mostly a mix of Nicolai's postgraduates past and present who gave papers plus others' (he mentions Sydney Anglo, in particular, a memorable paper on duelling).

Across the Seminar's first fifty-six years (1949–2005) a total of 841 people signed the register. That figure needs some glossing: it is likely that some attenders failed to sign (Bernadette Paton recalls thinking that signing was only for 'Important People'); some signed illegibly; and from a certain date the register seems to include the speaker. Nevertheless, this is an impressive body of scholars. Of these 841, the gender of 174 is unclear. Of the remaining 668, 393 (59 per cent) were women and 275 were men. This female dominance might be surprising, but it existed almost from the beginning. The attenders were evenly split between men and women in 1949, and a female superiority in numbers soon set in: three out five in 1955–6, six out of eight in 1956–7, three out of three in 1961–2. It may be that the 'femininity' of modern language student-cohorts explains this preponderance.[11] What is also striking from this total is the growth of new entrants: listing members by date of first attendance, the numbers are in single figures until the mid-1970s, but in double figures every year after 1978–9, over twenty every year between 1983 and 2003, over thirty every year between 1990 and 1995, reaching over fifty in two of those years. The number of students and scholars being newly drawn to this Seminar kept expanding in the central Rubinstein years, a testimony to his reputation, to the range and quality of the speakers, and to the relevance and popularity of Italian studies. Also important in the expansion was the inclusion of art-historical topics attracting art historians: Rubinstein himself noted that 'in 1969–70 there would have been no question of art historians attending the Seminar; by 1976 it had become routine' (Elam, notes on Rubinstein's retirement speech in 1996). At this period, funding for PhD study was more generous and more available, and choice of topic and supervisor less constrained than they later became.

The heyday of the Seminar under Rubinstein (and his eventual co-convenor David Chambers) was the 1970s and 80s, and this lasted into the 1990s: a solid core of Florentine historians, students of that city's society, politics and art/architecture, and with new members replacing erstwhile pillars such as the Kents. There was though also a consistent number of non-Florentinists, whether working on Siena (Peter Denley) or further afield on non-republican Italy such as Ferrara or Mantua, or on cognate disciplines such as archaeology. Once again, there were PhD students or postdocs from outside London, whether from Oxford or Cambridge (Denley, Elam) or from as far as Keele, thirsty for a kind of focused research debate that their own universities were unable to provide. 'As a Junior Research Fellow at King's College Cambridge (1972–76), I longed to experience the Seminar, and I finally plucked up courage to write to "Professor Rubinstein", whom I had not met, to ask if I could attend' (Elam). Art historians who attended tended to be those more interested in documents: 'We were art historians, but we wanted to be historians at the same level as [real] historians' (Haines).

Several of our respondents have conveyed to us their impressions of the character of the Seminar's programmes under Rubinstein: that the content was mainly Florentine, or that it was mainly political history, reflecting the major (but not exclusive) interests of the organizer – it is said, for example, that Nicolai was not interested in religion – or that the content was conservative and not interested in newer topics in social/cultural history or in new historiographical methods. According to Lauro Martines, 'Nicolai was not at home with discussions about social structure ... and the varieties of unconventional historical investigation ... [He] was wedded to the study of traditional political sources'. The earliest topic-lists that we have – from the late 1970s – do not wholly support these impressions. The balance between Florence and Italy, and between the political and the artistic, intellectual and economic did vary. In the spring term of 1977–8 three papers on Florentine humanist manuscripts, economy and topography were outnumbered by papers on central Italy and Mantua (art, confraternities and princely servants), and there were two other papers on non-Florentine topics. It may however be that the normal balance was the reverse: in the following term, only two papers looked outside Florence (John Law on Verona, Daniel Waley on the Roman region), and in the second term of 1981–2 five out of six papers addressed Florentine

# THE ITALY 1200–1700 SEMINAR     49

topics. Religion was certainly not neglected: the first session in October 1981 featured Rubinstein himself talking about reform of the religious orders in fifteenth-century Italy. Other religious topics followed too: Franciscan sermons (1981), piety and print (1981), church reform (1982), saints (1983) and confraternities (1978, 1980). There were papers on non-Florentine topics, such as frescoes in Cortona, tombs in Venice, Jews in Naples, and on non-political topics, such as Greek translations, Sicilian aristocrats, and wives' claims against insolvent husbands. It is true that there was a solid Florentine political theme: the politics of Dante's *Inferno*, the politics of Savonarola's sermons, the term '*politicus*' itself in Renaissance Italy (Rubinstein's own paper). And repeated attention to Lorenzo de' Medici: his library, his relations with Siena, his posthumous image. But the politics were not always Florentine – the papal states make an appearance – and the Florentine topics were not always political – taxation and education appear too. Nevertheless, the impression was certainly taken that 'Tuscany was the centre of the world as far as the Seminar was concerned' (Wright). And there is more force to the suggestion that newer historical interests and methods were not represented – for example, women's history, subaltern history, popular history, quantitative history – though Carlo Ginzburg (b. 1939) did once give a paper. Instead, there was a focus on individual, male historical actors – Lorenzo de' Medici, Dante, Savonarola, Machiavelli – or on institutions and monuments; but this was also because there were few scholars working on newer or alternative topics in British universities, and the seminars were not funded to bring in researchers from abroad.

It was in the mid-1990s that a supplementary seminar, 'Themes in Italian Renaissance History', conceived by Alison Brown and run in conjunction with Stefan ('Larry') Epstein and Dean, gave voice to fresher topics and non-British voices.[12] For five years, this themed seminar ran in the summer term on topics such as bodies, space, rules, groups and identities, and drew in speakers from France, Italy, Australia and the USA (Christiane Klapisch, Elizabeth Crouzet-Pavan, Andrea Zorzi, Ottavia Niccoli, Julius Kirshner, and others), as well as the UK.

When Rubinstein retired from convening the (parent) Seminar in 1996, the convenorship passed to Dean and Lowe, who were joined by a third convenor, first Alison Wright, art historian at UCL (until 2005), then Georgia Clarke, architectural historian at the Courtauld, and latterly (from 2009) by Serena Ferente, socio-political historian then at King's, now at Amsterdam. Frequent changes in the convenorship group reflected broader pressures on colleagues to participate more in their own local, departmental activities: these pressures came as academics and institutions adapted to the disintegration of the federal University of London (2007–19), and to the regularity of national research assessment exercises (2001, 2008, 2014), protecting the visibility of departmental research,[13] but needlessly duplicating and impoverishing the central facility. At this point there was a second major replacement of membership (see above). As a group of convenors, we did try to do things differently: fewer established figures, more early career scholars; more female speakers; minimal formalities; space for research students to ask questions; less focus on Florence and the Medici; sessions devoted to short presentations of research problems or to commemorative re-readings of works by recently deceased scholars, such as Rubinstein himself, or Don Weinstein.

The years after 2003 showed a strong contrast with the period 1986–92. The first and obvious observation is a rebalancing of the gender of speakers: only in a few terms were men now in a majority as speakers; in most terms, female speakers outnumbered them, and in 2010 the Seminar witnessed its first all-female programme. A second major observation is the absence of traditional political history in the papers presented, along with a clear move away from Florence as a major theme of the Seminar. The few overtly political papers were now more addressed to larger political processes ('state-building', 'urban systems of conflict') rather than specific historical moments or actors (though 'Caterina Sforza as political strategist' certainly fell into that category). It is true that at least one paper per term dealt with some aspect of Florentine history, and Machiavelli remained a definite favourite, but topics were now much less likely to focus on the Medici, more likely to address questions in that city's social history, such as women, children, trousseaux or working-class fashion. Religion and humanism continued as minor themes, whether picking up old debates on 'civic humanism' or thinking afresh about the relation between humanism and diplomacy, while papers on religion turned away from institutional church history and more to religious practice (miraculous images, private devotion, 'following in the footsteps of Christ'). The Seminar broadened its geographical range and expanded its inclusion of new kinds of cultural and social history. Naples, the South and Sicily became more regular topics: Neapolitan tombs, paintings, garden architecture and rape trials; southern lordships; government payment registers in Sicily. Previously untouched parts of northern Italy were now visited: sermons in Udine; a lady-in-waiting at the court of Savoy; trials, poisons and authors in Rome. Chronology broadened too: fewer papers on the fifteenth century (by far the majority in the 1980s), more on the sixteenth-seventeenth. New material history (armour, trinkets), performance (street-singers, 'charlatans' and 'male bodies on display') and broader socio-cultural history (the Renaissance tomato) were more to the fore. The working class came into better focus, whether it be the homes of Sienese artisans or the clothing choices of poorer Florentines. Historians at the Seminar also became more aware of theoretical and methodological issues, shown in the titles of two papers, 'How to read ...' (ambassadorial reports, letters). The word 'theory' makes its first appearance in a title in 2003, 'ideology' in 2005, 'sexuality' in 2016 (rather belated, some might think). Women's history continued its ascent: for a while every term brought new findings on the position, experience, objects or representation of women across Italy and from various classes. Geographical range was extended to consider Italians abroad and foreigners in Italy: Italian merchants in England, a Persian in Florence, Balkan émigrés in the south, Greeks in Ancona, the Genoese around the Black Sea. The kind of art history that discussed individual works and their origins or patronage was joined by more challenging attempts to look outside the frame: looking at the plinth not the statue, or the photographic reproduction not the artwork *in situ*. Finally, in a more playful spirit, a joint meeting with the European History 1150–1550 Seminar saw Dean 'trounce' (his word) David Carpenter in a debate 'Which country holds the record for records?' An unmistakable sense of going beyond old boundaries is the cumulative effect of the Seminar in the twenty-first century.

Seminar programmes are of course always a combination of the convenors' preferences and the availability of speakers, and there is a risk in drawing broader conclusions from them. Nevertheless, it can reasonably be argued that behind the fissiparity of topics in the first decades of this century lie broader explanatory developments in academia: the end of grand narratives, processes of decentring, the death of the canon, greater methodological awareness, decolonization.

An important final aspect to the membership is the shifting balance between regular and irregular attenders. For the first three decades (1949–78), all of the attenders attended most of the sessions: they were 'members' of the Seminar in a real and regular sense. The change to a different attendance pattern occurred suddenly and permanently in 1979–80, when only ten attenders, out of a total for the year of fifty-four, attended over half the sessions, and nineteen attended only once. This was perhaps the result of a more expansive menu of topics, as explained above; and it was certainly the start of a bifurcated membership: a core of about ten, a periphery of many more, occasional attenders attracted by topic or speaker. The Seminar thus assumed a different identity and function: no longer the professor and his friends, colleagues and students, but a broader constituency of historians and interested parties.

## Reminiscences

Reminiscences of forty-two attenders from across the life span of the Seminar form the basis of the second section of the chapter.[14] This personal and qualitative material provides a very different feel to an analysis of topics and speakers, gradually building a composite amalgam of how people later remembered and made sense of their experience of attending. Many commented on why they attended and what benefits they felt they accrued from doing so. The gender split of respondents – unplanned – was almost exactly half and half: twenty-two reminiscences from women and twenty from men. The early years and the most recent decades are the least well represented, while the middle period has generated more comment. Of the early years, two respondents first attended in the 1940s (Waley and Clementi), one in the 1950s (Alison Brown), and several sets of reminiscences emanate from respondents who first attended in the 1960s (Pesman Cooper, Webb, Jane Black, Bob Black, Dale Kent, Bill Kent, Moore and Pepper). The majority of the reminiscences focus on the period when Rubinstein was convenor; one reason for this is perhaps because Rubinstein is safely dead whereas the subsequent convenors are still all alive. Because Rubinstein is dead, however, there has been a tendency in some cases to write in hagiographical terms of his stewardship; attempts have been made to counter this by focusing on anecdote.

Virtually all of these reminiscences were written years after the seminar meetings they described, and what was written was undoubtedly coloured by lives and careers in the period in-between. Some attenders continued in academic life whereas others did not, as has been flagged earlier. Yet, for both sets, attendance at the Seminar came in retrospect to appear a watershed period in which they had imbibed (in most cases) or fought (in a few cases) the essential characteristics embodied by Rubinstein's approach to Italian Renaissance history. This might not have been the case had they been asked for reminiscences immediately after their attendance; memory adjustment is often evident. Another factor affecting the reminiscences is that Rubinstein's social networks were principally founded on his academic interests. Many of the attenders were or became lifelong friends of his, and were hardly impartial observers (Boucher raises this, as does Lippincott who remembers driving Rubinstein home in her Fiat 126 as she lived in the same block of flats as him in Hampstead), although it is worth stressing that friendship with Rubinstein was also in its way a hallmark of the Seminar during the years in which he was in charge. Rubinstein's position as founder of the Seminar in 1949, and his very long stewardship to 1996, meant that for forty-seven years the Seminar was considered his creation, his fiefdom. Several attenders

(Elam, Kraye, Marchand) reflected on the speech Rubinstein gave on his 'retirement' from the Seminar on 8 December 1996, in which he linked the way he ran the Seminar at the IHR to his formative experiences attending pro-seminars at the Friedrich-Wilhelms-Universität in Berlin in the early 1930s. Emphasizing his and the Seminar's lineage to great pre-war German institutions and scholarship was crucial (Marchand said Rubinstein 'described the German seminar as though it were yesterday'), but so too was difference, as he took account both of local conditions in England and of the constantly changing *zeitgeist*. The refugee both recreated and adjusted the tried and tested procedures he had witnessed in his youth in Berlin to fit with new circumstances in London.

Attenders were split over Rubinstein's stance on hierarchy. To everyone at the Seminar from at least the 1970s (it is not clear before this date – Bill Kent remembers calling him Professor Rubinstein), Nicolai chose to be 'Nicolai', and never Professor Rubinstein, which was clearly different to how teachers were addressed in 1930s Berlin. There was also a difference in how students behaved in relation to their teachers. As Rubinstein commented, 'No-one [at the IHR seminar] stood up for me', meaning no-one stood up when he entered the room as was the custom for a professor in Berlin. Yet Sam Cohn remembers the seating arrangements in 1975: there were 'three hierarchical circular rows ... with the professors in the inner chamber, ringed by a second seating of university lecturers and readers ... and then the hoi polloi of graduate students'. When Cohn raised his hand to ask a question, Rubinstein mistook it for a request to leave the room to go to the lavatory. This is countered by Bernadette Paton's memory of the Seminar in 1981–2 as 'a very egalitarian event ... students and lecturers were all in together, the famous and the obscure given equal weight both in invitations to speak and at question time'. Wright in the late 1980s 'found the atmosphere quite generous – no-one really hogging the question time and certainly sympathetic to a "youngster"'. Maybe the key to interpretation lies in the dating, and habits changed as the effects of the 1960s social revolution percolated into broader social relations in the course of the 1970s. Several early attenders who were PhD students reported being 'nervous' or 'terrified' or 'intimidated' by the Seminar in general (Pesman Cooper, Jane Black, Clarke), which impeded them from asking a question. Other attenders could be wary of the 'devastatingly hostile questions, often ending with an expressive sniff' (Elam) of another well-known combative attender, or remembered 'the biting force' conveyed by the word 'quite' (Cohn), or remembered a full-frontal attack (Denley); but these occurrences were acknowledged to be rare. One attender from the early 1970s, on the other hand, when the group was still small, remembered the 'marvellous discussions with Nicolai, Daniel Waley ... [and] John Hale' (Fox). A later attender described the question time as 'Civilized. Deference to Nicolai always seemed to keep things ... under control' (Knox), and this experience of the Seminar was echoed by others. Several attenders commented very favourably on the atmosphere and running of the IHR Seminar in comparison to other seminars they had known, either the director's seminar at the Warburg (Knox, Chambers, Lowe) or the medieval seminar at Oxford (Dean, Chambers, Paton) or the lack of relevant seminars in Cambridge – 'there wasn't much going on at Cambridge in the Renaissance field' – or even the Courtauld in the late 1970s and 1980s (Elam). 'Although we never spoke of inclusivity or porosity in the 1970s, those were characteristics of the seminar' (Lillie).

In the field of Italian medieval and Renaissance history, Rubinstein's IHR Seminar was 'celebrated'[15] or even 'legendary' (Kovesi), probably by the early 1970s, and not just in the United Kingdom, or in Europe, or in North America, but also in Australia, from which country he had a stream of PhD students.[16] Descriptions of the focus of the Seminar's meetings may be contested, with a clear split between those working on Florence and those with non-Florentine interests – 'the Seminar was fundamental intellectually for those who spoke and those who attended' (Elam) versus 'soporific ... anything but intellectually stimulating' (Moore) – but nearly everyone agreed on their social power, with comments ranging from 'the only venue for bringing together people in London interested in the Renaissance' (Clarke), 'a kind of club' (Boucher), 'a regular slot in which to feel part of a multi-generational scholarly community' (Lowe) to 'a very useful opportunity to catch up with friends who were scattered across the UK at various universities' (Lippincott). What they provided seems clear. First and foremost, they provided 'a sense of identity as an historian of Italy' (Dean) and a community of scholars: 'we were drawn in by the special sense of shared purpose and scholarly enquiry he created for and within the group' (Lillie). News of interest to the group was passed on at the Seminar. This could be exciting – such as success in applications for jobs – or sad: on 21 January 1982, after a paper by Elizabeth McGrath, on Medici allegories in Vasari's frescoes in the Palazzo Vecchio, Rubinstein announced that Rosemary Devonshire Jones, his first PhD student, was dead (Lowe).

There is a strong sense that an inner circle at the Seminar was performing for the benefit of an outer circle of PhD students and younger scholars. Rubinstein taught by example, believing that thus would best practice be transmitted. 'Week after week, it [the Seminar] taught the outer circle what scholarship was and how it should be presented' (O'Malley). Rubinstein aimed for rigour. 'The formal discipline of the Nicolai seminar encouraged us all to be at our absolute scholarly, critical best' (Kovesi). He was a living example of the benefits of deep and continuous archival research, and analysis of archival documents lay at the heart of his version of what Italian Renaissance history was. So, the Seminar was 'an introduction to archival research' (Jane Black) or 'a launch pad for archival work in Italy, where novices like myself gained some inkling of the strange crevices of deep research from scholars who had immersed themselves in documents for decades' (Lillie). During the first years, the Seminar's meetings had often consisted of an examination of an archival text (Bill Kent),[17] a practice resuscitated in part by the research clinics instituted by Dean and Lowe in the 2010s. These occasions, when attenders brought a research problem to be examined in detail by all those present, proved memorably effective, and were remembered by both convenors as amongst the best meetings they held. Documentary and textual analysis remained a leitmotif throughout, with papers that failed to do this being discussed more critically or altogether disparaged.

Another area of disagreement revolves around the extent to which the Seminar straightforwardly provided training for PhD students under Rubinstein's aegis. While some argue that it did (Chambers), at least in a meticulous technical sense (Bill Kent), others saw it as more of an arena than a training ground. The entry point for PhD students was high, as most received little or no formal palaeographical training, and what they learnt in the Seminar was not how to read a document but how to make sense of it and extract meaning from it, how to discuss or analyse it after they had read it. Research methods and skills were otherwise not addressed (except in one term's programme on 'Varieties of sources and techniques for research', 1996), and learning was passive rather than participatory. One attender, very early in his research, and on Rubinstein's advice, approached the *direttrice* of the Sala di manoscritti in the Biblioteca nazionale in Florence to ask the meaning of a particular contraction, to be told witheringly it meant 'et' (Black). Another fondly recalled a speaker who said, 'he only liked "scruffy" manuscripts and talked about a very scruffy one' (Holberton).

Meetings of the Seminar – instead of focusing on training – concentrated instead on Italian medieval and Renaissance history or history of art in action, allowing attenders to listen to and meet some of the most established scholars in the field, as well as giving PhD students the opportunity to test their hypotheses in front of an informed audience. Virtually everyone in the field in the UK was invited to give a paper – although years later Philip Jones claimed he had never been invited but that 'Trevor Dean had instead given a paper representing a "Jonesian" point of view' – but some were invited more often than others. One of the draws of the Seminar by the 1970s was its wide range of speakers: the attenders remembered a steady stream of Italians (Carlo Ginzburg, Domenico Maffei, Maria Monica Donato, Giovanni Ciappelli), often giving their paper in Italian, and many of the famous names from America came from the late 1960s onwards (Myron Gilmore, Felix Gilbert, David Herlihy, Melissa Bullard, Gene Brucker, Don Weinstein, Rudolph Bell, Richard Goldthwaite, Julius Kirshner, John Najemy, Tony Molho). Italians attached to the Warburg also swelled the numbers of speakers and attenders, 'loving the association with Nicolai that the seminars offered' (Ian Jones). These traditions continued – and, in the case of Italian speakers, expanded – after regime change, given impetus by the addition of the first Italian to become a seminar convenor, Serena Ferente.

One drawback of this discussion so far is that it has followed the 'great men of history' model by prioritizing Rubinstein, not least because most of the reminiscences focused on his stewardship. It is undoubtedly the case that his personality, his investment in the Seminar, and the longevity of his rule all led to a deep identification of it with him, or him with it. Yet even during this period there was another very significant player: the setting of the IHR. The space in which the Seminar was enacted has heavily influenced attenders' experiences, seeping into their consciousness in a similar way to the content of the papers. In some attenders' minds, the space influenced the memories, even if the room itself changed, from the Ecclesiastical History Room to the Low Countries Room to the British History Room to the Local History Room to two different rooms in the basement of the IHR, even with a period in exile in two further seminar rooms in Senate House (these last few perches were after Rubinstein's tenure). Peregrinations notwithstanding, the space (or lack of it) made a lasting impression. 'It seems always to have been hot, from the press of bodies and the unregulatable heating' (O'Malley), 'it took place in the very narrow very brown and green European History Room, then later in a barnlike space on the first floor' (Robertson), 'the rooms in which we met, lined with books, were usually small and cramped, dominated by dark green tables and with extraordinarily ugly stacking chairs of green metal with blue plastic upholstery' (Elam), 'you had to sit awkwardly, perched on the sort of bench-step that ran along the shelving ... the only place to rest the eyes always seemed to be the *Acta* of Requesens' (Dean). Often commented upon by members of the Seminar was the fact that the books in most of these rooms were not relevant to the topics under discussion, and seemed to have been assigned almost as a form of provocation – but Italy I and Italy II were far too small to accommodate talks.

Social mores dictated that, after the IHR, seminar members went to the pub, where many memorable and half-remembered discussions ensued. These too constituted a form of training. Attenders in the 1960s remembered going to the Museum Tavern on Great Russell Street and the original Pizza Express where there was a juke-box (Webb), but mostly the reminiscences coalesce around conversations in the University Tavern (now the College Arms) on Store Street, the haunt from the 1970s until its makeover in the 1980s, which was notably 'grubby' (Beverly Brown) and unglamorous. Sociability seeped through the pores of the Seminar, leading in a couple of cases (Jane and Bob Black, Wright and Marchand) to marriage. A third couple, having only met briefly, re-met there and later married (Zervas and Hirst). In addition, the Seminar led to notable academic partnerships, such as Dean and Lowe, and Chambers and Dean. Even without academic collaboration, the Seminar provided the occasion for meeting like-minded scholars and many lifelong friendships were forged after a first encounter there (Cohn and Lillie, Martines and Cohn). When new convenors took over in the 1990s, perhaps with a greater interest in the quality of wine, more convivial spots were found at the bar in the Royal Academy of Dramatic Art (RADA) on Malet Street and at the Life-Goddess in Store Street.

Yet the Seminar did not exist in a Rubinstein-only vacuum. It has had many convenors, all of whom introduced – or would have introduced – changes. Waley was apparently asked by Rubinstein whether he would share the running of the Seminar with him in the late 1960s, but a fortnight later he rescinded his offer, a change of mind explained by Waley 'because he [Waley] was not always polite when someone read a rotten paper'. Rubinstein continued to run the Seminar by himself until the late 1970s, when he invited Chambers to be co-convenor. Chambers's presence helped introduce changes, perhaps diluting Rubinstein's Florentine bias (even though there is little sense of it in the topics discussed above) and introducing a wider variety of speakers – although his tenure as co-convenor coincided with a period when academic fashions were changing too. When asked if he felt all types of history had been included, Chambers responded, 'There was no discussion of types of history. But this is a twenty-first-century question – it was not something thought of at the time'. Change through sharper boundary definition also occurred when the Seminar was involved in turf wars with other seminars, as chronological boundaries (with the Early Modern Italian History Seminar, founded by Robert Oresko) (Chambers and Pepper) and quotas of talks on Italian subjects (for the Early Modern European History Seminar, now European History 1500–1800) were imposed.

The importance of the Seminar for the study of Italian history in the UK cannot be overstated. This becomes clear if one asks what would have been different if the Seminar had not existed. Through all the vicissitudes of the transformation of universities from organizations fostering educational achievement to commercial enterprises with financial priorities, and the ever-changing fashions in academic history study and writing, the Seminar has maintained its focus on scholarly excellence and *Bildung*. In the absence of a relevant intellectual community in many university departments, it offered the possibility of an alternative group membership for students and scholars of medieval and Renaissance Italy. Perusing the names of the attenders of the Seminar, and analysing their scholarship, shows what an extraordinarily successful community of Italian historians it supported and nurtured.

# Notes

1. Institute of Historical Research, Wohl Library: IHR 3/3/29 and IHR 3/3/30.

2. We thank David Chambers for the earliest programmes we have recovered.

3. Unless signalled otherwise, all the quotations have come from these solicited reminiscences.

4. P. Denley and C. Elam, 'Introduction' and 'Nicolai Rubinstein', in *Florence and Italy: Renaissance Studies in Honour of Nicolai Rubinstein*, ed. P. Denley and C. Elam (London, 1988), pp. ix and xi–xiv; F. W. Kent, 'Nicolai Rubinstein, Teacher', in *Nicolai Rubinstein: In Memoriam*, ed. F. W. Kent (Florence, 2005), pp. 35–45; C. Russell, 'The Renaissance Comes to Bloomsbury: Studies in the Italian Renaissance in Twentieth-century London', in *The Art and Language of Power in Renaissance Florence: Essays for Alison Brown*, ed. A. Bloch, C. James and C. Russell (Toronto, 2019), pp. 377–406; D. Kent, *The Most I Could Be: A Renaissance Story* (Melbourne, 2021).

5. On Rubinstein's period in Oxford, see: K. Lowe, '"I Shall Snuffle About and Make Relations": Nicolai Rubinstein, the Historian of Renaissance Florence, in Oxford during the War', in *Ark of Civilization: Refugee Scholars and Oxford University, 1930–1945*, ed. S. Crawford, K. Ulmschneider and J. Elsner (Oxford, 2017), pp. 220–33.

6. See N. Rubinstein, 'Florentine Constitutionalism and Medici Ascendancy in the Fifteenth century', in *Florentine Studies: Politics and Society in Renaissance Florence*, ed. N. Rubinstein (London, 1968), pp. 442–62.

7. T. Dean, 'Daniel Waley', *Biographical Memoirs of Fellows of the British Academy*, xvii (2019), 305–24.

8. *Newnham College Roll Letter* (Cambridge, 2001), pp. 96–7. We thank Mary MacRobert for this information.

9. Birkbeck, University of London, Library Archives and Special Collections, Birkbeck College Annual Reports, 1954–65, GB 1832 BBK/10/1; University of Western Australia, University Archives, D. S. Duncan file. We are very grateful to Emma Illingworth at Birkbeck and Maria Carvalho at UWA for their help in tracing Donald Duncan.

10. Kent, *The Most I Could Be*, p. 108.

11. C. Evans, *Language People: The Experience of Teaching and Learning Modern Languages in British Universitie*s (Milton Keynes, 1988), p. 150.

12. For further details, see A. Brown, 'Renaissance Bodies: A New Seminar on the Renaissance', *Bulletin of the Society for Renaissance Studies*, xxii (1994), 20–24.

13. J. Hamann, 'The Visible Hand of Research Performance Assessment', *Higher Education*, lxxii (2016), 761–79.

14. Reminiscences about the Seminar were provided by: Bob Black, Jane Black (formerly Warner), Bruce Boucher, Michael Bratchel, Alison Brown (formerly Dyson), Beverly Brown, David Chambers, Paula Clarke, Dione Clementi, Sam Cohn, Trevor Dean, Peter Denley, Caroline Elam, Robert Fox, Richard Goldthwaite, Peggy Haines, Paul Holberton, Charles Hope, Ian Jones, Philip Jones, Bill Kent, Dale Kent, Catherine Kovesi, Dilwyn Knox, Jill Kraye, Amanda Lillie, Kristen Lippincott, Kate Lowe, Eckart Marchand, Lauro Martines, Jill Moore, Mick O'Malley, Bernadette Paton, Simon Pepper, Ros Pesman Cooper, Charles Robertson, Camilla Russell, Daniel Waley, Diana Webb (formerly Barron), Claudia Wedepohl, Alison Wright and Diane Zervas.

15. C. Brooke 'Obituary: Nicolai Rubinstein', *The Guardian*, 26 August 2002: https://www.theguardian.com/news/2002/aug/26/guardianobituaries.obituaries [accessed 20 Jun. 2023].

16. Russell, 'The Renaissance Comes to Bloomsbury', pp. 377–406.

17. Kent, 'Nicolai Rubinstein, Teacher', pp. 35–45.

# References

## Archived sources

Birkbeck University of London, Library Archives and Special Collections

Birkbeck College Annual Reports, 1954–65, GB 1832 BBK/10/1.

Institute of Historical Research, Wohl Library

IHR 3/3/29.
IHR 3/3/30.

University of Western Australia, University Archives

D. S. Duncan file.


## Published sources

Brooke, C., 'Obituary: Nicolai Rubinstein', *The Guardian*, 26 August 2002: https://www.theguardian.com/news/2002/aug/26/guardianobituaries .obituaries [accessed 20 Jun. 2023].

Brown, A., 'Renaissance Bodies: A New Seminar on the Renaissance', *Bulletin of the Society for Renaissance Studies*, xxii (1994), 20–24.

Dean, T., 'Daniel Waley', *Biographical Memoirs of Fellows of the British Academy*, xvii (2019), 305–24.

Denley, P., and Elam, C. (ed.), *Florence and Italy: Renaissance Studies in Honour of Nicolai Rubinstein* (London, 1988).

Evans, C., *Language People: The Experience of Teaching and Learning Modern Languages in British Universities* (Milton Keynes, 1988).

Hamann, J., 'The Visible Hand of Research Performance Assessment', *Higher Education*, lxxii (2016), 761–79.

Kent, D., *The Most I Could Be: A Renaissance Story* (Melbourne, 2021).

Kent, F. W., 'Nicolai Rubinstein, Teacher', in *Nicolai Rubinstein: In Memoriam*, ed. F. W. Kent, (Florence, 2005), pp. 35–45.

Lowe, K., '"I Shall Snuffle About and Make Relations": Nicolai Rubinstein, the Historian of Renaissance Florence, in Oxford during the War', in *Ark of Civilization: Refugee Scholars and Oxford University, 1930–1945*, ed. S. Crawford, K. Ulmschneider and J. Elsner (Oxford, 2017), pp. 220–33.

*Newnham College Roll Letter* (Cambridge, 2001).

Rubinstein, N., 'Florentine Constitutionalism and Medici Ascendancy in the Fifteenth Century', in *Florentine Studies: Politics and Society in Renaissance Florence*, ed. N. Rubinstein (London, 1968), pp. 442–62.

Russell, C., 'The Renaissance Comes to Bloomsbury: Studies in the Italian Renaissance in Twentieth-century London', in *The Art and Language of Power in Renaissance Florence: Essays for Alison Brown*, ed. A. Bloch, C. James and C. Russell (Toronto, 2019), pp. 377–406.

## Unpublished sources

Dean, T. and Lowe, K., Miscellaneous Private Correspondence and Notes.

Chapter 3

# The Economic and Social History of the Early Modern World Seminar

## David Ormrod*

Although the founders of the Institute of Historical Research were centrally concerned with English constitutional and political history, economic history would come to occupy an important place in its seminar programmes from the earliest years. In their pioneering collection of economic documents published in 1914, R. H. Tawney (1880–1962) and his co-editors had stressed that economic history 'cannot be studied apart from constitutional and political history', and singled out A. F. Pollard (1869–1948), the Institute's co-founder, as the only British historian to give equal weight to all three in his *Reign of Henry VII from Contemporary Sources* (1913).[1] With Eileen Power (1889–1940), Tawney started a joint seminar at the Institute in 1923 which by the 1925–6 session had expanded to comprise two strands, Power's on European trade in the later middle ages and Tawney's on European economic history of the sixteenth and seventeenth centuries.

Tawney and Power had been colleagues at the London School of Economics since 1921 and the latter's sudden death in 1940 deprived the profession of one of its most brilliant teachers and public intellectuals. It was Jack Fisher (1908–88), appointed to a lectureship in 1930, who developed Tawney's interests post-1945, and provided, in the running of the IHR seminar in early modern economic and social history, a link between Pollard's era and more recent times. In the summer of 1947, the Institute moved permanently to Senate House and Tawney resumed his research seminar there. By 1947–8, nineteen seminars were running, including

64  DAVID ORMROD

three in economic history: those of Eleanora Carus-Wilson (1897–1977), English Economic History in the later Middle Ages; Alwyn Ruddock (1916–2006), Tudor Economic History; and Tawney, Economic and Social History of England, 1600–42. As Leslie Clarkson recalled, Tawney's was still running successfully in the mid-1950s, with meetings interspersed by 'terrifying and stimulating' PhD supervisions with Fisher.[2] Fisher himself began teaching his undergraduate special subject on Tudor and early Stuart England in 1949 and took over the early modern survey lectures in preparation for Tawney's formal retirement in 1951.

It was during the 1950s and 60s that economic history acquired its identity as a fully independent sub-discipline, increasingly specialized, empirically based, and no longer troubled by debates about the place of economic theory in the social sciences which had unfolded in the wake of the Keynesian revolution of the later 1930s.[3] A period of expansion lasted until the mid-1970s, reflected in publication trends, the creation of separate university departments, and a growth in popularity amongst students at all levels, from sixth-formers to postgraduates. The dominant focus of interest lay in the British Industrial Revolution, an elephantine construct which required but failed to attract serious attention from theoreticians of growth and development in the UK. It is true that advances were made in the analysis of business cycles and commercial fluctuations, but much of the literature remained fixed in 'traditional, relatively atheoretical historical scholarship'.[4] The writings of W. W. Rostow (1916–2003), ambitious but deeply flawed, were widely drawn upon in attempts to fill the analytical vacuum, until more robust metrics emerged in the 1980s showing a much slower rate of industrial growth than previously suggested.[5] These changes overturned the primacy of the medieval and early modern periods in the development of the subject, first established by the work of William Cunningham (1849–1919) and Ephraim Lipson (1888–1960) and then promoted so successfully by Tawney and Power.

## The revived Seminar

During the 1960s, the LSE was very successful in attracting a steady flow of research students from home and abroad but Fisher was not minded to continue Tawney's early modern seminar at the Institute.[6] The social sciences, he admitted, had become much more specialized since 1945 and the preoccupation with economic growth had made the earlier focus on changes in economic and social structures look rather old-fashioned.[7] The history of capitalism, central to Tawney's concerns, was decidedly out of

THE ECONOMIC AND SOCIAL HISTORY OF THE EARLY MODERN WORLD SEMINAR   65

favour. As Fisher approached retirement, however, he was persuaded by three younger colleagues, Penelope Corfield, Negley Harte and Peter Earle, to revive the Seminar in 1974. Corfield and Harte had sat at Fisher's feet as PhD students and they were happy for him to preside over the Seminar in the traditional manner, assuring him that he would not be required to do any of the chores associated with running the programme.[8] Jack's brilliance and the attractive conviviality which he radiated were legendary, and talk often continued late into the evening. Post-seminar drinks in the University Tavern (now the College Arms), Store Street, followed by supper in Charlotte Street set a pattern which has hardly changed.[9] The Seminar has run continuously since then with the support of a growing number of convenors (see Figure 3.1), none of whom would aspire to the role of 'guru'.

The conviviality has continued, but in 2005, it was decided to reshape the Seminar and broaden its scope, reflected in a change of name from the Economic and Social History of Preindustrial England to that of the *Early Modern World*. Since we have a reasonably full record of speakers and topics since 1974, it is possible to show how we arrived at this metamorphosis – a gradual process, organic rather than planned – through which we accommodated new perspectives and approaches, whilst attempting to overcome, by degrees, the increasing fragmentation and insularity of the subject.[10] In reconstructing the predominant themes, we have adopted the categorization used by the editors of the *Economic History Review* from 1971 onwards, with minor modifications.[11] For convenience, these may be presented as two groups of 'core themes' from a range of newer spheres of interest associated more closely with social history.

During the years of Fisher's chairmanship, the overall direction and content of the programme were formed by two influences. The first of these was the Seminar's membership itself – comprising Fisher's former pupils in the early stages of their careers pursuing themes which he had either suggested, supervised or examined. Earle had worked on Mediterranean trade before 1550, Corfield on Norwich's history from 1650 to 1850, and Harte on the English linen industry in the long eighteenth century. Harte continued to pursue his interests in textile history, but all three went on to develop overlapping interests in urban history and London history, encouraged no doubt by Fisher's example. When Vanessa Harding became a convenor in 1986, the emphasis was further strengthened through her own work on medieval and early modern London in its demographic aspects, including health, housing and mortality. It was in the following year that the Women's Committee of the Economic History Society was formed, by which time the proportion of women members had fallen from

| | ‹1974 | ‹1980 | ‹1990 | ‹2000 | ‹2005 | ‹2010 | ‹2020 |
|---|---|---|---|---|---|---|---|
| | Economic & Social History of Preindustrial England | | | | Economic & Social History of the Early Modern World | | |
| Fisher | ====== | ======= | | | | | |
| Corfield | ====== | ======== | | | | | |
| Harte | ====== | ========== | ========== | ===== | ===== | ==== | |
| Earle | ====== | ========== | ========== | ===== | | | |
| Harding | | ==== | ========== | ===== | | | |
| Ormrod | | | ========= | ===== | ===== | ========== | |
| Zahedieh | | | | ==== | ===== | ========== | = |
| Epstein | | | | | == | | |
| Warde | | | | | = | | |
| Wallis | | | | | = | ======== | = |
| Hoppit | | | | | | ========== | = |
| Murphy | | | | | | ========= | |
| Irigoin | | | | | | ====== | = |
| Stephenson | | | | | | | = |
| Tunçer | | | | | | | = |

F. J. Fisher, 1974–86 (LSE/LSE); P. J. Corfield 1974–88 (Oxford & LSE/ Bedford-Royal Holloway) N. B. Harte 1974–2013 (LSE/UCL); P. Earle 1974–2004 (UCL & LSE/LSE); V. Harding, 1986–2004 (St Andrews/Birkbeck); D. J. Ormrod, 1991–2019 (LSE & Cambridge/Kent); N. Zahedieh, 2001–present (LSE/Edinburgh); S. R. Epstein, 2005–07 (Cambridge/LSE); P. Warde, 2009–10 (Cambridge/UEA, Cambridge); P. Wallis, 2009–present (York & Oxford/LSE); J. Hoppit, 2010–present (Cambridge/UCL); A. L. Murphy, 2010–18 (Cambridge/Hertfordshire); M. A. Irigoin, 2014–present (UNMDP & LSE/LSE); J. Stephenson, 2020–present (UCL & LSE/Oxford, UCL; A. C. Tunçer, 2020–present (NKUA & LSE/LSE, UCL)

**Figure 3.1** The Economic and Social History of the Early Modern World Seminar: chart of the Seminar's convenors, 1974–2020; © David Ormrod, 2022.

20 per cent at the time of the Society's foundation to only 10 per cent in 1987.[12] The Seminar saw women scholars well represented: at time of writing, we currently have equal numbers of men and women as convenors, with 26 per cent of papers presented by women speakers from 1974 to 2021, rising to 34 per cent over the past five years. Thanks to our hub location, we have also attracted regular attendees from outside London and overseas, especially North American students and researchers.

The second influence shaping the Seminar, in more diffuse ways perhaps, was the 'Preindustrial England' paradigm which acted as a wrapper for the fashionable textbooks of the 1970s.[13] By the mid-1980s, as we have already noted, interpretations of the Industrial Revolution came under increasing scrutiny following a wave of revisionist writing simultaneously questioning the rate of eighteenth-century growth and asserting its regional character and the diversification of rural occupations.[14] J. A. Sharpe (b. 1946) was one of the few textbook writers to complain of the obscurantist effect of the 'pre-industrial' label and reminded readers that Daniel Defoe had found 'manufactures' almost everywhere he went in his tours of the 1720s. Earle examined Defoe's language of economic growth at one of the first meetings of the Seminar in 1975 and, like Sharpe, complained that scholars of modern history had failed to understand the buoyancy of what they condescendingly regarded as a pre-industrial economy and society. The 'bustling prosperity' of the inland trade was what impressed Defoe most.[15]

If 'Tawney's Century' (1540–1640) barely emerged from the 'dark ages in economic history',[16] the challenge facing the convenors in the 1970s and 80s was to bring together new research findings that captured the dynamism of the century after 1660, especially with respect to the linkages between farming and the rural environment, industrial development, and the expansion of internal and overseas markets (core themes one and two, see Figures 3.3 and 3.4). By 1972 the concept of 'proto-industrialization' was being used to integrate these themes but scepticism prevailed in

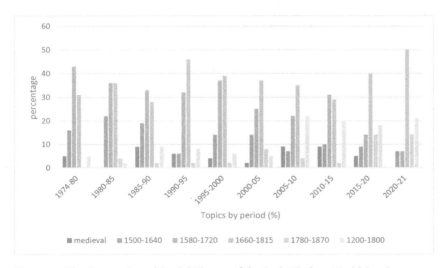

Figure 3.2 The Economic and Social History of the Early Modern World Seminar: graph of the Seminar's topics by period; © David Ormrod, 2022.

several quarters for some time, particularly in Britain.[17] The LSE's strengths lay in traditional industrial, commercial and financial history; its only major contribution to agrarian history was Tawney's *Agrarian Problem* (1912), rescued from obscurity by Jane Whittle and her collaborators a century later.[18] It was at Leicester and then Oxford that the subject flourished under the leadership of Joan Thirsk (1922–2013), and it was Thirsk's pioneering work on regional farming systems which provided the starting point for theories of proto-industrial growth and decline.[19] Questions about family size and the age and seasonality of marriage were also central to the thesis. Although the sociologist David Glass (1911–78) had paired up social and demographic research at the LSE in the post-war years, it was in Cambridge that historical demography developed apace in the hands of Peter Laslett (1915–2001), Roger Schofield (1937–2019) and Tony Wrigley (1931–2022). In the 1970s, Jack Fisher occasionally expressed his impatience with the rate of progress in Cambridge, demanding to know: 'when are they going to press the button?'[20]

The core themes of industrial and agricultural history retained their place in the Seminar programme throughout, but with a preponderance of papers in the former. The years 1985–90 saw a surge of interest in industrial history including papers on Durham mining, Derbyshire lead-working, Midlands metalwares, woollen fabrics, new draperies, table linen, housebuilding and London's luxury trades, to say nothing of earlier papers on Spitalfields and Canterbury silk, Staffordshire ceramics and the British

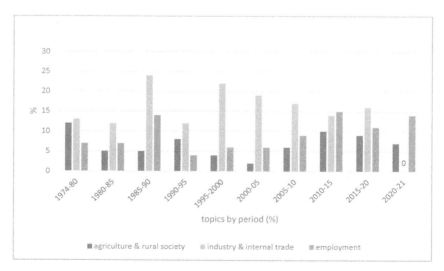

Figure 3.3 The Economic and Social History of the Early Modern World Seminar: graph of the Seminar's core themes (one): agriculture, industry and employment; © David Ormrod, 2022.

distillery.[21] Interestingly, many of these offerings involved an emphasis on urban manufacture and finishing, or centralized production; few impinged directly on the phenomenon of rural industrialization, which may have reflected the interests of the convenors and those working at the LSE. During the past fifteen years, however, increasing attention has been given to the history of work itself as the need for new research on specific industries has declined. Leisure preference and conditions of work were addressed earlier in papers by John Hatcher (b. 1951), Steve Hindle (b. 1965), Leonard Schwartz and Donald Woodward who went on to gather new wage series for Northern England, which helped to correct the southern bias and other deficiencies in the Phelps-Brown Hopkins series.[22] Interest in rural and agrarian history was strongest in the very early years of the Seminar. Joan Thirsk gave the opening presentation in 1974, and contributions to the history of farming, landownership and rural society came from her former students including John Broad, John Chartres, and later, Jane Whittle, together with other specialists outside the LSE orbit: Mark Overton, John Beckett, Anne Kussmaul and Keith Snell. The last two Cambridge researchers produced important new findings about women's work and seasonal employment in agriculture, leading Kussmaul to define late seventeenth-century England as the critical period in which regional specialization in farming created new opportunities for the expansion of rural industry.[23]

With the exception of a paper by Eckert Schremmer of Heidelberg, the Seminar was not especially concerned to examine the limitations or theoretical status of the proto-industrial model; it was gradually absorbed into the lexicon.[24] The question of de-industrialization and diverse regional experiences, usually concealed in sectoral analysis, emerged as a key issue in the proto-industrialization debate, and served to revise traditional views of the industrial revolution. In the long run of course, the northern heartlands of the 'industrial revolution' themselves de-industrialized, and this obvious but neglected consideration called for serious reappraisal of the broader social and political transformations sheltering behind the label. Maxine Berg (b. 1950), Pat Hudson (b. 1948) and Julian Hoppit (b. 1957), who became a convenor in 2010, called for a rehabilitation of the industrial revolution as the product of diverse and impermanent regional experiences.[25]

The most far-reaching revisions to the older 'pre-industrial' paradigm arose from a new focus on the early modern energy transition formulated by Tony Wrigley and sharpened by John Hatcher's definitive work on coal production and Paul Warde's research in environmental history, energy consumption and the pressure on timber supplies. In support of John Ulric Nef's earlier claims, Hatcher and Wrigley showed how exploitation of coal enabled England to escape at an early date from the constraints of the organic economy.[26] In 1560, coal consumption provided 10 per cent of total English energy requirements; by 1700, that figure had risen to 50 per cent, putting England in a uniquely favourable position compared with its neighbours.[27] Not only did this support early industrialization, it also facilitated London's exceptionally rapid rate of growth during the seventeenth century, albeit with costs attached. Paul Warde, who became a convenor in 2009, helped to give the programme an enhanced environmental dimension in two successful departures from our usual format. In 2010, we arranged a seminar/symposium with five speakers on 'Cities, Ecology and Exchange, 1600–1800', with Lex Heerma van Voss, Klas Ronnback and Leos Muller focusing on the North Sea–Baltic basin and the environmental costs of 'fuelling the city'. And in 2014, Warde led a round-table session with Geoffrey Parker (b. 1943) on the latter's *Global Crisis* (2013), with an emphasis on climate change, the significance of which was seriously underestimated by earlier writers.[28]

New work on overseas trade was slow to resurface after Ralph Davis's important mid-twentieth-century investigations based substantially on the Ledgers of the Inspector-General for the years 1697–1780 (see Figure 3.4). This chronological focus helps explain the general preoccupation with the possible contribution of the profits from foreign trade to economic growth and the 'industrial revolution'. There was, however, also a reluctance to accept the reality of mercantilist modes of thought

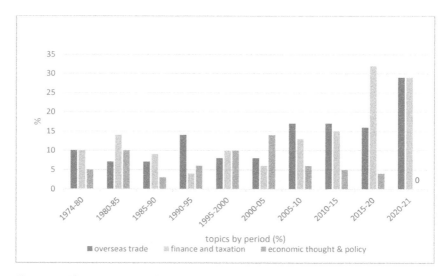

Figure 3.4 The Economic and Social History of the Early Modern World Seminar: graph of the Seminar's core themes (two): overseas trade; finance; economic thought and policy; © David Ormrod, 2022.

and practice (a view which now appears very dated). Relatively little attention was given to either the political contexts or the global structures within which commercial networks evolved. The measurement and analysis of trade flows continued along traditional lines, but it was especially Kirti Chaudhuri's work – his *Trading World of Asia* (1978) and his 1981 paper to the Seminar which pointed to wider horizons. An enthusiastic admirer of Fernand Braudel (1902–85) and Immanuel Wallerstein (1930–2019), Chaudhuri encouraged us to move beyond neo-Ricardian assumptions about early modern trade and consider the hierarchical order of leading cities and trading zones, underpinned by coercion and military power.[29]

This shift in thinking brought overseas expansion back to centre stage, with a transfer of emphasis from the intra-European trades to Eurasia and the Americas. It required a radically different approach to histories of empire and the unholy synergies between commerce, slavery, forced labour and the appropriation of 'new world' resources. Nuala Zahedieh, who became a convenor in 2001, contributed several papers which showed how London merchants made mercantilism work in the Atlantic trades before 1700 by manipulating the Navigation Acts and opening up rent-seeking opportunities to their advantage. As a result, the value of London's plantation trades roughly doubled from 1660 to 1700 and generated much larger trade flows than the mainland colonies.[30] Several speakers emphasized the transnational character of Atlantic commerce and the porous character of imperial boundaries, but it is only recently that the operation of the plantation system itself and the history of the enslaved have made their way into the seminar programme. Much Anglo-American writing, following eighteenth-century precedent, has tended to emphasize the high returns from Atlantic commerce, whilst disparaging the value of trade with Asia, with its associated drain of silver from the Americas, the connecting thread between the two.[31] Chaudhuri's volumes had already signalled the Eurocentric bias of such an outlook, and during the 1990s, interest in the trades and economies of South and Southeast Asia grew rapidly.

Increased interest in overseas expansion from the 1650s inevitably involved much closer examination of the consequences of inter-state rivalry, including extension of the state's capacity for revenue raising and the limitations and direction of its commercial policies. These concerns were represented in the Seminar's programme, which gradually shifted towards the second group of core themes (see Figures 3.3 and 3.4). Julian Hoppit had earlier pointed to the often contradictory and undisciplined character of much economic literature of the period and its frequent orientation towards the objectives of specific lobbies and interest groups. Few would argue now that the state possessed a masterplan guiding its approach to economic legislation or had the resources to enforce it consistently.[32] Nevertheless, as Zahedieh and Ormrod suggested in a joint presentation, the underlying presence of strong central tendencies in the commercial sphere more than justifies continued engagement with the concept of mercantilism.

Although more realistic conceptions of mercantilism have prevailed over the years, interest in the history of economic thought *per se* has declined, while contributions to financial history have grown alongside the build-up of work on overseas trade, credit networks and financialization. Anne Murphy, Alejandra Irigoin and Coskun Tunçer, who became convenors in 2010, 2014 and 2020 respectively, have helped to sharpen an existing focus on histories of financial and monetary history, which has encompassed a flood of new work on financial markets, property values, taxation and the rise of fiscal-military states. It was at a summer meeting of the Seminar in 1984 that John Brewer described the significance of the 'unfashionable work of the clerks and bureaucrats of the eighteenth-century Excise Office', which developed into one of the most persuasive approaches to the history of state formation in England, Europe and beyond.[33] D'Maris Coffman threw fresh light on the introduction of the excise which helped to place the origins of the British tax state firmly in the 1640s and 50s, in line with Patrick O'Brien and Michael Braddick's revisions of North and Weingast's simplified account. Papers by Patrick Walsh, Aaron Graham, Guido Alfani and Peter Wilson helped to break down the Anglocentric bias of the fiscal-military state paradigm.

The rapid expansion of economic history in the 1960s inevitably generated pressures to reconnect with, and explore, societal issues which did not necessarily impinge on the economic historian's concern with industrialization. Population history became a major focus. In 1965, Peter Laslett described the newly formed Cambridge Population Group as a reflection of the shift towards 'sociological history', a less Anglocentric history which would move beyond economic analysis and give greater weight to comparative studies of European, Asian, African and Oceanic societies.[34] Laslett's central interest lay in the history of family formation in the context of 'face to face societies', in which demographic characteristics were far from constant or uniform. Tony Wrigley went on to pioneer the application of quantitative techniques to the analysis of parish registers and anticipated the emerging results of *The Population History of England, 1541–1871* (1989) in a paper to the Seminar in 1981. This shifted the weight of demographic logic away from mortality to marriage and specifically, nuptiality. Papers in English demographic history dominated the programme in the late 1970s and early 80s and continued to add new layers of local information over the next two decades, especially in the areas of infectious disease and mortality which the Cambridge findings had to some degree relegated, from Justin Champion, Mary Dobson, Vanessa Harding, and indeed Tony Wrigley. Migration studies also flourished with contributions from Peter Clark, David Souden, Jeremy Boulton and John Landers, for a period which saw dramatically high rates of internal migration to London.

London was not included in the Cambridge Group's sample of 404 parish registers and the sources for the capital's demographic history remain numerous but fragmented, 'of varying degrees of rawness and reliability'.[35] Unsurprisingly, then, London history provided major opportunities for new research, especially from 1974 to 1995 (see Figure 3.5). As we have noted, all four of the original organizers had special interests in metropolitan history, which was strengthened when Vanessa Harding became a convenor in 1986. Penelope Corfield had already presented an inviting prospectus for describing the social and economic life of provincial capitals, at a time when urban history was experiencing a great surge of interest.

It was in 1976 that Lawrence Stone (1919–99) had rather unkindly described urban history as a new field in search of a project. If this contained even a grain of truth, that project would in due course materialize at the IHR with the establishment in 1988 of the Centre for Metropolitan History (CMH) directed by Derek Keene (1942–2021). By 1700, London had become the largest manufacturing centre in England, if not in Europe, and members of the CMH's 'skilled workforce project' – part of the larger

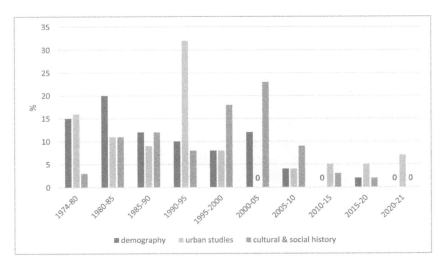

Figure 3.5 The Economic and Social History of the Early Modern World Seminar: graph of the Seminar's newer themes which experienced significant growth, only to decline in relative importance in the early twenty-first century; © David Ormrod, 2022.

'achievement project: intellectual and material culture in modern Europe' – presented new findings about the spatial clustering of skills in the city and the incremental nature of innovation, informed by close collaboration with museum curators. Robert Iliffe, Michael Berlin, David Mitchell and Lien Luu covered industries which included scientific and navigational instruments, shipbuilding, goldsmithing, luxury textiles and brewing.[36] The first two also considered the role of guilds as repositories of useful knowledge. More recently, Patrick Wallis, who became a convenor in 2009, reviewed current debates about the role of apprenticeship in the development of a skilled workforce from 1550 to 1800, and Judy Stephenson looked beneath London wage rates to discuss the categorization of skill, before becoming convenor in 2020.

To some extent, urban history provided us with a clear pathway into social and cultural history, the signposts for which had been provided by Jack Fisher's description of Jacobean London. The demands of the newly urbanized country gentry, Fisher stressed, led to a seasonal demand for leisure facilities, housing and hospitality that would persist for generations.[37] By the late seventeenth century, the divorce between elite and popular culture in London was becoming increasingly apparent as Peter Burke (b. 1937) emphasized, but London's expanding middling sorts were able to participate in new forms of sociability, refinement and material display which mimicked gentility, through an emerging 'culture of politeness', described by Larry Klein. A succession of papers explored print culture, art auctions, music performance, dining ceremony, and the world of clubs and coffee houses involving the formation of a culture-consuming public in the metropolis.[38]

If the consumption of culture had a strongly metropolitan and urban dimension, the demand for everyday items of household consumption opened an inexhaustible field for historians at almost every level of society in town and countryside. The 'world of goods' shifted our attention from histories of production to the material culture of domestic life in a way which seemed to echo the enthusiasms of Artur Hazelius and the Swedish folk-life museum movement of the late nineteenth century.[39] Lorna Weatherill's paper of 1983 on consumer behaviour and material culture, 1660–1760, proved to be a defining moment in establishing a new agenda for social and cultural history in both a rural and urban environment. The analysis of probate inventories which underlay Weatherill's work also informed a string of presentations on the consumption of clothing and textiles from Margaret Spufford (1935–2014), Beverly Lemire, Negley Harte, Catherine Richardson, John Styles and Darron Dean.

As Figure 3.3 shows, interest in urban history was strongest in the earlier years of the revived Seminar, peaking in 1990–95 and falling away thereafter.

Enthusiasm for social history came later, following in its wake, but also dwindled from 2005 onwards. From an early commitment to urban history, Penelope Corfield championed the reintegration of economic and social history with History, and in 1987–8 exchanged her role as a convenor of the Preindustrial England Seminar for convenorship of the Eighteenth Century Seminar. The two increasingly ran in parallel, and the former continued to include papers in urban, cultural and social history. Jack Fisher played a reduced role as seminar chair, as illness took its toll, a year or so before Penelope's move sideways. His death in January 1988 marked the conclusion of a remarkable period of intellectual growth in pre-modern English history which embraced the humanities and the social sciences. By 1989, the Seminar was left with three convenors, and David Ormrod joined the group soon afterwards, with interests in commercial history and museum practice, the latter via an attachment to the CMH and the Museum of London.

## New directions

These recollections show how, in several ways, the Seminar developed, responded to, and sometimes initiated efforts to broaden the thematic content of its programme. Nevertheless, it appeared to some that the tribe of economic historians in the wider world was losing its special dispensation, that of infinite promise. One of the darker prophets of doom was Donald Coleman (1920–95) who argued, uncharacteristically, that the subject was facing a series of self-inflicted problems arising from excessive respectability and loss of the subject's oppositional posture which had fired earlier writers like Tawney and J. L. and Barbara Hammond.[40] Jack Fisher also experienced disappointment in later years, and regretted that 'changing intellectual and cultural trends led to economic history losing its previously great research allure, with the 1960s and 70s rise of urban, social, gender and later cultural history'.[41] The appeal of specialized economic history degrees was indeed declining by the 1980s and required attention, but the outburst of self-criticism was overdone. Successive cuts in university funding made small departments particularly vulnerable – economic history amongst others – and administrative restructuring, with hindsight, was inevitable. Many faced closure or amalgamation. During the difficult years of the 1990s, the Institute's seminars and the encouragement offered by its then director, Patrick O'Brien, provided invaluable support for those seeking new ways forward.

As chair of the Economic History Society, Patrick arranged a series of four annual meetings of sixty heads of independent departments of economic and social history at the Institute from July 1997 to September 2000 to exchange information and consider strategies to protect and promote the future of the subject. Departments at risk, of course, had limited scope for manoeuvre and were forced to reshape their offer to meet the circumstances of their institutions, which usually involved 'moving in with the neighbours'. What was initially seen as a 'crisis of economic history' soon gave way to what the Women's Committee of the Society saw as a new start, a 'renaissance of economic and social history', announced at its annual workshop in November 1997. It was at this meeting and at the Seminar on the previous day that Jan de Vries developed his highly influential thesis of an 'industrious revolution', which shifted debates about eighteenth-century growth from technology and capital formation to consumer aspirations, an approach which had been underway, as we have seen, from the early 1980s.[42] To those earlier discussions, de Vries added a tighter logic which encompassed questions of labour supply and work intensity, agricultural specialization, household-level choices and the activities of women as consumers. This reconnected with earlier debates about proto-industrialization, but this time round, resistance to the idea of a 'long road to the industrial revolution' was much reduced.[43]

The Seminar continued to promote cultural and social history through the 1990s up to 2005 (Figure 3.5), but in that year, with Larry Epstein's encouragement, the decision was taken to place the emphasis further towards the economic end of the spectrum and to follow the turn towards global economic history. This came about in response to three sets of changes. First, many other seminars at the Institute were now dealing with cultural history, especially the Eighteenth Century Seminar. Second, the digital revolution of the 1990s had taken us into the world of big datasets utilizing national accounts and spanning several centuries which helped to end the traditional view of the earlier period in terms of unrelieved Malthusian stagnation, already prefigured in research on the Netherlands.[44] Third, some of us (including Epstein and Ormrod) had been closely involved in the launch of the IHR's Global History Seminar from 1996 onwards and had incorporated elements of comparative global history in our undergraduate teaching. The 'long road to the industrial revolution' made us increasingly aware of the need to make connections across large spaces and long timespans.

It was Patrick O'Brien who, following his appointment as director of the Institute in 1990, created its first seminar in global history. With a background in middle eastern and comparative European economic history and the backing of a scholarly philanthropist, Gerry Martin, Patrick developed the first master's degree in the UK for the subject.[45] Without his vision and energy, it has been said, 'the field of global economic history would not exist'.[46] The *Journal of Global History* was launched in 2006, and engagement with grand meta-narratives has gradually given way to more finely textured micro level analysis. Patrick regularly attended our Seminar in the 1990s, and several members took part in conferences and workshops arranged by the IHR-based 'achievement project' in London, Paris, Antwerp and Amsterdam, closely related to the emerging Global Economic History Network (GEHN) at LSE.[47] Giorgio Riello, a regular member of the Seminar and contributor became GEHN's research officer. Developing debates in global history, it seemed, were creating new opportunities for rethinking not only national history but also the variety of ways in which global dynamics impinged on local and regional economies.[48]

Soon after joining the LSE staff in 1992, Larry Epstein (1960–2007) became a regular member of the Seminar and gave papers on regional development in late medieval Italy and transfers of technological knowledge in Europe from 1200 to 1800. He agreed to become a convenor in 2005 in the session following the departure of Peter Earle and Vanessa Harding. The occasion was marked with a memorable relaunch party at which the Preindustrial England Seminar became the *Economic and Social History of the Early Modern World*. The change was not merely cosmetic but reflected the interests of the 2005 group of convenors in Atlantic, Northern and Southern European economic history, and our impatience with the pre-industrial paradigm. The proportion of non-English papers began to grow significantly: by the spring term of 2006, four out of five papers were devoted to non-British topics (see Figure 3.6). It would be impossible to overstate the sense of personal and intellectual loss that we felt with Larry's tragically early death in February 2007. His work on comparative European economic development was invaluable in helping to reshape our priorities. Paul Warde and Patrick Wallis became convenors in 2009 and their support enabled us to move forward.

The shift of emphasis from English to world history after 2005 has been beneficial in many respects but has brought with it the risk of incoherence and fragmentation, charges which many had levelled against the proliferating varieties of Anglocentric history of the 1960s and 70s. At the very least, we wanted to move away from the debilitating insularity and diffusionist perspectives of many traditional accounts of 'the first industrial nation'. As de Vries and van der Woude emphasized, the industrial revolution contributed to a 'larger process of economic modernization [which] involved more than industrial production [and] unfolded in a European zone larger than England', a zone best described as the North Sea Economy.[49] Bearing this in mind, we have paid special attention to new research in

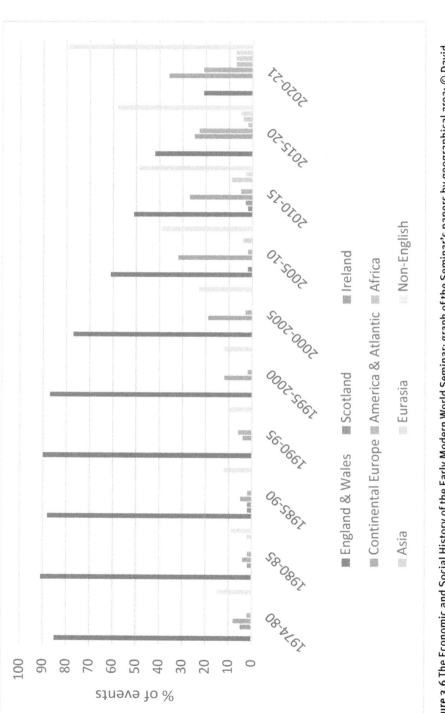

**Figure 3.6** The Economic and Social History of the Early Modern World Seminar: graph of the Seminar's papers by geographical area; © David Ormrod, 2022.

Dutch and Anglo-Dutch commercial, cultural and economic history. Our close links with the Low Countries Seminar have facilitated this, not least through occasional joint meetings to which Herman van der Wee, Jan Luiten van Zanden, Jan de Vries, David Ormrod, Oscar Gelderblom and David Freeman contributed.[50] In time, the movement of people, skills and ideas between the countries bordering the North and Baltic Seas, together with trade, shipping and financial transfers all combined to bring about a 'little divergence' between the fortunes of Northern and Southern Europe, providing an underlying meta-narrative capable of holding together these fragments of research.[51] Without this kind of selectivity and conceptual support, conversations within global history risk falling into 'polyphony at best, chaos at worst'.[52]

A second focus has been to pursue the kind of comparative work which the growing accumulation of big datasets has facilitated (see Figure 3.2, series 6, 1200–1800). Several individual scholars offered new long-run perspectives, especially on variations in wages and prices, central to constructing national income estimates, including Donald Woodward (wages in Northern England, 1450–1750), Jane Humphries (womens' wages in England, 1260–1850), Sevket Pamuk (wages and incomes in the Near East, 1100–1800). Especially important was Robert Allen's reassessment of European economic growth and the significance of England's high wage economy from the mid seventeenth century, arising from a buoyant protoindustrial base and the export of light worsteds.[53]

Of major interest was the collaborative work by Stephen Broadberry, Bruce Campbell and Mark Overton involved in estimating changes in GDP per capita over six centuries from 1270, bravely exposed at intervals to the Seminar, which, along with Alex Klein and Bas van Leeuwen's contributions resulted in their landmark volume *British Economic Growth, 1270–1870* (2015). For early modernists, the most striking outcome of Broadberry and others is its affirmation that the years 1651–1770 were characterized by a measurable dynamism comparable to that experienced during the century after 1770, with GDP per capita approximately doubling in both sub-periods (increases of 97.7 per cent and 97.5 per cent). It is, of course, the reduction of population pressure which underlies this favourable assessment of the long century following the civil wars; for the period 1470–1651, the corresponding figure is minus 4.3 per cent.[54] The value of historical national accounts for the centuries before 1850 is nevertheless limited and, as Pat Hudson reminded us, GDP per capita measures tell us nothing about the social distribution of resources, human wellbeing or environmental sustainability.[55]

Regarding the larger question of the 'great divergence' between western Europe and east Asia, it was inevitable that the Seminar would begin to prioritize Asian economic history following publication of Kenneth Pomeranz's landmark text *The Great Divergence* (2000).[56] As Richard Drayton emphasized some years later, the history of globalization is easier to grasp once we regard Europe as a peninsula of Asia.[57] Several papers addressed different aspects of the trade and organization of the European India companies, with a predominant domestic or metropolitan emphasis in each case. More recently, however, we have included contributions with a sharper Asian focus, centring especially on Indian textile production and the transfer of skills between the Indian and British silk and cotton industries. In 2009 and 2016, Giorgio Riello contributed papers on the trades in raw cotton and cotton fabrics and framed the history of the first 'global industry' outside the conventional Anglocentric (or Lancastrian) pattern.[58] These and a series of papers from earlier contributors owed much to the familiar turn towards consumer behaviour represented especially in Maxine Berg's contributions, focused initially on the Birmingham metal trades before moving on to the growing taste for Asian imports, especially of luxuries and semi-luxury goods.

The appetite for exotic Asian commodities in Europe is conventionally seen as a major driving force behind early modern consumer culture but rising silver prices in seventeenth-century China resulting from the Ming dynasty's shift from paper money, played an equally important if not a determining role. Shortly before joining the organizing group, Alejandra Irigoin highlighted American–Eurasian exchange in her important discussion of trans-Pacific bullion and commodity flows carried by the Manila galleons from Acapulco to Manila, the basis for the first integrated global trade flows from the late 1560s. With her encouragement, we have paid increasing attention to Spanish, Portuguese and Latin American history in ways which have counterbalanced the hitherto predominant Northern European emphasis. Access to Spanish-American silver and its recirculation between Southern and Northern European markets emerged as a central issue in papers by Alejandro Garcia-Monton and Claudio Marsilio. Several speakers have recently examined regional aspects of Iberian economic and financial history, starting with Leandro Prados de la Escosura's magisterial survey of Spain's overall economic performance in a European perspective from 1270 to 1850.

## Conclusion

Broadly speaking, we have continued along the path which we set in 2005, one which leads beyond Protestant Anglophone views of the world to encompass divergence and global interconnectedness. The grand narrative which Tawney and Power embraced, the rise of capitalism, has been replaced by a series of smaller scale configurations which lend themselves more readily to measurement and modelling for those inclined in that direction. This has caused some to complain that the subject 'too often deploys its methodology on its face, like scaffolding on a building abandoned by bankrupt builders'.[59] But this is too pessimistic, and the turn towards global histories of material culture and consumption is now sufficiently embedded in the literature to generate a flow of engaging new paradigms and research questions. Far from ignoring 'new economic history' and quantitative methods, we have maintained a very broad understanding of what comprises 'economic and social history', seeing them as mutually dependent. Despite the increasing strength of more technical economic history, we have cultivated a 'middle furrow' and have followed a broadly historical approach.

The danger we now face, it could be argued, arises from a drift towards incoherence and fragmentation in a virtual world of unlimited possibilities. It was in the autumn term of 2020 that we moved the Seminar onto an online platform, enabling us to provide a programme of seven speakers located in Paris, Pittsburgh, Frankfurt, Tokyo, Georgetown, Stanford and Porto. It remains to be seen whether and to what extent we will revert to our pre-Zoom format of face-to-face meetings, drinks, dinner and the uninhibited sociability for which we are famous. Hopefully we will. Video conferencing, however, has enabled us to discuss global history *globally*, at minimal cost, and it may be that we could in future combine real gatherings at the IHR with speakers and participants joining us from across the world – at least sometimes. If so, we might consider a more thematic and integrated programme to avoid undue fragmentation.

## Notes

\* I am grateful to Penelope Corfield, Vanessa Harding, Pat Hudson, Negley Harte, Julian Hoppit, Nuala Zahedieh and Patrick Wallis for comments, suggestions and recollections.

1. A. E. Bland, P. A. Brown and R. H. Tawney, *English Economic History: Select Documents* (London, 1914), p. v.

2. L. A. Clarkson, 'From England to Australia to Ireland: A Cultural Odyssey', in *Living Economic and Social History*, ed. P. Hudson (Glasgow, 2001), pp. 42–6 at p. 45.

3. S. Howson, 'Keynes and the LSE Economists', *Journal of the History of Economic Thought*, xxxi (2009), 257–80.

4. R. Floud interviewed by Danny Millum (2008): archives.history.ac.uk /makinghistory/resources/interviews/Floud_Roderick.html [accessed 1 October 2022].

5. C. K. Harley, 'British Industrialization before 1841: Evidence of Slower Growth during the Industrial Revolution', *Journal of Economic History*, xlii (1982), 267–89; N. F. R. Crafts, *British Economic Growth during the Industrial Revolution* (Oxford, 1985).

6. R. Dahrendorf, *A History of the London School of Economics and Political Science, 1895–1995* (Oxford, 1995), pp. 430–31.

7. F. J. Fisher, 'The Department of Economic History', *LSE Magazine*, iv (Nov. 1971), 3.

8. N. B. Harte, 'In Memory of F. J. Fisher', in *London and the English Economy, 1500–1700*, ed. P. J. Corfield and N. B. Harte (London, 1990), p. 28.

9. Wine in the Common Room has replaced beer-drinking, and speakers no longer face a 'trek' to the Neel Kamal on Charlotte Street as this restaurant has closed down.

10. W. Clarence-Smith, 'Editorial', *Journal of Global History*, i (2006), 1.

11. N. B. Harte, 'Trends in Publications on the Economic and Social History of Great Britain and Ireland, 1925–74', *Economic History Review*, xxx (1977), 20–41 at pp. 33–4.

12. N. B. Harte, 'The Economic History Society, 1926–2001', in *Living Economic and Social History*, ed. Hudson (Glasgow, 2001), pp. 1–12 at p. 8.

13. L. A. Clarkson, *The Pre-Industrial Economy in England, 1500–1750* (London, 1971); B. A. Holderness, *Pre-Industrial England: Economy and Society from 1500–1700* (London, 1977); and T. K. Derry and M. G. Blakeway, *The Making of Pre-Industrial Britain* (London, 1973).

14. P. Hudson, 'The Regional Perspective', in *Regions and Industries: A Perspective on the Industrial Revolution in Britain*, ed. P. Hudson (Cambridge, 1989), pp. 5–38; P. Hudson, *The Industrial Revolution* (London, 1992), pp. 101–32; J. Stobart, *The First Industrial Region: North-west England, 1700–60* (Manchester, 2004).

15. J. A. Sharpe, *Early Modern England: A Social History, 1550–1760* (London, 1987), p. 142; P. Earle, *The World of Defoe* (London, 1976), p. 108.

16. F. J. Fisher, 'Tawney's Century', in *Essays in the Economic and Social History of Tudor and Stuart England in Honour of R. H. Tawney*, ed. F. J. Fisher (Cambridge, 1961), pp. 1–14; F. J. Fisher, 'The Sixteenth and Seventeenth Centuries: The Dark Ages in English Economic History?' *Economica*, xxiv (1957), 2–18.

17. D. C. Coleman, 'Proto-Industrialization: A Concept too Many', *Economic History Review*, xxvi (1983), 435–48; R. Houston and K. D. M. Snell, 'Proto-Industrialization? Cottage Industry, Social Change, and Industrial Revolution', *Historical Journal*, xxvii (1984), 437–92.

18. J. Whittle (ed.), *Landlords and Tenants in Britain, 1440–1660* (Woodbridge, 2013).

19. J. Thirsk, 'Industries in the Countryside', in *Essays in the Economic and Social History of Tudor and Stuart England*, ed. F. J. Fisher (Cambridge, 1961), pp. 70–88; J. Thirsk (ed.), *The Agrarian History of England and Wales, 1640–1750, Vol. 1, Regional Farming Systems* (Cambridge, 1984).

20. Templeman Library, University of Kent: Barker Oral History Tapes, BAR/10.

21. Respectively: Keith Wrightson, Andy Wood, Marie Rowlands, Richard Conquest, Luc Martin, Ronald Berger, David Mitchell, Elizabeth McKellar, Helen Clifford; and Natalie Rothstein, Lorna Weatherill, John Chartres.

22. D. Woodward, *Men at Work: Labourers and Building Craftsmen in the Towns of Northern England, 1450–1750* (Cambridge, 1995). H. Phelps-Brown and S. V. Hopkins, 'Seven Centuries of Building Wages', *Economica*, xxii (1955), 195–206.

23. A. Kussmaul, *A General View of the Rural Economy of England, 1538–1840* (Cambridge, 1990), pp. 170–80.

24. For example, see: R. Allen, 'Progress and Poverty in Early Modern Europe', *Economic History Review*, lvi (2003), 403–43.

25. M. Berg and P. Hudson, 'Rehabilitating the Industrial Revolution', *Economic History Review*, xlv (1992), 24–50; J. Hoppit, 'Counting the Industrial Revolution', *Economic History Review*, xliii (1990), 173–93; J. Hoppit, 'Understanding the Industrial Revolution', *Historical Journal*, xxx (1987), 211–24.

26. E. A. Wrigley, *Continuity, Chance and Change: The Character of the Industrial Revolution in England* (Cambridge, 1988); E. A. Wrigley, *Energy and the Industrial Revolution* (Cambridge, 2010); J. Hatcher, *The History of the British Coal Industry: Volume 1 Before 1700* (Oxford, 1993).

27. P. Warde, *Energy Consumption in England and Wales, 1560–2000* (Rome, 2007), p. 59.

28. G. Parker, *Global Crisis: War, Climate Change and Catastrophe in the Seventeenth Century* (New Haven, 2013).

29. K. N. Chaudhuri, *The Trading World of Asia and the English East India Company, 1660–1760* (Cambridge, 1987); K. N. Chaudhuri, *Asia before Europe* (Cambridge, 1990).

30. See N. Zahedieh, *The Capital and the Colonies: London and the Atlantic Economy, 1660–1700* (Cambridge, 2010).

31. N. Zahedieh, 'Overseas Trade and Empire', in *The Cambridge Economic History of Modern Britain, I, 1700–1870*, ed. R. Floud, J. Humphries, and P. Johnson (Cambridge, 2014).

32. J. Hoppit, 'The Contexts and Contours of British Economic Literature, 1660–1760,' *Historical Journal*, xlix (2006), 79–110; J. Hoppit, *Britain's Political Economies: Parliament and Economic Life, 1660–1800* (Cambridge, 2017).

33. J. Brewer, *The Sinews of Power: War, Money and the English State, 1688–1783* (New York, 1989).

34. P. Laslett, *The World We Have Lost* (London, 1965), pp. 231–3.

35. V. Harding, 'The Population of London, 1550–1700: A Review of the Published Evidence', *London Journal*, xv (1990), 111–28 at p. 111.

36. *Centre for Metropolitan History: Annual Report 1997–8 and Tenth Anniversary Conference Papers* (London, 1998), pp. 52–8. See also: https://archives.history.ac.uk/cmh/projects.html [accessed 1 Oct. 2022].

37. F. J. Fisher, 'The Development of London as a Centre of Conspicuous Consumption in the Sixteenth and Seventeenth Centuries', *Transactions of the Royal Historical Society*, xxx (1948), 37–50.

**38.** From Adrian Johns, David Ormrod, Rosamond McGuiness, Carole Taylor, David Mitchell, Peter Clark, Brian Cowan.

**39.** S. Rentzhog, *Open Air Museums: The History and Future of a Visionary Idea* (Kristianstad, 2007), pp. 4–32.

**40.** D. C. Coleman, *History and the Economic Past: An Account of the Rise and Decline of Economic History in Britain* (Oxford, 1978), pp. 116–19.

**41.** P. Corfield, 'Fellow Historians' (2018): https://www.penelopejcorfield.com /history-making/fellow-historians/ [accessed 1 Oct. 2022].

**42.** Seminar Paper 7, Women's Committee Workshop (7–8 Nov. 1997). J. de Vries, 'The Industrial Revolution and the Industrious Revolution', *Journal of Economic History,* liv (1994), 249–70; J. de Vries, *The Industrious Revolution: Consumer Behaviour and the Household Economy, 1650 to the Present* (Cambridge, 2008).

**43.** J. L. van Zanden, *The Long Road to the Industrial Revolution: The European Economy on a Global Perspective, 1000–1800* (Leiden, 2009), pp. 1–14.

**44.** J. de Vries and A. M. van der Woude, *The First Modern Economy* (Cambridge, 1997).

**45.** A. Macfarlane, 'Interviews with Leading Thinkers: Patrick O'Brien, 28 May 2005': https://sms.cam.ac.uk/media/1141911 [accessed 1 Oct. 2022]. P. K. O'Brien, 'Global History' (2008): https://archives.history.ac.uk/makinghistory/resources/articles /global_history.html [accessed 1 Oct. 2022].

**46.** T. Roy and G. Riello (ed.), *Global Economic History* (London, 2019), p. v.

**47.** P. O'Brien et al. (ed.), *Urban Achievement in Early Modern Europe: Golden Ages in Antwerp, Amsterdam and London* (Cambridge, 2001).

**48.** M. Berg, P. Hudson and K. Bruland, 'Writing the History of Global Challenges for the 21st Century', A Discussion hosted by the British Academy and the Global History and Culture Centre, University of Warwick: https://www.youtube.com/watch?v =84Tq2VsAH40 [accessed 9 Jan. 2022]

**49.** De Vries and Van der Woude, *First Modern Economy*, p. 716; D. Ormrod, *The Rise of Commercial Empires: England and the Netherlands in the Age of Mercantilism, 1650–1770* (Cambridge 2003), p. xiii.

**50.** Our limited contact with French colleagues, except for Guillaume Daudin and Phillippe Minard, is regrettable; recent papers in French economic history by Richard Drayton and Joseph La Hausse de Lalouvière focused on the Caribbean.

**51.** A. M. de Pleijt and J. L. van Zanden, 'Accounting for the Little Divergence', *European Review of Economic History*, xx (2016), 387–409.

**52.** E. Frankema, G. Sood and H. Tworek, 'Editors' Note: Global History after the Great Divergence', *Journal of Global History*, xvi (2021), 1–3.

**53.** R. Allen, 'Reassessing European Economic Growth, 1500–1800' (unpublished seminar paper, 16 Apr. 2004), and Allen, 'Progress and Poverty', 406–9.

**54.** S. Broadberry, B. M. S. Campbell, A. Klein, M. Overton and B. van Leeuwen, *British Economic Growth, 1270–1870* (Cambridge, 2015), pp. 226–44, esp. appendix 5.3.

**55.** P. Hudson, 'The Industrial Revolution, Relatively Speaking' (unpublished seminar paper, 9 Jun. 2017); P. Hudson, '*British Economic Growth 1270–1870*, by S. Broadberry et al. (Cambridge, 2015)', *Economic History Review*, lxix (2016), 363–5. See also: P. Hudson, 'Industrialization, Global History and the Ghost of Rostow' [The Economic History Society's Annual Tawney Lecture] (University of Warwick, 2014): https://ehs.org.uk/multimedia/tawney-lecture-2014-industrialisation-global-history -and-the-ghost-of-rostow/ [accessed 1 Oct. 2022].

56. K. Pomeranz, *The Great Divergence: China, Europe and the Making of the Modern World Economy* (Princeton, 2000). See also S. Broadberry and S. Hindle 'Editors' Introduction', *Economic History Review* [Special Issue: Asia in the Great Divergence], lxiv (2011), 1–7.

57. R. Drayton, 'France and the World Economy in the Eighteenth Century' (unpublished seminar paper, 9 Dec. 2011).

58. See also G. Riello and P. Parthasarathi (ed.), *The Spinning World: A Global History of Cotton Textiles, 1200–1850* (Oxford, 2009).

59. Clarkson, 'From England to Australia to Ireland', p. 45.

# References

## Archived sources

Templeman Library, University of Kent

Barker Oral History Tapes, BAR/10.

## Published sources

Allen, R., 'Progress and Poverty in Early Modern Europe', *Economic History Review*, lvi (2003), 403–43.

Berg, M., and Hudson, P., 'Rehabilitating the Industrial Revolution', *Economic History Review*, xlv (1992), 24–50.

Berg, M., Hudson, P., and Bruland, K., 'Writing the History of Global Challenges for the 21st Century', A Discussion hosted by the British Academy and the Global History and Culture Centre, University of Warwick: https://www.youtube.com/watch?v=84Tq2VsAH40 [accessed 9 Jan. 2022].

Bland, A. E., Brown, P. A., and Tawney, R. H., *English Economic History: Select Documents* (London, 1914).

Brewer, J., *The Sinews of Power: War, Money and the English State, 1688–1783* (New York, 1989).

Broadberry, S., and Hindle, S., 'Editors' Introduction', *Economic History Review* [Special Issue: Asia in the Great Divergence], lxiv (2011), 1–7.

Broadberry, S., et al., *British Economic Growth, 1270–1870* (Cambridge, 2015).

*Centre for Metropolitan History: Annual Report 1997–8 and Tenth Anniversary Conference Papers* (London, 1998).

Centre for Metropolitan History Projects: https://archives.history.ac.uk/cmh/projects.html [accessed 1 Oct. 2022].

Chaudhuri, K. N., *The Trading World of Asia and the English East India Company, 1660–1760* (Cambridge, 1987).

Chaudhuri, K. N., *Asia before Europe* (Cambridge, 1990).

Clarence-Smith, W., 'Editorial', *Journal of Global History*, i (2006), 1.

Clarkson, L. A., *The Pre-Industrial Economy in England, 1500–1750* (London, 1971).

Clarkson, L. A., 'From England to Australia to Ireland: A Cultural Odyssey', in *Living Economic and Social History*, ed. P. Hudson (Glasgow, 2001), pp. 42–6.

Coleman, D. C., *History and the Economic Past: An Account of the Rise and Decline of Economic History in Britain* (Oxford, 1978).

Coleman, D. C., 'Proto-Industrialization: A Concept too Many', *Economic History Review*, xxvi (1983), 435–48.

Corfield, P., 'Fellow Historians' (2018): https://www.penelopejcorfield.com/history-making/fellow-historians/ [accessed 1 Oct. 2022].

Crafts, N. F. R., *British Economic Growth during the Industrial Revolution* (Oxford, 1985).

Dahrendorf, R., *A History of the London School of Economics and Political Science, 1895–1995* (Oxford, 1995).

Derry, T. K., and Blakeway, M. G., *The Making of Pre-Industrial Britain* (London, 1973).

Earle, P., *The World of Defoe* (London, 1976).

Fisher, F. J., 'The Development of London as a Centre of Conspicuous Consumption in the Sixteenth and Seventeenth Centuries', *Transactions of the Royal Historical Society*, xxx (1948), 37–50.

Fisher, F. J., 'The Sixteenth and Seventeenth Centuries: The Dark Ages in English Economic History?' *Economica*, xxiv (1957), 2–18.

Fisher, F. J., 'Tawney's Century', in *Essays in the Economic and Social History of Tudor and Stuart England in Honour of R. H. Tawney*, ed. F. J. Fisher (Cambridge, 1961), pp. 1–14.

Fisher, F. J., 'The Department of Economic History', *LSE Magazine*, iv (Nov. 1971), 3.

Floud, F., 'Interview by Danny Millum at the Institute of Historical Research' (2008): archives.history.ac.uk/makinghistory/resources/interviews/Floud_Roderick.html [accessed 1 October 2022].

Frankema, E., Sood, G., and Tworek, H., 'Editors' Note: Global History after the Great Divergence', *Journal of Global History*, xvi (2021), 1–3.

Harding, V., 'The Population of London, 1550–1700: A Review of the Published Evidence', *London Journal*, xv (1990), 111–28.

Harley, C. K., 'British Industrialization before 1841: Evidence of Slower Growth during the Industrial Revolution', *Journal of Economic History*, xlii (1982), 267–89.

Harte, N. B., 'Trends in Publications on the Economic and Social History of Great Britain and Ireland, 1925–74', *Economic History Review*, xxx (1977), 20–41.

Harte, N. B., 'In Memory of F. J. Fisher', in *London and the English Economy, 1500–1700*, ed. P. J. Corfield and N. B. Harte (London, 1990), p. 28.

Harte, N. B., 'The Economic History Society, 1926–2001', in *Living Economic and Social History*, ed. P. Hudson (Glasgow, 2001), pp. 1–12.

Hatcher, J., *The History of the British Coal Industry: Volume 1 Before 1700* (Oxford, 1993).

Holderness, B. A., *Pre-Industrial England: Economy and Society from 1500–1700* (London, 1977).

Hoppit, J., 'Understanding the Industrial Revolution', *Historical Journal*, xxx (1987), 211–24.

Hoppit, J., 'Counting the Industrial Revolution', *Economic History Review*, xliii (1990), 173–93.

Hoppit, J., 'The Contexts and Contours of British Economic Literature, 1660–1760,' *Historical Journal*, xlix (2006), 79–110.

Hoppit, J., *Britain's Political Economies: Parliament and Economic Life, 1660–1800* (Cambridge, 2017).

Houston, R., and Snell, K. D. M., 'Proto-Industrialization? Cottage Industry, Social Change, and Industrial Revolution', *Historical Journal*, xxvii (1984), 437–92.

Howson, S., 'Keynes and the LSE Economists', *Journal of the History of Economic Thought*, xxxi (2009), 257–80.

Hudson, P., 'The Regional Perspective', in *Regions and Industries: A Perspective on the Industrial Revolution in Britain*, ed. P. Hudson (Cambridge, 1989), pp. 5–38.

Hudson, P., *The Industrial Revolution* (London, 1992).

Hudson, P., 'Industrialization, Global History and the Ghost of Rostow' [The Economic History Society's Annual Tawney Lecture] (University of Warwick, 2014): https://ehs.org.uk/multimedia/tawney-lecture -2014-industrialisation-global-history-and-the-ghost-of-rostow/ [accessed 1 Oct. 2022].

Hudson, P., '*British Economic Growth 1270–1870*, by S. Broadberry et al. (Cambridge, 2015)', *Economic History Review*, lxix (2016), 363–5.

Kussmaul, A., *A General View of the Rural Economy of England, 1538–1840* (Cambridge, 1990).

Laslett, P., *The World We Have Lost* (London, 1965).

Macfarlane, A., 'Interviews with Leading Thinkers: Patrick O'Brien, 28 May 2005': https://sms.cam.ac.uk/media/1141911 [accessed 1 Oct. 2022].

O'Brien, P. K., 'Global History' (2008): https://archives.history.ac.uk /makinghistory/resources/articles/global_history.html [accessed 1 Oct. 2022].

O'Brien, P., et al. (ed.), *Urban Achievement in Early Modern Europe: Golden Ages in Antwerp, Amsterdam and London* (Cambridge, 2001).

Ormrod, D., *The Rise of Commercial Empires: England and the Netherlands in the Age of Mercantilism, 1650–1770* (Cambridge, 2003).

Parker, P., *Global Crisis: War, Climate Change and Catastrophe in the Seventeenth Century* (New Haven, 2013).

Phelps-Brown, H., and Hopkins, S. V., 'Seven Centuries of Building Wages', *Economica*, xxii (1955), 195–206.

Pleijt, A. M. de, and Zanden, J. L. van, 'Accounting for the Little Divergence', *European Review of Economic History*, xx (2016), 387–409.

Pomeranz, K., *The Great Divergence: China, Europe and the Making of the Modern World Economy* (Princeton, 2000).

Rentzhog, S., *Open Air Museums: The History and Future of a Visionary Idea* (Kristianstad, 2007).

Riello, G., and Parthasarathi, P. (ed.), *The Spinning World: A Global History of Cotton Textiles, 1200–1850* (Oxford, 2009).

Roy, T., and Riello, G. (ed.), *Global Economic History* (London, 2019).

Sharpe, J. A., *Early Modern England: A Social History, 1550–1760* (London, 1987).

Stobart, J., *The First Industrial Region: North-west England, 1700–60* (Manchester, 2004).

Thirsk, J., 'Industries in the Countryside', in *Essays in the Economic and Social History of Tudor and Stuart England*, ed. F. J. Fisher (Cambridge, 1961), pp. 70–88.

Thirsk, J. (ed.), *The Agrarian History of England and Wales, 1640–1750, Vol. 1, Regional Farming Systems* (Cambridge, 1984).

Vries, J. de, 'The Industrial Revolution and the Industrious Revolution', *Journal of Economic History*, liv (1994), 249–70.

Vries, J. de, *The Industrious Revolution: Consumer Behaviour and the Household Economy, 1650 to the Present* (Cambridge, 2008).

Vries, J. de, and Woude, A. M. van der, *The First Modern Economy* (Cambridge, 1997).

Warde, P., *Energy Consumption in England and Wales, 1560–2000* (Rome, 2007).

Whittle, J. (ed.), *Landlords and Tenants in Britain, 1440–1660* (Woodbridge, 2013).

Woodward, D., *Men at Work: Labourers and Building Craftsmen in the Towns of Northern England, 1450–1750* (Cambridge, 1995).

Wrigley, E. A., *Continuity, Chance and Change: The Character of the Industrial Revolution in England* (Cambridge, 1988).

Wrigley, E. A., *Energy and the Industrial Revolution* (Cambridge, 2010).

Zahedieh, N., *The Capital and the Colonies: London and the Atlantic Economy, 1660–1700* (Cambridge, 2010).

Zahedieh, N., 'Overseas Trade and Empire', in *The Cambridge Economic History of Modern Britain, I, 1700–1870*, ed. R. Floud, J. Humphries, and P. Johnson (Cambridge, 2014).

Zanden, J. L. van, *The Long Road to the Industrial Revolution: The European Economy on a Global Perspective, 1000–1800* (Leiden, 2009).

## Unpublished sources

Allen, R., 'Reassessing European Economic Growth, 1500–1800', Seminar Paper (16 Apr. 2004).

Drayton, R., 'France and the World Economy in the Eighteenth Century', Seminar Paper (9 Dec. 2011).

Hudson, P., 'The Industrial Revolution, Relatively Speaking', Seminar Paper (9 Jun. 2017).

Chapter 4

# The British History in the Seventeenth Century Seminar

## Jason Peacey

Writing the history of a long-lived seminar series at the Institute of Historical Research poses a challenge, albeit one that has merit in terms of addressing important aspects of, and shifts within, academic culture. It is salutary to reflect upon something that has been a significant part of many people's lives. My own involvement with what is now the Seventeenth Century British History Seminar began while I was a PhD student – based outside London – in the early 1990s. The Seminar became a fixture in my diary upon my joining the History of Parliament project in 1994 and then more seriously so upon becoming a convenor after securing a post at University College London in 2006.[1] I thus followed in the footsteps of others whose responsibility for finding, chairing and hosting speakers, as well as for guarding the registers, is more or less directly linked to holding a permanent academic position within the University of London. I am *loyal* to a seminar that has been part of my life for thirty years, and proud to be associated with an institution – often described simply as the 'Thursday Seminar' – that was established in 1951, and that is now in its eighth decade of fortnightly sessions. At the same time, this kind of relationship with one particular seminar corresponds with a distinct phase in the IHR's history; it was not how things worked originally and is a model that is no longer adhered to very strictly. In that sense, reflecting on the history of a specific seminar contributes to the wider history of the IHR, and of English academia. As such, this chapter teases out phenomena – regarding convenors, audiences and speakers – that speak to broader patterns of continuity and change, all of which are relevant to debates about the IHR's future, rather than just its past.

Of course, such comments can only be suggestive, and the potential for relating the Seminar's history is limited. Sadly, the opportunity has been missed to produce a satisfactory oral history; as with aged grandparents, there was scope to ask more questions, to pay more attention to stories from yesteryear, and to have a better memory. More importantly, we possess inadequate documentary records, and it is embarrassing not to be able to draw upon a systematic seminar archive. As things stand, it has not been possible to locate the registers of attendees, speakers and papers for the period after 1984–5. Moreover, registers for earlier decades are frustratingly cryptic, not least in terms of how rarely evidence survives about who delivered papers, let alone about the topics upon which they spoke.

What follows is therefore an imperfect history of the Seventeenth Century British History Seminar, based upon extant registers, upon memories (my own as well as those of others), and upon a fairly complete list of papers delivered since 2001, and maintained for my own purposes.[2] This chapter will hopefully do justice to the Seminar's distinctive and valuable qualities, and raise questions about the role of seminars within the scholarly landscape. At the very least it will begin the process of teasing out what can be gleaned from available sources about the Seminar's convenors, its audience and its papers, as well as how it conducts its business, and its 'culture'.

For much of its life, the Seminar has been less celebrated than its elder sibling – the 'Monday Seminar', formally the Tudor and Stuart History Seminar, convened over the years by A. F. Pollard (1869–1948), Joel Hurstfield (1911–80), John Neale (1890–1975), and Conrad Russell (1937–2004), amongst others.[3] That seminar has its own revealing history and, as anyone who has attended both groups will attest, they have always had rather different atmospheres. That these two seminars – and indeed others – have co-existed for so long, despite their thematic and chronological similarities, is significant and is probably more or less comprehensible. Rightly or wrongly, the Thursday Seminar has sometimes been treated as less high-powered than the Monday Seminar, but for a long time it was also less austere and intimidating. Some have certainly wondered whether the Seventeenth Century Seminar could do with being *more* robust, in terms of its discussions of specific papers. Nevertheless, the success and longevity of the Seminar reflects its welcoming atmosphere, and its culture of support and sociability, all of which have been cultivated by successive convenors, and have engendered the loyalty that is so apparent from its history, thereby helping to make it an IHR institution.

## Convenors

As with all historical phenomena, there is a pre-history to what became the Seventeenth Century British History Seminar, and one that perhaps set the tone for later decades. The early registers reveal the existence of a seminar on 'English History, 1603–1660', convened by Miss I. G. Powell from 1926–7 until around the Second World War, although this may have been essentially an internal Royal Holloway seminar catering for its all-female student body (the college went co-educational in 1965).[4] Another precursor – on English political history in the seventeenth century – was established by the 1925–6 session and overseen by Norman Sykes (1897–1961: Oxford DPhil, 1923) and Esmond de Beer (1895–1990).[5] Sykes began his academic career at King's College London in 1924, the same year he was ordained in the Church of England, and was later appointed Dixie professor of ecclesiastical history at Cambridge in 1944 and dean of Winchester Cathedral in 1958.[6] De Beer, meanwhile, was a New Zealander who inherited from his mentor, C. H. Firth, a passion for great editing projects, including the diary of John Evelyn and the correspondence of John Locke.[7]

Cosmopolitanism and big editorial ventures would remain important to later incarnations of the Seminar, the convening of which also reveals other patterns. The formal creation of the Thursday Seminar can be attributed to Robert Latham (1912–95), who moved to Royal Holloway from a lectureship at KCL in 1942, and who was a reader there by the time that he established the Seminar in 'English Political and Constitutional History in the Seventeenth Century'. Whatever motivated Latham, it is striking that the Thursday Seminar was so beholden to one prominent historian, and Latham ran the Seminar single-handed from 1951 until 1968. Of course, it should be noted that Latham was then much less celebrated than he later became, as one of the editors of Samuel Pepys's diary. It is also noteworthy that the Pepys project was an early example of modern transnational scholarship for it involved William Matthews who, despite being an Englishman with a London PhD, was in post at the University of California, Los Angeles.[8]

Latham's departure from the Seminar in 1968 – for a professorship at the University of Toronto, before becoming Pepys Librarian at Magdalene College, Cambridge – perhaps signalled a change at the IHR, whereby seminars were increasingly overseen by groups of historians from across London, rather than by a dominant individual. Initially, this meant Roger Lockyer, Henry Roseveare and Ian Roy, a team that took over with the 1968–9 session, and one presumably designed to offer a blend of seniority and youthful enthusiasm, as well as a broader range of expertise. Lockyer

(1927–2017) had been a lecturer at Royal Holloway since 1961 and had already produced *Tudor and Stuart Britain 1471–1714* (1964): a hugely successful textbook which appeared in a revised fourth edition in 2018.[9] Roseveare and Roy had both begun attending the Seminar in 1960, within weeks of each other, and while still pursuing postgraduate research. By this stage, at least, the Seminar clearly had the ability to attract attendees from outside London. Roseveare, who brought expertise in economic history, completed his PhD at Cambridge in 1962, while Roy completed his Oxford DPhil on the royalist army during the civil wars in 1963. Both enjoyed long careers at KCL and remained involved with the Seminar until their respective retirements, and indeed for much longer in Roy's case. That neither Roy nor Roseveare produced huge quantities of published work says less about the importance of their scholarship – which in both cases included important source editions – than about changes within the profession. Here, the Seminar's long history reveals important shifts from amateur (or gentlemanly) to professional scholarship, as well as the gradual re-balancing of scholarly endeavours from teaching (and postgraduate supervision) to publication, and it may be no coincidence that such developments were accompanied by seminars adding more convenors. Roy and Roseveare might be thought to symbolize a phase when academia had become professionalized but not yet obsessed with research publications.

The next addition to the roster of convenors was John Miller (b. 1946), who completed his Cambridge PhD – on the 'Catholic factor' in English politics from 1660 to 1688 – in 1971, and who is first listed as a convenor during the 1975–6 session. Miller's work contributed to historiographical development in the politics of religion, and subsequently a new generation – with its own interests, as well as very different sartorial tastes – became represented on Thursday evenings. Indeed, Miller would later commend the Seminar for its 'papers and discussions afterwards, formal and informal' as a 'constant source of stimulation and information' and a means of keeping 'in touch with the work being done on the period by a number of impressive younger historians on both sides of the Atlantic'.[10]

This change was augmented with the addition of Justin Champion (1960–2020), who gained his PhD from Cambridge in 1989 and secured a lectureship at Royal Holloway and Bedford New College in 1992.[11] At that point the Thursday Seminar shifted from being known – colloquially – as the 'three wise men' seminar, to being dubbed the seminar of the 'three wise men … and young pretender', with Champion affectionately referred to as the 'Lion King' for his resplendent blond hair.

Thus far, the evolution of the Seminar had involved continuity as well as change. The number of convenors grew, and the development of more specialized scholarship became evident. What convenors shared, however, was a formal association with the University of London, as 'permanent' members of academic staff at one college or another. That tradition was upheld into the twenty-first century. That my own formal involvement did not begin until my appointment at UCL did not seem noteworthy, and other convenors likewise joined upon becoming lecturers. Neither did it seem significant that, even as the number of convenors grew, the Seminar acknowledged seniority. While all of the convenors generally attended each seminar, and helped to entertain the speakers, the programme was formally organized by John Miller, even if he was very open to suggestions about possible speakers, and even if he did not *invariably* chair sessions.

That Miller felt like the leader of the Seminar, particularly following the retirements of Roy and Roseveare, did not seem remotely odd, but it is notable how much the Seminar has changed since his retirement in 2012. The Seminar now boasts an expanded and more diverse group of nine convenors. This shift has occurred naturally, rather than as a result of a determined policy, and it reflects the kinds of people whose enthusiasm for the Seminar has made them obvious candidates to be co-opted as convenors. Some convenors have retained their association with the Seminar after leaving the University of London; others have always been employed elsewhere; and at least one might be thought to be a member of the 'precariat' – in this case a postdoctoral scholar with no permanent position – that is now such a controversial aspect of the university sector. A new structure has been accompanied by new processes, and the Seminar is now more collaborative, in terms of how speakers are identified, sessions are conducted and administration is handled. This is appropriate, but also necessary; the lives of modern academics involve different pressures from those witnessed by previous generations and running a seminar single-handed now seems less manageable, not least in a situation where university managers treat it as a less worthwhile dimension of our work, and where the University of London is a less meaningful entity.

## Audiences

Not all changes have been planned, or strategized, but convenors have certainly reflected upon the 'culture' of the Seminar, not least in terms of thinking about its 'audience', the second theme of this chapter. This is partly a matter of tone and atmosphere, and the determination to make proceedings welcoming. Key here is sociability, and however formal things may once have been, it is striking how informal things have been since at least the early 1990s. This is particularly true in terms of post-seminar proceedings, which have sometimes involved local restaurants, and *always* local pubs. The point here is not simply that such places were chosen because they appealed to the convenors, even if Ian Roy was partial to the homely delights of the Trattoria Mondello on Goodge Street, and even if John Miller was partial to a pint of ESB (extra special bitter). The real point is that venues were chosen so as not to exclude postgraduate students, either in terms of price or the ability to accommodate a large group of scholars. Mondello, while hardly pricey, was actually a rare treat; more often during the 1990s we dined at a very basic (and long-gone) Italian canteen on Charlotte Street, and even there the bill was massaged to ensure that students were subsidized by more senior colleagues. It also meant that conversations continued in a range of less than glitzy pubs. The lure of a new Fuller's pub on Tottenham Court Road eventually gave the Seminar not just a venue that served both food and beer, but also a base which soon became a firm association, at least until the area's gentrification prompted the move to a quieter venue, and one more convenient for those who needed to catch a late train.

The point of such stories is that sociability has long been integral to the culture and intellectual vibrancy of the Seminar, rather than simply a function of the need to feed and water the speaker, usually at the convenors' expense.[12] For many people, long evenings in the Jack Horner or Skinners' Arms have been as important as, if not more important than, the papers themselves, and while pub-based sociability risks excluding some people, this has certainly not been the aim, and such a culture is surely relevant to the Seminar's success and longevity, and to the allegiance that it engenders.[13] Of course, appreciating the importance of loyalty involves more than food and drink, although such things are hard to separate from the kinds of pattern that can be detected when reflecting on who has frequented the seminar over the years, not least with the aid of surviving registers.

Latham's Seminar started small, with an audience of four to five people per meeting in its first year, but it soon became established, and by the mid-1950s papers were generally attracting twelve to fourteen people. Over the years the average audience has sometimes been smaller than this, but it has frequently been larger, and it has often been gratifying – if claustrophobic – when we have crammed thirty or more people into a small seminar room. The early registers prove revealing in fascinating ways, even in terms of how names were recorded. For example, it is striking that, while the Seminar was very far from being a male preserve, there was a tendency to refer to men with their initials, or perhaps only a surname, while female attendees were generally referred to with a title (Miss Roberts, Miss Jenkins, and so on). That most members of the Seminar were students appears clear from the fact that very few people were accorded their academic or professional titles, whether professor or indeed 'reverend'. (Unfortunately, the recording of institutional affiliations was also erratic.) That said, such patterns and associated prejudices were not rigidly enforced. 'Miss Hodge' from Royal Holloway soon became 'Susan Hodge'; Mrs Glow soon became 'Miss Lottie Glow'; and 'Miss Rowe' – who had attended Miss Powell's seminar back in the 1930s – soon became 'Violet A. Rowe'. In its own way, and rather slowly, the Seminar moved with the times.

Beyond signalling cultural change, the registers also prove revealing in other ways. A full prosopography of the Seminar is obviously impossible, particularly in terms of those who never completed their postgraduate studies, published their research or remained within academia. Nevertheless, striking patterns can be discerned on the basis of those whose names are recognizable from the historiography of early modern Britain.

Very often, of course, the Seminar was frequented by, and dependent upon, local talent, in terms of those studying for London PhDs. This was true from the very start, and an early stalwart was Alan Everitt (1926–2008), who later found success as a pioneer of the 'county community' school of local history, but who was then one of Latham's PhD students.[14] Another young scholar who benefitted from Latham's support was William Lamont (1934–2018), the historian of puritanism, who began attending in 1956–7, having just completed his BA degree, and who was training to be a teacher alongside undertaking his PhD (1956–61). As noted already, these successful students were not always men. One example is Violet Rowe, who attended the Seminar from 1955 until 1964, for at least some of which time she was completing what would be her 1965 London PhD, with a thesis on Sir Henry Vane junior. Many other names are also recognizable. These include Brian Quintrell, who attended while completing his 1965 Royal Holloway PhD – on early Stuart government in Essex – before taking up a post at Liverpool, as well as Madeline Jones, who received her London PhD – on the history of parliamentary representation in Kent during the English Revolution – in 1967.[15] They also include students of Ian Roy, such as R. H. Silcock (1971–2) and Lawson Nagel (1975–6); students of Lockyer such as Alan McGowan (1965–6) and Frances Condick (1975–6); and students of Conrad Russell, such as David Hebb (1973–4), Jacqueline Eales (1981–2) and Richard Cust, the last of whom began attending the Seminar in 1976–7, shortly before moving to a lectureship at Birmingham. Beyond this, of course, the Seminar benefitted from having on its doorstep – in Woburn Square – numerous early modernists at the History of Parliament, including Gillian Hampson, Peter Lefevre, John Ferris and Stuart Handley, as well as Ted Rowlands, at least before he became MP for Cardiff North (1966). For generations of PhD students, the Seminar has taken the place of a more general departmental research seminar, helping to make their experiences somewhat different from students in other universities.

What also made the experience different was that it was always possible to meet students from further afield, and there is mileage in the suggestion that IHR seminars are less insular than those elsewhere. Early visitors, in 1952–3, included John MacCormack, the historian of the Irish Adventurers and of the Long Parliament, as well as David Underdown (1923–2009), the latter of whom had begun his PhD at Oxford under Christopher Hill (1912–2003), before completing his studies at Yale, and who had not yet taken up his first teaching post in Tennessee. Neither MacCormack nor Underdown was then a published author. Another Oxford student who attended that year was D. T. Whitcombe, who was in the final stages of a PhD supervised by Donald Pennington (1919–2007). Whitcombe, whose subsequent career lay in school teaching, certainly acknowledged the influence of Latham, 'at whose seminar I received constant advice and encouragement'.[16] Others pursued university careers, including many who studied at Oxford and Cambridge. Robin Clifton, who began attending the Seminar in 1955–6, later completed his thesis on anti-popery at Oxford (1967), having already begun teaching at Warwick. The year 1960–61 saw visits from two Oxford students: A. M. Johnson, who studied the history of Chester before moving to University College, Cardiff; and Robert Beddard, the historian of the Restoration church, who had been an undergraduate in London, and who subsequently held college fellowships in both Cambridge and Oxford. In subsequent years, the registers reveal other visitors, including Colin Brooks, who was researching taxation and public opinion during the Restoration (1968–9), Lionel Glassey, who was working on the commission of the peace in later Stuart and Hanoverian England (1967–9), and Julia Buckroyd, who was studying ecclesiastical affairs in Restoration Scotland (1974–5); not to mention historians of Restoration political thought like Mark Goldie, and of the Cromwellian army like Henry Reece (both 1975–6), as well as the historian of seventeenth-century taxation and state formation, Mike Braddick (1985–6). Such students presumably had other opportunities for attending specialist seminars, and as such few became very regular attendees. For those studying further afield, trips to London may have been less feasible, although the Seminar certainly attracted postgraduates from beyond the 'golden triangle'. John Newton, who attended in 1954–5, had studied at Hull under the Reformation historian and sometime IHR director, A. G. Dickens (1910–2001), before becoming an IHR research fellow during the closing stages of his PhD (1955), and then becoming a Methodist minister.[17] G. V. Chivers presumably came to London in 1957–8 to research relations between the City and the state, the subject of his 1962 Manchester PhD. Other students from Manchester included P. R.

Seddon (1963–4) and Keith Lindley (1964–6). Others attended from Lancaster, Southampton and Birmingham.

For at least some non-London students, attendance at the Seminar marked the end of a day at the old Public Record Office (PRO) in Chancery Lane, which closed in 1997, or else in the old British Library, until 1998.[18] For some, there were practical reasons for prolonging their day in London, in terms of not being able to get cheap trains or buses home until later in the evening, but it would be unwise to dismiss the intellectual attractions of the IHR. Even if the Thursday Seminar has sometimes been regarded as less rigorous than others, 'junior' members of the audience, especially PhD students, certainly found it intimidating. This doubtless reflects the fact that the Seminar has always attracted some of the brightest students from further afield. As early as 1955–6 the Seminar was attended by a graduate student from Australia, Donald Kennedy, who subsequently taught for forty years at the University of Melbourne. More often, students came from the USA. During 1953–4, the attendees included G. R. Abernathy, years before he became an assistant professor at the University of Alabama (1960) and began to publish.[19] The following year saw visits from C. R. Niehaus during the research for his 1957 Harvard thesis on law reform during the 'Puritan revolution', and before his appointment as an assistant professor at MIT (1960). From Boston University came John Battick (1961–2), who completed his PhD on Cromwell's 'Western design' in 1967, before moving to the University of Maine, where he remained until 1997. Later in the decade the Seminar was attended by Sears McGee from Yale (1967–9), who subsequently had a distinguished career at Santa Barbara, as well as Robert (Roy) Ritchie from UCLA (1967–8), who later became a professor at San Diego and research director at the Huntington Library. For many scholars who went on to have illustrious careers, in other words, the Seminar was part of their induction into, and involvement with, academia; those who attended regularly during extended research trips to England invariably enlivened proceedings with fresh perspectives, and for them the seminar clearly performed a useful social function. The PhD process can be a lonely one, all the more so during prolonged trips away from one's home country, and the Seminar – as well as its sociability – can clearly be invaluable.

What also emerges from the registers is how reliant the Seminar has always been upon PhD supervisors to encourage – and perhaps instruct – their students to frequent the IHR. Some came to London to study, presumably having been advised by teachers and mentors. In the case of Lotte Glow (later Mulligan) this presumably meant George Yule, her undergraduate tutor at Melbourne (1948–50). Glow attended the Seminar from 1955 to 1958, before completing her research in Adelaide, and then teaching at La Trobe until her retirement in 1995. Influential US scholars in this respect included D. H. Willson at Minnesota, whose students included the historian of parliamentary elections, J. K. Gruenfelder, who attended as a PhD student (1961–2) before taking up a post at Wyoming. Visitors from Berkeley included students of Thomas Barnes such as Karl Bottigheimer (1962–3), Stephen Stearns (1962–4) and Howard Nenner (1966–7). Students from Yale included those supervised by J. H. Hexter, including Caroline Hibbard (1968–70); those from Princeton included Robert Brenner (1966–7) and Rachel Weil (1985–6), both of whom were supervised by Lawrence Stone (1919–99). Indeed, the value of attending the Seminar has evidently been instilled by supervisors into their students over successive 'generations'. Having attended as an Australian student in the 1950s, Donald Kennedy perhaps ensured that Carolyn Polizzotto, his student at Melbourne, attended the seminar while studying civil war Puritanism in London in the early 1970s. Similarly, Ann Hughes began attending the Seminar as a student of Brian Quintrell, who had himself attended during postgraduate research. Hughes has been attending ever since, and at least one of her own students, Sean Kelsey, has become a noted 'friend of the seminar'. Such lineages can be traced back to the origins of the Seminar, which was attended in its first year by David Underdown, in later years by his student Mark Kishlansky (1948–2015), who was in London as a PhD student from Brown in 1973–4, and then by Kishlansky's own students, such as Victor Stater (1983–4).

In addition to students, the Seminar has also benefitted from attendance by more 'senior' academics, some of whom appeared more or less regularly and frequently, sometimes over decades. This is true of many scholars from around the UK. The registers reveal that David Hebb, who completed a Bedford College PhD on piracy in early Stuart England (1985), attended from 1973 until at least 1986. Having begun attending as a PhD student in the mid-1960s, Keith Lindley's name appears in the registers into the 1980s, and he certainly continued to attend thereafter. The same was true of Rosemary O'Day, who first attended in the late 1960s as a student working on clerical patronage at King's, and whose name appears throughout the 1970s and into the 1980s, while she was working at the Open University. Ruth Spalding, the biographer of the civil war MP, Bulstrode Whitelocke, and the editor of his substantial diary, attended the Seminar every year from 1966 until at least 1986.[20] More strikingly, such loyalty is also evident with scholars based further away, for many of whom the rhythm of the academic year involved trips to London as soon as teaching ended. Anyone familiar with the IHR will have noted the tendency for attendance at seminars to change in the last weeks of the summer term, as people like Henry Horwitz (1938–2019) arrived from the USA.[21] Some scholars, moreover, spent prolonged periods of research leave in London, to the great benefit of many seminars. During 1960–61, Paul Seaver (1932–2020) – then of Reed College and later of Stanford – attended every session, and although not everyone was so assiduous, the registers certainly reveal a succession of visiting scholars, including Royce MacGillivray (Waterloo, 1966–7), Wilfrid Prest (Adelaide, 1973), Stephen Foster (Northern Illinois, 1971–2), and Brian Levack (Texas, 1975), as well as Fritz Levy (Washington, 1979–80). Another, Charles Korr, from the University of Missouri at St Louis, was probably introduced to the IHR by his mentor, S. T. Bindoff (1908–80). Having attended as a student, Howard Nenner returned to the Seminar during sabbatical leave from Smith College (1972–3). Like so many others, Levy and Nenner became familiar faces at the Seminar for many years, sometimes long after their retirement, and the registers confirm just how many visiting historians return at least once and sometimes several times. Howard Reinmuth – another student of D. H. Willson at Minnesota – attended the Seminar whilst in London in 1973–4 and 1985–6, presumably while on leave from the University of Akron. Roy Schreiber attended in the mid-1960s, while completing his London PhD, and then again as an IHR fellow, and subsequently returned to the Seminar in 1974–5 and in 1983–4, while on leave from the University of Indiana. Likewise, Patricia Crawford, who began attending as a graduate student from Australia in 1965, returned fairly regularly during periods of leave from the University of Western Australia until at least 1981. It was surely this devotion – rather than just cultural change – which ensured that she moved from being recorded as Mrs Crawford to P. M. Crawford, Dr P. Crawford, and Patricia Crawford, and eventually as 'Pat' or 'Trish'.[22]

## Speakers

Such patterns – as well as others relating to shifts in intellectual trends – can also be discerned using evidence about the third dimension of the Seminar's history: its speakers. Here too the evidence is imperfect. The identity of speakers was only recorded – sporadically – from the mid-1970s, and little survives about paper titles before 2001. Nevertheless, the extant material still reveals something of the culture at the IHR and permits broader conclusions to be drawn about the ongoing value of its seminars.

In memory and reputation, the Seventeenth Century Seminar is held to have sourced its programme from within the ranks of regular attendees, and this is somewhat true. In 2003–4, three convenors – Champion, Roy and Miller – gave *four* papers between them, while three further talks came from people at the History of Parliament. Sometimes this involved convenors stepping in to fill gaps in the schedule, or established members of the Seminar being prevailed upon to help out. Indeed, five of these speakers reappeared on the programme the following year. These are extreme examples, although they reflect the challenges that all convenors face: being able to find speakers, particularly for slots at the start of the autumn term; needing to fill in when speakers pull out at short notice; and – perhaps most importantly – the limited budgets that are available to bring speakers to London. In that sense, it is a miracle that the Seminar has survived. That it *thrives* reflects careful management and curation. Here, of course, such challenges have been offset by IHR fellowship schemes, including those sponsored by the Mellon Foundation, the great merit of which has been to attract scholars from outside London. Such fellowships – which are really valuable in a context where few university departments of history can offer postdoctoral funding – are often thought about in terms of the advantages they give to younger scholars; equally important is the dynamism that such people bring to the seminars within which they become embedded.

However much each year's programme is a product of necessity, it also involves virtues. IHR seminars clearly have a role in supporting the discipline, nationally and globally, but they also need to serve the interests of the scholarly community in London, where university departments often lack research seminars. As such, there is value in providing a forum for local PhD students – as part of their induction into the scholarly community – as well as for more established scholars. This was evident on 11 March 1976, for example, when a paper was given by Hans Pawlisch, a PhD student at King's, working on the Tudor conquest of Ireland.[23] It has, quite rightly, been evident ever since, in terms of papers by the convenors' own PhD students. Traditionally, such presentations are some of the first that graduate students deliver, and since the prospect can be daunting there is comfort in being able to do so before familiar faces. Similarly, since the skills involved in asking questions and contributing to discussions tend to be acquired only gradually, this too is something that can best be fostered within a familiar setting.

More broadly, the image of an insular seminar – with speakers drawn from London colleges – needs modification. While not much is known about every speaker from the 1975–6 session, it is noteworthy that they included Julia Buckroyd and Henry Reece, PhD students from Cambridge and Oxford respectively, as well as Lynn Beats, a student of Anthony Fletcher's at Sheffield. Other papers were delivered by Robin Gwynn and Ian Gentles, to both of whom we shall return. The following year saw another paper by Buckroyd, while 1979–80 saw a paper from Michael Weinzierl, a PhD student from Austria, and another from Stephen Roberts,

THE BRITISH HISTORY IN THE SEVENTEENTH CENTURY SEMINAR    103

who was in the final stages of a PhD with Ivan Roots at Exeter, and who was then an IHR fellow. Then, as now, the Seminar recruited speakers from the widest pool of bright PhD students, and as far as possible the aim has always been to offer a 'blended' programme, involving scholars both local and international, and those at different stages of their career. In 1983–4, an unusually large audience – including luminaries like Nicholas Tyacke, Peter Lake, Linda Levy Peck and Mark Kishlansky – heard a paper from Pauline Croft, a colleague from Royal Holloway. Recent years have seen papers from some of the most important scholars in the field of early modern studies, including Lake himself, Tom Cogswell, Tim Harris, David Cressy, John Marshall, Kenneth Fincham, Colin Davis, Mark Jenner, Adam Fox, Alan Macinnes, Bernard Capp, Brian Cowan and Steve Pincus, and many more. As this selective list also indicates, the Seminar has retained strong transatlantic relations.

The Seminar has always benefitted from its enduring membership. Having attended in the 1960s, while producing a PhD on puritanism in Old and New England, Michael Finlayson returned as a speaker in 1976–7, as a tenured historian at Toronto. Michael Braddick, whose most recent paper was in February 2021, has been associated with the seminar since 1985, when he first appeared in the registers as a Cambridge PhD student. Jaqueline Eales, who last gave a paper in 2019, has been attending since being a PhD student in the early 1980s. Ann Hughes, who most recently appeared in June 2022, has been attending since 1973. Such examples could be replicated, and the list of speakers in recent years confirms patterns that are evident from the earlier registers, in terms of the frequency with which the Seminar attracts a following amongst key players in the field. Furthermore, those who first attended the Seminar as students and junior academics – such as Mark Kishlansky, Tim Harris, Steve Pincus, Peter Lake, Ann Hughes and Michael Braddick – have also gone on to encourage the younger generation to follow suit. Here, it is possible to discern evidence of scholarly lineages. In recent years, papers have been given not just by Lake, but also by his PhD students (David Como, Bill Bulman), and even by their students in turn (Noah Millstone, Richard Bell). Similarly, the Seminar's heritage can be traced from Sonia Tycko – recently appointed to a lectureship at Edinburgh – all the way back to its very earliest incarnation, via her supervisor, Mark Kishlansky, and then his supervisor, David Underdown.

Another somewhat unfair characterization of the Thursday Seminar involves the notion that papers have tended to lack thematic range, as well as methodological and conceptual sophistication. Thus, while the quality of papers – and discussions – may always have varied, the Seminar has always been ecumenical, and although there may always have been a tendency to favour some kind of 'political history', this has always been defined very broadly. Nowadays, the IHR boasts a huge range of seminar series, and while some of these specialize on particular themes and approaches (such as cultural, social, economic and religious history), the Thursday Seminar can legitimately claim to be generalist, and to have reflected shifting scholarly interests over time. Whether or not the quality of papers has sometimes been mixed, the *diversity* of papers is central to the Seminar's appeal, and to the value of the seminar format.

In part, this can be demonstrated through the interests of the convenors. Latham and Lockyer ranged widely, at least in terms of the students they supervised, and the 'political' scope of the Seminar has always included local dimensions, as well as religious perspectives, at least in terms of church politics. As academic specialisms have solidified, this intellectual breadth was maintained more obviously by means of a larger group of convenors, who brought expertise in economic history (Roseveare) and intellectual history (Champion). Champion's involvement certainly positioned the Seminar as a venue for new kinds of intellectual history, which ranged beyond canonical thinkers like Hobbes and Locke, and which explored connections between canonical thinkers and their political, religious and economic contexts. Other convenors helped to ensure chronological range, at least from the civil wars (Roy) through to the later Stuarts (Miller); that the Seminar has focused less obviously on the pre-civil war decades of the seventeenth century reflects relations with the Tudor–Stuart Seminar, to which we will return.

Since 2001, the Seminar has remained a focal point for scholarship on traditional aspects of seventeenth-century British history, in terms of the civil wars and Restoration, as well as broader themes in religious, economic, local and urban history. The Seminar has illuminated how these sub-disciplines have evolved in dialogue with other fields of expertise whilst bearing witness to the emergence of interdisciplinary concerns – such as print culture – as major dimensions of early modern studies, as well as the waxing and waning of the 'new British history'. Likewise, and more recently, it is possible to trace a resurgence of interest in the 1650s, and in the kind of political and religious radicalism that was somewhat side-lined by 'revisionist' scholars in the 1970s and 1980s. The Seminar is also now providing a forum for scholarship on colonial, imperial and transnational history, and on state formation, as well as work that relates to literary studies, art history, social history and gender history, not to mention newer fields like environmental history, memory studies, medical history and the history of emotions. Fairly frequently, moreover, the Seminar hosts papers that might otherwise be expected to be given at one of the other seminars at the IHR or within the University of London. This may reflect the reality that loyalty to a seminar sometimes involves being 'tribal'. It may also indicate that there is value in attending a 'generalist', yet chronologically focused seminar, that considers different topics and sub-disciplines and provides speakers with informed feedback from an audience with contrasting perspectives.

## Conclusions and prospects

As befits a gathering of historians, the story of the Seventeenth Century British History Seminar involves both continuity and change, and sheds light not just upon the value of the IHR but also of the kinds of seminars that it hosts, while also prompting reflections about the future of such activities.

That the Thursday Seminar has continued to evolve is clear. Recent years have seen different formats being embraced, from joint papers to book launches and round-table discussions. Convenors are rightly concerned not just with offering a 'mixed economy' of presentations by both senior and junior scholars, but also about achieving a healthy gender balance. The onset of the COVID-19 pandemic, of course, necessitated other changes, some of which may become permanent. After a few papers were cancelled in the midst of 'lockdown', meetings quickly resumed 'remotely' – via Zoom – and while this format was sub-optimal in many respects, it also attracted larger and more diverse audiences. Attendance thus involved old friends as well as new faces from across the globe, who would otherwise be unable to attend. It was also possible to secure speakers who might not otherwise have been able to offer papers. As possibilities for 'in person' seminars have returned, moreover, convenors are determined to run 'hybrid' seminars that combine the advantages of 'remote' and 'in person' formats.

The response to COVID-19 indicates that the seminars must and can adapt, and there are clearly other challenges to be overcome. The broad history of IHR seminars indicates that specific groups have come and gone, and there is no necessary reason for any one seminar to remain on the books indefinitely. As noted earlier, there are anomalies in the range of seminar series that currently exist. Some were created following personality clashes amongst convenors, and they have then survived long after such disputes were forgotten.

One particular oddity involves the existence of – or overlap between – the Monday (Tudor and Stuart) and Thursday (Seventeenth Century British)

Seminars. Historically, this awkwardness was navigated through an informal temporal boundary – set at 1640 – which is now honoured in the breach. Discussions have periodically taken place about the possibility – or desirability – of merging these two groups (perhaps to create a weekly early modern British history seminar), only to encounter logistical difficulties and the conservatism of some convenors. Other challenges might be even more intractable. The IHR clearly suffered when the British Library moved to new premises on Euston Road; fewer people now pop across to the IHR for a cuppa and a seminar after a day's research. The death of the Anglo-American conference in 2015 makes the IHR a less obvious focal point for visiting scholars towards the end of the summer term, and seminars might now be less central to the evolving mission of the IHR, which has dramatically diversified its activities in recent years. Limited budgets make it harder to sustain full programmes of speakers, and pressures are increasing to find other funding models – including external sponsorship – that might only be feasible for certain seminars. It also seems that fewer PhD supervisors make students aware of the IHR, and of the benefits that seminars offer.

Perhaps the most serious challenge to seminar culture involves the inexorable rise of the kinds of academic conferences that lack a tight chronological, thematic or disciplinary focus, that are curated from applications rather than involving invited speakers, and that revolve around panels of short papers, or even conference posters. To the extent that this trend has prompted debate, fears have been expressed about the quality of papers and discussions as well as about how delegates involve themselves in instrumental 'networking' to the detriment of participating in a more meaningful *community*. Too often, conference programmes lack time to discuss papers properly, and many people lament that the short-paper format is poorly suited to the development of serious arguments. Some worry that the art of writing a fifty-minute paper, which typically serves as the basis of a chapter, article or essay, and which can support debate for thirty minutes or more, is being lost, and that speakers no longer think it worth investing time in preparing a formal presentation. While the Seventeenth Century Seminar has certainly experimented with different formats, it remains committed to speakers delivering substantial papers, which can be subjected to meaningful interrogation by a somewhat stable group of attendees who serve as an informed body of experts, albeit of diverse specialisms.

Such challenges mean that IHR seminars face a difficult future, and only time will tell whether they continue to inspire the kind of steadfast support that has been evident in the past. In the case of the Thursday

Seminar, two further examples of such allegiance are striking, not least because they highlight its international importance. The first involves Robin Gwynn, the leading expert on Huguenots in early modern Britain. Remarkably, by the time that Gwynn completed his London PhD, in 1976, he had been attending the seminar for more than a decade. Moreover, after securing an academic post at Massey University in New Zealand – where he taught from 1970 to 1995 – Gwynn continued to attend the Seminar, as in 1983–4 and 1984–5, and then into his retirement. His most recent paper was in 2015. The second example involves Ian Gentles, who first attended in 1966–7 as a young PhD student working with Ian Roy, who continued to attend after securing a post at York University in Toronto, and who appears in the register throughout the 1970s and 1980s, as both a speaker and audience member. Indeed, this commitment – to both supervisor and seminar – ensured that Ian has continued to attend since then, and that he is one of those loyal friends who has also directed his own students towards it. His most recent appearance involved a special trip to London for a meeting in honour of Ian Roy in 2019, over half a century after first attending the IHR.

The final instructive example of loyalty involves Stephen Porter (1949–2021), who completed his PhD – on property destruction in the civil wars – with Ian Roy in 1983.[24] Porter's attendance at the Seminar is first recorded in 1975, and it continued until at least 1986, the point at which the paper trail goes cold; yet Porter's time at the IHR highlights perhaps the most important dimension of seminar culture. Porter is fondly remembered as someone who was hugely influential in making the Seventeenth Century Seminar a welcoming and helpful forum, and whatever qualms may once have been expressed about its intellectual rigour, there can be little doubt about its supportive atmosphere. Whether or not the Thursday Seminar has been an unusually relaxed gathering, lacking the stuffiness and hierarchy that were evident elsewhere, its key strengths have always been those of the seminar format more generally. At their best, seminars offer a distinctive kind of scholarly community, making it possible to interact with a diverse group of people, whether IHR regulars or visitors from further afield, and to develop lasting relationships with other attendees. The utility of the seminar, in other words, is not just a matter of the papers that are delivered, but also of the expertise upon which it is possible to draw on a regular basis. The benefits also include being able to encounter a diverse range of topics, and to engage with substantial papers in a meaningful fashion. In both contexts, the sociability involved, and even the 'silo' effect – whereby many people confine their attendance to one seminar group – might be valuable rather than problematic. At their best, seminars demonstrate the advantages of loyalty, sociability and eclecticism, things which are linked and mutually reinforcing, and which foster scholarly development for individuals and the 'field' alike. Such things cannot easily be replicated with other research and learning formats, and as such they should be both cherished and nurtured.

# Notes

1.  For the earliest links between members of the IHR and the History of Parliament project, see D. W. Hayton, 'Colonel Wedgwood and the Historians', *Historical Research*, lxxxiv (2011), 328–55.

2.  Institute of Historical Research, Wohl Library: IHR/3/3/18 (Register, 1926–7 to 1984–5); IHR/3/3/19 (Register, 1985–6).

3.  For selected further details, see A. G. Dickens, 'Joel Hurstfield', and N. Fuidge, 'Joel Hurstfield and the Tudor Seminar', in *The English Commonwealth 1547–1640: Essays in Politics and Society Presented to Joel Hurstfield*, ed. P. Clarke, A. G. R. Smith and N. Tyacke (Leicester, 1979), pp. 13–16 and 17–21; W. T. Jones, 'The Seminar Today', *The Pollardian* (1956), 8–11, reproduced in D. Birch and J. Horn (comp.), *The History Laboratory: The Institute of Historical Research 1921–96* (London, 1996), pp. 132–3; R. F. Leslie and A. G. Dickens, 'S. T. Bindoff: an Appreciation', in *Wealth and Power in Tudor England: Essays Presented to S. T. Bindoff*, ed. E. W. Ives, R. J. Knecht and J. J. Scarisbrick (London, 1978), pp. xvi–xxi; P. Lake, *Moderate Puritans and the Elizabethan Church* (Cambridge, 1982), vi; and J. Murphy, 'History Owns Many Meanings' (online, n.d.): http://john-murphy.co.uk/?page_id=1255 [accessed 1 Dec. 2022].

4.  *Institute of Historical Research: Sixth Annual Report 1926–27* (London, 1928), p. 20; C. Bingham, *The History of Royal Holloway College, 1886–1986* (London, 1986), p. 147 and dustjacket blurb.

5.  *Institute of Historical Research: Fifth Annual Report 1925–26* (London, 1927), p. 19.

6.  J. S. Bezzant, 'The Very Reverend Norman Sykes 1897–1961', *Proceedings of the British Academy*, xlvii (1961), 417–28.

7.  J. Trapp, 'Beer, Esmond Samuel de (1895–1990)', *Oxford Dictionary of National Biography* (online, 2004): https://doi.org/10.1093/ref:odnb/39804 [accessed 1 Dec. 2022].

8.  E. Duffy, 'Robert Clifford Latham, 1912–1995', *Proceedings of the British Academy*, clxvi (2010), 201–11; 'Robert Latham', *Independent*, 16 Jan. 1995: https://www .independent.co.uk/news/people/robert-latham-obituaries-1568235.html [accessed 1 Dec. 2022]. 'William Matthews Dead at 69; Editor of Definitive Pepys Diary', *The New York Times*, 14 June 1975, p. 30.

9.  J. Caplan, 'Roger Lockyer Obituary', *The Guardian*, 28 November 2017: https://www .theguardian.com/books/2017/nov/28/roger-lockyer-obituary [accessed 1 Dec. 2022].

10.  J. Miller, *After the Civil Wars: English Politics and Government in the Reign of Charles II* (Harlow, 2000), p. viii.

11.  'Professor Justin Champion', 15 June 2020: https://www.royalholloway.ac.uk /about-us/news/professor-justin-champion/ [accessed 1 Dec. 2022]. Champion served as President of the Historical Association (2014–7) and was one of the UK's foremost proponents of public history, see J. Champion, 'What Are Historians for?', *Historical Research*, lxxxi (2008), 167–88.

12.  The extremely limited budget that seminars possess – £150 per annum – provides another incentive for frugality.

13.  One transatlantic friend recently acknowledged the 'Skinners' Arms seminar', see R. Ingram, *Reformation Without End: Religion, Politics and the Past in Post-Revolutionary England* (Manchester, 2018), p. xv. Some members of the Seminar come to the pub more often than they attend seminar papers themselves, perhaps to enjoy less restrained discussion, especially after the speakers of less than brilliant papers have departed.

**14.** J. Thirsk, 'Alan Everitt', *The Guardian*, 5 Feb. 2009: https://www.theguardian.com/education/2009/feb/06/obituary-alan-everitt [accessed 1 Dec. 2022].

**15.** 'Brian Quintrell – A Tribute', The Record Society of Lancashire and Cheshire: http://rslc.org.uk/blog/brian-qunitrell-a-tribute/ [accessed 1 Dec. 2022].

**16.** D. T. Whitcombe, *Charles II and the Cavalier House of Common, 1663–1674* (Manchester, 1966), p. x.

**17.** J. Newton, 'A. G. Dickens (1910–2001): A Personal Appreciation', *Historical Research*, lxxvii (2004), 5–8.

**18.** J. Hopson, 'The British Library and Its Antecedents', in *The Cambridge History of Libraries in Britain and Ireland: Volume III 1850–2000*, ed. A. Black and P. Hoare (Cambridge, 2006), pp. 299–315; M. Leapman, *The Book of the British Library* (London, 2012); J. Cantwell, *The Public Record Office, 1959–1969* (Richmond, 2000).

**19.** For an example, see G. R. Abernathy, 'Clarendon and the Declaration of Indulgence', *Journal of Ecclesiastical History*, xi (1960), 55–73.

**20.** J. Thirsk, 'Ruth Spalding', *Independent*, 26 May 2009: https://www.independent.co.uk/news/obituaries/ruth-spalding-actor-and-director-who-also-wrote-a-whitbread-prizewinning-biography-1690656.html [accessed 1 Dec. 2022].

**21.** Horwitz, who certainly attended the Seminar in 1977–8, completed his Oxford DPhil in 1963, and taught at the University of Iowa, 1963–2004.

**22.** S. Mendelson, 'Patricia M. Crawford, 1941–2009', *History Workshop Journal*, lxxi (2011), 289–92.

**23.** Pawlisch was an IHR fellow in 1976–7; his paper was subsequently published: 'Sir John Davies, the Ancient Constitution, and Civil Law', *Historical Journal*, xxiii (1980), 689–702.

**24.** 'Tribute to Stephen Porter', The Charter House: https://thecharterhouse.org/blog/tribute-to-stephen-porter/ [accessed 1 Dec. 2022].

# References

## Archived sources

Institute of Historical Research, Wohl Library

IHR/3/3/18.
IHR/3/3/19.

## Published sources

Abernathy, G. R., 'Clarendon and the Declaration of Indulgence', *Journal of Ecclesiastical History*, xi (1960), 55–73.

Bezzant, J. S., 'The Very Reverend Norman Sykes 1897–1961', *Proceedings of the British Academy*, xlvii (1961), 417–28.

Bingham, C., *The History of Royal Holloway College, 1886–1986* (London, 1986).

Birch, D., and Horn, J. (comp.), *The History Laboratory: The Institute of Historical Research 1921–96* (London, 1996).

'Brian Quintrell – A Tribute', The Record Society of Lancashire and Cheshire: http://rslc.org.uk/blog/brian-qunitrell-a-tribute/ [accessed 1 Dec. 2022].

Cantwell, J., *The Public Record Office, 1959–1969* (Richmond, 2000).

Caplan, J., 'Roger Lockyer Obituary', *The Guardian*, 28 November 2017: https://www.theguardian.com/books/2017/nov/28/roger-lockyer-obituary [accessed 1 Dec. 2022].

Champion, J., 'What Are Historians for?', *Historical Research*, lxxxi (2008), 167–88.

Dickens, A. G., 'Joel Hurstfield', in *The English Commonwealth 1547–1640: Essays in Politics and Society Presented to Joel Hurstfield*, ed. P. Clarke, A. G. R. Smith and N. Tyacke (Leicester, 1979), pp. 13–16.

Duffy, E., 'Robert Clifford Latham, 1912–1995', *Proceedings of the British Academy*, clxvi (2010), 201–11.

Fuidge, N., 'Joel Hurstfield and the Tudor Seminar', in *The English Commonwealth 1547–1640: Essays in Politics and Society Presented to Joel Hurstfield*, ed. P. Clarke, A. G. R. Smith and N. Tyacke (Leicester, 1979), pp. 17–21.

Hayton, D. W., 'Colonel Wedgwood and the Historians', *Historical Research*, lxxxiv (2011), 328–55.

Hopson, J., 'The British Library and Its Antecedents', in *The Cambridge History of Libraries in Britain and Ireland: Volume III 1850–2000*, ed. A. Black and P. Hoare (Cambridge, 2006), pp. 299–315.

Ingram, R., *Reformation Without End: Religion, Politics and the Past in Post-Revolutionary England* (Manchester, 2018).

*Institute of Historical Research: Fifth Annual Report 1925–26* (London, 1927).

*Institute of Historical Research: Sixth Annual Report 1926–27* (London, 1928).

Lake, P., *Moderate Puritans and the Elizabethan Church* (Cambridge, 1982).

Leapman, M., *The Book of the British Library* (London, 2012).

Leslie, R. F., and Dickens, A. G., 'S. T. Bindoff: An Appreciation', in *Wealth and Power in Tudor England: Essays Presented to S. T. Bindoff*, ed. E. W. Ives, R. J. Knecht, and J. J. Scarisbrick (London, 1978), pp. xvi–xxi.

Lockyer, R., *Buckingham: The Life and Political Career of George Villiers, First Duke of Buckingham, 1592–1628* (London, 1981).

Mendelson, S., 'Patricia M. Crawford, 1941–2009', *History Workshop Journal*, lxxi (2011), 289–92.

Miller, J., *After the Civil Wars: English Politics and Government in the Reign of Charles II* (Harlow, 2000).

Murphy, J., 'History Owns Many Meanings' (online, n.d.): http://johnmurphy.co.uk/?page_id=1255 [accessed 1 Dec. 2022].

Newton, J., 'A. G. Dickens (1910–2001): A Personal Appreciation', *Historical Research*, lxxvii (2004), 5–8.

Pawlisch, H. S., 'Sir John Davies, the Ancient Constitution, and Civil Law', *Historical Journal*, xxiii (1980), 689–702.

'Professor Justin Champion', 15 June 2020: https://www.royalholloway.ac.uk/about-us/news/professor-justin-champion/ [accessed 1 Dec. 2022].

'Robert Latham', *Independent*, 16 January 1995: https://www.independent.co.uk/news/people/robert-latham-obituaries-1568235.html [accessed 1 Dec. 2022].

Thirsk, J., 'Alan Everitt', *The Guardian*, 5 February 2009: https://www.theguardian.com/education/2009/feb/06/obituary-alan-everitt [accessed 1 Dec. 2022].

Thirsk, J., 'Ruth Spalding', *Independent*, 26 May 2009: https://www.independent.co.uk/news/obituaries/ruth-spalding-actor-and-director-who-also-wrote-a-whitbread-prizewinning-biography-1690656.html [accessed 1 Dec. 2022].

Trapp, J., 'Beer, Esmond Samuel de (1895–1990)', *Oxford Dictionary of National Biography* (online, 2004): https://doi.org/10.1093/ref:odnb/39804 [accessed 1 Dec. 2022].

'Tribute to Stephen Porter', The Charter House: https://thecharterhouse
.org/blog/tribute-to-stephen-porter/ [accessed 1 Dec. 2022].
Whitcombe, D. T., *Charles II and the Cavalier House of Common, 1663–1674* (Manchester, 1966).
'William Matthews Dead at 69; Editor of Definitive Pepys Diary', *The New York Times*, 14 June 1975, p. 30.

## Unpublished sources

Peacey, J., Miscellaneous Private Correspondence and Notes.

Chapter 5

# The British History in the Long Eighteenth Century Seminar

## Penelope J. Corfield*

On its best form, the Long Eighteenth Century Seminar can generate a genuine intellectual excitement, which is truly energizing and inspiring. It doesn't happen at every meeting. Yet it happens often enough to keep participants mentally on their toes with expectation. As a result, the Seminar's sessions on alternate Wednesday afternoons at 5.15 p.m., during London University terms, are almost invariably both crowded and attentive.

One key contributing factor is that the standard of presentations is high. Colleagues know the Seminar's reputation for probing debates. Wisely, therefore, they tend to present their best work, hoping for a stimulating mix of criticisms and constructive responses. In effect, they are getting a free consultancy from a large congregation of experts.

Another significant component is the dedicated participation of the 'regulars'. They embody continuity. Well versed in the seminar style, the regulars often ask incisive questions. But they don't all feel obliged to intervene every time. Their intent listening is enough to foster a receptive atmosphere.

Simultaneously, the Seminar attracts many 'occasionals'. They are just as welcome. Characteristically, they are scholars from out of town, who attend when they can. They add the spice and zest of the unexpected. And that applies to 'known' occasionals as much as it does to complete newcomers. The Seminar's popularity means that, for the last thirty years, it has been one of the IHR's largest, attracting large numbers in the range of thirty to sixty people. And in the Zoom era of 2020–21, literally hundreds of scholars, from across the UK and overseas, have joined online.

The variety of colleagues in attendance can cause surprises. Once a young postgraduate was giving a strong critique of an eminent scholar, who lives in Australia. As the presentation began, the Antipodean expert in question opened the door and slipped in quietly. Head-to-head confrontations do happen from time to time. But it's fairer when both parties know that their antagonist is present. Accordingly, the chair discreetly alerted the speaker, who paused briefly before resuming with intellectual rigour combined with personal courtesy (as best practice prescribes). A rousing debate ensued, in which all participated. It was a shining example of how to confront basic disagreements with frankness and dignity. The moral is that any scholar from any country may join an open-access seminar at any time, without prior notice.[1]

With the dynamic mix of regulars and occasionals, another essential requirement is a strong team of organizers, with a range of ages and expertise. They propose speakers for the programme, while a sub-team settles the details. Another valiant colleague simultaneously manages the communications network – an ever more vital task as seminar numbers grow. Turn by turn, the organizers chair the sessions. They ask timely questions, being prompt to intervene should debates flag. They all attend without fail (emergencies excepted). And they act as unofficial hosts for the crucial 'après-seminar' sociability, ensuring that no-one is left moping on the fringes.

Collectively, the aim is to get a scintillating debate after every presentation. That's exciting for speakers, even if being under the spotlight for an entire evening can be tiring. And it's energizing for everyone. In earlier eras, it often happened that the most senior professor asked the first question, followed by colleagues in rank-order. Yet today, happily, procedures are less formal. The chairs usually take questions as they come, though sometimes grouping interventions on one specific point. They also try to get contributions from all corners of the room, to uphold inclusivity.

There is no quest for unanimity – fortunately, as there is no standard seminar 'line'. Yet there is collective intellectual effort, neither designed to refute totally nor to uphold the speaker's case entirely, but instead to give it a good work-out. And, afterwards, the après-seminar drinks and dinner provide a splendid time for all to wind down and to reflect upon the shared experience.[2] Incidentally, postgraduates pay a pre-set price, since otherwise the cost of dining in central London would preclude their attendance. The convenors cover the costs, with spontaneous contributions from any generous colleagues who also wish to sustain the scholarly community.

In the late 1990s, there were some complaints that questions at this Seminar were too tough and aggressive. A number of feminists, in particular, found the style too 'macho'. If the speaker hesitated or evaded the point, then people would press robustly to get an answer. Yet not all agreed with the critics. Professor Karen Harvey, who began her London PhD in 1995 and became a seminar regular, has a different memory. Writing in 2021 (in response to an appeal for reminiscences), she recalled that the 1990s style was tough but fair:

> I myself experienced what I felt had been a pretty gruelling encounter at the Seminar as a PhD student, but I understood that the work needed to be improved and that I was being held to an academic standard that applied to everybody ... And this principle – that I would be charged on the basis of my work, not my identity [as a young woman] – was terrifically important to me. What mattered was my research, my ideas and my arguments. I found this liberating and remarkably enabling.[3]

That said, no seminar is an island. As further noted below, the twenty-first century has seen a general 'softening' in academic debating styles. And the Long Eighteenth Century Seminar has not avoided the trend. Yet Harvey ended her account with the reasonable hope that scholars would continue to speak their minds. Cooing approval for every presentation – good, bad or indifferent – would not help anyone. A rigorous but fair exchange is the desideratum.

Today, the crowds at this Seminar indicate that things continue to go well. Nonetheless, nothing is set in stone. The format has changed since 1921, as shown in the next section – and will continue to evolve.

## Updating the format

Interestingly, there are no surviving myths or memories of this Seminar's very early days. Not only is the membership transient over the decades, but the format has changed substantially. So, while today's participants are pleased to learn that they are contributing to one of the foundational seminars at the esteemed Institute of Historical Research, they know little more.

This centenary exercise of retrieval thus provides a welcome chance to put current practices into a long-term framework. Historically, a seminar (from the Latin *seminarium* or seed-bed) referred to a teaching class of students, led by a professor.[4] Indeed, in many universities today, entire courses are known as seminar programmes. Yet there is also a more specific application. Special research seminars were organized for postgraduates, who were learning their craft. Such sessions constituted an updated forum for Socratic dialogue between tutor and pupil, extended into a collegial network.

First adopted in nineteenth-century German universities, the research seminar was gradually adopted in progressive academic institutions in Britain. Advanced classes were attended by senior historians and their postgraduates. Sessions were select, not open to everyone. The postgraduates usually reported their latest findings, while the academics responded with crisp assessments.

Within London University, the nascent seminar culture gained a massive boost in 1921, when historians began to convene in the friendly ambience of the new Institute of Historical Research. Sharing a common venue encouraged the sense of a community of historians. Scholars and postgraduates attended from many, though not absolutely all, of London University's constituent Colleges.

Among the foundational seminars was that focusing upon eighteenth-century history. Its original emphasis was upon political and constitutional affairs (reflecting the then current state of research), although, as will be seen, many changes were to follow. In 1921, its first convenor was Hugh Hale Bellot (1890–1969), a newly appointed history assistant at University College London. His time at the Seminar lasted until 1927, when he moved to Manchester, as the next step in a varied career that included wartime secondment to the Board of Trade (1940–44) and a later stint as president of the Royal Historical Society (1952–6).[5] Bellot's commitment and affability (he was later described as 'an old-fashioned English gentleman'[6]) launched the Seminar well. In effect, he was one of those pioneer historians – himself without a doctorate – who encouraged the professionalization of postgraduate studies among following generations.

Then from 1927 to 1932, the baton was passed to Guy Parsloe (1900–85), also history assistant at University College London.[7] He was notably devoted to the Institute of Historical Research, where he became its secretary and librarian from 1927 to 1943.[8] Historians of the eighteenth century were thus leading activists within the IHR and, in parallel, on London University's history board of studies.

Initially, this Seminar was named *English Political History: Eighteenth Century*. And at times, specific dates were added to delimit the chronological range. From 1931 to 1975, however, the name was standardized into an ecumenical *English History in the Eighteenth Century*: the Anglocentric focus, which seemed 'natural' to first convenors, was subsequently shed. Throughout the 1930s, the lead organizer was Mark A. Thomson (1903–62), who moved to a chair at Liverpool in 1945. But he returned to London in 1956, leading the Seminar again until his death in 1962.[9] His fellow organizer from the mid-1950s was Ian R. Christie (1919–98).

THE BRITISH HISTORY IN THE LONG EIGHTEENTH CENTURY SEMINAR    119

Between 1962 and 1972, he carried the baton single-handedly, then continuing the task, with colleagues, until his retirement in 1984.[10]

During these post-war years, the seminar format changed decisively. It was no longer a closed class but became a discussion forum, as is the preferred model today. That innovation enabled students to learn, not just from a few teachers but from the wider historical profession as well. Instead of many short reports from postgraduates, one invited scholar (whether a regular or not) gives an opening paper, followed by another hour of questions and discussion. Those attending come not simply to hear a lecture but to debate it. That format allows the programme to be advertised in advance; and much greater numbers to attend, both from within and outside London University. Over time, the Long Eighteenth Century Seminar has sought to invite a great range of external speakers. The aim is to test the entire field, not to advance one seminar 'line'.

Booking a full roster of speakers did initially increase the organizers' workload and anxiety levels. In the era before email and social media, they chiefly relied upon exchanges of letters, which could be agonisingly slow to arrive – as well as occasional phone-calls. By such efforts, however, the pedagogic experience, in this as in other seminars, was decisively transformed.

Postgraduates continue to learn; but they do so by taking their turn as the lead presenters – and by witnessing a cross-section of senior and junior experts in the profession do likewise. It is instructive to work out what it takes to give a strong presentation and how to answer questions well. And it can be an eye-opener when (rarely) a great name in the profession arrives without adequate preparation and offers nothing more than a few anecdotes. The postgraduate indignation is then vociferous. It's a sign that they have high expectations, which motivates them to perform well themselves, when the time comes.

A further change, in the later 1970s or early 1980s, made the whole seminar experience much healthier. It was always considered impolite to smoke a pipe or cigarette during the presentation. Once the speaker ended, however, inveterate smokers would immediately reach for their nicotine fix. The kerfuffle acted as a boundary-marker, giving people a moment to think of good questions. Nonetheless, the resulting fug of smoke was unhealthy and disagreeable. Participants among this particular group were not among the IHR's heaviest smokers. But it was still a relief when the practice was stopped by agreement within each seminar (long before any official ban upon indoor smoking).

Ending the rustle of reaching for cigarettes then left scope for the advent of a new ritual, although these two habits were not direct alternatives. Initially, no-one dreamed of clapping at the end of a presentation. It seemed far too theatrical. And it might imply that fellow scholars were passive audiences.

Nonetheless, sporadic applause began in the 1990s. Initially, the organizers in this Seminar discouraged the practice. They thought that hosting the speakers for drinks and dinner afterwards was a better form of thanks. Yet wider *zeitgeist* shifts are hard to resist. When crowds began clapping, the organizers could hardly sit on their hands. From the 2000s onwards, applause became more common. By *c.*2010, it was routine, adding to the performative element of presentations, then usually given by PowerPoint. Today, chairs often close the evening with another round of clapping. And, in the era of virtual meetings by Zoom (2020–21), indications of silent applause or thumbs-up helped to counteract the chill of remote debate. Collective appreciation of effort encourages debates that are both frank and mutually respectful.

Culturally, this shift towards a softer, gentler debating style had many roots. At its most basic, it reflected a welcome desire, among seminar organizers and participants alike, to broaden access to academe and to prevent its procedures from seeming intimidating. Clapping presentations, and prefacing questions with kind words, are necessary preludes to inclusive debate in the twenty-first century. The Seminar has shifted seamlessly into this style, without losing its capacity for intellectually tough interventions.

Developing an open-door policy has also taken the form of designating at least one session per year as an 'outreach' event. It is held in a novel venue, outside the IHR, to attract a different audience. So, for example, in February 2015, a panel on 'Exhibiting the Eighteenth Century' was hosted at Kensington Palace, jointly by this Seminar and by the Centre for Eighteenth-Century Studies at London's Queen Mary College. It was a stimulating event, with searching exchanges, attended by seventy (plus) colleagues, including many from the museum world.

Since 2014, such innovations have been funded by the Seminar's two sponsors: Mark Storey and Carey Karmel. Their generous support, which came out of the blue, has also permitted the introduction of an annual prize for the best presentation by a postgraduate or early career scholar. So, while the format mutates, the Seminar's key aim, to encourage the next generation of scholars, endures.

## Expanding the thematic remit

Continuities as well as change apply to the big questions for research and debate. Throughout its first fifty years, the Seminar's chief focus was undoubtedly upon political history. Bellot, Parsloe and Thomson were all interested in the advent of constitutional and legal norms. And in the 1950s and 1960s, the Seminar was absorbed in the debates which followed the explosive impact of Lewis Namier's new approach to eighteenth-century British politics.[11] He focused not upon laws and constitutions but upon place, patronage and politicking. Those interested in other key eighteenth-century themes, such as colonial expansion or commercial/industrial growth, would have been directed to other London seminars, such as those in imperial or economic history.

Particularly under the aegis of Ian Christie in the 1950s and 1960s, the Seminar was a known centre of support for Namier (1888–1960), and his allies, known as Namierites. Not that dissent was excluded. Arguments over Namier were conducted with vigour, as they were over the continuing strength (or otherwise) of the Jacobite cause post-1715. The tenacious Eveline Cruickshanks (1926–2021), then and for many years a seminar regular, was quick to remind colleagues of surviving support for Toryism and, in 1745, for Bonnie Prince Charlie[12] – arguing with her characteristic force, knowledge and good humour.

Namier offered a conservative vision of historical individualism. He opposed both Marxist doctrines of class conflict and Whig/liberal theories of the march of ideas. Namier had in his youth attended lectures at Lausanne University by the influential Italian sociologist/economist, Vilfredo Pareto. A determined anti-Marxist, he saw history as an endless circulation of 'elites'.[13] Namier was no direct disciple. But Pareto's claim struck a chord. Focusing upon the 1750s and 1760s, Namier put England's leaders – in both government and opposition – under his research microscope. Thereupon he argued that an individualized quest for place and patronage was far more significant than was competition between rival ideals or competing political parties.[14]

Instant debates generated both great heat and fresh light.[15] Namier's biographical approach was borrowed for application to other periods, with mixed results. As the widespread dust died down, it became clear that political parties cannot be air-brushed from British history, though their format and power vary greatly over time. In the same way, the role of ideas, and the role of sectoral/class economic interests, can be highly important, but not always, and not always in the same way.

Yet, equally, it is notable that the quest for place and the power of patronage operate, even if diversely, within many political systems. Personal motivations, as well as links and contacts between individuals have impact. Thus, Namier proved to be one parent of a powerful research technique, known as prosopography or group biography.[16] The methodology is widely used today by both historians and sociologists, though users have no obligation to endorse Namier's ideological stance and his down-playing of ideas.

Immediately, one big new prosopographical enquiry into the History of Parliament project, re-launched in 1951,[17] received input from participants at London's eighteenth-century seminar.[18] Many wrote model biographies of individual MPs, whether famous statesmen or unknown back-benchers. Two notably active contributors were Eveline Cruickshanks and Ian Christie. They disagreed on many points, but concurred on the significance of the eighteenth century.

Animated by such interests, the Seminar's atmosphere was purposive. Fortnightly numbers rose from the ten or so who gathered in pre-war days, to twenty or more. Alice Prochaska, who later became IHR's librarian, secretary and deputy director (1984–92), recalled the presence in the 1970s of scholars with distinctly varied approaches: 'The much-admired George Rudé turned up, on a sabbatical year, with his insights into the links between the French Revolution and politics in Britain.'[19]

All these London seminars were confident gatherings, far from deferential to the traditional claims of 'Oxbridge'. This Seminar certainly shared that collective spirit. Most students were by now studying for a doctorate, although many went on to get jobs before they had completed. Topics for debate were also diversifying. It is true that Prochaska still recalled some tedious sessions on old-style administrative and military history,[20] but the vigorous tides of research diversification were impossible to resist.

Throughout, Ian Christie was a reticent but diligent chair. Professor Kent Hackmann, who arrived in 1978 as a new visiting postgraduate from Idaho, gave a short presentation on the mid-century merchant-politician William Beckford. And got an immediately impressive response:

> Professor Christie ... took command of the table. For about forty minutes, without having taken notes, he critiqued my paper with a professional expertise and human kindness that I came to realize were hallmarks of his personality. He reviewed my paper, pointing out generalizations that could be clarified and ideas that needed to be developed. More importantly, he pointed me in directions I had not considered.[21]

Again, Kent Hackmann had an equally positive experience, when he re-joined the Seminar on sabbatical leave in 1987–8. Colleagues advised on his new project; and four senior professors, including Ian Christie, provided constructive criticisms of draft chapters. It was a fine practical example of the strong Anglo-American links that the IHR had always encouraged.

Nonetheless, Christie's plain, terse manner was not always productive.[22] In 1980, Professor Kathleen Wilson, then just arrived in the UK to work on her PhD, outlined her topic to the Seminar. Thereupon, she writes: 'Professor Christie looked at me and said, matter-of-factly: "You'll never do it; at least not from those sources."'[23] He feared that the Georgian provincial press would not yield the information that Wilson was seeking. Undeterred, if somewhat irked, Wilson completed her doctorate successfully and progressed to a productive academic career.[24] Later she noted, charitably, that Christie was probably 'in his own way' trying to warn her of pitfalls ahead – as no doubt he was. Yet this response was symptomatic of his growing conservatism – about themes, sources and even access into the profession – which was not helpful. As always, rival viewpoints are best offered with tact and ecumenical inclusivity.

Agreeably, meanwhile, a pleasant coda to Christie's time at the Seminar ensued in 1992, eight years after his retirement. He had ceased to attend. But, one evening, he arrived in radiant good humour to announce that he had just got married for the first time, at the age of seventy-three. It was touching that he wanted the Seminar to know. And, from such a reserved man, this acknowledgement of academic comradeship was positively startling.

By the 1990s, the Seminar's thematic remit was becoming much more adventurous. Adaptations had begun under the aegis of John Dinwiddy (1939–90), a humane and witty scholar.[25] He became joint seminar organizer in October 1972 and strove to broaden the themes. There were presentations on trade unionism, crime and madness. Discussions regularly stretched beyond the strictest century boundaries.[26] In acknowledgement, the Seminar's name was extended to include explicitly the early nineteenth century. In October 1989, it became *British History in the Long Eighteenth Century 1688–1848*. And by 1991, when the concept had become familiar, the restraining dates were quietly dropped.[27]

When making these adaptations, the organizers were keen to extend the Seminar's remit from 'England' to 'Britain'. But they were unfussed by precise start and end dates. The 'long eighteenth century' acted as an umbrella term, used by researchers of many specialisms. And it avoided programmatic names such as 'Age of Enlightenment'. The new term was quick-and-easy to use and soon became popular. There were a few nervous jokes about the eighteenth century's 'imperialist' chronology-grabbing from the adjacent 'Victorian' seminar. However, a mutual flexibility in crossing artificial time-barriers and acceptance of overlap had long operated in practice, and continued to apply.

Sadly, there followed, in spring 1990, a major blow. John Dinwiddy's abrupt death by drowning, at the age of 50, was a grievous loss. Thereupon Penelope Corfield, recruited as fellow organizer in 1984, resolved to continue and extend his work. She had been earlier involved in the IHR's Early Modern Economic and Social History Seminar and also helped co-found the new Women's History Seminar. (All groups worked together amicably, and from time to time held joint sessions together.) But Corfield eventually decided to concentrate upon this Seminar. She particularly welcomed the challenge of resynthesizing many specialisms in the round, as well as in the long.

As the Seminar developed an inclusive and adventurous agenda, the aim was not to drop political history. Far from it. A broader and deeper political history remains a vital part of the Seminar's expanding remit. Indeed, the task of studying and understanding the past, properly viewed, is always and must be cross-disciplinary. From this period onwards, the number of seminar participants rose into the thirties and often well above. A 'big name' or a 'hot' topic might lift attendance into the sixties, or sometimes even above.

Gathering a broad team of co-organizers, with diverse interests, was an essential step. Julian Hoppit (University College London) joined in 1988, followed in the early 1990s by Arthur Burns (King's College, London) and Tim Hitchcock (then at the University of North London, and later Sussex University). The invitation to a colleague from outside London University seemed to the organizers an entirely natural step, and was received without comment by the IHR. Other seminars were doing the same. And this trend further strengthened the IHR's ecumenical role as a regional and national hub for all historical researchers.

Later in 2010, Hoppit left to focus on the Early Modern Economic History Seminar. But new organizers include Joe Cozens (Essex University), Margot Finn (University College London), Amanda Goodrich (Open University), Sally Holloway (Oxford Brookes University), Sarah Lloyd (Hertfordshire University) and Gillian Williamson (independent scholar). A further vital change in 2015 was the recruitment of early career and postgraduate representatives, bringing fresh perspectives. This last initiative particularly enhances the Seminar's inclusivity.

Expanding themes have no limit. Eighteenth-century studies during the last forty years have been transforming themselves. The result is a veritable 'exploding galaxy'.[28] Impetus comes partly from deepening research into old themes, plus much scintillating new research into new themes, using the mass of under-studied eighteenth-century materials in archives, museums and libraries. Social, urban, cultural, linguistic, ethnic and women's history have thereby been joined by studies in 'identities' (personal and collective) and emotions – all aided by the democratized access provided by digital history.[29]

Big arguments add further fuel. Poised between the (controversially defined) 'early modern era' and the (equally controversial) 'modern times', the eighteenth century calls for re-definition. Was it a crucible of change? And, if so, from what to what? Among many lengthy debates were those prompted by E. P. Thompson's *Making of the English Working Class* (1963).[30] Did an earlier social structure of ordered ranks shift into a new society of competing classes? Or, if not, what (if anything) happened instead? Such debates were paralleled by even longer-running arguments in economic history. Did Britain experience industrial revolution – industrial evolution – or neither – or elements of both?[31] (And today climatologists and eco-historians ask pointedly: with what long-term impacts upon the global climate?)

Separate contests were then newly triggered by Michel Foucault's *Madness and Civilization* (in English, 1965) and his later *Discipline and Punish* (in English, 1975).[32] He detected drastic eighteenth-century shifts in welfare and penal policy. Furthermore, he argued that all social order is constituted by a collective 'discourse', which Foucault defined as the summation of knowledge-systems, underpinned in turn by power relations.[33] These intelligence-grids dictate the nature of 'reality'. Discuss. And they did.

Related questions about the role of language immediately became a recurrent theme for debate, from many perspectives. For instance, in March 1993 the eminent German historian Reinhart Koselleck (1923–2006) addressed a joint meeting of this Seminar with the German Historical Institute of London.[34] His theme was 'People and Nation: Structural and Semantic Approaches'. It was a packed session. Colleagues came to debate both the specifics and the theory. Similar issues were crystallized by a panel on 'History and Language: Post the "Linguistic Turn"'. Held in January 2002, the speakers were Alun Munslow (1947–2019), Gareth Stedman Jones and John Shaw. Their disagreements invited everyone to consider the challenge of defining precisely the remit and power of 'language'.

Further stirring these complex brews, in 1985 Jonathan Clark (a frequent seminar visitor in the 1970s) urged a return to a conservative interpretation of the eighteenth century.[35] He dubbed Britain an 'ancien regime' on a par with the absolute monarchies of Austria or pre-revolutionary France. To support his case, he cited the continuing power of kingship and of the Anglican Church. Clark's revisionism was explicitly anti-Marxist and anti-Whig/liberal. Yet it was not at all pro-Foucault. Nor did Clark revive Namier's methodology or Namier's dismissal of the importance of ideas.

Thus, while controversies often circle around repeated issues, the claims and evidence may vary significantly.

Similarly diverse conclusions are emerging from recent research into 'identity' – whether sexual, gendered, ethnic, religious or cultural – and from meditations about how best to respond to a world-historical crime (albeit legal in the eighteenth century), like the trans-Atlantic trade in enslaved Africans. Complex questions, with complex data, evoke complex debates, within which individuals seek to find and share valid pathways.

Accordingly, the Seminar participants from time to time take collective stock. Panels entitled *'Where stands the Eighteenth Century?'* or *'Was there a Long Eighteenth Century?'* – or some variant – appeared in its programme in January 1992, in January 2000, and in November 2007. Moreover, a day-long outreach Conference on the state-of-play was held on a sunny Saturday in April 2019. It attracted well over 170 participants. Such events sharpen definitions and debates. They also encourage both consolidation and further renewal.

## Summary reflections

Positive memories feature a powerful opening from Roy Palmer (1932–2015), talking in October 1986 on songs as a source for social history.[36] With no other preliminaries, he launched into a solo rendering of a 1720s ballad which had survived purely in oral transmission, until he first recorded it. His performance brought the house down. And then, by way of conclusion, Palmer orchestrated communal singing of early nineteenth-century protest songs. Unforgettable.

Quixotic memories include the time in 2011 when a mouse ran in to sit on the speaker's shoe, while he, unaware, discussed environmental degradation in eighteenth-century London. Cue muffled laughter from those in the front rows. Another occasion in December 2016 was marred by insistent drilling, produced by repair work in the IHR basement. The sound echoed along the leaden pipework, giving the impression that an irately buzzing giant was about to pulverize the entire building. The speaker, Professor Jeremy Black (Exeter University), carried things off with characteristic panache. But it was deeply disappointing, and should not have happened.

Plentiful intellectual memories, meanwhile, confirm that most scholars who publish on the long eighteenth-century history do, at some stage, talk to this Seminar. In June 1989, for instance, the ever-fertile ever-debating E. P. Thompson presented his paper on 'The Moral Economy Revisited'. He energetically scribbled notes on all criticisms, as part of his retrospective self-criticism and self-justification, which before long appeared in print.[37]

Participants and speakers attend regularly from across Britain, Ireland and continental Europe. Colleagues from North America visit whenever they can. As do scholars worldwide. Notably in the 1990s and 2000s, the Seminar gained from a goodly contingent of Japanese scholars, either studying or on sabbatical leave in London. And international contributors continue to make their welcome presence felt in today's virtual sessions.

London's Long Eighteenth Century Seminar is thus like a long-running river: its course outwardly similar but its flow always in renewal. There are deeps as well as shallows; patches of turbulence, as well as calm. There is scope for pioneering new routes, as well as deepening existing ones. No-one has to attend. Many do. The result is the creation of a genuine intellectual community.[38]

Finally, this Seminar not only contributes to the life of the IHR but has a wider hinterland too. Historians now attend in growing numbers the annual meetings of the British Society for Eighteenth-Century Studies (founded 1971).[39] And, through that body, they belong to the International Society (founded 1967),[40] with its thirty-five national and regional affiliates.

Impressively, indeed, this global network forms an updated version of the eighteenth-century Republic of Letters. It links scholars across disciplines and national boundaries. These societies are voluntary bodies, without an institutional base. Their bond is not place or patronage but a shared fascination with all aspects of the long eighteenth century in the round. No participants and organizers are paid specifically for these tasks. They labour for love. *Where stands the long eighteenth century today?* Answer: thriving – looking outwards – and keenly debating the full significance of this pivotal era in world history.

## Notes

\* With warm thanks for recollections from Arthur Burns, Mary Clayton, Amanda Goodrich, Kent Hackmann, Karen Harvey, Tim Hitchcock, Sarah Lloyd, Mary-Clare Martin, David Ormrod, Alice Prochaska, Robert Shoemaker, Michael Townsend and Kathleen Wilson. This chapter is dedicated to all participants and organizers post-1921.

1. PJC adds: As a young postgraduate at another seminar, I once referred favourably but rather loftily to a rare work, published many decades earlier, with a clear implication that the author was long since dead and buried. A sepulchral voice responded: 'Thank you'. The venerable but very much alive author was present in the room. It was a useful lesson.

2. It is helpful to find a roomy restaurant that can seat everyone at one long table (even if re-arranged as rectangle or L-shape), to ensure an inclusive atmosphere.

3. Recollections from Karen Harvey, professor of cultural history at Birmingham University, sent to PJC, 28 May 2021.

4. See A. Goldgar, *Impolite Learning: Conduct and Community in the Republic of Letters, 1680–1750* (London, 1995); A. Grafton, *Worlds Made by Words: Scholarship and Community in the Modern West* (London, 2009), esp. pp. 1–2, 6–7, 197–204, 211–15; and J. Östling, *Humboldt and the Modern German University: An Intellectual History* (Lund, 2018).

5. H. H. Bellot, an expert on constitutional law, who also wrote the centenary history of his institution: H. Hale Bellot, *University College London, 1826–1926* (London, 1928).

6. I. Poulton, 'Remembering the Bellots' (2019), https://somersetlad.com/2019/11/10/remembering-the-bellots/ [accessed 1 Sept. 2021].

7. For an affectionate biography, see J. Parsloe, *Charles Guy Parsloe, 1900–85* (Epsom, 2018).

8. Parsloe then moved to become secretary of the Institute of Welding (1943–67) and secretary-general of the International Institute of Welding (1948–66): a highly unusual move, even by the eclectic standards of the early historical profession.

9. M. A. Thomson published an Historical Association booklet *Macaulay* (London, 1959) as well as *A Constitutional History of England, 1642–1801* (London, 1938).

10. I. R. Christie began his career (1948) as assistant lecturer in history at University College London and ended by holding the prestigious Astor professorship (1979–84), Notable among his publications are *The End of North's Ministry, 1780–2* (London, 1958); *Wilkes, Wyvill and Reform: The Parliamentary Reform Movement in British Politics, 1760–85* (London, 1962); *Crisis of Empire: Great Britain and the American Colonies 1754–83* (London, 1966); *Myth and Reality in Late-Eighteenth-Century British Politics, and Other Papers* (London, 1970); and *Stress and Stability in Late Eighteenth-Century Britain: Reflections on the British Avoidance of Revolution* (London, 1984).

11. For Namier, see L. Colley, *Lewis Namier* (London, 1989); D. Hayton, *Conservative Revolutionary: The Lives of Lewis Namier* (Manchester, 2019).

12. E. Cruickshanks, *Political Untouchables: The Tories and the '45* (London, 1979).

13. See J. Femia, *Vilfredo Pareto* (London, 2016), and T. Bottomore, *Elites and Society* (London, 1993).

14. Esp. in L. B. Namier, *The Structure of Politics at the Accession of George III* (London, 1929).

15. Contrast H. Butterfield, *George III and the Historians* (London, 1957), pp. 10–11, 200–15, 293, 297–9, with J. Brooke, 'Namier and Namierism', *History and Theory*, iii

(1964), 331–47. For further context, see M. Bentley, *Modernizing England's Past: English Historiography in the Age of Modernism, 1870–1970* (Cambridge, 2005).

**16.** K. S. B. Keats-Rohan, *Prosopography Approaches and Applications: A Handbook* (Oxford, 2007). For the related technique of network analysis, see I. A. McCulloh, H. L. Armstrong and A. N. Johnson, *Social Networks Analysis with Applications* (Hoboken, NJ, 2013).

**17.** The project, long mooted, was re-launched in 1951 with cross-party support and Treasury funding: see *The History of Parliament Project*, https://www.history ofparliamentonline.org [accessed 1 Sept. 2021].

**18.** Among the project's earliest fruits were L. B. Namier and J. Brooke, *The House of Commons, 1754–1790* (London, 1964), and R. Sedgwick, *The House of Commons, 1715–54* (London, 1970).

**19.** George Rudé (1910–93) had a distinguished academic career in Australia and Canada, writing numerous studies including *The Crowd in History: A Study of Popular Disturbances in France and England, 1730–1848* (New York, 1964). Quotation from Alice Prochaska, for whose recollections, see fn. 20.

**20.** Recollections from Alice Prochaska, later (2010–17) principal of Somerville College, University of Oxford, sent to PJC, 29 July 2021.

**21.** Recollections from Kent Hackmann, professor of history at University of Idaho, sent to PJC, 17 Nov. 2020.

**22.** For some examples, see N. B. Harte, 'Obituary: Ian R. Christie', *The Independent*, 5 Dec. 1998.

**23.** Recollections from Kathleen Wilson, professor of history at Stony Brook University, New York, sent to PJC, 9 Aug. 2021.

**24.** Yale University PhD (1985), expanded into a prize-winning book: K. Wilson, *The Sense of the People: Politics, Culture and Imperialism in England, 1715–85* (Cambridge, 1995).

**25.** J. R. Dinwiddy (Royal Holloway, London University) was author of *From Luddism to the First Reform Bill: Reform in England, 1810–32* (Oxford, 1986) and *Bentham* (Oxford, 1989). From 1977–83, he was also senior editor of the Bentham Project at University College London. See I. R. Christie, 'John Rowland Dinwiddy, 1939–90', *Utilitas*, ii (1990), i–ii.

**26.** For example, in January 1990, J. R. Jones (University of East Anglia) gave a presentation on Hanoverian blue-water naval policy, followed by discussion ranging from Elizabethan times to Britain post-Second World War.

**27.** The term emerged in research circles in the later 1980s, first appearing in a book title by F. O'Gorman, *The Long Eighteenth Century: British Political and Social History, 1688–1832* (London, 1997).

**28.** P. J. Corfield, 'British History: The Exploding Galaxy', *Journal for Eighteenth-Century Studies*, xxxiv (2011), 517–26: also available at https://www .penelopejcorfield.com/PDFs/3.1.1-CorfieldPdf24-Exploding-Galaxy.pdf [accessed 1 Sept. 2021].

**29.** In 2003, a path-breaking project in eighteenth-century digital history was launched by seminar organizer Tim Hitchcock (University of Sussex) and frequent contributor Robert Shoemaker (University of Sheffield), with the digitization of London's criminal records from *The Proceedings of the Old Bailey, 1674–1913*: https://www.oldbaileyonline.org [accessed 1 Sept. 2021].

**30.** E. P. Thompson (1924–93), *The Making of the English Working Class* (London, 1963); and esp. 'Postscript', in ibid. (1968 edn), pp. 916–39, for EPT's response to critics.

31. See overview in P. N. Stearns, *Debating the Industrial Revolution* (London, 2015).

32. M. Foucault (1926–84), *Madness and Civilisation: A History of Insanity in the Age of Reason* (Paris, 1961), trans. R. Howard (New York, 1965); idem, *Discipline and Punish: The Birth of the Prison* (Paris, 1975), trans. A. Sheridan (New York, 1977).

33. A. W. McHoul and W. Grace, *A Foucault Primer: Discourse, Power and the Subject* (London, 1995).

34. For context, see N. Olsen, *History in the Plural: An Introduction to the Work of Reinhart Koselleck* (New York, 2011).

35. J. C. D. Clark, *English Society, 1688–1832: Ideology, Social Structure and Political Practice during the Ancien Regime* (Cambridge, 1985).

36. R. Palmer, *The Sound of History: Songs and Social Comment* (Oxford, 1988).

37. Published as E. P. Thompson, 'The Moral Economy Revisited', in idem., *Customs in Common* (London, 1991), pp. 259–351.

38. For a distillation of shared seminar experiences, see P. J. Corfield and T. Hitchcock, *Becoming a Historian: An Informal Guide* (London, 2022).

39. The British Society for Eighteenth-Century Studies: https://www.bsecs.org.uk /the-society [accessed 15 Sept. 2021].

40. The International Society for Eighteenth-Century Studies: https://oraprdnt.uqtr .uquebec.ca/pls/public/gscw031?owa_no_site=304 [accessed 15 Sept. 2021].

## References

### Published sources

Bellot, H. H., *University College London, 1826–1926* (London, 1928).

Bentley, M., *Modernizing England's Past: English Historiography in the Age of Modernism, 1870–1970* (Cambridge, 2005).

Bottomore, T., *Elites and Society* (London, 1993).

The British Society for Eighteenth-Century Studies: https://www.bsecs.org.uk/the-society [accessed 15 Sept. 2021].

Brooke, J., 'Namier and Namierism', *History and Theory*, iii (1964), 331–47.

Butterfield, H., *George III and the Historians* (London, 1957).

Christie, I. R., *The End of North's Ministry, 1780–2* (London, 1958).

Christie, I. R., *Wilkes, Wyvill and Reform: The Parliamentary Reform Movement in British Politics, 1760–85* (London, 1962).

Christie, I. R., *Crisis of Empire: Great Britain and the American Colonies 1754–83* (London, 1966).

Christie, I. R., *Myth and Reality in Late-Eighteenth-Century British Politics, and Other Papers* (London, 1970).

Christie, I. R., *Stress and Stability in Late Eighteenth-Century Britain: Reflections on the British Avoidance of Revolution* (London, 1984).

Christie, I. R., 'John Rowland Dinwiddy, 1939–90', *Utilitas*, ii (1990), i–ii.

Clark, J. C. D., *English Society, 1688–1832: Ideology, Social Structure and Political Practice during the Ancien Regime* (Cambridge, 1985).

Colley, L., *Lewis Namier* (London, 1989).

Corfield, P. J., 'British History: The Exploding Galaxy', *Journal for Eighteenth-Century Studies*, xxxiv (2011), 517–26. Also available at https://www.penelopejcorfield.com/PDFs/3.1.1-CorfieldPdf24-Exploding-Galaxy.pdf [accessed 1 Sept. 2021].

Corfield, P. J., and Hitchcock, T., *Becoming a Historian: An Informal Guide* (London, 2022).

Cruickshanks, E., *Political Untouchables: The Tories and the '45* (London, 1979).

Dinwiddy, J. R., *From Luddism to the First Reform Bill: Reform in England, 1810–32* (Oxford, 1986).

Dinwiddy, J. R., *Bentham* (Oxford, 1989).

Femia, J., *Vilfredo Pareto* (London, 2016).

Foucault, M., *Madness and Civilisation: A History of Insanity in the Age of Reason*, trans. R. Howard (New York, 1965).

Foucault, M., *Discipline and Punish: The Birth of the Prison*, trans. A. Sheridan (New York, 1977).

Goldgar, A., *Impolite Learning: Conduct and Community in the Republic of Letters, 1680–1750* (London, 1995).

Grafton, A., *Worlds Made by Words: Scholarship and Community in the Modern West* (London, 2009).

Harte, N. B., 'Obituary: Ian R. Christie', *The Independent*, 5 December 1998.

Hayton, D., *Conservative Revolutionary: The Lives of Lewis Namier* (Manchester, 2019).

*The History of Parliament Project*: https://www.historyofparliamentonline.org [accessed 1 Sept. 2021].

The International Society for Eighteenth-Century Studies: https://oraprdnt.uqtr.uquebec.ca/pls/public/gscw031?owa_no_site=304 [accessed 15 Sept. 2021].

Keats-Rohan, K. S. B., *Prosopography Approaches and Applications: A Handbook* (Oxford, 2007).

McCulloh, I. A., Armstrong, H. L., and Johnson, A. N., *Social Networks Analysis with Applications* (Hoboken, NJ, 2013).

McHoul, A. W., and Grace, W., *A Foucault Primer: Discourse, Power and the Subject* (London, 1995).

Namier, L. B., *The Structure of Politics at the Accession of George III* (London, 1929).

Namier, L. B., and Brooke, J., *The House of Commons, 1754–1790* (London, 1964).

O'Gorman, F., *The Long Eighteenth Century: British Political and Social History, 1688–1832* (London, 1997).

Olsen, N., *History in the Plural: An Introduction to the Work of Reinhart Koselleck* (New York, 2011).

Östling, J., *Humboldt and the Modern German University: An Intellectual History* (Lund, 2018).

Palmer, R., *The Sound of History: Songs and Social Comment* (Oxford, 1988).

Parsloe, J., *Charles Guy Parsloe, 1900–85* (Epsom, 2018).

Poulton, I., 'Remembering the Bellots' (2019) in https://somersetlad.com/2019/11/10/remembering-the-bellots/ [accessed 1 Sept. 2021].

*The Proceedings of the Old Bailey, 1674–1913*: https://www.oldbaileyonline.org [accessed 1 Sept. 2021].

Rudé, G., *The Crowd in History: A Study of Popular Disturbances in France and England, 1730–1848* (New York, 1964).

Sedgwick, R., *The House of Commons, 1715–54* (London, 1970).

Stearns, P. N., *Debating the Industrial Revolution* (London, 2015).

Thompson, E. P., *The Making of the English Working Class* (London, 1963).

Thompson, E. P., *Customs in Common* (London, 1991).

Thomson, M. A., *A Constitutional History of England, 1642–1801* (London, 1938).
Thomson, M. A., *Macaulay* (London, 1959).
Wilson, K., *The Sense of the People: Politics, Culture and Imperialism in England, 1715–85* (Cambridge, 1995).

## Unpublished sources

Corfield, P. J., Miscellaneous Private Correspondence and Notes.

Chapter 6

# The Low Countries History Seminar

## Ulrich Tiedau*

When the COVID-19 pandemic forced the Low Countries History Seminar to convene online for the first time in 2020–21, many participants embraced the move with enthusiasm. A supportive comment on Twitter noted how historians from all over the world would now be able to attend this 'fabled' academic occasion, giving an indication of the esteem in which one of the oldest seminars offered by the Institute of Historical Research is held. The aim of this chapter is to reconstruct the Seminar's institutional and intellectual history, re-appraising its stories and analysing its changing topics, themes, methods and demographics over time.

## Beginnings under Pieter Geyl

The Seminar's origins were associated with the early life of the University of London's department of Dutch studies, co-hosted by Bedford College and University College and founded in 1919 with funds donated by members of the *Nederlandsche Vereeniging te London,* a London-based gentlemen's club for Dutch expats whose membership included executives from Royal Dutch Shell and other Anglo-Dutch companies. The department was established with a library, a readership and a professorship, with the first incumbent of the latter being the former London correspondent of the *Nieuwe Rotterdamsche Courant* newspaper Pieter Geyl (1887–1966).[1] One guiding motivation here was a desire to revive the reputation of the Netherlands, whose neutrality during the First World War was widely, if not necessarily correctly, seen as having been more favourable to Germany. Geyl's inaugural lecture laid out a bold plan for developing

Dutch studies pertaining to 'the whole field of Dutch civilization', which from Geyl's 'Greater Netherlands' point of view also included the Flemish part of Belgium and the Cape Dutch (Afrikaans) speakers in South Africa. In 1920, Geyl was joined by the reader Pieter Harting (1892–1970), a philologist from Utrecht who had originally specialized in Sanskrit; however, the two men did not work well together for long. Apparently, Harting conspired with Gregory Foster, the powerful provost of University College, to replace Geyl as chair on the occasion of the scheme's initial five-year review in 1924, but the attempt failed.[2] The resulting acrimony between Geyl and Harting led to the department being split into two: Harting took sole control of Dutch language and literature at Bedford College (before accepting a professorship at Groningen shortly thereafter), whilst Geyl's remit was reduced to Dutch history and institutions at UCL.[3] Stripped of the responsibility of running a full department, he turned his attention to the fledgling IHR. In his autobiography (written in 1942 in a Nazi hostage camp and posthumously published in 2009), Geyl recalled:

> Pollard had at about this time achieved one of his great life goals and founded an institution to which the more advanced, postgraduate historical work of the entire university would be concentrated: the Institute for Historical Research, for the time being housed in a temporary building behind the British Museum. I was given a room there for my historical books from the Dutch library, which I could build up with a Dutch government grant and which until then had been somewhat hidden away in Bedford College. I have always enjoyed that little library; it helped me a lot for my own work, and it was admired by English colleagues: there were especially many source publications that they could use.[4]

This contingent arrangement furthered Pollard's design of the IHR's seminar library, wherein 'points made, and queries raised in seminars could be instantly checked by pulling a book of documents off the surrounding shelves'.[5]

These developments facilitated the emergence of a postgraduate teaching seminar in Low Countries history. As Geyl himself noted:

> I was also asked to take the lead, along with [Hugh Hale] Bellot, a seminar in European diplomatic history. Only a few students came there, but it immediately got a good name: it was found interesting. Generating and leading a discussion was something that went well for me. Bellot soon left it entirely to me, he himself went in a different direction, but I know that he spoke about me with the greatest appreciation. The next step – and this had to be approved in the

board of studies – was that to the list of 'special' and 'optional' topics that made up the BA exam, two of mine were added ... Optional: the Low Countries in European history 1648–1839; special: diplomatic history of the War of the Spanish Succession. Those subjects were now indeed chosen by a few students every year, so that I had a small group of my own, with whom I always got along excellently. And some of them went on after their BA for the MA or PhD and came to the Institute at my seminar, where I had some outside students, by the way, from Edinburgh, Oxford, Berlin, and then Renier [Geyl's favourite student and protégé]! And under my leadership they produced a few not insignificant 'theses' ... All of this was extremely satisfying and enjoyable.[6]

Organized on a regular basis throughout term time, Geyl's seminar ran from 1924–5 to 1934–5. Whilst ostensibly focused on European diplomatic history, studies of the Low Countries figured prominently. From 1927–8 onwards, after Geyl had arranged for a major book donation from the Dutch government (1925), the room for diplomatic history was repurposed for studying the history of the Netherlands, making this national specialism somewhat distinct from those supported by the room for the rest of European history.[7]

Attendance at Geyl's Seminar was modest (although not out of keeping with that of many other of the early seminars), at between three and six participants. Geyl made every effort to ensure that readings were 'accessible to English students, and not so Dutch that they would scare everyone away'.[8] To complement these activities, Harting's successor, Jacob Haantjes (1864–1953), organized a reading group at the IHR on Dutch historical texts.[9] This drew in students such as Mary Fischer, who was working on Dutch Guiana under the supervision of Arthur Percival Newton (1873–1942), Rhodes professor of imperial history at King's College, and the New Zealand born E. S. de Beer (1895–1990) – later famed for editing the diary of John Evelyn and the correspondence of John Locke, but then an assistant in UCL's department of history.[10]

Geyl's students played a formative role in the early life of the Seminar. Gustaaf Renier (1892–1962), who would succeed Geyl as chair in 1935, attended right from the beginning from 1924–5 through to 1929–30. After completing a master's degree at the University of Edinburgh, Isabel A. Montgomery, née Morison, started doctoral studies under Geyl's supervision and participated in the Seminar in 1925–6 and 1927–8.[11] Mary Trevelyan (1905–94) joined in 1926–7 as she studied Anglo-Dutch relations during the 'Glorious Revolution', resulting in a monograph on *William the Third and the Defence of Holland, 1672–74* (1930).[12] Margaret

Olivia Campbell, *née* Noël-Paton, worked on the Triple Alliance of 1668 and attended the Seminar from 1927–8 to 1929–30. She would later assist the German émigré pedagogue Kurt Hahn in founding Gordonstoun School in Scotland.[13] The number of female seminarists at this time is striking, probably in part a consequence of the University's Dutch programme being based at the female-only Bedford College (although students of Dutch from UCL and other London colleges attended the classes there as well).

In the early 1930s, another of Geyl's protégés, Stanley Thomas Bindoff (1908–80), not only worked on the Scheldt controversy between the Treaty of Paris of 1814 and the Treaty of London of 1839, but also translated the second and third volumes of Geyl's magnum opus *Geschiedenis van de Nederlandsche Stam* into English and became an assistant librarian of the IHR; in later years, Bindoff switched to Tudor history and became the first professor of history at Queen Mary College in 1951.[14] Margaret Cobb addressed the breakdown of the Anglo-Austrian alliance (1748–56); R. R. Goodison focused on England and the Orangist party (1665–72), a work to which Geyl acknowledged he owed a lot for his own preparations of *Oranje en Stuart* (1939); and Alice Carter, *née* Le Mesurier (1909–86), studied Anglo-Dutch diplomatic relations from 1756 to 1763, before developing an academic career at the London School of Economics.[15] As she put in the preface to her *The Dutch Republic in Europe in the Seven Years War* (1971):

> I was one of the many English students Professor Geyl taught to love his mother country, and to want to learn about relations between the Netherlands and England, which Geyl had come to regard as his second fatherland. Professor Boogman, also a student of Geyl's, has written recently of the freedom with which we were allowed to choose our own area of research, and make our own discoveries therein in our own way and at our own time. We could draw our own conclusions, to which Geyl would listen courteously before kindly revealing to us the fallacies apt to beset the young student who starts working on his own. We were not submitted to unsought direction, though it was always to be had on request. Nor were we intimidated by *obiter dicta*, though we would not, I think, have been permitted to harbour doubts about the Greater Netherlands theory. With that one exception his seminars were meetings of free minds.[16]

The dynamism of the Seminar also owed much to Geyl's formidable reputation within and beyond the University of London. As one of the most senior historians from the Low Countries to be publishing regularly in English, Geyl was instrumental in shaping both the perception of the history of this European region in Britain and the wider Anglophone world (Henri Pirenne's magnum opus *Histoire de Belgique* had not been translated into English, and still has not been fully to this day).[17] During the interwar period, he also used and abused his position for political purposes, in particular for advancing the cause of *Groot-Nederland* and supporting the Flemish-nationalist movement, oscillating between moderate federalist and radical anti-Belgian positions, to the point that in 1929 he was declared *persona non grata* by the Belgian authorities.

After he left London to take up a chair in Utrecht (1935) and after the Second World War, which he largely spent in Buchenwald and German hostage camps in the Netherlands (1940–44), Geyl renewed his position in Anglophone intellectual culture in the post-war period by sparring with Arnold Toynbee and other British scholars on matters of historiographical controversy, including two highly influential BBC radio broadcasts in 1948.[18] He continued to be regarded as 'well acquainted with – indeed a part of – the English historical scene', in spite of being located elsewhere.[19]

## Continuation under Gustaaf Renier

Geyl was succeeded in 1935 by the 'licensed eccentric' Gustaaf Renier (1892–1962).[20] Born in Flushing to Belgian parents, Renier considered himself a Francophone Zeeuw. He started his historical studies in Ghent under the noted medievalist Henri Pirenne (1862–1935), but fled Belgium at the outbreak of the First World War, first to his parents in Zeeland, then on to England. After initially working as a journalist, he took up postgraduate studies under Geyl's supervision at the University of London. In 1930 his thesis was published as *Great Britain and the Establishment of the Kingdom of the Netherlands, 1813–1815*.[21] This marked the beginning of an extraordinary period of writing which included the irreverent *The English: Are They Human?* (1931), in which Renier, who struggled to fully integrate into British society, gave 'a satirical description of the English among whom he had lived for many years without ever losing his sense of wonder at their social and mental habits',[22] short biographies of *William of Orange* [the Silent] (1932) and *Oscar Wilde* (1933), as well as serving as the translator for P. J. Blok's *The Life of Admiral de Ruyter* (1933) and other works.[23]

In 1934 Renier was appointed part-time lecturer in modern history as well as tutor to the Evening School of UCL's history department, which had effectively subsumed Geyl's nominal department for Dutch history and institutions.[24] After Geyl's departure for Utrecht, Renier was not the department's first choice to replace Geyl, despite there being a mutual understanding between them to that effect, but after a protracted process he was appointed as reader (elevated to the chair of Dutch history in 1945).[25]

Having been a member of the Seminar since 1924, he took over its convenorship in 1936, with Stanley Thomas Bindoff as his first seminar assistant.[26]

One seminar member and former student of Renier's, Ragnhild Hatton, remembered upon the occasion of his retirement in 1957: 'In the twenty-one years of [Renier's] guidance, the Seminar has grown tremendously: in scope, as the amendment of its title to "International History of the Seventeenth and Eighteenth Centuries" indicates, and in size.' The Seminar's enlargement was partly 'due to the post-war expansion of postgraduate studies and the influx of scholars from Europe and America to London', which was reflected by the move from the small pipe-smoked room in the old IHR-barrack before the war to the stately Senate House in 1948, but also due to Renier's growing reputation as a seminar convenor. While initially clearly orientated around postgraduate learning, in later years the emphasis shifted more to professional academic discussions. As Hatton further noted: 'one of the distinguishing features of the Seminar in recent years has been the number of university teachers who have become regular members of it'.[27] Throughout, the defining rule of Renier's *colloquium doctum* was, as Hatton expanded, that:

> no written paper is ever read at the seminar (we have had some fine displays of temper when anyone has as much as suggested this), Renier insisting that scholars meet in a seminar to *talk* about their work and that to talk well about one's work means a command of one's material so disciplined that a learned *conversation* can take place. The speaker therefore (aided, if necessary in the case of a beginner, by some pencilled brief notes) must be able to get the results of his work, or problems relating to it, across to the rest of the seminar without too much detail and he must be willing to be interrupted – without losing the thread of his own thought – by the others for comments and questions at any moment.[28]

In contrast to this detail on the format of the Seminar, little is known about its subject content under Renier's convenorship; however, the titles of the theses his students produced are indicative. Master's dissertations included P. J. Welch's *The Maritime Powers and the Evolution of the War Aims of the Grand Alliance, 1701–4* (1939–40) and E. N. La Brooy's *The Dutch East Indies* (1939–40). From 1945–6 to 1946–7, William Gerald Beasley worked on Anglo-Dutch relations in the seventeenth century. He had intended to follow this up with doctoral research on Anglo-Dutch rivalry in South-east Asia but, having learned Japanese whilst serving in the Royal Navy and been a part of the British Liaison Mission in Tokyo, Beasley was hired as lecturer in far eastern history at the School of Oriental and

African Studies (SOAS) in 1947 and settled on Great Britain and the opening of Japan, 1834–58, as a topic, encouraged by Renier.[29] Incidentally, Renier's own wartime service included time with the BBC's European Monitoring Unit in Evesham and then work as an adviser to the Dutch Press and Information Service for the Dutch Government-in-Exile, for which he received two Dutch decorations.[30] Beasley would later become professor of the history of the Far East at SOAS until his retirement and offer an IHR seminar on the history of the Far East from 1955–6.[31]

Occasionally, the Seminar was also the subject of external inquiries. In one documented instance from 1948, it was asked for its expert opinion on a contested seventeenth-century royal grant of William III of large parts of Labrador, Canada, to the Dutch merchant of Portuguese descent Joseph de la Penha (1697). Signed by William as King of England but filed in a Dutch archive without official seal in either capacity, descendants of de la Penha repeatedly used the document to claim ownership of the territory in Canadian courts. The Seminar was able to establish the credibility of the deed by proving that William had indeed been at Het Loo palace, where the document had been drawn up, at the time in question, but also commented that the grant could only have been made in William's role as sovereign of the principality of Orange and not as *stadholder* of the Dutch Republic.[32]

By the early 1950s the Seminar was flourishing, and the number of participants regularly reached double figures. This success hid a more painful sense of failure for Renier, however. For his book *History: Its Purpose and Its Method* (1950), which he regarded as his masterpiece, not only received a generally indifferent reception but was savaged in the *Times Literary Supplement* (26 January 1951) by an anonymous reviewer – widely known to be none other than Lewis Namier (1888–1960), who would soon move to the IHR to embark upon the re-launched History of Parliament project. So hurt was Renier that 'not only would he never publish anything about history again, but not a word in English anymore'.[33] Looking back at his achievements on the occasion of his retirement, Renier wrote:

> Comparisons are bound to be made. Geyl will come out of them better than I. He gave the chair scholarly distinction and that aura of controversy that is the lifeblood of the humanities. But he will also be remembered as the man who dined as Toynbee's guest, before slaughtering him at the microphone. A man who neither looked to the right nor to the left and yet a kindly colleague and a gentleman. I shall be recalled, during the brief period that is covered by academic memory, as a touchy provincial looking down upon Hollander, Fleming and Englishman alike, the man who quarrelled with all but his students, who sent to Coventry [i.e. ostracized] the

Dutch Ministry of Education, Long-skirt College [i.e. Bedford College] the Board of Studies in History, and all those who refused to live up to his theory that there is no evil in the world, but only folly and craziness.[34]

## Transition under Ragnhild Hatton

According to the IHR records, Ragnhild Hatton also was co-convenor of the Seminar for the years 1954–5 to 1956–7. Hatton, *née* Hanssen, (1913–95) – a native of Norway who married an Englishman in 1936 – had her studies interrupted by the Second World War, but after turning down a research fellowship at Girton College, Cambridge, she undertook doctoral studies in London, producing a dissertation which was published as *Diplomatic Relations between Great Britain and the Dutch Republic, 1714–1721* (1950).[35] Maintaining a presence at the Seminar, Hatton then started teaching at the London School of Economics (where she rose through the ranks to become professor of international history in 1968). Informally she appears to have taken over the *de facto* leadership of the Seminar from Renier, as Andrew Lossky noted that she 'directed two graduate seminars in the Institute of Historical Research, one of which she had inherited from G. J. Renier'.[36] This would tally with Renier's general retreat from academe after the Namier incident and probably also extend further back than 1954–5, as Renier in a letter to the IHR director from May 1954 argued that '[i]n listing this seminar as a joint undertaking by Dr Hatton and myself we shall do no more than recognize an existing situation'.[37] In later reflections (1957) Hatton acknowledged that the Seminar

> helped young research students to take an objective view of their subjects and to express their aims and their results with clarity and precision. It must also have helped to combat that isolation from which young research workers following the unsociable disciplines seem to suffer to a marked extent in the absence of any generally accepted standard of supervision.[38]

In complementary fashion, Andrew Lossky (1985) remembered: 'the friendly and informal atmosphere of these meetings', in which

> one could present for general discussion any problem of the seventeenth or eighteenth century, no matter how tentative or inchoate one's own ideas on it were, and the resulting exchange of views was of inestimable value for everybody in attendance. Many a good and

novel idea that later found its way into the published works of the participants had its origin in Dr Hatton's seminar.[39]

## Renewal under Ernst Kossmann

In 1957 Ernst Heinrich Kossmann (1922–2003) succeeded Renier, initially as reader and then in 1962 as professor of Dutch history. Born in Leiden and partially of German-Jewish descent, Kossmann had suffered under the Nazis, being made a forced labourer in German-annexed Strasbourg, an experience captured in the 1950 novel *De Nederlaag* ('the Defeat') by his twin brother Alfred.[40] After the Second World War, Kossmann spent time in Paris and Leiden cultivating a commitment to historical scholarship with his wife, Johanna, *née* Putto. He received his PhD in 1954 from the University of Leiden with a thesis on France's seventeenth-century civil war, *La Fronde*, as Johanna established a reputation as an historian of the Low Countries in her own right.[41] Under the auspices of Geyl's recommendation, the couple then moved to London in 1957, where Ernst's new position at University College went hand-in-hand with him taking over the Seminar at the IHR. His arrival in turn precipitated a change in nomenclature, for henceforth the seminar was titled the Seminar on Dutch History, Domestic and International.[42] In some ways this shift marked the culmination of what Geyl had started back in the mid-1920s, for Dutch history had now fully supplanted diplomatic history as the Seminar's focus; and, in contrast, Hatton made the Seminar on International History of the Eighteenth Century her own. Kossmann later (2003) remembered his arrival at the IHR as follows:

> And then there was the postgraduate seminar, the highest form of education in existence. It was an honour for an academic to lead such a seminar of his own. I inherited one from Renier and did not know at all what to do with it. After all, Renier had only left two undergraduates and not a single postgraduate student – deliberately, for he had not taken on any more students for some time since, he said, he could not be sure that these would be in as good hands with his successor as in his. In fact, in the beginning, this Seminar was only attended by colleagues who had some connection with Geyl, Renier, the Netherlands and Dutch history. Among them were women and men of quality, creative people with well-known *œuvres* to their name or in the process of writing them, experienced researchers who knew many languages, had lived in all kinds of foreign countries for a long time and had worked in the archives:

the lively and original Charles Boxer, the young Graham Gibbs, Alice Carter, who taught at the London School of Economics, the Norwegian historian Ragnhild Hatton, who had completed a PhD under Renier, the Spanish Isabel de Madariaga, and many others.[43]

As the Seminar found new strength and vigour, Kossmann was struck by the quality of the intellectual exchanges between the seminarians, who by now were almost exclusively professional historians. In his reminiscences, he recalled:

> a company that met every other week, expecting something would happen and debated with an eloquence that was completely overwhelming to me in the beginning. Especially the women made an impression. Most certainly I have never known a group of historians who, at such a breath-taking pace, exchanged their insights with so much erudition, such a mastery of the finest details of the sometimes rather exotic subjects in which they were interested, in such a powerful tone. What did I, a provincial from Leiden, have to offer these people?[44]

Kossmann's self-deprecation here can be counterbalanced by the insights of his former student, the intellectual historian Frank Ankersmit (2007):

> He had an unusually strong and fascinating personality – I never met anyone even remotely coming close to what he was like. Just to give you an idea: he was all that one might associate with François Guizot, very much aloof, very intelligent, both impossible to get close to and yet very much accessible and blessed with the rhetorical powers of a Pericles. If he had chosen a political career, the recent history of my country would have been unrecognisable from what it is now. It rarely happened, but if he really felt that it was necessary, he could raise a rhetorical storm blowing away everything and everybody. Indeed, when thinking of him, I never am sure what impressed me most, his scholarship or his personality. He was a truly wonderful man.[45]

But Kossmann's intellectual leadership not only reinvigorated the Seminar but also elicited innovation. A collaboration with the historian John Selwyn Bromley (initially of Keble College, Oxford, and then of the University of Southampton) established a series of conferences on Anglo-Dutch history, resulting in five volumes of essays between 1960 and 1975.[46] These developments provided opportunities for cross-fertilization with the activities of the Seminar. Several times a year, Ernst and Johanna presented to the Seminar extensive critical reviews of newly published

THE LOW COUNTRIES HISTORY SEMINAR       145

literature on the history of the Low Countries. These interventions provided both the academic calendar and individual seminar discussions with a greater degree of structure and established a formative relationship with the Kossmanns' contributions to the 'bulletin critique de l'historiographie néerlandaise' in the historical journal *Revue du Nord* (est. 1910). Of these activities, Kossmann recalled:

> we divided the material into equal portions as much as possible; mostly it boiled down to Johanna taking care of prehistory and the Middle Ages, as well as of economic and church history, whereas I looked after the rest and edited the whole thing in French. Since we viewed this bulletin as a means of raising interest in Dutch historiography abroad, we made our judgments in benevolent prose without, by the way, forcing ourselves to praise if we did not like a particular publication ... thanks to our diligent missionary work, we have now and then been able to give a certain meaning to the difficult seminar that I had inherited.[47]

Taken together, the conferences and seminars, which now even more frequently than before were attended by visitors and guest speakers from the Low Countries, helped internationalize the field, which until then had too often been seen through the narrow prism of *Vaderlandse geschiedenis* (history of the Fatherland).[48] While this fact may sound banal in an age when international scholarly communication and exchange is taken for granted, at the time this was highly innovative and paved the way for scholarly practices of today. The Seminar had also, quite organically and imperceptibly, changed its remit from postgraduate teaching to a broader sense of scholarship and research.

## The Seminar under Koen Swart

After the Kossmanns left for Groningen in 1966, Koenraad (Koen) Swart (1916–92) took on the chair of Dutch history: an appointment not much to the liking of Geyl, who passed away later that year. That said, Swart was the first convenor of the Seminar to arrive at the IHR as a senior academic with considerable experience. He had studied law and history at Leiden as one of the last students of the pioneering cultural historian Johan Huizinga (1872–1945) and then attended the Nuremberg Trials on behalf of the *Rijksinstituut voor Oorlogsdocumentatie* ('National Institute for War Documentation') in 1947–9. Thereafter he taught at institutions in the USA, including the University of Illinois at Urbana (1950–52), Georgetown University (1952–3), Brenau College (1954–6) and Agnes Scott College

(1956–66); and he became a naturalized American.[49] Having worked mainly on French history during this period, it came as a great surprise to him to be approached to fill the prestigious chair of Dutch history at UCL.[50]

Swart's leadership of the Seminar worked to exemplify a now established tradition of setting Dutch and Belgian history in an international context with a view to furthering an interest in the subject in Britain and the wider English-speaking world. The Seminar continued the practice begun by the Kossmanns to produce surveys of recent Dutch historiography, but this time as a collaborative effort and in English, not French. From 1973 to 1982, the Seminar published a bibliography of recent Dutch and Belgian historiography in volumes six to ten of the *Acta Historiae Neerlandicae* (renamed in 1978 as *The Low Countries Yearbook*), and then in 1981, bundled and complemented by indexes, as volume one of the *Nederlands Historisch Genootschap*'s new bibliographical series.[51] The writing of the annual surveys of historical literature gave the Seminar a certain solidarity and cohesion, which was further enhanced by social adjuncts and meals with speakers that had become a regular fixture by this time. Furthermore, Swart was recognized as 'the central figure in the Seminar in the history of the Low Countries, where he stimulated young English researchers in their study of Dutch history from, in his opinion, a healthy distance'.[52] Indeed, Swart certainly did much to encourage a new generation of Low Countries historians, including Geoffrey Parker, Leslie Price, Alastair Duke, Rosemary Jones, Renée Gerson, Chris Emery and Jonathan Israel.

Of Swart's own works, his *William of Orange and the Revolt of the Netherlands, 1572–84* is known best: incomplete at the time of Swart's passing in 1992, it was published posthumously first in 1994 and then in English translation with accompanying introductory chapters by Alastair Duke and Jonathan Israel in 2003.[53]

## The Seminar under Jonathan Israel, and after

In 1984, Jonathan Israel (b. 1946) was appointed as Swart's successor as the chair of Dutch history. Having been educated at Oxford and Cambridge, Israel had been working at UCL for a decade when he took up the post, and significantly he was the first British academic to do so. His second book *The Dutch Republic and the Hispanic World* (1982) was followed by other ground-breaking works on Low Countries history as well as on the 'radical' Enlightenment and the intellectual origins of modern democracy more widely.

As Swart eased himself into retirement he co-convened the Seminar with Israel for the academic year 1985–6. Thereafter, Israel took on sole responsibility of the convenorship. However, perhaps in recognition of the intensification of university teaching and research, it was not long before a more fluid arrangement of co-convenorship became the norm. When Israel undertook research leave in 1991–2, Alastair Duke of the University of Southampton and Graham Gibbs of the University of Oxford stood in as co-convenors, before all three of them continued the role jointly afterwards. In 1994–5, Gibbs moved to the University of Liverpool and was replaced by Lesley Gilbert from the Department of Dutch Studies, which had re-joined UCL after Bedford College merged with Royal Holloway in 1985. However, Gilbert herself departed in 1996–7. The following year, Israel and Duke were joined by Renée Gerson of London Guildhall University, Judith Pollmann of Somerville College, Oxford, and Stuart Moore of the University of Southampton; the latter four continued running the seminar after Israel moved to the Institute of Advanced Study, Princeton, in 2000–2001.[54]

In 2002–3 the newly appointed, and still present, incumbent of the chair of Dutch history, Benjamin Kaplan, arrived at the IHR. Educated at Harvard, he specializes in religious history of early modern Europe, in particular of the Low Countries. A year after that, Gerson and Moore retired from the convenorship, Duke left in 2005–6, and then Pollmann in 2008–9, after her appointment as professor for early modern Dutch history at Leiden in 2005. New co-convenors included Anne Goldgar of King's College London and Raingard Esser of the University of the West of England, Bristol. In 2011–12, this author (like Lesley Gilbert from the UCL Department of Dutch) joined for the outgoing Esser, who had taken up a professorship in Groningen. Joanna Woodall of the Courtauld Institute also provided much needed art historical expertise throughout. In 2017–18, Liesbeth Corens of Queen Mary became the latest co-convenor. In 2019–20, Goldgar moved to the University of Southern California, Los Angeles; however, due to the Seminar's temporary move online, necessitated by the COVID-19 pandemic, she has been able to continue as a convenor for the time being. The great success of the first season of the Low Countries History Seminar in this new medium, which allowed the 'fabled' events to be followed worldwide, make it seem likely that some form of hybrid seminar will emerge in the post-COVID-19 age.

Extant records make it possible to consider the Seminar's speakers and their papers only from 1990–91 onwards. In terms of geographical distribution over these past thirty years, about two thirds of the speakers had UK-based affiliations, of which over a third were from the University of

London, whilst about a quarter were from Dutch institutions. Speakers were also, unsurprisingly, drawn from the USA and Belgium, but also from other European countries, as well as from Canada and Israel. About two thirds of the speakers were male, one third female, with an upwards trend: in the past decade the percentage of female speakers has been approaching 40 per cent.

Organizational pragmatism has played an increasing role in shaping the Seminar's calendar. It operates with gratefully received financial support from the *Stichting Professor van Winter Fund*, the Friends of the IHR, Flanders House (the diplomatic representation of the Government of Flanders in the UK) and an anonymous donor. Inevitably, however, travel expenses remain modest and so many speakers are invited while staying in the London-Oxford-Cambridge 'golden triangle' for archival research or visiting fellowships and the like, often irrespective of the type of history they are pursuing. This phenomenon complements the way the personal choices and networks of co-convenors inform the content of the Seminar for any given year. Close collaboration between the Low Countries Seminar and the Seminar for Economic History, both scheduled on Friday afternoons, has also led to regular joint seminar meetings since the early 2000s.

In looking at the topical change over the decades, one thing that is striking is that the Seminar has diversified a lot and become more interdisciplinary. Art historians started making regular appearances in the mid-1990s, with not just scholars but also practitioners from galleries and museums, including the National Gallery, the Ashmolean Museum and the Rijksmuseum. Whereas political, international and religious aspects of Low Countries history remain popular throughout the recent life of the Seminar, a gradual increase in papers on social, cultural and intellectual history can be witnessed, reflecting both general trends in the field (for example, moving away from privileging elites) and the convenors' evolving interests and preferences. A renewed emphasis on the history of colonization emerged in the mid-2000s. Considerations of gender history started to appear in the late 2000s with the history of minorities growing through the 2010s. There have also been a number of papers on the history of science and technology and the odd foray into digital history. In terms of chronological coverage, there has been a widening of scope to include occasional seminars on medieval times as well as nineteenth- and twentieth-century history, although overall a focus on the early modern period has remained largely intact.[55] In terms of format, the focus on intense learned discussion continues, although the Seminar has accommodated changes, such as the way speakers now typically rely on PowerPoint slides for the presentation of the initial paper.

## Conclusion

The Low Countries History Seminar has evolved over the decades, constantly reinventing something of the ethos of Pollard's 'history laboratory'.[56] From the late 1950s onwards, it became an incubator of, or else a catalyst for, an astonishing surge of research publications on Low Countries history in English, embedding the subject in a more international perspective – or the 'colonization of Dutch history' by British historians, as Swart called it in 1984.[57] However, Swart also reminds us to see this against the background of Britain having become less insular and more European in its political culture at the time. Obviously, after recent political events, the situation is different now; and it will be interesting to see how post-Brexit life will affect Anglo-Dutch relations in academia as well as in wider society.

## Notes

\* I would like to thank my co-convenors, past and present, as well as David Manning, Warren Oliver and Reinier Salverda for their help and support in writing this chapter. I am also grateful to Zoë Karens, former archivist at the IHR, for providing me with access to and valuable advice on the material.

1. For an in-depth evaluation of Geyl's time in London, see S. van Rossem and U. Tiedau (ed.), *Pieter Geyl and Britain: Encounters, Controversies and Impact* (London, 2022): http://doi.org/10.14296/vfsr7023 [accessed 20 Dec. 2022].

2. We only have Geyl's account of the conflict. Given his pugnacious nature it is not unreasonable to assume that there might have been another side to the story as well.

3. Harting subsequently went on to inaugurate the Anglo-Dutch student exchange programme that still carries his name, one of the oldest such internationalization schemes in European Higher Education, see Harting Scheme: https://hartingscheme .wordpress.com/history-of-the-scheme/ [accessed 21 Dec. 2021].

4. P. Geyl, *Ik Die Zo Weinig In Mijn Verleden Leef: Autobiografie 1887–1940*, ed. W. Berkelaar, L. Dorsman and P. van Hees (Amsterdam, 2009), p. 151. N.B. The translation from the original Dutch, like for all quotations in this chapter, is my own.

5. M. Thompson, '"Making History": A Short History of the Institute of Historical Research' (2008): https://archives.history.ac.uk/makinghistory/resources/articles /IHR.html [accessed 10 Nov. 2020].

6. Geyl, *Autobiografie*, p. 152.

7. Once relocated to Senate House in 1947–8, a designated Low Countries Room was kept for the Seminar until 2014, when 'modernization' decreed that this space sadly had to give way to a computer training room.

8. Geyl, *Autobiografie*, p. 152.

9. Institute of Historical Research, Wohl Library: IHR/2/1/13, J. Haantjes to A. F. Pollard (15 Jan. 1926); IHR/1/1/5, IHR committee minutes (20 Jan. 1926). For details on Haantjes, see the biography in Frisian language by J. H. Brouwer, *Oantinkens oan Jacob Haantjes, 1899–1956, meast út syn briefwiksel* (Ljouwert, 1960).

10. J. B. Trapp, 'Beer, Esmond Samuel de (1895–1990)', *Oxford Dictionary of National Biography* (online, 2004): http://doi.org/10.1093/ref:odnb/39804 [accessed 1 Dec. 2022].

11. For evidence of Montgomery's scholarship, see R. Geikie, *The Dutch Barrier 1705–1719*, ed. I. Montgomery, with a memoir of the author by G. M. Trevelyan and intro. by P. Geyl (Cambridge, 1930).

12. M. C. Trevelyan, *William the Third and the Defence of Holland, 1672–4* (London, 1930). For Mary Caroline Moorman [née Trevelyan] (1905–94), see D. Cannadine, 'Trevelyan [née Ward], Janet Penrose (1879–1956)', *ODNB* (2019): http://doi.org/10 .1093/odnb/9780198614128.013.369122 [accessed 1 Dec. 2022].

13. See the biography of her son 'Douglas Oran Keir Campbell', in *Dictionary of Scottish Architects* (2016): http://www.scottisharchitects.org.uk/architect_full.php?id =403281 [accessed 8 May 2021].

14. S. T. Bindoff, *The Scheldt Question: To 1839* (London, 1945); P. Geyl, *The Netherlands Divided, 1609–1648*, transl. S. T. Bindoff (London, 1936); P. Geyl, *The Netherlands in the Seventeenth Century*, transl. S. T. Bindoff (London/New York, 1964); P. Collinson, 'Bindoff, Stanley Thomas [Tim] (1908–1980)', *ODNB* (2004): http://doi.org/10.1093/ref:odnb/58737 [accessed 1 Dec. 2022].

15. E. H. Kossmann, *Familiearchief: Notities over voorouders, tijdgenoten en mijzelf* (Amsterdam, 2003), p. 74. For a brief biography of Carter-Le Mesurier, see

Netherlands Institute for Advanced Study, Amsterdam: https://nias.knaw.nl/fellow/carter-le-mesurier-a-c/ [accessed 8 May 2021].

**16.** A. C. Carter, *The Dutch Republic in Europe in the Seven Years War* (London, 1971), p. ix.

**17.** A. Duke, '*Ik die zo weinig in mijn verleden leef ... Autobiografie 1887–1940*, by Pieter Geyl', *Dutch Crossing: Journal of Low Countries Studies*, xxxvi (2012), 88–90, at p. 88.

**18.** For more details, see R. Ensel, 'Debating Toynbee after the Holocaust: Pieter Geyl as a Post-war Public Intellectual', in *Pieter Geyl and Britain: Encounters, Controversies and Impact*, ed. S. van Rossem and U. Tiedau (London, 2022), pp. 147–63.

**19.** V. Mehta, *Fly and the Fly Bottle: Encounters with British Intellectuals* (London, 1963), p. 122. The author was a prominent journalist of the *New Yorker* magazine.

**20.** P. Geyl, 'Prof. G. J. Renier: The Dutch and the English', *The Times*, 6 Sept. 1962, p. 12.

**21.** G. Renier, *Great Britain and the Establishment of the Kingdom of the Netherlands, 1813–1815: A Study in British Foreign Policy* (London, 1930).

**22.** Geyl, 'Prof. G. J. Renier: The Dutch and the English', p. 12.

**23.** O. Renier, *Before the Bonfire* (Shipston-on-Stour, 1984), p. 131.

**24.** UCL Calendar 1934–35, p. lxix and p. 67. G. Renier, 'Dutch History in England', *Pollardian*, xvii (Spring Term, 1957), 3–4.

**25.** Geyl, *Autobiografie*, pp. 277–80. Also see P. van Hees, 'Utrecht-Londen: De briefwisseling tussen Pieter Geyl en Gustaaf Renier', *Maatstaf*, 35 (1987): 162–8.

**26.** R. Hatton, 'Professor G. J. Renier as the Leader of a Postgraduate Seminar', *Pollardian*, xvii (Spring Term, 1957), 7–8, at p. 8. See also: Renier, *Before the Bonfire*, p. 129.

**27.** Hatton, 'Professor G. J. Renier', p. 7.

**28.** Hatton, 'Professor G. J. Renier', p. 8.

**29.** *Institute of Historical Research: Twenty-fifth Annual Report 1945–46* (London, 1946), p. 13; W. G. Beasley, 'Introduction: A Personal Memoir', in *Collected Writings of W. G. Beasley* (Richmond, 2001), pp. 1–10.

**30.** O. Renier and V. Rubinstein, *Assigned to Listen: The Evesham Experience, 1939–43* (London, 1986); 'Prof. G. J. Renier: The Dutch and the English', *The Times*, 6 Sept. 1962, p. 12.

**31.** *Institute for Historical Research: Thirty-fifth Annual Report 1955–56* (London, 1957), p. 17.

**32.** Cambridge University Library (CUL) MS RCMS 240/2/4: Remarks by Dutch History Seminar (6 Apr. 1948), associated correspondence and documents in CUL MS RCMS 240/2/1–5. For more on the the de la Penha family's claim, see L. M. Freeman, *Early American Jews* (Cambridge, MA, 1934), pp. 146–51; 'Who Owns Labrador? The Historic Facts of an Unsolved Mystery', *The Knickerbocker: The Magazine of the Low Countries*, (1945), pp. 28f. The family's claims were dismissed by Canadian courts in 1927, 1950 and 1983.

**33.** Kossmann, *Familiearchief*, p. 160.

**34.** G. Renier, 'Dutch History in England', p. 4. Cf. O. Renier, *Before the Bonfire*, p. 132.

**35.** A. Lossky, 'Ragnhild Marie Hatton', *Studies in History and Politics / Études d'Histoire et de Politique* [special issue *Essays in European History in Honour of Ragnhild Hatton*, ed. K. Schweizer and J. Black], iv (1985), 13–17, at p. 13: curiously there is an account of how her interest in Low Countries history was inspired by an English cannon ball stuck in the brickwork of Bergen Cathedral, a relic of the second Anglo-Dutch war (1665–7).

**36.** A. Lossky, 'Ragnhild Marie Hatton', p. 15.

37. Institute of Historical Research, Wohl Library: IHR/2/1/418: G. J. Renier to J. G. Edwards (13 May 1954) and T. Milne to G. J. Renier (2 Jul. 1954). The request was granted by the IHR committee on 30 Jun. 1954.

38. Hatton, 'Professor G. J. Renier', pp. 7–8; quoted after Renier, *Before the Bonfire*, p. 129.

39. Lossky, 'Ragnhild Marie Hatton', p. 17.

40. H. L. Wesseling., 'Ernst Heinrich Kossmann', *Jaarboek van de Maatschappij der Nederlandse Letterkunde, 2003–2004*, 106–25, at p. 108.

41. F. R. Ankersmit, 'Ernst Kossmann, 31 Januari 1922–8 November 2003', *Levensberichten en herdenkingen 2005* (Amsterdam, 2005), pp. 66–75, at p. 69.

42. Institute of Historical Research, Wohl Library: IHR/1/1/32: IHR committee meeting minutes for 15 May 1957.

43. Kossmann, *Familiearchief*, p. 149. For details on Isabel de Madariaga, see S. Dixon, 'Madariaga, Isabel Margaret de (1919–2014)', *ODNB* (2018): http://doi.org/10.1093/odnb/9780198614128.013.108901 [accessed 1 Dec. 2022]. For details on Charles Boxer, see J. S. Cummins, 'Boxer, Charles Ralph (1904–2000)', *ODNB* (2007): http://doi.org/10.1093/ref:odnb/74008 [accessed 1 Dec. 2022].

44. Kossmann, *Familiearchief*, p. 149.

45. M. Moskalewicz, 'Sublime Experience and Politics: Interview with Professor Frank Ankersmit', *Rethinking History*, xi (2007), 251–74.

46. For the first, see J. S. Bromley and E. H. Kossmann (ed.), *Britain and the Netherlands*, intro. P. Geyl (London, 1960). Kossmann himself published widely on the theory of history, amongst other topics, but his most famous publication in English is *The Low Countries, 1780–1940* (Oxford, 1978), published in the Oxford History of Modern Europe series.

47. Kossmann, *Familiearchief*, p. 150.

48. B. Kaplan, *Reformation and the Practice of Toleration: Dutch Religious History in the Early Modern Era* (Leiden, 2019), pp. 1–26.

49. J. Israel, 'K. W. Swart: His Career as a Historian', in *William of Orange and the Revolt of the Netherlands, 1572–84*, ed. R. P. Fagel et al. (Aldershot, 2003), pp. 1–7, at p. 2.

50. M. Witlox, 'Interview met Professor K. W. Swart', *Spiegel Historiael* (Feb. 1984), p. 103, quoted after Israel, 'K. W. Swart', p. 2.

51. A. C. Carter et al. (ed.), *Historical Research in the Low Countries 1970–1975* (The Hague, 1981).

52. S. Groenveld, 'Koenraad Wolter Swart. Rotterdam 16 Oktober 1916–Wassenaar 27 Juli 1992', *Jaarboek van de Maatschappij der Nederlandse Letterkunde* (Leiden, 1993), pp. 133–8, at p. 138.

53. K. W. Swart, *Willem van Oranje en de Nederlandse opstand, 1572–84* (The Hague, 1994); K. W. Swart, *William of Orange and the Revolt of the Netherlands, 1572–84*, trans. J. C. Grayson, ed. R. P. Fagel et al., intro. chaps. A. Duke and J. Israel (Aldershot, 2003).

54. This information is drawn from the IHR's annual reports, but sometimes the reality might have been slightly different to that which was noted for the record.

55. Cf. M. Wintle, 'Research and Teaching in Dutch History in the United Kingdom: A First Survey', *Dutch Crossing: Journal of Low Countries Studies*, xiv (1990), 104–11.

56. A. F. Pollard, *Factors in Modern History* (London, 1924); cited in D. Birch and J. Horn (comp.), *The History Laboratory: The Institute of Historical Research 1921–96* (London, 1996), p. 127. See also A. Cobban, 'Small Seminars in History', *The Times, Supplement on University College London*, 3 Mar. 1965, p. ii.

57. Witlox, 'Interview met Professor K. W. Swart', quoted after Israel, 'K. W. Swart', p. 2.

# References

## Archived sources

Cambridge University Library

> MS RCMS 240/2/1–5.

Institute of Historical Research, Wohl Library

> IHR/1/1/5.
> IHR/1/1/32.
> IHR/2/1/13.
> IHR/2/1/63.
> IHR/2/1/418.

University College London, Special Collections

> *Pollardian: Journal of the History Department, University College London* (College Collection, Pers).

## Published sources

Ankersmit, F. R., 'Ernst Kossmann, 31 Januari 1922–8 November 2003', *Levensberichten en Herdenkingen 2005* (Amsterdam, 2005), pp. 66–75.

Beasley, W. G., 'Introduction: A Personal Memoir', in *Collected Writings of W. G. Beasley* (Richmond, 2001).

Bindoff, S. T., *The Scheldt Question: To 1839* (London, 1945).

Birch, D., and Horn, J. (comp.), *The History Laboratory: The Institute of Historical Research 1921–96* (London, 1996).

Bromley, J. S., and Kossmann, E. H. (ed.), *Britain and the Netherlands*, intro. P. Geyl (London, 1960).

Brouwer, J. H., *Oantinkens oan Jacob Haantjes, 1899–1956, Meast út syn Briefwiksel* (Ljouwert, 1960).

Cannadine, D., 'Trevelyan [née Ward], Janet Penrose (1879–1956)', *Oxford Dictionary of National Biography* (2019): http://doi.org/10.1093/odnb /9780198614128.013.369122 [accessed 1 Dec. 2022].

Carter, A. C., *The Dutch Republic in Europe in the Seven Years War* (London, 1971).

Carter, A. C. et al. (ed.), *Historical Research in the Low Countries 1970–1975* (The Hague, 1981).

Cobban, A., 'Small Seminars in History', *The Times, Supplement on University College London*, 3 March 1965.

Collinson, P., 'Bindoff, Stanley Thomas [Tim] (1908–1980)', *Oxford Dictionary of National Biography* (2004): http://doi.org/10.1093/ref:odnb/58737 [accessed 1 Dec. 2022].

Cummins, J. S., 'Boxer, Charles Ralph (1904–2000)', *Oxford Dictionary of National Biography* (2007): http://doi.org/10.1093/ref:odnb/74008 [accessed 1 Dec. 2022].

Dixon, S., 'Madariaga, Isabel Margaret de (1919–2014)', *Oxford Dictionary of National Biography* (2018): http://doi.org/10.1093/odnb/9780198614128.013.108901 [accessed 1 Dec. 2022].

'Douglas Oran Keir Campbell', in *Dictionary of Scottish Architects* (2016): http://www.scottisharchitects.org.uk/architect_full.php?id=403281 [accessed 8 May 2021].

Duke, A., '*Ik Die zo Weinig in Mijn Verleden Leef ... Autobiografie 1887–1940*, by Pieter Geyl' [book review], *Dutch Crossing: Journal of Low Countries Studies*, xxxvi (2012), 88–90.

Ensel, R., 'Debating Toynbee after the Holocaust: Pieter Geyl as a Post-war Public Intellectual', in *Pieter Geyl and Britain: Encounters, Controversies and Impact*, ed. S. van Rossem and U. Tiedau (London, 2022), pp. 147–63.

Freeman, L. M., *Early American Jews* (Cambridge, MA, 1934), pp. 146–51.

Geikie, R., *The Dutch Barrier 1705–1719*, ed. I. Montgomery, with a Memoir of the Author by G. M. Trevelyan and intro. by P. Geyl (Cambridge, 1930).

Geyl, P., *The Netherlands Divided, 1609–1648*, transl. S. T. Bindoff (London, 1936).

Geyl, P., 'Prof. G. J. Renier: The Dutch and the English', *The Times*, 6 September 1962.

Geyl, P., *The Netherlands in the Seventeenth Century*, transl. S. T. Bindoff (London, 1964).

Geyl, P., *Ik Die Zo Weinig In Mijn Verleden Leef: Autobiografie 1887–1940*, ed. W. Berkelaar, L. Dorsman and P. van Hees (Amsterdam, 2009).

Groenveld, S., 'Koenraad Wolter Swart. Rotterdam 16 Oktober 1916–Wassenaar 27 Juli 1992', *Jaarboek van de Maatschappij der Nederlandse Letterkunde* (Leiden, 1993), pp. 133–8.

Harting Scheme: https://hartingscheme.wordpress.com/history-of-the-scheme/ [accessed 21 Dec. 2021].

Hatton, R., 'Professor G. J. Renier as the Leader of a Postgraduate Seminar', *Pollardian*, xvii (Spring Term, 1957), 7–8.

Hees, P. van, 'Utrecht-Londen: De briefwisseling tussen Pieter Geyl en Gustaaf Renier', *Maatstaf*, 35 (1987): 162–8.

*Institute of Historical Research: Twenty-fifth Annual Report 1945–46*
(London, 1946).

*Institute for Historical Research: Thirty-fifth Annual Report 1955–56*
(London, 1957).

Israel, J., 'K. W. Swart: His Career as a Historian', in *William of Orange and the Revolt of the Netherlands, 1572–84,* ed. R. P. Fagel et al. (Aldershot, 2003), pp. 1–7.

Kaplan, B., *Reformation and the Practice of Toleration: Dutch Religious History in the Early Modern Era* (Leiden, 2019).

Kossmann, E. H., *The Low Countries, 1780–1940* (Oxford, 1978).

Kossmann, E. H., *Familiearchief: Notities over Voorouders, Tijdgenoten en Mijzelf* (Amsterdam, 2003).

Lossky, A., 'Ragnhild Marie Hatton', *Studies in History and Politics / Etudes d'Histoire et de Politique* [special issue *Essays in European History in Honour of Ragnhild Hatton*, ed. K. Schweizer and J. Black], iv (1985), 13–17.

Mehta, V., *Fly and the Fly Bottle: Encounters with British Intellectuals* (London, 1963).

Moskalewicz, M., 'Sublime Experience and Politics: Interview with Professor Frank Ankersmit', *Rethinking History*, xi (2007), 251–74.

Netherlands Institute for Advanced Study, Amsterdam: https://nias .knaw.nl/fellow/carter-le-mesurier-a-c/ [accessed 8 May 2021].

Pollard, A. F., *Factors in Modern History* (London, 1924).

'Prof. G. J. Renier: The Dutch and the English', *The Times*, 6 September 1962.

Renier, G., *Great Britain and the Establishment of the Kingdom of the Netherlands, 1813–1815: A Study in British Foreign Policy* (London, 1930).

Renier, G., 'Dutch History in England', *Pollardian*, xvii (Spring Term, 1957), 3–4.

Renier, O., *Before the Bonfire* (Shipston-on-Stour, 1984).

Renier, O., and Rubinstein, V., *Assigned to Listen: The Evesham Experience, 1939–43* (London, 1986).

Rossem, S. van, and Tiedau, U. (ed.), *Pieter Geyl and Britain: Encounters, Controversies and Impact* (London, 2022): http://doi.org/10.14296 /vfsr7023 [accessed 20 Dec. 2022].

Swart, K. W., *Willem van Oranje en de Nederlandse opstand, 1572–84* (The Hague, 1994).

Swart, K. W., *William of Orange and the Revolt of the Netherlands, 1572–84,* trans. J. C. Grayson, ed. R. P. Fagel et al., intro. chaps. A. Duke and J. Israel (Aldershot, 2003).

Thompson, M., '"Making History": A Short History of the Institute of Historical Research' (2008): https://archives.history.ac.uk /makinghistory/resources/articles/IHR.html [accessed 10 Nov. 2020].

Trapp, J. B., 'Beer, Esmond Samuel de (1895–1990)', *Oxford Dictionary of National Biography* (Online, 2004): http://doi.org/10.1093/ref:odnb/39804 [accessed 1 Dec. 2022].

Trevelyan, M. C., *William the Third and the Defence of Holland, 1672–4* (London, 1930).

Wesseling, H. L., 'Ernst Heinrich Kossmann', *Jaarboek van de Maatschappij der Nederlandse Letterkunde, 2003–2004*, 106–25.

'Who Owns Labrador? The Historic Facts of an Unsolved Mystery', *The Knickerbocker: The Magazine of the Low Countries*, iv (1945), 28–9.

Wintle, M., 'Research and Teaching in Dutch History in the United Kingdom: A First Survey', *Dutch Crossing: Journal of Low Countries Studies*, xiv (1990), 104–11.

Witlox, M., 'Interview met Professor K. W. Swart', *Spiegel Historiael* (February 1984).

Chapter 7

# The Modern French History Seminar

## Pamela Pilbeam* with David Manning

During the academic year of 1912–13, the University of London made use of grants allocated to it by the London County Council (LCC) to endow a chair in French history and institutions.[1] Exactly how, when and why this happened may be unclear, but the initiative reflected an intellectual culture that had seen the founding of the University of London Institute in Paris (1894) and the Institut Français du Royaume-Uni (1910), set against wider social, political and diplomatic contexts associated with not just a burgeoning of the 'French colony' in London but the increasing stability of the French Third Republic (1871–1941) and the start of the *Entente cordiale* (1904).[2] The new professorship – the first of its kind in Britain – carried with it teaching responsibilities at University College and the London School of Economics. It was taken up first in 1913 by the prominent economic historian Paul Mantoux (1877–1956). His tenure was, however, short-lived. Having served as a translator for Franco-British diplomatic meetings during the First World War, Mantoux moved in 1921 to a position at the League of Nations Secretariat and became the first director of the Graduate Institute of International Studies, Geneva (est. 1927).[3] He was succeeded in the following year by Paul Vaucher (1887–1966), a noted authority on eighteenth-century English and French history, and a protégé of the historian Émile Bourgeois (1857–1934) and the philosopher-historian Élie Halévy (1870–1937), who had introduced Vaucher to the Fabian-socialist milieu of Sidney Webb and R. H. Tawney.[4] It was Vaucher, then listed as a teacher at the LSE, who held the first Modern French History Seminar during the 1923–4 session. This was the start of a series of intermittent and sparsely attended meetings between 1923 and 1929. Although it is not certain where Vaucher's early seminars were held nor how many people attended, we do know that they were held under the auspices of the Institute of Historical Research. The records mention just two students who were present at the very beginning: Jean Brookes, a visiting doctoral researcher from the University of Chicago working on the nineteenth-century Anglo-French rivalry in the Pacific Islands, and Mildred Whibley, formerly of the London Day Training College, who was preparing an MA at UCL with a thesis on mid-nineteenth-century Anglo-Sardinian relations.[5] After taking parts of both the history and law tripos at Girton College, Cambridge, Rosamund White became Vaucher's first MA student and possibly the only seminar attendee during the 1924–5 session. By 1928–9, the Seminar had its first doctoral researcher, Agnes King, who in 1931 completed a thesis, on the 'relations of the British government with the émigrés and royalists of western France, 1793–5'.[6] After the 1930–31 session, Vaucher stopped convening the Seminar, possibly for health reasons. However, while increasingly absent from London, he presumably stayed on as professor until moving to the Sorbonne in 1945.

## Alfred Cobban's Seminar

The first regular seminar series in modern French history commenced in 1947–8 under the stewardship of Alfred Cobban (1901–68).[7] Cobban was an Englishman who had obtained a PhD in history from the University of Cambridge in 1926. Up to that point, Cobban could be considered as much a political philosopher as an historian: his doctoral thesis focused on Edmund Burke; but from this it was not too much of a leap to Jean-Jacques Rousseau and the French Revolution.[8] Cobban was a secular liberal who joined the Fabians in 1920 while an undergraduate. He was first a lecturer at the University of Newcastle and moved in 1937 to become reader in French history at UCL,[9] where he was promoted to professor in 1953 and remained until his death in 1968. The import and scope of Cobban's academic work can hardly be underestimated; it has recently been the subject of a forum discussion in *French History*.[10] His most notable intervention came from his inaugural lecture, 'The Myth of the French Revolution' (1954, publ. 1955), given in the presence of René Massigli, the French ambassador to Britain. Out of it grew *The Social Interpretation of the French Revolution*, presented first for the 1962 Wiles Lectures at the Queen's University Belfast, and then published in 1964 as a book, which rapidly became 'the handbook of revisionism for a new generation of Anglo-Saxon scholars'.[11] Cobban's rejection of an established French-Marxist interpretation of the Revolution provoked historians such as George Lefebvre (1874–1959) and Albert Soboul (1914–82) into controversy.[12] More generally,

Cobban's fifteen books – including the *History of Modern France* (published by Penguin in three volumes, 1957–65) – and numerous scholarly articles made him the most respected and influential English-language historian of modern France in his generation.[13] From 1957 to 1967 he was editor of *History: The Journal of the Historical Association*, and he also contributed to the Historical Association Pamphlets series which inspired a generation of school students and their teachers.[14] In addition to convening the Seminar at the IHR, his presence was widely felt within the University of London: most significantly as head of the history department at UCL between 1961 and 1966.[15]

Cobban was also a devoted teacher. He ran an undergraduate special subject on the French Revolution at UCL and convened the IHR's Modern French History Seminar, usually once a week during term time on Monday evenings from 1947 to 1967. During this period, the Seminar was first and foremost concerned with training doctoral students, who typically never missed a meeting unless they were out of the country doing archival research in France. Cobban assumed that his students had a good working knowledge of the French language, and that they would be doing research in French archives, so they were expected to spend at least a year in France. The Seminar met in the 'France Room' at IHR, where the bookshelves were filled, floor to ceiling, with volumes on French sources. Cobban's students considered this area their own, frequently used the splendid collection of documents it contained and felt intruded upon when students with other interests wandered in to do their own work there. Seminars consisted of sessions on preparing the doctoral thesis and historical methodology, papers by those who had recently completed their doctoral studies, other scholars teaching at the University of London, and occasionally people from farther afield like Richard Cobb (1917–96), a doctoral student of Lefebvre who became professor of modern history at Oxford in 1972 – and, of course, student presentations.[16] Research students had to make regular progress reports to the group, which could become a terrifying prospect; and anyone near completion or recently examined would be invited to give a full-length paper. Cobban himself would also regularly give a presentation on recent research in French history, and all attendees busily took notes. At some point, presumably in the late 1950s or early 1960s, a tradition developed whereby seminar members, although never Cobban himself, would often retire to a modestly priced, but often excellent, restaurant; there was, for example, Kwai's, a Chinese establishment nearby on Tottenham Court Road, as well as the Spaghetti House on Goodge Street and Schmidt's on Charlotte Street.[17] These outings, as well as visits to nearby pubs, helped seminar members share ideas and form life-long bonds just as much as the seminars themselves. After the last seminar of the academic year, students would be invited for a delightful supper, cooked by Cobban's wife Muriel (1906–88/9) at the couple's flat in Bayswater. Cobban's Seminar was later remembered by one of his students as 'an inspiring occasion' where fellow learners 'enjoyed his warmth and humour as well as the originality of his thought'; the discussion, it was noted, 'often saved us from losing our way in insignificant detail or vague speculation, for through those years Alfred Cobban never failed to teach that research must serve intellectual purposes and general ideas must be tested by research'.[18]

Many of Cobban's doctoral students went on to become significant scholars.[19] The most academically outstanding of his first recruits, George Rudé (1910–93), enjoyed a remarkable career.[20] The Norwegian-born Rude – the accented surname Rudé was not adopted until around 1953 – came to history as both a 'mature student' and as a member of the British Communist Party, while teaching modern languages at St Paul's School, a task for which he had been prepared by a BA in French and German from Trinity College, Cambridge. His fascination with the past then drove him to study for a BA (1948) and then a PhD (1950) in history from the University of London. Rudé's activity as a Party member was such that he was forced to resign from St Paul's, but he found a conditional intellectual ally in Cobban and common cause with the London-based Historians' Group of the Communist Party of Great Britain. A heavily revised version of his doctoral thesis was published by Oxford University's Clarendon Press as *The Crowd in the French Revolution* (1959): a work that was prefaced with dutiful thanks to Cobban 'for his help and guidance over a number of years' and yet tellingly dedicated to Cobban's critic and Rudé's friend and collaborator George Lefebvre.[21] Rudé benefitted from both Cobban's supervisions and seminars, but Cobban briefly excluded him from attending the Seminar after he refused to condemn the Soviet occupation of Hungary in 1956 (the two later made up their differences). Throughout the 1950s, Rudé's politics may have hindered him from securing employment at a British university, though jobs of any kind in French history were not abundant at that time. Nearing the age of fifty, he finally started his academic career in 'exile', as senior lecturer at the University of Adelaide, Australia. Except for an aborted appointment to a chair at the newly founded University of Stirling, Scotland, Rudé cultivated his reputation as one of the leading social historians of his generation overseas at the Universities of Adelaide and Flinders, and then latterly in Canada at Sir George Williams (now Concordia) University, from 1970 until his retirement in 1987. Despite all these difficulties, Cobban always acknowledged Rudé's exceptional scholarship; and, for his part, Rudé contributed to the memorial volume of essays dedicated to his supervisor.

Cobban gained a strong following amongst young Canadian scholars. The prestige of his London chair and his reputation as an historian of ideas had an allure. However, when Cobban visited the USA in the late 1940s and 1950s it was evident that leading American scholars of French history, such as Leo Gershoy (1897–1975), R. R. Palmer (1909–2002), and Crane Brinton (1898–1968), worked largely within an historiographical tradition established by specialists in France, most notably the towering figure of Georges Lefebvre. Appropriately, the 1958 first issue of the US-based *French Historical Studies* was dedicated to Lefebvre and included a printed version of his patriotic words that 'praised Robespierre as the great historical defender of democracy'.[22] But Cobban was a little younger than most of his American counterparts, and much younger than the octogenarian Lefebvre. Cobban's work therefore signalled something of a changing of the guard, beginning with the publication of his widely read *History of Modern France* (1957), and followed by his bold attempt (described above) to question and recast the very terms in which the history of the Revolution had hitherto been written. By the late 1950s, it was becoming increasingly clear to Canadians and others that to study with Cobban was to work with the leading English-language specialist in the field.

The experience of one of his earliest Canadian students, John Bosher (1929–2020), illustrates this attraction. Having obtained a BA in history from the University of British Columbia (UBC) in 1950, Bosher found his way to London a couple of years later on honeymoon, but also used the trip to strike up an acquaintance with Professor S. T. Bindoff (1908–80), a prime mover within both the University of London and the IHR during the 1950s, with whom he had previously corresponded about undertaking postgraduate study. Bindoff recommended his friend and colleague 'Cobby' as a supervisor and the two conspired first to send their young charge to the Sorbonne to prepare a *diplôme d'études supérieures* (DES, the equivalent of an MA by thesis) with Vaucher and the celebrated historian of medieval England, Edmond Perroy (1901–74). Bosher then returned to London to undertake a PhD, duly completed in 1957 with a thesis entitled 'The Movement for Internal Free Trade in France during the Eighteenth Century'.[23] The department of history at UBC presently offered Bosher a position and he, along with his wife and children, returned to Canada. As a university teacher, Bosher helped foster an interest in French history amongst the next generation of students at UBC, among them Tim Le Goff and Fred Affleck, whom he encouraged to undertake postgraduate study under Cobban's supervision.[24]

The academic appeal of studying under Cobban was also enhanced for Canadian students by institutional factors. The specialization of the Canadian BA in history lent itself to moving straight on to research training in a way that was more suited to the postgraduate offerings in England than America. By the 1960s, Canadians could draw upon not only the collective example and experience of former students who had already prepared their doctorates in London but also more credible financial support, notably from the Canada Council and the Commonwealth Scholarship Programme.[25] By 1966–7, the membership of Cobban's Seminar included no less than six Canadians, several of whom became close friends: there was Le Goff (PhD 1970, professor emeritus at York University, Toronto); Edward Whitcomb (PhD, 1970, sometime university teacher, civil servant, and, in retirement, writer on Canadian music and provincial history); Fred Affleck (PhD 1972, retired after a career as an Australian civil servant, railway executive, and holder of a university chair in Transport Economics at the University of Western Australia); Glennis Parry (former civil servant and Canadian media executive); John Robinson (retired diplomat and former Canadian High Commissioner to Jamaica); and D. M. G. Sutherland (PhD 1974, professor emeritus at the University of Maryland).

And, of course, Cobban attracted British students, including some who had first attended his special subject and option courses in French history as undergraduates. Cobban was both discerning and responsible in his choice of postgraduate students. Pamela Pilbeam recalled how, when he accepted her for postgraduate study in 1962, he encouraged Richard Sims, another former undergraduate from his special subject group, to work on Franco-Japanese relations. This ensured that Cobban could devote his time and expertise to Pilbeam whilst also seeking to do the best for Sims, who went on to complete his PhD in 1968 and pursue a distinguished academic career at SOAS. Cobban also drew students from Cambridge, including Keith Baker (London PhD 1964), J. E. Wallace Sterling professor in humanities at Stanford University, Julian Dent (1957–2020: London PhD 1965), formerly emeritus professor at the University of Toronto; and Roger Mettam (1939–2022: Cambridge PhD 1967), whom Cobban supervised, presumably as an external candidate.[26] A specialist in the seventeenth century, Roger had a significant career at Queen Mary College and served with distinction for many years as co-convenor of the Early Modern European History Seminar at the IHR.

Women constituted another noticeable group in Cobban's Seminar. Cobban tried his best to advance women in university careers, particularly women from less advantaged backgrounds; this was a time when only around 6 per cent, or less, of the A-level cohort went on to university. Among them were Nicola Sutherland (b. 1925: PhD 1958, retired from the chair of modern history at Royal Holloway in 1987), Olwen Hufton (b. 1938: PhD 1961–2, emeritus fellow Merton College, Oxford), and Pamela Pilbeam (née Cartlidge; PhD 1966, professor emeritus in French history at Royal Holloway).[27] The most illustrious was Hufton, a grammar-school girl raised on a council estate. Hufton's revised doctoral thesis was published by Oxford's Clarendon Press as *Bayeux in the Late Eighteenth Century: A Social History* (1967); the last words of the preface gave thanks to her 'friends in the seminar of French History at the University of London who discussed with me many of the themes treated here and to whom my debt is great'.[28] Hufton soon began to develop these and other ideas in a series of pioneering and widely read works on French and European history, such as *The Poor of Eighteenth-Century France* (1974), and *The Prospect Before Her: A History of Women in Western Europe* (1995). She went on to hold chairs at the European University Institute, Harvard and Oxford; she is also Dame Commander of the British Empire (2004).

In the final years of Cobban's life, his Seminar started to become a more 'varied group' comprising not just his latest 'students but also several former students or current colleagues who had teaching jobs in or around London ... and others from more distant UK universities ... but we got along well when we were together in the seminar and afterwards in the pub'.[29]

## Transitions

Cobban's successor to the chair of French history at UCL was Douglas Johnson (1925–2005), previously professor of modern history at Birmingham and then mainly known for his 1963 study of the nineteenth-century French historian, political thinker and politician François Guizot (1787–1874).[30] A graduate of Worcester College, Oxford, Johnson found both an aptitude for French history and his future wife, Madeleine Rébillard, while studying in Paris at the École Normale Supérieure (ENS) in the late 1940s. His academic credits included *The French Revolution* (1970), *Michelet and the French Revolution* (1990) and the editorship of the *Fontana History of Modern France*; but by the late 1970s he was also a central figure of the Franco-British Council (established in 1972 by a joint initiative of President Georges Pompidou and Prime Minister Edward Heath) and a notable commentator and journalist writing regularly for the right-of-centre *Spectator*. Indeed, he even became Margaret Thatcher's advisor on France when she was prime minister.[31] Although Johnson was almost as discreet about his own politics in academic company as Cobban had been, he believed firmly that leading academics ought to be public intellectuals, a view that resonated especially well in France. His dual commitment to French history and intellectual life were duly recognized by the French government, which made him a *Chevalier* of the Legion of Honour in 1978, raised later to the rank of *Officier* in 1997.

Johnson managed Cobban's remaining doctoral students through to completion and took the lead in running the Modern French History Seminar from 1968 onwards.[32] The Seminar had already begun to broaden in scope during Cobban's last years, with papers by more visiting scholars than previously. Under Johnson's direction this process continued, and the Seminar became a more broadly based research forum for working historians of France at all stages of their research and careers. Johnson frequently invited distinguished French colleagues, often also friends of his, to give papers. Among the first was Annie Kriegel (1925–95), who had been active in the Jewish-Communist Resistance and then the French Communist Party, later becoming a leading student of French Communism (her thesis, *Aux origines du communisme français, 1914–1920* was published in 1964), though she eventually rejected the Party itself; by the early 1970s she had come to be associated with Raymond Aron's circle and wrote columns for the right-leaning *Le Figaro*.[33] Douglas had first met Kriegel in 1949 when Rébillard shared a room with her at the women's ENS. He later took delight in saying that in those days Kriegel used to sleep with an AK-47 rifle at the head of her bed. When Kriegel spoke at the IHR, she did so to an eager audience in the France Room; alas, there was no sign of the Kalashnikov.

Douglas further enhanced the Seminar's scope by encouraging members of the Institut Français du Royaume-Uni (IFRU) to attend its meetings at the IHR, an invitation to which they responded enthusiastically. The expansion of the British university sector in the 1960s also furnished the IHR with new possibilities. The Universities of York and Sussex soon acquired distinguished historians of France, and Rod Kedward (b. 1937) at Sussex established a close working relationship with the Seminar. Through such endeavours the group expanded from about fourteen attendees to as many as thirty on some occasions.

After 1975, Johnson withdrew as an active seminar organizer, but it was agreed that his name could remain as a convenor. Pamela Pilbeam – a former doctoral student of Cobban, long-serving member of the Seminar, and lecturer at Bedford College since 1965 – took the lead in planning programmes, which she did a year in advance, in consultation with other members. She established new contacts and firmed up invitations by letters and phone calls, an onerous task in those days, now much simplified by today's online communications. Outside speakers who had made a notable contribution to French history were invited to give papers, although preference was given to academics and doctoral students at the University of London and other regular seminar members. Now very much a research group, the Seminar met regularly about ten or twelve times, mainly in the first and second terms of the academic year, with the sessions now almost exclusively given over to presenting research papers. In the early 1980s, specialists in pre-1789 history, notably Nicola Sutherland and Roger Mettam, moved to the IHR's Early Modern European History Seminar, although joint meetings between the two seminars were subsequently held for appropriate topics. Through much of the 1980s and 1990s, Pilbeam worked tirelessly to keep the Seminar going despite the increasing demands of her own developing academic career; fortunately, however, she was able to share the burden latterly with Tom Gretton, lecturer in the history of art department, and Rebecca Spang, lecturer in history department, at UCL. Both were members of the Seminar's organizing committee at various points. Pilbeam also revived the tradition of inviting everyone for a meal at the end of the academic year, and recalls her daughter Ashka commenting, after handing round drinks at one large gathering, that there was *even* one handsome *young* man (Julian Swann, now professor of history at Birkbeck) in attendance.

## Anglo-French collaborations

In 1998 Geraldine d'Amico, cultural attaché at the French Embassy and the London IFRU, helped organize a very advantageous arrangement that brought several fully funded speakers from France to deliver papers at the IHR. This led to the Modern French History Seminar being jointly run for a time by the IHR and the IFRU.[34] This magnificent and unusual opportunity served a mutual benefit, for the French were keen to have their scholarly pre-eminence recognized more widely while British specialists in French history and culture made the most of learning from and engaging with their French counterparts. These links were also made more immediate and frequent by the recent (1994) opening of the Eurostar rapid train service through the new channel tunnel. In 1998, French guests included Maurice Agulhon (1926–2014), recently retired from his chair at the Collège de France and just appointed Officer of the Legion of Honour, who spoke on 'De Gaulle et la symbolique nationale de la France'.[35] In 1999 the Seminar heard the renowned historian of nineteenth-century French society Alain Corbin (b. 1936) present his 'Réflexions sur le paysage sonore parisien au XIXème siècle'.[36] He was followed in 2000 by Odile Krakovitch, head archivist at the Archives Nationales, on 'La Repression des imprimeurs sous Napoleon'; in the same year Pascal Dupuy, from Université de Rouen, addressed a combined seminar meeting at the IFRU on 'History and Films: Methods and New Approaches'. In 2001, the Seminar heard from Jean-François Sirinelli, professor at the Institut d'Études Politiques de Paris (Sciences Po). This highly prestigious and beneficial arrangement lasted into 2003–4, when Hervé Ferrage was cultural attaché. The last meeting held in this format featured Professor Jean-Pierre Azéma who filled the IFRU cinema with an expectant audience for a talk about Vichy France; Azéma delivered an excellent public lecture, but the event was not really a seminar.

The demise of the joint seminar series was symptomatic of a broader change in the French government's cultural policy. French decision-makers lost interest in bringing researchers to London to talk about their special research, and seminars ceased to be subsidized; they now wanted events that could attract *le grand public*. In another sign of the times, the IFRU's library in London was made to remove research works considered of no interest to the general public, and instead fill its shelves with magazines. Films now took precedence over talks. Yet the fact that the French government had been willing for a number of years to fund visits by French researchers chosen by the Seminar organizers indicates the strong reputation of the IHR and the recognition of history as a worthy subject of enquiry. Equally impressive was the willingness of senior French academics and archivists to come and speak, and the way in which interested parties from other institutions such as the British Library were able to use the IHR Seminar to establish personal contact with their counterparts in France. And the link between the IFRU and academic history continues with occasional lectures, most notably the annual Douglas Johnson Memorial (est. 2010), which in 2023 was co-organized by the Society for the Study of French History and the Association for the Study of Modern and Contemporary France and hosted at the London IFRU.[37]

For two academic years, 2004–6, the Modern French History Seminar, in association with the IHR's Europe from 1500–1800 Seminar (convened by Roger Mettam) and the Medieval France Seminar (convened by Jinty Nelson), entered a joint arrangement with Université Paris IV Sorbonne, the British Institute in Paris, and the Vice-Chancellor's Development Fund. Speakers from Paris IV came to speak at IHR and in return IHR members went to speak at Paris IV. The establishment of this Seminaire d'Histoire Franco-Britannique contributed greatly to raising the profile of the IHR, not just in Paris but within France as a whole. It enabled the participating seminars to invite rising young researchers to take part in their proceedings and made it possible for British and French scholars to develop dynamic reciprocal relations. Through this collaboration, the Modern French History Seminar welcomed Fabrice Bensimon from

Paris-X, François Poirier from Paris-XIII, Eric Fassin of the ENS and the École des Hautes Études en Sciences Sociales, and Tim Le Goff, then at Paris-Sorbonne.

## Renewal

Between the early 2000s and the present, the organization, format and intellectual scope of the Seminar have changed considerably, and continue to do so. At the same time, younger generations of scholars have come to assume leadership roles.

Through the late twentieth century, the Seminar had functioned with a leading convenor, Pamela Pilbeam, supported by an organizing committee that by 2004 included Julian Jackson (Queen Mary), Rebecca Spang (UCL), Geraldine d'Amico (IFRU) and Debra Kelly (Westminster); they were joined in 2006 by two other senior colleagues from Queen Mary, Jeremy Jennings and Colin Jones, the latter replacing Pilbeam as the main convenor. But gradually the Seminar's organization became collective in nature and by 2022 the committee consisted of a dozen members: Venus Bivar (University of York), Ludivine Broch (Westminster), James Connolly (UCL), Alison Carrol (Brunel), Charlotte Faucher (Sorbonne Nouvelle), Julian Jackson (Queen Mary), Colin Jones (Queen Mary), Daniel Lee (Queen Mary), Tyson Leuchter (King's College), Julia Nicholls (King's College), Robert B. Priest (Royal Holloway) and Andrew W. M. Smith (Chichester).

In the early 2000s, doctoral students in the final stages of their theses were still encouraged to give full-length seminar papers. After about 2006, however, this practice became rarer as doctoral students began to deliver shorter talks. Another innovation saw authors of recent scholarly publications introduce their work, followed by a group discussion. These formats proved especially popular when the Seminar had to move online during the COVID-19 pandemic. An online book launch of Natalya Vince's *The Algerian War, The Algerian Revolution* (2020) hosted by the Seminar in February 2021 attracted 140 participants, many of them North Americans and affiliates of the Society for French Historical Studies. The new online format has made possible a much larger, and indeed global, sense of group participation. However, the advantages of the traditional in-person format will be hard to replace: to take just one example, Andrew Smith recalled how in 2016 he had profited within the brief moments between the formal seminar discussion and the ensuing socializing to get candid but constructive support for a draft book manuscript from one Pamela Pilbeam.[38]

In recent times, the subject matter of the Seminar has also broadened, following the increasing interest in the French Empire and the Francosphere, as can be readily seen by looking up the collection of select summaries and recordings of past papers at the Seminar on the French History Network blog.[39] Until twenty or so years ago, scholars could write about the history of France with perhaps only a passing mention of colonization and/or decolonization. Yet, in January 2021, the Seminar held a full debate on Pan-Africanism. Now, the Seminar 'welcomes a range of scholarship on France, its empire, and its people from the French Revolution to today', considering a 'spectrum of approaches ... from political history to environmental history, comparative studies to interdisciplinary reflections'.[40] These developments encapsulate the dynamism and respect that the Modern French History Seminar has retained throughout its nearly century-old existence; they also hint at even more and better offerings in the decades to come.

# Notes

\* Grateful thanks to Clive Church (who sadly died in December 2021, aged 82), Negley Harte, Malcolm Crook, Julian Jackson, Rebecca Spang and Tim Le Goff for reading, commenting upon and helping to improve this chapter.

1. *University of London: The Historical Record (1836–1912), being a Supplement to the Calendar Completed to September 1912* (London, 1912), pp. 181–2.

2. For further context, see M. Rapoport, 'The London French from the Belle Epoque to the End of the Inter-War Period (1880–1939)' and C. Faucher and P. Lane, 'French Cultural Diplomacy in Early Twentieth-Century London', in *A History of the French in London: Liberty, Equality, Opportunity*, ed. D. Kelly and M. Cornick (London, 2013), pp. 241–80 and 281–302; G. Banner, 'The Early Years: A Department in the Making, 1895–1920', in *Political Science at the LSE: A History of the Department of Government, from the Webbs to Covid*, ed. C. Schonhardt-Bailey and G. Bannerman (London, 2021), pp. 21–52; R. Dahrendorf, *LSE: A History of the London School of Economics and Political Science 1895–1995* (Oxford, 1995), pp. 72–134; and N. Harte, *The University of London 1836–1986: An Illustrated History* (London, 1986), pp. 162–213, esp. p. 180.

3. Paul Mantoux graduated DLitt. from Paris in 1905. His thesis, which was extensively researched and written in England, was published as *La Révolution Industrielle au XVIIIe Siècle* (1906, English trans. 1927). In 1910, he was appointed professor at *École des Hautes Études Commerciales de Paris*. For wider context, see P. D. Boer, *History as a Profession: The Study of History in France, 1818–1914*, trans. A. Pomerans (Princeton, 1988), pp. 309–57. For the history of the Graduate Institute of International Studies, see https://www.graduateinstitute.ch/sites/internet/files/2020-12/Book_90years_Institute_web.pdf [accessed 1 Nov. 2022].

4. J. Rule, 'Paul Vaucher: Historian', *French Historical Studies*, iv (1967), 98–105. For more on the complex and idiosyncratic figure of Halévy, see S. Vincent, *Élie Halévy: Republican Liberalism Confronts the Era of Tyranny* (Philadelphia, 2020).

5. Institute of Historical Research, Wohl Library: IHR 3/3/21, f. 21; *Institute of Historical Research: Third Annual Report 1923–1924* (London, 1925), p. 7; G. G. Coulton et al., 'University Research, Session 1923–24', *History*, ix (1925), 361.

6. Rosamund White went on to write several history textbooks for the Macmillan's Senior School Series, edited by F. W. Chambers, sometime HM Inspector of Schools and presumably a relative of Rosamund's husband, G. A. Chambers. Under her married name, Rosamund also published a serious work of historical fiction that dealt with the 'first five years of the married life of Napoleon and Josephine, from Josephine's point of view', based upon 'extensive reading in a great variety of sources' and quoting directly from 'Napoleon's letters': see R. Chambers, *Little Creole: A Story of Napoleon and Josephine* (London, 1952), p. 7.

7. O. Hufton, 'Alfred Bert Carter Cobban', *Oxford Dictionary of National Biography* (online, 2007): https://doi.org/10.1093/ref:odnb/56344 [accessed 1 Nov. 2022]. This is now largely superseded by the 2020 forum discussion in *French History*, see below.

8. P. Pilbeam, 'The Impact of Alfred Cobban on approaches to 1789' [Conference Paper], *H-France Salon*, xii (online, 2020): https://www.youtube.com/watch?v=Bkgijuo_pmI [accessed 1 Nov. 2022].

9. P. Pilbeam, 'A Liberal Voice and a Fabian: Alfred Cobban', *La Révolution Française*, xxiii (online, 2022): https://doi.org/10.4000/lrf.6819 [accessed 1 Nov. 2022].

10. M. Crook et al., 'Forum: The Legacy of Alfred Cobban', *French History*, xxxiv (2020), 512–60.

11. G. Lewis, 'Introduction', in A. Cobban, *The Social Interpretation of the French Revolution*, second edition (Cambridge, 1999), pp. xiii–xlix at p. xiv.

12. C. Behrens, 'Professor Cobban and His Critics', *Historical Journal*, ix (1966), 236–41.

13. For a bibliography of Cobban's main writings, see J. F. Bosher (ed.), *French Government and Society 1500–1850: Essays in Memory of Alfred Cobban*, (London, 1973), pp. xv–xviii.

14. A. Cobban, *Historians and the Causes of the French Revolution* (London, 1946). This work was then superseded in the Historical Association Pamphlet series by G. Rudé, *Interpretations of the French Revolution* (London, 1961).

15. For further details, see P. Pilbeam, 'Alfred Cobban, His Writing and His Teaching', in 'Forum', *French History*, 519–30. See, also V. Wedgwood, 'Alfred Cobban (1901–1968)', in *French Government and Society 1500–1850: Essays in Memory of Alfred Cobban*, ed. J. F. Bosher (London, 1973), pp. xi–xiv.

16. For Cobb's own illuminating memoir, see his 'Introduction: Experiences of an Anglo-French Historian', in R. Cobb, *A Second Identity: Essays on France and French History* (London, 1969), pp. 1–50.

17. Amongst the student community, Schmidt's had a reputation for its surly German waiters – reflecting something of the culture of the time, UCL undergraduates once joked that 'Martin Bormann is alive and well and working in Schmidt's'.

18. J. F. Bosher, 'Preface', in *French Government and Society 1500–1850: Essays in Memory of Alfred Cobban*, p. v.

19. For an annotated list of Cobban's doctoral students, see 'Forum', *French History*, 559–60.

20. J. Friguglietti, 'Rudé, George Frederick Elliot (1910–1993)', *ODNB* (2004): https://doi.org/10.1093/ref:odnb/53299 [accessed 1 Nov. 2022]; D. Munro, 'The Strange Career of George Rudé – Marxist Historian', *Journal of Historical Biography*, xvi (2014), 118–69; J. Friguglietti, 'A Scholar "In Exile:" George Rudé as a Historian of Australia', *French History and Civilization*, i (online, 2005): https://h-france.net/rude/wp-content/uploads/2017/08/vol1_Friguglietti1.pdf [accessed 1 Nov. 2022]; and for Rudé's bibliography see The George Rudé Society: https://h-france.net/rude/who/ [accessed 1 Nov. 2022]

21. G. Rudé, *The Crowd in the French Revolution* (Oxford, 1959), pp. i and iii.

22. J. Harvey, 'Alfred Cobban as a Transnational Voyager to America', in 'Forum', *French History*, 541–58 at p. 554.

23. T. Le Goff, 'Reminiscences of a Canadian Postgraduate Student in London: The Seminars of Alfred Cobban and Douglas Johnson (1965–1970 and After)', in 'Forum', *French History*, 530–40 at pp. 531–2. At p. 559 the 'Forum' mistakenly presents the title of Bosher's PhD thesis as 'French Finances, 1770–1795'; this is the title of a later (1970) monograph. N.B. In conversation, Tim Le Goff has noted that it would have been all but impossible for a Canadian or an American to do a *doctorat d'état* in France before the French doctoral system was reformed in the 1970s and 1980s. One could prepare various inferior postgraduate degrees, such as a *doctorat de l'université*, a diploma awarded by the Sorbonne, although not recognized by the French State. Or you could do as Bosher did, and prepare a DES, which indeed was a State-recognized degree. However, the real doctorate in France, the one that counted for jobs, was the *doctorat d'état*, in those days an arduous, often decade-long task that presupposed the candidate's time of preparation would be paid for till completion by a reliable job in the educational establishment.

24. There were other students of Bosher's at UBC, like Gillian Thompson, Angus McLaren and William Irvine, who pursued active scholarly and university careers as historians of France.

25. Le Goff, 'Reminiscences', in 'Forum', *French History*, 530–40.

**26.** While the Drapers professorship of French was established in 1919 and the professorship of modern history in 1930, the University of Cambridge had no chair in French history at the time; however, scholars such as John P. T. Bury (1908–87) and C. M. Andrew (PhD, Cambridge 1965) provided teaching expertise in modern French history.

**27.** For some reminiscences of life at Royal Holloway see Royal Holloway, University of London: https://www.royalholloway.ac.uk/about-us/our-alumni/for-alumni/alumni-news/a-grown-ups-view-of-bedford-college/ [accessed 1 Nov. 2022].

**28.** O. Hufton, *Bayeux in the Late Eighteenth Century: A Social History* (Oxford, 1967), p. viii.

**29.** Le Goff, 'Reminiscences', in 'Forum', *French History*, 534.

**30.** R. Gildea, 'Douglas William John Johnson', *ODNB* (online, 2009): https://doi-org.ezproxy4.lib.le.ac.uk/10.1093/ref:odnb/95778 [accessed 1 Nov. 2022]; S. Reynolds, 'Douglas Johnson 1925–2005', *Modern & Contemporary France*, xiii (2005), 483–87; M. Cornick and C. Crossley, *Problems in French History* (Basingstoke, 2000).

**31.** Franco-British Council: https://francobritish.org/en/about/ [accessed 1 Dec. 2022].

**32.** Students who started with Cobban and ended with Johnson included Tim Le Goff, Donald Sutherland and Ed Whitcomb. N.B. Nicola Sutherland provided valuable service in helping to organize the Seminar through Cobban's declining health in 1967–8 and oversaw things until Johnson took over.

**33.** For further details, see S. Hoffmann and R. Tiersky, 'Hommage à Annie Kriegel', *French Politics and Society*, xiii (1995), 63–7.

**34.** There are no records for the joint IHR-IFRU seminars. The planning was rather informal with Pamela Pilbeam taking a lead to agree with Geraldine d'Amico whom to invite from France and on what date. At first the speakers presented at IHR, but later meetings were hosted at the IFRU.

**35.** R. Chartier and P. Rosanvallon, 'Hommage à Maurice Agulhon', Collège de France Newsletter (2015), 88–90: https://doi.org/10.4000/lettre-cdf.2210 [accessed 1 Nov. 2022].

**36.** S. Godfrey, 'Alain Corbin: Making Sense of French History', *French Historical Studies*, xxv (2002), 381–98.

**37.** For details, see French History Society, 'Fourteenth Douglas Johnson Memorial Lecture in French History': http://frenchhistorysociety.co.uk/douglas-johnson/ [accessed 1 Dec. 2022].

**38.** A. W. M. Smith, 'Doing History: A Timeline of My Book's Publication': https://awmsmith.wordpress.com/2016/09/27/doing-history-a-timeline-of-my-books-publication/ [accessed 1 Nov. 2022].

**39.** French History Society Network Blog: http://frenchhistorysociety.co.uk/blog/?cat=7 [accessed 1 Nov. 2022]. Cf. Institute of Historical Research, French History Collections: https://www.history.ac.uk/library/collections/french-history [accessed 1 Nov. 2022].

**40.** Institute of Historical Research, Modern French History: https://www.history.ac.uk/seminars/modern-french-history [accessed 1 Nov. 2022].

# References

## Archived sources

Institute of Historical Research, Wohl Library

IHR 3/3/21.

## Published sources

Banner, G., 'The Early Years: A Department in the Making, 1895–1920', in *Political Science at the LSE: A History of the Department of Government, from the Webbs to Covid*, ed. C. Schonhardt-Bailey and G. Bannerman (London, 2021), pp. 21–52.

Behrens, C., 'Professor Cobban and His Critics', *Historical Journal*, ix (1966), 236–41.

Boer, P. D., *History as a Profession: The Study of History in France, 1818–1914*, trans. A. Pomerans (Princeton, 1988).

Bosher, J. F. (ed.), *French Government and Society 1500–1850: Essays in Memory of Alfred Cobban* (London, 1973).

Chambers, R., *Little Creole: A Story of Napoleon and Josephine* (London, 1952).

Chartier, R., and Rosanvallon, P., 'Hommage à Maurice Agulhon', Collège de France Newsletter (2015), 88–90: https://doi.org/10.4000/lettre-cdf.2210 [accessed 1 Nov. 2022].

Cobb, R., *A Second Identity: Essays on France and French History* (London, 1969).

Cobban, A., *Historians and the Causes of the French Revolution* (London, 1946).

Cornick, M., and Crossley, C., *Problems in French History* (Basingstoke, 2000).

Coulton, G. G. et al., 'University Research, Session 1923–24', *History*, ix (1925), 361.

Crook, M. et al., 'Forum: The Legacy of Alfred Cobban', *French History*, xxxiv (2020), 512–60.

Dahrendorf, R., *LSE: A History of the London School of Economics and Political Science 1895–1995* (Oxford, 1995).

Faucher, C., and Lane, P., 'French Cultural Diplomacy in Early Twentieth-Century London', in *A History of the French in London: Liberty, Equality, Opportunity*, ed. D. Kelly and M. Cornick (London, 2013), pp. 281–302.

Franco-British Council: https://francobritish.org/en/about/ [accessed 1 Dec. 2022].

French History Society, 'Fourteenth Douglas Johnson Memorial Lecture in French History': http://frenchhistorysociety.co.uk/douglas-johnson/ [accessed 1 Dec. 2022].

French History Society Network Blog: http://frenchhistorysociety.co.uk /blog/?cat=7 [accessed 1 Nov. 2022].

Friguglietti, J., 'Rudé, George Frederick Elliot (1910–1993)', *Oxford Dictionary of National Biography* (2004): https://doi.org/10.1093 /ref:odnb/53299 [accessed 1 Nov. 2022].

Friguglietti, J., 'A Scholar "In Exile:" George Rudé as a Historian of Australia', *French History and Civilization*, i (online, 2005): https://h -france.net/rude/wp-content/uploads/2017/08/vol1_Friguglietti1.pdf [accessed 1 Nov. 2022].

The George Rudé Society: https://h-france.net/rude/who/ [accessed 1 Nov. 2022]

Gildea, R., 'Douglas William John Johnson', *Oxford Dictionary of National Biography* (online, 2009): https://doi-org.ezproxy4.lib.le.ac .uk/10.1093/ref:odnb/95778 [accessed 1 Nov. 2022].

Godfrey, S., 'Alain Corbin: Making Sense of French History', *French Historical Studies*, xxv (2002), 381–98.

Graduate Institute of International Studies, Geneva: https://www .graduateinstitute.ch/sites/internet/files/2020-12/Book_90years _Institute_web.pdf [accessed 1 Nov. 2022].

Harte, N., *The University of London 1836–1986: An Illustrated History* (London, 1986).

Harvey, J., 'Alfred Cobban as a Transnational Voyager to America', in Crook, M. et al., 'Forum: The Legacy of Alfred Cobban', *French History*, xxxiv (2020), 541–58.

Hoffmann, S., and Tiersky, R. 'Hommage à Annie Kriegel', *French Politics and Society*, xiii (1995), 63–7.

Hufton, O., *Bayeux in the Late Eighteenth Century: A Social History* (Oxford, 1967).

Hufton, O., 'Alfred Bert Carter Cobban', *Oxford Dictionary of National Biography* (Online, 2007): https://doi.org/10.1093/ref:odnb/56344 [accessed 1 Nov. 2022].

Institute of Historical Research, French History Collections: https://www .history.ac.uk/library/collections/french-history [accessed 1 Nov. 2022].

Institute of Historical Research, Modern French History: https://www .history.ac.uk/seminars/modern-french-history [accessed 1 Nov. 2022].

*Institute of Historical Research: Third Annual Report 1923–1924* (London, 1925).

Le Goff, T., 'Reminiscences of a Canadian Postgraduate Student in London: The Seminars of Alfred Cobban and Douglas Johnson

(1965–1970 and After)', in Crook, M. et al., 'Forum: The Legacy of Alfred Cobban', *French History*, xxxiv (2020), 530–40.

Lewis, G., 'Introduction', in A. Cobban, *The Social Interpretation of the French Revolution*, second edition (Cambridge, 1999), pp. xiii–xlix.

Mantoux, M., *La Révolution Industrielle au XVIIIe Siècle* (Paris, 1906).

Munro, D., 'The Strange Career of George Rudé – Marxist Historian', *Journal of Historical Biography*, xvi (2014), 118–69

Pilbeam, P., 'Alfred Cobban, His Writing and His Teaching', in Crook, M. et al., 'Forum: The Legacy of Alfred Cobban', *French History*, xxxiv (2020), 519–30.

Pilbeam, P., 'The Impact of Alfred Cobban on Approaches to 1789' [Conference Paper], *H-France Salon*, xii (Online, 2020): https://www .youtube.com/watch?v=Bkgijuo_pmI [accessed 1 Nov. 2022].

Pilbeam, P., 'A Liberal Voice and a Fabian: Alfred Cobban', *La Révolution Française*, xxiii (online, 2022): https://doi.org/10.4000/lrf.6819 [accessed 1 Nov. 2022].

Rapoport, M., 'The London French from the Belle Epoque to the End of the Inter-War Period (1880–1939)', in *A History of the French in London: Liberty, Equality, Opportunity*, ed. D. Kelly and M. Cornick (London, 2013), pp. 241–80.

Reynolds, S., 'Douglas Johnson 1925–2005', *Modern & Contemporary France*, xiii (2005), 483–87.

Royal Holloway, University of London: https://www.royalholloway.ac.uk /about-us/our-alumni/for-alumni/alumni-news/a-grown-ups-view-of -bedford-college/ [accessed 1 Nov. 2022].

Rudé, G., *The Crowd in the French Revolution* (Oxford, 1959).

Rudé, G., *Interpretations of the French Revolution* (London, 1961).

Rule, J., 'Paul Vaucher: Historian', *French Historical Studies*, iv (1967), 98–105.

Smith, A. W. M., [Personal Blog], 'Doing History: A Timeline of My Book's Publication': https://awmsmith.wordpress.com/2016/09/27 /doing-history-a-timeline-of-my-books-publication/ [accessed 1 Nov. 2022].

*University of London: The Historical Record (1836–1912), Being a Supplement to the Calendar Completed to September 1912* (London, 1912).

Vincent, S., *Élie Halévy: Republican Liberalism Confronts the Era of Tyranny* (Philadelphia, 2020).

## Unpublished sources

Pilbeam, P., Miscellaneous: Private Correspondence and Notes.

Chapter 8

# The Imperial and World History Seminar

## Sarah Stockwell*

The Imperial and World History Seminar has been at the Institute of Historical Research since the Institute's foundation in 1921.[1] With possibly earlier antecedents still, it is either the oldest or second oldest seminar in British imperial history and one of the earliest history research seminars in Britain.[2] The Seminar has been pioneering on multiple fronts, and not simply because it was among the very first of its kind. Its long history – unbroken except during the Second World War – offers an unrivalled vantage point for exploring the development of historical approaches to empires and colonialism, and, even more so, the long tradition of imperial studies in London.

The Seminar's history serves as a lens through which to view a British imperial academic world. Imperial studies (encompassing imperial history and other subjects related to empire) at the University of London have not received the same attention as those at the Universities of Oxford and Cambridge.[3] This neglect may seem curious given that the Rhodes Professorship of Imperial History (recently renamed the Professorship of Imperial and Global History), with which the history of the Seminar is intimately related, was established at King's College London in 1919 and was only the second chair in the subject anywhere in the world.[4] Perhaps this neglect is because there was nothing sufficiently singular about imperial history in London as to constitute a 'London school', at least in comparison to studies at Oxford and Cambridge. Nevertheless, the early Seminar was crucial to the development of the field, and in the 1950s and 60s, the University of London's relationship with new universities in the empire-Commonwealth helped to make London's imperial studies distinctive. The architecture of higher education in a British academic world – and its asymmetries of power – brought generations of graduate students from colonies and former colonies to London. However, by the 1960s and 70s the Seminar's intellectual importance came to lie not just in its advancement of imperial history but, paradoxically, in its contribution to the decolonization of this academic world. As the Seminar's alumni returned home, they played leading roles in the formation of new national schools of history, and in the evolution of new area studies that departed from the imperial histories – if not necessarily the methodologies – associated with those at the Seminar's helm. By the 1970s and 80s forces that the Seminar had helped progress saw it experience the full effects of the 'wind of change' that had led a decade before to Britain's retreat from empire. But, in something of an ironic turn, decolonizing projects also rescued the Seminar, as postcolonial studies, and then world history, contributed to the subject's reinvention and reinvigoration.

## Origins

Between 1921 and 1938, the Seminar was convened by and synonymous with the first Rhodes chair, Arthur Percival Newton (1873–1942), a King's graduate and lecturer in imperial history there since 1914.[5] In fact initially Newton ran two postgraduate seminars: an 'Introductory Course on Sources for Modern History' – later retitled as 'Preliminary Class' – and, on Tuesdays, the 'Seminar in Colonial History'.[6] The latter rapidly established itself as the most important centre for training postgraduate students in British imperial history: the Cambridge historian of empire, Ronald Hyam, later conceded that Cambridge had 'nothing to compare' with Newton's imperial history group at the time.[7] Newton's own work set a formidable agenda. Starting with *The Colonising Activities of the English Puritans* (1914) and *The Empire and the Future* (1916), he extended with huge chronological and geographical reach to pay attention to the 'broad sweep of Imperial policy as seen from London'. He was also general editor of the *Cambridge History of the British Empire* and editor of the Longman series of 'Imperial Studies' which between 1927 and 1942 published nineteen volumes.

The 1921–2 session of the Seminar attracted up to eleven participants, mostly Newton's postgraduate students. Initially, the numbers attending grew rapidly: to fifteen in 1922–3, then eighteen the following year and twenty-six in 1926–7.[8] One early member was Eveline Martin (1894–1960). After studying history at Westfield College, Martin was supervised by Newton for her PhD dissertation, published as *The British West African Settlements, 1750–1821: A Study in Local Administration* (1927), the second volume in Newton's Longman series. Her research subject exemplified Ronald Robinson's claim that 'Newton studied "areas" with his pupils' even though he himself had a sense of the empire as an organic whole.[9] Martin became university reader of African and imperial history in 1932, and subsequently taught at the University of Ibadan, Nigeria. Just a few decades after the partition of Africa, those associated with the Seminar were making a remarkable contribution to the pre-colonial, if not pre-imperial, history of the continent from the sixteenth century onwards, albeit with a focus on Europeans in Africa.[10] Another earlier attendee was Richard Pares (1902–58), an Oxford graduate in *literae humaniores* who in the mid-1920s was briefly an assistant lecturer at University College London.[11] Pares would go to have an illustrious academic career which contributed to the advance of imperial history with *War and Trade in the West Indies, 1739–1763* (1936) and *A West India Fortune* (1950).

Of the eleven participants in the Seminar's inaugural session, eight were women. Before 1927–8, women formed a majority in all but one year: a position that, as far as this author is aware, would not again be replicated during the rest of the twentieth century. One leading light here was Lilian Penson (1896–1963), who had transferred from Birkbeck College to University College to undertake doctoral studies co-supervised by Newton and A. F. Pollard (1869–1948). In 1921 she became one of the first, and possibly the first, of either sex to be awarded a PhD from the University of London. Penson's thesis was published as *The Colonial Agents of the British West Indies* (1924), beginning a distinguished career that would include becoming chair of modern history at Bedford College and from 1948 to 1951 the first female vice-chancellor of the University of London.[12] The University had, of course, played a pioneering role in women's higher education. Bedford College was founded as a dedicated women's college in 1849, and in 1878 London became the first British university to admit women to degrees. Not long after, King's College for Women opened. In 1923, the first year in which the college affiliation of those attending the Seminar is given, twelve of the fifteen attending were women: three from Bedford, four possibly from Imperial, with one unspecified and a further seven probably from King's. It seems likely that the initially high number of women at the Seminar reflected both the wider London environment, and more specifically that at King's, as well as possibly the impact of the war on male recruitment. By the mid-1930s the proportion of women to men had fallen to around one third. The overall attendance declined a little in the later decade, reaching only fourteen in several years, while the number of non-King's students also dwindled.

From an early date, overseas, and especially Commonwealth, students were among the Seminar's other attendees. Having been born in the

Netherlands and raised in South Africa, the naturalized Afrikaner Cornelis de Kiewiet (1902–86) moved to London to undertake doctoral studies under Newton's supervision. He participated in the Seminar in 1927, the same year he completed his thesis, subsequently published as *British Colonial Policy and the South African Republics, 1848–1872* (1929): this was the third volume in Newton's Longman series. Later, de Kiewiet served as President of Rochester University, President of the American Association of Universities and chairman of the American Council of Learned Societies, making a significant impact upon mid-twentieth-century academic policy in the USA, and indeed internationally.[13] Another Commonwealth student was the Canadian, William Stewart MacNutt. The award of the Imperial Order of Daughters of the Empire scholarship enabled him to study for an MA with Newton. In the 1950s he became an important figure in the Canadian historical profession, producing influential accounts of Loyalists in the Canadian Maritime Provinces.[14] The first postgraduate student of colour to attend the Seminar may have been the Ceylonese/Sri Lankan, G. P. Tambayah in the academic year 1935–6. Educated at the Catholic St Joseph's College, Colombo, he commenced an MA dissertation with Newton in January 1936. Thereafter, Tambayah appears to have entered Ceylonese public administration and received an MBE for his services as government agent in Ceylon's Western Province in the Queen's birthday honours in 1954, at which date the Queen was still head of state in Ceylon.[15]

Newton himself was visiting professor at the University of the Punjab and reader at the University of Calcutta in 1928–9. He also visited American and dominion universities under the auspices of both the Institute of International Education (est. 1919) and the Universities Bureau of Empire (est. 1913), the London-domiciled body that subsequently became the Association of Commonwealth Universities.[16] In varied ways the Seminar was therefore at the heart of what Tamson Pietsch characterizes as an 'expansive British academic community' that spanned the globe, facilitated by the development of doctoral research and the interwar expansion of travelling scholarship schemes that encouraged the flow of foreign, and, especially, Commonwealth and colonial students to Britain.[17]

Newton's successor at King's, Vincent Todd Harlow (1898–1961), was appointed to the Rhodes chair in 1938, following posts at the Universities of Southampton and Oxford.[18] In the 1930s, he and Richard Pares had run Oxford's weekly Commonwealth history seminar, 'working the 1830–60 period so hard and in such intense detail that it was almost killed off'.[19] Once in London, Harlow renamed the IHR's seminar 'British Colonial History'. But Harlow convened the Seminar for only one year before the outbreak of war, whereupon he transferred to the Ministry of Information.

The Seminar recommenced in 1946, when Harlow began co-convening the Seminar with Martin (the first, and until 1977, only, female convenor). Numbers were initially small, with only thirteen others present. The following year the Seminar was restyled 'The History of British Imperial Policy and Administration'.[20] While Harlow authored what constitutes in many respects the most enduringly influential work of any individual associated with the Seminar, *The Founding of the Second British Empire, 1763–1783* (2 vols, 1952–64), this was published after he returned to Oxford in 1948 to take up the Beit professorship of colonial history. Back in Oxford, Harlow re-founded the Commonwealth history seminar. Like its London equivalent, this was '*his* seminar' and in its new iteration may have been influenced by the London model.[21]

## New directions

International student recruitment resumed following the war. In what would become a trend, some students began following intellectual trajectories very different to those leading the Seminar. One was the Guyanese historian Elsa Goveia (1925–80), who, having completed a BA at University College London (UCL), commenced a doctorate under Martin's supervision in 1948. She eschewed an imperial perspective in preference for a subaltern approach. Mary Chamberlain writing about Goveia found it 'enjoyable to speculate on the kind of contrapuntal impact' Goveia's ideas might have had as she doubted that some of the emerging ideas Goveia espoused had 'penetrated Dr Martin's seminar on the [Institute's] third floor'. She wondered what Harlow or Martin, with her emphasis on administrative history, 'made of Goveia's "West Indian" mind as it grasped and then applied the insights from anthropology into explaining how the cultural, social and racial complexity of the West Indies had been historically forged';[22] in fact there is no evidence Goveia attended the Seminar in Harlow's era, as her name first appears in the register in 1949.[23] Chamberlain notes Goveia was part of a new cohort of historians, social scientists and activists, whose lives in the late 1940s connected the distinct worlds of the West Indian Students Union (WISU) and the Institute's seminars.[24] Goveia's contemporaries included the Nigerian Kenneth Dike (1917–83), later heralded by Chieka Ifemesia as the 'father of modern African historiography'.[25] Dike began work under Harlow. He would subsequently recall that Harlow was perceived by his colonial students as close to the Colonial Office and inclined to hold it 'against them' if they were critical of British colonial rule.[26] Dike was likely the first Black African scholar who had completed a PhD in history to be appointed to a lectureship in an African university.

His thesis was later published as *Trade and Politics in the Niger Delta, 1830–1885* (1956).

Harlow's departure coincided with a new phase in the Seminar's history. Martin ceased to be a convenor, and the Seminar was for the next thirty years dominated by Harlow's successor as Rhodes chair, Gerald (Gerry) Sandford Graham (1903–88), who renamed the Seminar 'British Imperial History', the title it would retain until the twenty-first century. In 1950–51 it moved to what became its regular slot on a Monday.[27] Graham was a Canadian who had transferred to London for wartime service in the historical section of the Canadian Army Overseas, following doctoral studies in Cambridge and posts at Harvard and his alma mater, Queen's University Ontario.[28] The scope of Graham's work was indicated by *Empire of the North Atlantic: The Maritime Struggle for North America* (1950) and *The Politics of Naval Supremacy: Studies in British Maritime Ascendancy* (1965). Martin may have acted as temporary convenor during some of Graham's (many) travels but is not listed as such in the registers.

By the 1960s there were also other academics associated with the Seminar. These included Graham's colleagues at King's: the Canadian-born historian of colonial Africa, John E. Flint (1930–2021), and Glyndwr Williams (1932–2022), a seminar member from 1956, who took up a lectureship at Queen Mary College in 1959. Both were Graham's former postgraduate students. In 1969, Graham's last year in post, Williams as well as another King's lecturer and former Graham student, the Canadian George Metcalf, are jointly listed as convenors. But while others played significant roles in the Seminar's intellectual life, and Graham left the menial tasks of seminar organization to his junior colleagues, he presided over the weekly meetings in a room at the end of a corridor on the Institute's third floor, 'with a long table with ten or so chairs on each side and a large ashtray at its head'. Williams recalled that 'No seminar began until Graham was in place and managed to get his pipe going, sometimes a lengthy business.'[29] This was very much the 'professor's seminar'. The number of those attending fluctuated between twelve (1951–2) and twenty-eight (1964–5). Among the many names appearing in the registers in the 1950s and 60s are A. G. Hopkins (1960–61) and John MacKenzie (1966–7, before listed as having 'gone to Rhodesia'), each of whom would make singular contributions to the field. Another is John Mercer, who first appears in the registers in 1968–9, and whom generations of seminar alumni will remember from his continued involvement over many decades.[30]

Under Graham the Seminar functioned explicitly as a form of graduate training. As he advised attendees in 1967, 'This a [sic] research seminar in the sense that you are apprentices (I hesitate to call myself Master) and this room, and the Round Room [in the old Public Record Office, Chancery Lane] and the Reading Room in the B. M. etc are your workshops'.[31] Research students, as well as visiting academics, applied to join the Seminar, and, at least in the early 1950s, their names were forwarded to Graham by the Institute's librarian. Although there is no evidence of any real selection process, Graham was advised on at least one occasion that the applicant might lack 'an adequate degree for research purposes'.[32] This probably reflected the Institute's expectation that students participating in seminars should be enrolled on research degrees.[33] Graham appears to have created an index card for each applicant, including those from other institutions.[34]

In what is perhaps the most striking claim made about the Seminar, Flint judged that on Graham's watch the Seminar became 'an engine for the decolonization of imperial history', influencing the profession in every country of the Commonwealth', with Graham the unlikely 'midwife to major nationalist revisionism'.[35] The truth of the matter was perhaps both more and less than this. But, as Flint also remarked, the Seminar's impact was certainly not the result of Graham's own intellectual agenda. There was 'no "Graham school" of imperial history'. Instead, Graham's scholarship corresponded to an established form of imperial history characteristic of the pre-war period but increasingly out of touch with newer approaches being pioneered elsewhere, notably by Ronald Robinson and Jack Gallagher.[36] In the three years he attended the Seminar, Graham's former doctoral student, the Canadian Phillip Buckner, did not recall Graham or any of his students ever talking about their work. London remained 'a lingering outpost of an older historiography'.[37] In contrast, Freddie Madden recalled how, after Harlow's death and Gallagher's appointment to the Beit chair in 1963, the Oxford Seminar ceased to be 'largely a Commonwealth promotional industry' and how Commonwealth history became 'fun'.[38] Graham, who frequently seemed to be napping during the presentation, would invariably ask the same first question of his graduate students: 'What have you told us that is new?' More penetrating questions from Flint and Williams 'saved the Seminar from being a total loss'.[39] Richard Price, then a doctoral student working under the radical Indian-born historian Ranajit Guha, who later helped to found subaltern studies, similarly considered the Seminar old fashioned. However, as Flint's claim indicates, the Seminar's importance lay elsewhere: notably in its cohort of international members.[40] Most were among Graham's extraordinarily large number of postgraduate students: Flint put this at 200, although only around half that number can be readily verified, and some may well not have completed their studies.[41] As well as from the USA, these came from across the old Commonwealth and the new, a trend likely assisted in the 1960s by the introduction of Commonwealth studentships.[42]

Most numerous were Canadians. In the 1960s they included Phillip Buckner, Marilyn Barber, Barry Gough and Hugh Johnston. There were several reasons for this strong Canadian presence. Only some Canadian universities offered doctoral programmes, and, where they did, these took longer to complete than British ones, an important consideration for Canadians seeking tenure track positions as quickly as possible. Canadian Council fellowships provided funding for some and from the early 1960s Canadians also had access to Commonwealth scholarships. The Commonwealth connection probably also acted as a draw, notably for Anglophone Canadians. Once these had decided upon postgraduate study in Britain, Graham's own Canadian nationality and contacts among what was still a small Canadian historical community ensured many of them applied to work with him, as Buckner recalls. When he was awarded a scholarship, Buckner thought initially of applying to Cambridge. But his advisers at the University of Toronto urged him to work with Graham, after Graham himself – a member of the scholarship committee – had contacted one of Buckner's referees for the scholarship to propose he supervise Buckner.[43] At least six of Graham's students came from the University of New Brunswick, where Newton's former student, MacNutt, was now working: an illustration of the value of 'old boy' networks.

Graham and his colleagues at the Seminar also attracted a significant number of African postgraduates. These included Dike, whom Graham inherited when Harlow moved to Oxford, and who was described by Graham as 'for two years the outstanding student in my seminar'.[44] On completion, Dike took up a post at the University of Ibadan (est. 1948), quickly rising to become head of the history department there and generating for Graham another association that proved fruitful for recruitment. Jacob F. Ade Ajayi (1929–2014), another 'first-rate' young Nigerian scholar whom Graham hoped 'may be a second Dike', applied to work with Graham because he had been Dike's supervisor, commencing work in London in the 1950s.[45] Other notable Nigerian seminar members included Emmanuel A. Ayandele, supervised by Flint.

As these international students returned home, a growing diaspora of former Graham supervisees and of the Seminar's alumni developed. They went on to occupy posts in Commonwealth countries, old and new. Others took up posts in the USA and Britain. By Graham's retirement, Buckner estimates that at least sixteen former seminar members were at Canadian universities, notably at Dalhousie University, where Flint had taken up a position. Equally striking were the number of those whom one former Nigerian student, I. A. Akinjogbin, recently appointed head of history at the University of Ife, referred to in a letter to Graham in 1971 as 'your boys in Nigeria'.[46] Many were at Ibadan, especially before civil war caused – as Graham lamented – 'division between my old, and cherished seminar students'.[47] By 1963–4 seven lecturers at Ibadan were 'G. S. G.'s former students', as annotated by Graham on an Ibadan history prospectus.[48]

This notable record reflected asymmetrical power relationships between London and new colonial and Commonwealth institutions, such as the Universities of Ghana and Ibadan, as well as those formed from existing colleges in Khartoum (Sudan) and Makerere (Kampala, Uganda) in 1947 and 1949. In the 1940s a new body, the Inter-University Council for Higher Education in the Colonies (IUC), was formed to facilitate the development of the new university colleges, including through the secondment of staff from British universities. The IUC worked in close association with London whose academics oversaw the creation and accreditation of the new universities' syllabuses and examinations. But for Nigerian students the connection to Graham also provided an opportunity to get round these structural inequalities. For example, in 1956 Dike asked Graham to 'use whatever <u>discreet</u> [sic] influence you can' with the IUC to secure his promotion to chair. Graham replied 'the chair is in the bag, and nothing can prevent you now from ascending the Golden Stool', a reference to the traditional throne of the Ashanti kingdom.[49] By 1960, Dike had become principal at Ibadan, and, when it became a fully independent university in 1962, its vice-chancellor, a position he held until, at the start of the civil war he, as an Igbo, was forced out, moving instead to Harvard. As Dike later commented, the 'new attitudes to the history of the non-white Commonwealth and to the cultures of Black Africa ... owes more than is realized to GSG's encouragement of young scholars from these areas'.[50] Yet biographical entries on these distinguished African scholars rarely, or never, mention Graham, perhaps because the connection to an imperial historian sat uncomfortably with those celebrating these pioneers in African studies.

At the crux of Flint's claim about 'decolonization' was that the Seminar's alumni played a crucial part in developing area studies and founding new 'national' schools of history that got away from Eurocentric perspectives. There is some evidence that this was the case. Buckner estimates that Graham may have produced more university professors teaching Canadian and/or imperial history in Canadian universities than any other graduate programme except perhaps for those of the Université Laval and University of Toronto, although Canadian history was already established in Canadian universities in the 1950s. Three of the Seminar's alumni served as presidents of the Canadian Historical Society: Buckner (1992–3), John Kendle (1981–2) and Judy Fingard (1997–8).[51]

In Nigeria, Graham's students were instrumental in the development of what is identified as an Ibadan school of history, a distinct nationalistic Nigerian history.[52] This school was of seminal importance in the development of African studies generally, that put the colonial era in its place as (to employ Ajayi's memorable turn of phrase) merely an 'episode' in the *longue durée* of African history.[53] But it was not without its critics, for it was traditional in method and subject, being focused overwhelmingly on matters of politics. In this respect, although the Ibadan school represented a departure from, and a challenge to, imperial history, in other ways it bore resemblance to precisely the kind of history nurtured in Graham's Seminar. Another feature of some of the scholarship was a focus on religion and the history of Christian mission, perhaps reflecting KCL's religious foundation.[54] Graham was a source of practical support to his African graduates, not only reviving Newton's Imperial Studies series, but also, at a time when African history was not perceived as a commercial proposition, inaugurating the West African History book series. Published by Oxford University Press, this was supported financially by West African Newspapers Ltd.[55] He was to be of help in other ways too. For example, in 1956 Dike sought Graham's assistance in persuading the IUC and London historians, notably Lilian Penson, a member of the IUC as well as chair of the committee on London's relations with new universities, to agree to his curriculum reforms at Ibadan.[56]

A diversification of subject matter emerged initially out of necessity. Perpetuating the Seminar's function in doctoral training, the speakers were mostly postgraduate students who were expected to present chapters of their theses: this was perhaps the only manageable way for Graham to cope with so many supervisees. This resulted in a seminar that pulled in different directions. Graham himself acknowledged the increasingly fragmented nature of a field in which scholars sought to incorporate the experience of the colonized. Indeed, in one presentation given at the start of the academic year in 1954, and apparently recycled in 1955, 1956, 1960, 1961 and 1962, he advised that unity was difficult to achieve in the Seminar 'unless one picks a theme, and makes demands for papers that might trespass heavily on thesis time'.[57] Ajayi recalled the Seminar, 'increasingly dealt more with the history of the countries of the Commonwealth than with imperial history as such'.[58] Similarly Buckner remembered that whereas in the 1950s Canadian members of the Seminar were primarily interested in British imperial history, by the 1960s only one of the Canadians 'thought of himself as an Imperial historian', although most (but not all) were working on topics which had an imperial dimension'. Since the Canadians 'knew little or nothing about fields other than Canada and the other groups in the Seminar knew nothing about Canada', discussion lacked depth. The division was reproduced outside the Seminar, with little social contact between the Canadian and African contingents, perhaps because the Africans were generally older and married, while the Canadians were younger and single.[59]

While seminar alumni played leading roles in the creation of new national schools of history, the development of area studies was not only at odds with Graham's own imperially focused scholarship but his scepticism about the readiness of African states for independence.[60] In one double-edged comment, Graham worried about this 'generation of African intellectuals' whose lives may be 'shortened by the enormous weight of responsibilities which African self-government is slowly bringing to bear upon them'.[61] Around 1957 he canvassed opinion among other historians teaching imperial history in Britain, including E. E. Rich, Jack Fisher and Harlow, about the necessity for those doing area studies of developing a knowledge of the broader colonial context. This was apparently prompted by developments at Makerere, where in 1957 the introduction of single honours degrees enabled the institution's historians to be 'more adventurous' in their teaching of African history.[62] Robert Latham, reader in history at Royal Holloway College and, under London's external degree programme, examiner for Makerere, responded that it was 'dangerous for Makerere etc to be allowed their heads', explaining 'as you know this new syllabus scares me'. Graham also put pressure on Dike to retain imperial history. In response, Dike who led a transition to African history in 1956, was non-committal.[63] However, perhaps because of Graham's intervention, students at Ibadan continued to be offered courses in the history of the British Commonwealth, but as these were optional, they did not undermine the curriculum reforms.

The challenge posed by regional studies was felt close to home and for many years led to a turf war with a new African History Seminar at the School of Oriental and African Studies (est. 1916). This seminar was presided over by Roland Oliver (1923–2014), who in 1946 was appointed as the School's first lecturer in African history; he was later holder of the London University chair in African history (1963–86).[64] Oliver was determined to foster an African history that was about more than colonialism and untainted by association with those working in imperial history. His African History Seminar, originating in a 1953 conference, was the first of its kind in the world.[65] Oliver, whose tenure in London overlapped with Graham's for twenty-one years, was instrumental in the launch of *The Journal of African History*, and determined to hold his own in the face of growing 'competition' from a new generation of American Africanists.[66]

Like Graham, Oliver expected his graduate students to attend his seminar, while participation in the Imperial Seminar was discouraged – although in a memoir Oliver acknowledged considerable 'interchange' with Graham's seminar. His former student and, from 1969, colleague Richard Rathbone remembers that for Africanists the IHR was 'enemy territory, one of the nests of those who questioned whether African history was "proper history"'. This position reflected too the struggle Africanists experienced to attain their rightful place within the academy generally and within the local context of the University of London History Board of Studies.[67] Intriguingly, the Imperial Seminar may have been influential in shaping the African seminar at least initially. In 1953 Oliver took responsibility for what he refers to as 'Graham's seminar' while Graham was in Ghana. By bringing him into touch with Graham's Nigerian students Oliver recalled he was able to reorganize his own seminar so that, instead of being a discussion group for colleagues with a marginal interest in African history', it became a 'place of training for future teachers in the subject'.[68]

There was not the same conflict with Asian studies or Indian history, which had a seminar domiciled at SOAS. The IHR's seminar paid little attention to Indian history until after Graham's departure. This in part reflected the research specialisms of those associated with the Seminar in its first fifty years. However, in contrast to African history, Indian history, which emerged from 'Oriental studies', was long established as a distinct field, as evident in the publication of the *Cambridge History of India* (6 vols, 1922–37) alongside a separate *Cambridge History of the British Empire* (8 vols, 1929–61). That the Raj also had a separate institutional history, administered by the India Office, rather than the Colonial Office, may have contributed to this separation. Moreover, because few Britons took up posts in Indian universities (which recruited locally) there were not the same networks and associations between the Seminar and South Asia comparable to those that existed in the case of Africa.[69]

Within London, the Institute of Commonwealth Studies constituted a third base for scholars of Commonwealth and empire, and a place for these to pursue agendas distinct from those associated with either the Imperial History or the SOAS Seminars. This was the case with the 'Societies of Southern Africa in the 19th and 20th Centuries' Seminar launched by Shula Marks (b. 1938) at the Institute in 1969.[70] This attracted a new generation of radical Africanists who associated with a Marxist, or at least Marxisant, outlook that contrasted with both the 'liberal scholarship' of the SOAS seminar and the more Eurocentric focus of the IHR.[71] With two internationally significant Africanist seminars to attend, very few from SOAS participated in the IHR seminar. The pattern only changed in the 1990s, when Rathbone, and William Gervase Clarence-Smith, began attending.

## Collaboration and reinvention

Attendance at the Seminar remained steady, varying between a peak of twenty-six (1970–71) and a low of fifteen in 1978–9.[72] However, relative stability masked distinct changes. In the 1970s a growing proportion of these attendees were academics in post rather than graduate students. The dynamics which had formerly brought large numbers to Britain were no longer as favourable. Whereas previously there had been under-provision at higher education level in many Commonwealth countries, more overseas universities now had their own doctoral programmes: developments that ironically the University of London, through its external degree programme,[73] and the Seminar, had played a part in fostering. Simultaneously postgraduate study in Britain became more expensive for foreign students. Differential fees for home and overseas students, first introduced in 1967, rose steeply in the 1970s. For a while the changes suppressed overseas recruitment,[74] and imperial history was likely among the subjects most affected by measures which changed the situation of students from Commonwealth countries. The rise of area studies also served as something of an existential threat. By 1984, David Fieldhouse (1925–2018), newly appointed to the Vere Harmsworth chair in imperial history at Cambridge, was led to ask if 'Humpty Dumpty' could be put back together again.[75] As the field fragmented, more attendees started cherry picking, attending only when the Seminar corresponded to their interests.[76] With a growing trend for individuals to drop in on an occasional basis, the number of signatories in the register in the 1980s climbed steeply, and even more so in the 1990s, when they ran to many pages, but a 'hard core' of regulars was much smaller.[77] Indeed, through the 1970s and 80s numbers in any one week rarely exceeded twenty.[78] Douglas Peers, bucking the broader downward trend, arrived from Canada in 1984 to do doctoral research with Graham's successor as Rhodes chair, Peter James Marshall (b. 1933). Attendance, he recalls, was 'often quite sparse'. Despite the austere surroundings, with participants 'hemmed in by steel bookshelves, dusty volumes, and with hard wooden chairs', some still managed to doze off. With cuts to university funding, there was a wider sense of history under threat with few students around the tearoom (that is, the Common Room).[79] Regular attendees were mostly male, although there were a few female graduate students, including in the 1980s Penny Carson and Judith Rowbotham – a gender pattern still very evident when I arrived in London in 1992.

Graham's retirement in 1970 also constituted something of a hiatus, since he was not replaced as Rhodes chair for ten years until, in 1981, Marshall, a lecturer at King's since 1959, was promoted to the position. Marshall retired in 1993 and was succeeded by another King's colleague,

188    SARAH STOCKWELL

Andrew Porter (1945–2021). Porter held the post until ill-health forced his premature retirement in 2008, when the Guyanese/Barbadian historian, Richard Drayton (b. 1964), was appointed to the chair. While all three have been significant influences on the Seminar – Drayton presided over its renaming as the Imperial and World History Seminar – their tenure saw the Seminar become, like others at the Institute, less about one individual. The interlude between Graham's retirement and Marshall's appointment was particularly decisive for in the intervening period the Seminar was jointly stewarded by Williams and Marshall, as well as initially Metcalf. A collegial mode of working was typical of Marshall and Williams, and, on his promotion to the Rhodes professorship, Marshall, unlike his predecessors, did not think of this as 'his seminar'.[80] Williams and Marshall were joined in 1971 by Trevor Reese, a reader in imperial history at the Institute of Commonwealth Studies until his premature death in 1976, in 1977 by Freda Harcourt, senior lecturer at Queen Mary and Westfield, and in 1978 by Porter, who took up a lectureship at King's in 1971 on Metcalf's death. From 1985 Jim Sturgis, a Canadian expatriate at Birkbeck, was added to the team, and later David Killingray, an historian of Africa and the African diaspora at Goldsmith's College.[81]

Beginning with Marshall and Williams, those now in charge were less invested in the empire and provided stronger intellectual leadership than Graham. Robinson and Gallagher's scholarship had become the new canon, and, at the Seminar there was much talk of 'metropole and periphery', the 'official mind', and informal and formal empires. There was no programme as such but with Marshall and Williams in charge there was a new engagement with Asia, as well as the Pacific, reflecting their own period and regional expertise.

Under Marshall and Williams, the Seminar had a reputation for friendliness and conviviality, the latter maintaining traditions dating back at least to the Graham era. At the end of his seminars Graham had taken members to Olivelli's, an Italian restaurant on Store Street and reportedly the first place to serve pizza in London, where he footed most of the drinks bill. At the end of the academic year the last meeting of the Seminar was a sociable occasion at the Grahams' London house in Norland Square. There students were treated to an account, often with film, of Graham's travels, while his wife, Mary, supplied food and drink.[82] Proceedings followed a similar fashion under Marshall and Williams, but with less hierarchy. Seminar participants would collect over tea in the Institute. With the Seminar over they proceeded to drinks at Birkbeck bar and thence to dinner. For many years, the Seminar patronized a nearby, self-service, Italian, until its closure led attendees to dine at a greater variety of restaurants. It was far from grand, and on one memorable occasion, one of the staff, familiar with the weekly visits, advised Marshall that no professor in Italy would deign to frequent such a lowly establishment. But the modest venue ensured that in contrast to many an Oxbridge seminar where speakers might be entertained at college dinners, the occasion was open to all so that everyone, including students, had their opportunity to chat informally with the speaker. The end-of-year tradition was continued too, although relocated to the Institute. A speaker, selected to convey a sense of occasion, generally kicked off proceedings, before a buffet supper prepared by the convenors and (since, with the exception of Freda Harcourt, and later myself, the convenors were male) their wives. After, washing up was done in one of the small kitchenettes.

The Institute's location in the heart of London ensured a regular stream of visitors passing through, contributing to a sense of collegiality and sociability. Visitors included Dane Kennedy, then a graduate student at Berkeley, who attended the Seminar while in London in the 1970s.[83] Another was Shigeru Akita, initially during a research year in London and then on subsequent travels to the UK. He found the Seminar useful for Japanese scholars who wished to learn 'easily and quickly, the latest research by British & European/American scholars'. The post-seminar drinks provided informal opportunities to talk, and the IHR seminar 'became a kind of "gateway" for Japanese scholars to contact and broaden their relationship with foreign (British) scholars'. On Akita's return to Osaka, he tried to re-create a similar atmosphere, but, since it was not possible to do this fully, the IHR seminar continued to offer 'quite unique and valuable' opportunities for Japanese scholars temporarily resident in London.[84]

The 1990s marked a period of renewed optimism. The wider academic environment became more positive with more appointments to academic posts. Aided by overseas economic growth, recruitment also increased. Marshall retired as Rhodes professor in 1992, but he and Williams stayed on as convenors, and by 1993 the Seminar was led by Marshall, Porter, Williams, Harcourt, Killingray and Sturgis. Buckner, by then teaching in Canada, returned, joining the panel of convenors, when in 1993–4 on an academic exchange with Sturgis.[85] Later Harcourt retired as convenor, and I joined. By the early 2000s Marshall and Williams had stepped down, leaving three of us: Porter, Killingray and me. Postgraduate students associated with the Seminar continued to be engaged on a diverse range of projects, but there were notable concentrations on late nineteenth-century imperialism, missionary studies and Africa. Alongside British students, Canadians were still numerous relative to those of other national origin. However, by the 2000s the Seminar's graduate students were an increasingly cosmopolitan group. With a few notable exceptions (such as Miguel Bandeira Jerónimo), most came from beyond Europe, with a growing number from East Asia. In the 2010s and 2020s this trend has continued although now with more Chinese, Korean and Taiwanese than Japanese graduates.

Imperial history was also undergoing a revival, invigorated by a fresh generation of scholarship – subaltern, postcolonialism and the 'new imperial history', and by other approaches that emphasized connectivity in different 'worlds', imagined and geographical, including the Atlantic and 'British'. The latter saw the academic debate turn full circle as scholars of Britain's 'old' dominions like Canada and Australia sought once again to reinsert British imperial connections into their national histories but in ways that emphasized networks rather than a 'centre-periphery' axis common to older scholarship. The development of 'British world' studies also saw historians of empire once again pay attention to the old white settlement colonies after several decades in which scholarship had focused more on Asia and Africa.

Initially the Seminar was slow to embrace some of these historiographical developments. Politics, capitalism and the military were staple fare; culture, discourse and gender (the focus of the new imperial history) less so. Religion was one notable exception, however, and in the 1990s it was discussed to a degree perhaps unusual in modern history seminars at the time. In line with Porter's shifting research focus from South Africa and capitalism to religion, the Seminar listened to many papers on the history of missiology, including from one seminar alumnus, Ajayi. By providing a platform for those working principally in religious and missionary studies, the Seminar made a significant contribution to reinserting religion, commonly neglected, back into imperial history. Porter secured funding to help pay for some speakers through his association with the North Atlantic Missiology Project and Currents in World Christianity Project (1996–2001).

The Seminar became gradually more attentive to the new imperial history in the 1990s, with speakers including Catherine Hall. By the end of the decade and the early 2000s culture and the ways in which Britain was constituted by empire were more commonly discussed. Those at the helm of the Seminar took the new scholarship seriously, with Marshall taking it as the subject of his 1994 Creighton Lecture, 'Imperial Britain'. Porter meanwhile engaged with the concept of cultural imperialism from the perspective of his own research on the history of Christian mission. However, for Porter especially serious engagement with any aspect of imperial history inevitably entailed robust criticism and, in the Seminar, penetrating questioning. In the case of the new imperial history, this may have contributed to a perception that he was hostile to it. When Catherine Hall (b. 1946), a leading figure in the new imperial history, arrived in London to take up a position at UCL, she and Linda Colley (b. 1949) launched a new seminar, 'Reconfiguring the British: Nation, Empire, World, 1600–1800', to provide an alternative forum for its discussion.

Porter's hallmark forensic style was also brought to bear on the other key interpretative development of the 1980s and 90s that, like the new imperial history, placed Britain at the centre of analysis: Peter Cain and A. G. Hopkins's conceptualization of a 'gentlemanly capitalism' centred on the City of London as the driving force behind British imperialism over the *longue durée*.[86] Their thesis was the subject of several papers, including two in the autumn of 1992 alone. For Akita this focus proved 'the turning point' of his research career, cementing a shift in his research towards the comparative economic history of South and East Asia and thence to global history, and notable interventions in debates around 'gentlemanly capitalism'.[87]

In the 1990s, while much scholarly attention was directed at analysing imperialism in its British context, a focus on Africa, Asia and the Caribbean continued to be a distinguishing feature of the Seminar. Contributions from area specialists were common and speakers' expertise in multiple languages and world archives notable. In this respect the Seminar continued to provide a forum for an established imperial history, but one that had much in common with an emergent world history school, in which the economics and politics of empires came once more to the fore of scholarly agendas propelled by new scholarly interest in globalization and a new era of Anglo-American overseas intervention.

The Seminar's evolution in 2009 to become the 'Imperial and World History Seminar' represented a natural development and corresponded to a transition already under way elsewhere, including at Oxford and Cambridge. In its latest iteration, the Seminar has proven a broad church, hosting area specialists alongside researchers in transnational, imperial and global history; connectivity is commonly, but not always, addressed. From 2009, the Seminar also ceased to meet weekly and became fortnightly: a realistic arrangement in view of the increasing difficulties academics with young families and with significant teaching and administrative commitments had in attending a weekly early evening seminar. A new seminar led by early career researchers was begun which interleaved with the Seminar. Academic posts in world and imperial history proliferated in London, including at King's, and there were by the 2010s new convenors. At the time of writing, the current team comprises Richard Drayton, Sarah Stockwell, Jon Wilson, Toby Green, Leslie James, Simon Latham, David Motadel, Gavin Sood and Kim Wagner.

## Conclusion

The Seminar, one of the oldest of its kind, has been a significant centre for imperial history for over a century. There was not one London 'school', but in its earliest decades the Seminar was notable for its part in the development of imperial history as a distinct field, including by the many women graduates attending. In its middling years, under the convenorship of Marshall and Williams, it held a focus on the eighteenth century; and in the later twentieth century it established a singular attention to religion. But the Seminar's importance also lies in its role as the unlikely vehicle for the emergence of new nationalist historiographies, with which imperial history was frequently in tension. In this way the Seminar's history is that of the history of empire itself. It encompasses the period when the empire was still an ongoing concern, and those teaching and researching the history of imperialism in London were themselves ideologically attached to it, and London, as the empire's centre, attracted a large intake of colonial and Commonwealth students; through the challenges both to the Seminar and the wider field of imperial history that accompanied the end of empire, and then, finally, in the twenty-first century when, with its refashioning as the Imperial and World History Seminar, it has undergone its own decolonization.

# Notes

\* I am immensely grateful to the following for allowing me to interview them and/or for sending me reminiscences about the Seminar: Shigeru Akita, Phillip Buckner, David Killingray, Peter Marshall, Douglas Peers, Richard Rathbone and the late Glyn Williams. Their written testimonies, solicited for this chapter, are referenced on first citation as 'X's notes for this author'. Thanks also to Michael Townsend (IHR) and the archivists at King's College London (KCL) for their help and for permission to cite papers in their collections; to attendees at the Seminar in October 2021 when a version of this paper was presented; and to David Manning, John Darwin and Richard Drayton. I first discovered the IHR, like so much else in my life, in the company of the late Arthur Burns. This chapter is dedicated with love and gratitude to his memory.

1. Institute of Historical Research, Wohl Library: IHR/3/3/5, seminar registers.

2. Archival records at the IHR and KCL shed no light on the precise origins although there may have been a link to the annual public lectures in imperial history organized at King's College from 1913, funded by the Rhodes Trust: see R. Drayton, 'Imperial History and the Human Future', *History Workshop Journal*, lxxiv (2012), 156–72, at pp. 164–5. The Commonwealth History Seminar at Oxford existed by the 1930s, see F. Madden, 'The Commonwealth, Commonwealth History, and Oxford', in *Oxford and the Idea of Commonwealth: Essays Presented to Sir Edgar Williams*, ed. F. Madden and D. K. Fieldhouse (London, 1982), pp. 7–29, at p. 16.

3. Drayton, 'Imperial History', 156–72.

4. The oldest is the Beit professorship of colonial history at Oxford (est. 1905).

5. King's College London Archives (KCLA), catalogue entry for Newton.

6. It was once suggested that the latter had two strands in 1925–6: 'The African Trade, 1660–1837' and 'British North America, 1763–1837', see D. Birch and J. Horn (comp.), *The History Laboratory: The Institute of Historical Research 1921–96* (London, 1996), p. 130.

7. R. Hyam, *Understanding the British Empire* (Cambridge, 2010), pp. 473–508, at p. 487; R. Hyam, 'The Study of Imperial and Commonwealth History at Cambridge, 1881–1981: Founding Fathers and Pioneer Research Students', *Journal of Imperial and Commonwealth History*, xxix (2001), 75–93. It was not until 1958 that a comparable seminar, in Commonwealth and European expansion, was established at Cambridge by Nicholas Mansergh.

8. IHR/3/3/5, seminar registers.

9. R. Robinson, 'Oxford in Imperial Historiography', in *Oxford and the Idea of Commonwealth: Essays Presented to Sir Edgar Williams*, ed. F. Madden and D. K. Fieldhouse (London, 1982), pp. 30–48, at pp. 33–5.

10. Early Master's theses included: Kate Eliot, 'The Beginnings of English Trade with Guinea and the East Indies, 1550–1559' (1915), Elsie Harrington, 'British Measures for the Suppression of the Slave Trade upon the West Coast of Africa, 1807–33' (1923), and R. Mellor, 'British Policy in Relation to Sierra Leone, 1808–52' (1935). For more, see A. D. Roberts, 'The British Empire in Tropical Africa', in *The Oxford History of the British Empire. Volume V. Historiography*, ed. R. W. Winks (Oxford, 1999), pp. 463–85, at pp. 466–70 and 475–7.

11. IHR/3/3/5, seminar registers. A. L. Rowse, 'Richard Pares', *Proceedings of the British Academy*, xlviii (1962), 345–62.

12. R. Greaves, 'Penson, Dame Lillian Margery (1896–1963), Historian', *Oxford Dictionary of National Biography* (online, 2004): https://doi.org/10.1093/ref:odnb /35468 [accessed 1 Nov. 2022].

**13.** R. Glotzer, 'C. W. de Kiewiet, Historian of Africa: African Studies and the American Post-War Research University', *Safundi: The Journal of South African and American Studies*, x (2009), 419–47.

**14.** D. Green, 'William Stewart MacNutt', *New Brunswick Literary Encyclopaedia* (2010): https://nble.lib.unb.ca/browse/m/william-stewart-macnutt [accessed 7 Jan. 2022].

**15.** IHR/3/3/6. KCLA, Registry Slip Books, 1936–8. *The London Gazette*, sup. to 1/10 Jun. 1954 (no. 40191), p. 3304: thanks to Emily Dourish at Cambridge University Library for this reference.

**16.** KCLA, catalogue entry for Newton Papers.

**17.** T. Pietsch, *Empire of Scholars: Universities, Networks and the British Academic World, 1850–1939* (Manchester, 2013), p. 93, p. 154, and p. 192.

**18.** W. D. McIntyre, 'Harlow, Vincent Todd (1898–1961)', *ODNB* (2008): https://doi.org/10.1093/ref:odnb/63794 [accessed 17 Mar. 2021].

**19.** Madden, 'The Commonwealth', p. 16.

**20.** IHR/3/3/6.

**21.** According to David Fieldhouse's unpublished memoir: written communication from John Darwin; quote from Madden, 'The Commonwealth', p. 19.

**22.** Mary Chamberlain, 'Elsa Goveia: History and Nation', *History Workshop Journal*, lviii (2004), 167–90, at pp. 177–9. I owe this reference to Dongkyung Shin. See also L. Braithwaite, *Colonial West Indian Students* (Kingston, Jamaica, 2001).

**23.** IHR/3/3/6.

**24.** Chamberlain, 'Elsa Goveia', 177–9.

**25.** E. Raymond, 'Kenneth Onwuka Dike' (n.d.): https://www.abdn.ac.uk/stories/kenneth-dike/ [accessed 1 Nov. 2022].

**26.** K. Dike, 'Gerald S. Graham: Teacher and Historian', in *Perspectives of Empire: Essays Presented to Gerald S. Graham*, ed. J. Flint and G. Williams (London, 1973), pp. 1–8, at p. 5.

**27.** IHR/3/3/7.

**28.** J. Flint, 'Graham, Gerald Sandford (1903–1988)', *ODNB* (2004): https://doi.org/10.1093/ref:odnb/50759 [accessed 17 Mar. 2021].

**29.** Williams's notes for this author. IHR/3/3/7 and IHR/3/3/15, seminar registers.

**30.** IHR/3/3/7.

**31.** KCLA, Graham papers, 12/2/11: 'Seminar file', paper 9 Oct. 1967. Cf. A. F. Pollard, *Factors in Modern History*, third edition (London, 1932), p. 312.

**32.** KCLA, Graham papers, 12/2/11: 'Seminar file', Taylor Milne to Graham, 2 Oct. 1952; 2 Oct. 1953.

**33.** *Institute of Historical Research: First Annual Report, 1921–22* (London, 1923), pp. 5–8.

**34.** KCLA, Graham papers, 4/12.

**35.** J. Flint, 'Professor Gerald Sandford Graham, 1903–1988', *Journal of Imperial and Commonwealth History*, xvii (1989), 297–300.

**36.** Flint, 'Graham', 297–300.

**37.** P. Buckner, 'Defining Identities in Canada: Regional, Imperial, National', *Canadian Historical Review*, xciv (2013), 290–311, at p. 295.

**38.** Madden, 'The Commonwealth', p. 21.

39. Buckner's notes provided for this author.

40. H. Perraton, *A History of Foreign Students in Britain* (Basingstoke, 2014), p. 65 and pp. 103–4.

41. Flint, 'Graham', *ODNB*.

42. Perraton, *History of Foreign Students*, p. 65 and pp. 103–4.

43. Above, all from notes, Buckner.

44. KCLA, Graham papers, 1/7: letter of reference for Dike addressed to US Educational Commission (n.d., prob. 1950s).

45. KCLA, Graham papers, 1/1: Graham to the 'Director of Nigerian Students', 28 Sept. 1956.

46. Buckner, notes; KCLA, Graham papers 1/1: Akinjogbin to Graham, 7 Sept. 1971.

47. KCLA, Graham papers 1/1: Graham to Ayandele, 3 May 1967.

48. KCLA, Graham papers 3/22.

49. KCLA, Graham papers 1/7: Dike to Graham, 2 May 1956, and Graham's reply.

50. Dike, 'Graham', p. 7.

51. Buckner, notes and correspondence with author.

52. P. Lovejoy, 'The Ibadan School of Historiography and Its Critics', in *African Historiography: Essays in Honour of Jacob Ade Ajayi*, ed. T. Falola (Harlow, 1993), pp. 195–202.

53. J. F. A. Ajayi, 'Colonialism: An Episode in African History', in *Colonialism in Africa 1870–1960: Volume 1: The History and Politics of Colonialism 1870–1914*, ed. L. H. Gann and P. Duignan (Cambridge, 1969), pp. 497–509.

54. J. F. A. Ajayi's PhD diss. (LSE, 1958) was published as *Christian Missions in Nigeria, 1841–1891: The Making of a New Elite* (London, 1965) and E. A. Ayandele's PhD diss. (KCL, 1964) was published as *The Missionary Impact on Modern Nigeria, 1842–1914* (London, 1966).

55. J. Flint and G. Williams, 'Preface', in *Perspectives of Empire*, x.

56. KCLA, Graham papers, 1/7: Dike to Graham, 23 Nov. 1956.

57. KCLA, Graham papers, 12/2/11: 'Seminar file', notes, dated 12 Oct. 1953; subsequent dates annotated on paper.

58. J. F. A. Ajayi, 'African History at Ibadan', in *The Emergence of African History at British Universities*, ed. A. H. M. Kirk-Greene (Oxford, 1995), pp. 91–109, at p. 96.

59. Notes, Buckner.

60. Flint, 'Graham', *ODNB*.

61. KCLA, Graham papers, 1/7: Graham to Franklin D. Scott, 13 Dec. 1955 [recommending Dike for a fellowship at Northwestern University].

62. K. Ingham, 'Makerere and After', in *Emergence of African History*, ed. Kirk-Greene, pp. 113–33, at p. 121.

63. KCLA, Graham papers 3/21: Graham's papers; and Latham to Graham, 6 Mar. [1957]. On reforms at Ibadan, see: Ajayi, 'African History', p. 100, where it is implied that the change occurred on Dike's watch.

64. For further details, see 'Roland Oliver (1923–2014)': https://africanstudies.org/individual-membership/in-memory/roland-oliver-1923-2014/ [accessed 1 Dec. 2022].

65. R. Oliver, 'African History: SOAS and Beyond', in *Emergence of African History*, ed. Kirk-Greene, pp. 13–38, esp. p. 17.

66. Rathbone's notes for this author, and interview, 12 Mar. 2021; notes, Williams.

67. Notes and interview, Rathbone; Oliver 'African History', p. 26 and p. 19.

68. Roland Oliver, *In the Realms of Gold: Pioneering in African History* (London, 1997), p. 147.

69. Marshall notes for this author, and interview, P. J. Marshall, 19 Mar. 2021.

70. S. Marks, 'The Societies of Southern Africa Seminar at the Institute of Commonwealth Studies' (2012): https://sas-space.sas.ac.uk/3557/1/ShulaMarks-ICS_Societies_of_Southern-Africa_seminar.pdf [accessed 2 Mar. 2022].

71. Notes and interview, Rathbone.

72. IHR/3/3/7.

73. See D. Shin, '"Partnership in Universities", British Strategies for New Universities at the End of Empire' (unpublished King's College London PhD thesis, 2022).

74. Perraton, *History of Foreign Students*, pp. 108–11 and p. 131.

75. D. Fieldhouse, 'Can Humpty Dumpty Be Put Together Again? Imperial History in the 1980s', *Journal of Imperial and Commonwealth History*, xii (1984), 9–23.

76. Interview, Marshall.

77. IHR/3/3/15 and IHR/3/3/42.

78. Notes, Marshall.

79. Peers's notes for this author.

80. Interview, Marshall.

81. IHR/3/3/7 and IHR/3/3/15.

82. Notes, Williams.

83. D. Kennedy, 'An Education in Empire', in *How Empire Shaped Us*, ed. A. Burton and D. Kennedy (London, 2016), pp. 95–105, at p. 99.

84. Akita notes for this author.

85. Buckner, 'Defining Identities', p. 304.

86. First expounded in articles and then in P. Cain and A. G. Hopkins, *British Imperialism* (Harlow, 1993).

87. S. Akita, 'From South Asian Studies to Global History: Searching for Asian Perspectives', in *How Empire Shaped Us*, ed. A. Burton and D. Kennedy (London, 2016), pp. 117–28, esp. p. 122.

# References

## Manuscript and archival sources

Institute of Historical Research, Wohl Library

IHR/3/3/5.
IHR/3/3/6.
IHR/3/3/7.
IHR/3/3/15.
IHR/3/3/42.

King's College London Archives

Catalogue entry for Newton, Arthur Percival (1873–1942)
Graham Papers, 1/1.
Graham Papers 3/21.
Graham Papers, 3/22.
Graham Papers, 4/12.
Graham Papers, 1/7.
Graham Papers, 12/2/11.
Registry Slip Books, 1936–8.

## Printed and online sources

Ajayi, J. F. A., *Christian Missions in Nigeria, 1841–1891: The Making of a New Elite* (London, 1965).

Ajayi, J. F. A., 'Colonialism: An Episode in African History', in *Colonialism in Africa 1870–1960: Volume 1: The History and Politics of Colonialism 1870–1914*, ed. L. H. Gann and P. Duignan (Cambridge, 1969), pp. 497–509.

Ajayi, J. F. A., 'African History at Ibadan', in *The Emergence of African History at British Universities*, ed. A. H. M. Kirk-Greene (Oxford, 1995), pp. 91–109.

Akita, S., 'From South Asian Studies to Global History: Searching for Asian Perspectives', in *How Empire Shaped Us*, ed. A. Burton and D. Kennedy (London, 2016), pp. 117–28.

Ayandele, E. A., *The Missionary Impact on Modern Nigeria, 1842–1914* (London, 1966).

Birch, D., and Horn, J., (comp.), *The History Laboratory: The Institute of Historical Research 1921–96* (London, 1996).

Braithwaite, L., *Colonial West Indian Students* (Kingston, Jamaica, 2001).

Buckner, P., 'Defining Identities in Canada: Regional, Imperial, National', *Canadian Historical Review*, xciv (2013), 290–311.

Cain, P., and Hopkins, A. G., *British Imperialism* (Harlow, 1993).

Chamberlain, M., 'Elsa Goveia: History and Nation', *History Workshop Journal*, lviii (2004), 167–90.

Dike, K., 'Gerald S. Graham: Teacher and Historian', in *Perspectives of Empire: Essays Presented to Gerald S. Graham*, ed. J. Flint and G. Williams (London, 1973), pp. 1–8.

Drayton, R., 'Imperial History and the Human Future', *History Workshop Journal*, lxxiv (2012), 156–72.

Fieldhouse, D., 'Can Humpty Dumpty Be Put Together Again? Imperial History in the 1980s', *Journal of Imperial and Commonwealth History*, xii (1984), 9–23.

Flint, J., 'Professor Gerald Sandford Graham, 1903–1988', *Journal of Imperial and Commonwealth History*, xvii (1989), 297–300.

Flint, F., 'Graham, Gerald Sandford (1903–1988)', *Oxford Dictionary of National Biography* (2004): https://doi.org/10.1093/ref:odnb/50759 [accessed 17 Mar. 2021].

Flint, J., and Williams, G., 'Preface', in *Perspectives of Empire: Essays Presented to Gerald S. Graham*, ed. G. Williams and J. Flint (London, 1973), p. x.

Glotzer, R., 'C. W. de Kiewiet, Historian of Africa: African Studies and the American Post-War Research University', *Safundi: The Journal of South African and American Studies*, x (2009), 419–47.

Greaves, R., 'Penson, Dame Lillian Margery (1896–1963), Historian', *Oxford Dictionary of National Biography* (online, 2004): https://doi.org/10.1093/ref:odnb/35468 [accessed 1 Nov. 2022].

Green, D., 'William Stewart MacNutt', *New Brunswick Literary Encyclopaedia* (2010): https://nble.lib.unb.ca/browse/m/william-stewart-macnutt [accessed 7 Jan. 2022].

Hyam, R., 'The Study of Imperial and Commonwealth History at Cambridge, 1881–1981: Founding Fathers and Pioneer Research Students', *Journal of Imperial and Commonwealth History*, xxix (2001), 75–93.

Hyam, R., *Understanding the British Empire* (Cambridge, 2010).

Ingham, K., 'Makerere and After', in *The Emergence of African History at British Universities*, ed. A. H. M. Kirk-Greene (Oxford, 1995), pp. 113–33.

*Institute of Historical Research: First Annual Report, 1921–22* (London, 1923).

Kennedy, D., 'An Education in Empire', in *How Empire Shaped Us*, ed. A. Burton and D. Kennedy (London, 2016), pp. 95–105.

*The London Gazette*, sup. to 1/10 Jun. 1954 (no. 40191).

Lovejoy, P., 'The Ibadan School of Historiography and Its Critics', in *African Historiography: Essays in Honour of Jacob Ade Ajayi*, ed. T. Falola (Harlow, 1993), pp. 195–202.

Madden, F., 'The Commonwealth, Commonwealth History, and Oxford', in *Oxford and the Idea of Commonwealth: Essays presented to Sir Edgar Williams*, ed. F. Madden and D. K. Fieldhouse (London, 1982), pp. 7–29.

Marks, S., 'The Societies of Southern Africa Seminar at the Institute of Commonwealth Studies' (2012): https://sas-space.sas.ac.uk/3557/1/ShulaMarks-ICS_Societies_of_Southern-Africa_seminar.pdf [accessed 2 Mar. 2022].

McIntyre, W. D., 'Harlow, Vincent Todd (1898–1961)', *Oxford Dictionary of National Biography* (2008): https://doi.org/10.1093/ref:odnb/63794 [accessed 17 Mar. 2021].

Oliver, R., 'African History: SOAS and Beyond', in *The Emergence of African History at British Universities*, ed. A. H. M. Kirk-Greene (Oxford, 1995), pp. 13–38.

Oliver, R., *In the Realms of Gold: Pioneering in African History* (London, 1997).

Perraton, H., *A History of Foreign Students in Britain* (Basingstoke, 2014).

Pietsch, T., *Empire of Scholars: Universities, Networks and the British Academic World, 1850–1939* (Manchester, 2013).

Pollard, A. F., *Factors in Modern History*, third edition (London, 1932).

Raymond, E., 'Kenneth Onwuka Dike' (n.d.): https://www.abdn.ac.uk/stories/kenneth-dike/ [accessed 1 Nov. 2022].

Roberts, A. D., 'The British Empire in Tropical Africa', in *The Oxford History of the British Empire. Volume V. Historiography*, ed. R. W. Winks (Oxford, 1999), pp. 463–85.

Robinson, R., 'Oxford in Imperial Historiography', in *Oxford and the Idea of Commonwealth: Essays Presented to Sir Edgar Williams*, ed. F. Madden and D. K. Fieldhouse (London, 1982), pp. 30–48.

'Roland Oliver (1923–2014)': https://africanstudies.org/individual-membership/in-memory/roland-oliver-1923-2014/ [accessed 1 Dec. 2022].

Rowse, A. L., 'Richard Pares', *Proceedings of the British Academy*, xlviii (1962), 345–62.

## Unpublished sources

Eliot, K., 'The Beginnings of English Trade with Guinea and the East Indies, 1550–1559', MA Thesis (University of London, 1915).

Harrington, E., 'British Measures for the Suppression of the Slave Trade upon the West Coast of Africa, 1807–33', MA Thesis (University of London, 1923).

Mellor, R., 'British Policy in Relation to Sierra Leone, 1808–52', MA Thesis (University of London, 1935).

Shin, D., '"Partnership in Universities", British Strategies for New Universities at the End of Empire', PhD Thesis (King's College London, 2022).

Stockwell, S., Miscellaneous Private Correspondence and Notes.

Chapter 9

# The Postgraduate Seminar in Theory and Method (1986–2008)

## Rohan McWilliam

Unlike those who attended university in the 1960s and (maybe) the 1970s, the students of the 1980s lack a mythology. In politics at large, it was a time of Thatcherism; in higher education a period of retrenchment.[1] The great age of academic expansion that followed the 1963 Robbins Report and the confident political radicalism that often accompanied it had hit the buffers. In some respects, this made both student politics and the larger academic climate more interesting; the 1980s proved to be a time of intellectual energy amongst historians. The assumptions that had governed a lot of historical research (about economic and materialist explanations for change) were tested and new ideas came forward. The creation of the Postgraduate Seminar in Theory and Method at the Institute of Historical Research in 1986 provides a lens through which to view the forces that shaped historical enquiry in the Thatcher decade and assess the new generation of historians who emerged at that time.

This chapter explores the reasons why the Postgraduate Seminar was founded and the distinctive spirit that animated it. It is based on my memories of the Seminar in its formative years as well as those of some others who participated in it. I have endeavoured in a minor way to write a cultural and intellectual history of this group. The Seminar may no longer exist, but it has left a legacy: it was a staging post for a number of historians who went on to have important academic careers and served as a precursor to the IHR's current History Lab Postgraduate Seminar. I explore here the paradigms that the Seminar concerned itself with. Some of these still inform academic discussion today, even though (as will become clear) the Seminar was very much the product of its time.

## The origins of the Seminar

The Postgraduate Seminar in Theory and Method was really the outcome both of some wider changes in academic culture and of a group of younger scholars entering the profession. None of this would have been possible if the IHR had not itself changed in some respects. The IHR was an institution that felt in the mid-1980s like an annex of the British Library, at that time just a short walk away in the British Museum; it displayed a slightly other-worldly quality, which was part of its charm for some and yet daunting for others. Like many of the figures involved in the foundation of the Postgraduate Seminar, I was not part of the University of London. There were postgraduates at the IHR who were attached to many universities in the UK and other countries.

In 1983 I commenced my PhD at the University of Sussex in Brighton where I worked under the supervision of the pioneering scholar of history from below, J. F. C. Harrison (1921–2018), on Victorian populism.[2] I first encountered the IHR in 1985 because, while in Brighton, I was invited up by Virginia Berridge (b. 1946) – later to become one of the leading scholars of public health policy – to deliver a paper to her Newspaper History Seminar. Speaking at this event alerted me to the possibilities of the IHR both in terms of its seminars and library but also the opportunity to socialize with other postgraduates.

At the time, my department at Sussex (like other university history departments) paid for a number of postgraduate places at the IHR. This carried the benefit of IHR membership but also much-coveted borrowing rights at Senate House Library. Coming up from Brighton to live in the metropolis, I looked to the IHR as an alternative institutional home. Like many postgraduates from institutions outside London, I identified with the IHR as the hub of the historical community in Britain (but not necessarily with the University of London). A year after I joined, the IHR actually became my employer as I was paid to set up the seminar rooms and purchase cakes from a local supermarket for teatime. I only gave this up when I started part-time teaching.

The Institute in those days felt conservative, run by a group of men and women who were the products of Harold Macmillan's Britain. There was also a significant young fogey contingent, all bow ties and Harris Tweed. In the Common Room there was a consistent cast of misfits and eccentrics sipping coffee while reading old volumes of *Punch* and who could be found in the numerous nooks and crannies of the library upstairs. Some turned out, on closer inspection, to be leading historians. We postgraduates imagined how a cosy Agatha Christie-type murder mystery could be set there whose title would be 'The Clio Conspiracy'.

Yet, whilst some history departments elsewhere (especially in new, plate-glass universities, polytechnics and adult education) were throwing up challenging ideas about history from below, women's history and the linguistic turn, this tide of new historical inquiry seemed to stop just short of the entrance to Senate House. Notoriously, it had taken the IHR a long time even to subscribe to *Past and Present*.

Attendance at seminars was a slightly mysterious process. New members were informed that they needed to write to convenors in order to get permission to attend a seminar (although I admit I never bothered with this). A pecking order existed at seminars when it came to contributions from the floor: regulars usually got to contribute the initial points. There were seminars where women had a tough time being called upon to ask a question. Some discussions could also be gladiatorial: questioning could be fierce and aggressive.

Yet the mid-1980s was also a period of transformation for the IHR. Some of this derived from F. M. L. (Michael) Thompson's time as director (1977– 90). Despite his own instincts, Michael showed a willingness to engage with new ideas and recognized how the academic world was changing. Another reason was the then secretary and librarian of the IHR, Alice Prochaska, who, from 1984 until 1992, developed an inclusive spirit and helped open the Institute up, once again, to postgraduate students. Librarians such as Donald Munro and Robert Lyons also showed a commendable openness to young scholars and became cherished in their turn. When I first joined, Robert Lyons gave me a tour of the four floors of the IHR, showing me how the place worked. This allowed me to get to know him. Donald Munro had been active in producing a series of bibliographies on British history which in retrospect were the predecessors of the modern online Bibliography of British and Irish History.[3] He was always happy to chat about history, politics or anything else over tea. If there was a strong sense of hierarchy at the IHR, there was also a spirit of welcome (although many postgraduates still found the Institute forbidding). The launch of the Women's History Seminar in 1986 (see Chapter 10 by Kelly Boyd) was another sign that the historical 'winds of change' were sweeping through the IHR. Even a year after I joined, the Institute seemed a different place.

Given my interests, I not only attended the Victorian and Edwardian Britain Seminar but also the two seminars devoted to the twentieth century: one run by Alice Prochaska (and others) on modern British policy and administration and the other co-ordinated by Pat Thane and Jonathan Zeitlin on state and society in modern Britain. The long nineteenth century seminar was run by Michael Thompson and Roland Quinault, and it was followed by drinks and then a meal at an Indian restaurant in Fitzrovia. Michael usually ordered for everybody, and no one minded.

Why did the Postgraduate Seminar come into existence? It derived from an event that shook up the IHR and proved a catalyst for change. At this time the Seminar on British Policy and Administration in the Twentieth Century established, as part of its mission, invitations to key political figures, asking them to reflect on their careers and their participation in significant political events. These 'Witness Seminars' gave rise to talks by Tony Benn and Douglas Jay, as well as a number of civil servants. But, in 1986, Enoch Powell, then MP for South Down, was asked to speak at a witness seminar on the Conservative governments of the 1950s (of which he was a part).[4] A group of postgraduates, led by Clare Midgley (Kent PhD, 1989), objected to the invitation on the grounds that it lent academic legitimacy to a man whose notorious 'Rivers of Blood' speech in 1968 had fuelled racism and incited racial violence.[5]

The arguments that went back and forth between the IHR and the students anticipated a lot of the current arguments about no-platforming and cancel culture.[6] The organizers of the witness seminar made the case that Powell was not being asked to speak about his views on race and that, in any case, the purpose of the event was to probe the memories of a former cabinet minister. Postgraduates in the IHR's Common Room were themselves divided, some arguing for free speech and for the opportunity to listen to a key figure in modern British politics (whatever they thought about his views on race).

The episode blew up into a larger challenge to the ethos of the IHR itself. Why were there no formal channels to make student voices heard? Why was the choice of historical subjects at seminars so conservative? Even the subject of Powell's talk was criticized. Why ask a cabinet minister to speak and not an ordinary person who had lived through the 1950s? This illuminated the distance between the organizers of the witness seminar and the postgraduates who were calling for a different kind of history. As it was, the talk by Enoch Powell went ahead, but, whilst he was speaking, postgraduates held an alternative informal seminar on the politics of history in the Common Room. Powell was brought into the building through a route avoiding the main entrance in order to avoid any potential encounter with protestors and it is still unclear if he ever knew there had been a controversy over his invitation. Ironically, many of the protestors would have sympathized with the contents of Powell's testimony. Much of it was devoted to attacking Britain's reliance on the nuclear deterrent.

In the wake of Powell's talk, the management of the IHR agreed to a debriefing session in which the protestors and representatives of the Seminar on British Policy and Administration in the Twentieth Century were invited to give papers to state their case. What was then the Local History Room (the biggest room in the building at that point) was packed out. A large number of postgraduates were there but so were many established historians, concerned about the issues raised by the protest. It was a defining moment for the IHR. Michael Thompson chaired the event. John Turner (b. 1949) of Royal Holloway made the case for the witness seminar organizers, insisting that the invitation to Powell did not involve any endorsement of his views on race. The postgraduates were led by Clare Midgley and Amanda Vickery (London PhD, 1991) who gave short papers making the case against the Powell invitation. In retrospect, this was an extremely brave thing to have done. There was much dark talk among the postgraduates that they might have ruined their careers by speaking out (although, as things turned out, this was far from the case).[7] From the floor there were comments from Ben Pimlott (1945–2004) and Roger Mettam (1939–2022) supporting the invitation, with Anna Davin (b. 1940) and Jinty Nelson (b. 1942) criticizing it. Some of the exchanges were heated. Would one ask members of the far right to speak? Whose views were so offensive that they would not be invited? Was not the invitation to Powell, at the very least, extremely distasteful? The postgraduates insisted they were not in favour of getting rid of Powell's books in the library but against (as they saw it) giving him the legitimacy of an invitation to speak.

A number of issues then got thrown up in the discussion that posed a profound challenge to the ethos of the IHR itself. Why was there no representation for students on the board of the IHR (something common in many universities after the 1960s)? This might have provided a conduit through which such issues as the Powell invitation could be discussed. There were also complaints about the culture of seminars and some suggestion that students should be able to run their own seminars. The meeting ended with Michael Thompson saying he would take note of these points.

Whilst the issue of the Powell invitation was not resolved (he attended at least one IHR seminar later on), the IHR moved on the question of representation. A position was made available on the board for a postgraduate representative; the first was Pamela Edwards (London PhD, 1995).[8] It was also agreed that postgraduates could have their own seminar although it had a slightly unofficial quality, being allowed to meet in mid-afternoons at two-thirty and not in the usual slot around five o'clock preferred by most seminars.

For reasons that were never clear to me, Julie Wheelwright (researching an ahead-of-her-time topic on women who dressed as men and fought in wars) asked me, on behalf of the postgraduates, if I would organize this new seminar.[9] It was thought best if it would be a seminar devoted to theory and methodology as that was a space that could unite all postgraduates regardless of the topics or periods they were working on and which was also different from the kind of history promoted by other seminars. We decided that we would have papers by postgraduates but would also invite talks from senior academics. Setting it up, I had the feeling that we were tolerated by the IHR but were not quite part of its established seminar culture. We were not (at that time) given a red book as an attendance register though we were allowed to advertise the seminar's existence on the ground-floor noticeboard. We used our own register in which we recorded details of each event.[10] The first annual report of the IHR to even mention the Seminar was in the 1991–2 session, five years after its formation.

## The early spirit of the Seminar

The Postgraduate Seminar in Theory and Method was meant to abandon any sense of hierarchy; hence it employed a rotating chair who had to be a postgraduate. The main idea was to provide a space in which postgraduates could speak, experiment and build their confidence. Not all postgraduates thought the Seminar a good thing; some regarded it as an indulgence and a distraction from their dissertations.

I did not have a firm agenda for the Seminar which, in retrospect, was a good thing. In my mind, I took inspiration from the Sussex University History Workshop group where I had heard papers whilst a student there (I helped run it at one point). This was an informal offshoot of the main History Workshop movement, which was still at that time running its remarkable conferences which were jamborees of people's history, offering new perspectives on the past that were not being heard in the academy, and deploying categories of class, race, gender and sexuality.[11] The Sussex University group had been quite rigorous in its discussions, and I thought we could do something similar at the IHR.

In the 1980s most history departments did not put on events about preparing for the job market that are routinely found today in many places. There was also, among postgraduates, a lot of discussion about the poor quality of supervision. Why was there so little actual training in the mechanics of historical research (apart from classes in palaeography for those who needed it)? Why was the relationship with supervisors often so distant? One postgraduate met his supervisor in the first week of his PhD and was told to come back and see him in a year's time after he had done some work. I recall another student telling me how he had asked his supervisor who his external examiner might be, only to be told 'none of your business'. The Postgraduate Seminar therefore provided a space to explore what a PhD was. Was it just a passport to the academic community or something more? We were concerned about the PhDs that had been completed in the 1970s where it seemed some candidates had put in ten years of work. How could we compete with that given the pressure to complete our theses in a much shorter time frame? Some students who were aged over thirty were concerned that universities would not hire them as they would be too expensive on account of their age. We did not use the word 'networking' but that was essentially what some of our discussions were about. The Seminar was a forum where we could train each other not only in how to be historians but also in how to deliver a thesis that would pass.

What we did not realize was that the academic world was changing. Universities increasingly expected students to compete their PhDs within an allotted time, usually three years. There would be increasing numbers of training events for students as part of the professionalization of graduate teaching. The first Research Assessment Exercise (RAE) was in 1986 and reshaped academia in the UK. During the 1990s, age became less of a criterion for employment (something that particularly discriminated against women); instead, the RAE (the precursor to the current Research Excellence Framework [REF]) tended to favour the hiring of people who were likely to produce strong outputs, regardless of age.

At the time, however, the conversation amongst us was very much about whether we would ever get jobs. The supply of academic positions had dried up (although, taking the long view, each generation of scholars feels this way). We would read the *Times Higher Education Supplement* or the education section of the *Guardian* and complain about how little hiring was taking place. There was some resentment about people (as we saw it) who had walked into cushy jobs in the 1960s whereas we were consigned to an academic precariat. University departments were increasingly middle-aged. Little did I know that it would take me six years to secure a permanent academic position. In many ways the situation eerily foretold the current state of the job market for scholars entering the profession.

One important dimension to the Postgraduate Seminar was that it did have a spirit of welcome. Newcomers would be dragged off for tea afterwards. The layout of the IHR's Common Room helped: its tables, chairs and stools could be quickly moved around and re-assembled. It was a true haunt for postgraduates, acting like a magnet where one could find like-minded people (although it was occasionally described by us as the 'vortex of inactivity'). Conversations could be loud and sometimes boisterous. Postgraduates and senior scholars mixed on what felt like equal terms, ripping apart the hierarchical atmosphere of the IHR. The introduction of fresh coffee, available all-day round, from 1986 was important, making it feel like a slightly downmarket version of a gentleman's club. Although women were tolerated (and indeed there was a relatively even gender spilt among postgraduates), there was outrage among the old guard when one postgraduate breast-fed her baby in the Common Room.

The Seminar (from its foundation in 1986 onwards) gained from the explosion of young historians who had fetched up at the IHR (doing their PhDs, trying to start an academic career or going in for the very few post-docs that existed). Their relationship to the profession felt extremely precarious. Some were already finding their way into part-time teaching, sometimes at various American universities in London.

The later 1980s and 1990s saw more postgraduates from North America visit London to do research for their PhDs back home, including a remarkable number of students supervised by Judith Walkowitz (b. 1945) who was then at Rutgers and who encouraged her students to make use of the IHR: Anna Clark (PhD, 1987), Pamela Walker (PhD, 1992), Erica Rappaport (PhD, 1993), Joy Dixon (PhD, 1993). They all attended the Seminar at various times and went on to become established academics. Given the research interests of the kind of people involved, we had strong links to two seminars at the IHR: Women's History and the Eighteenth Century British History Seminar. Tim Hitchcock (Oxford DPhil, 1985), Lee Davison (Harvard PhD, 1990), Tim Kiern (London MSc, 1982) and Robert Shoemaker (Stanford PhD, 1985) would spend endless hours in the Common Room discussing the 'weak but strong' eighteenth-century state.[12] These discussions formed the basis of their edited volume, *Stilling the Grumbling Hive*.[13]

From the start we adopted the (what was by then) conventional model of IHR seminars with a fifty-minute seminar followed by discussion. Many people at the Seminar were not postgraduates at all; everybody was welcome. Age was not an issue, though most were between about twenty-two and thirty-two. The way papers were chosen was pretty *ad hoc*, based on friendships and informal connections. It was not unusual for a person to show up to listen to a seminar and be asked to give a paper a few months later. Long post-event discussions in the Common Room would be followed by further conversation in the Students' Union Bar in the School of Oriental and African Studies (SOAS) and, frequently, a cheap meal off Boswell Street in Holborn at Dee's Thai restaurant (which, alas, no longer exists).

Clare Midgley and I spoke at the first seminar in late 1986 which examined the uses of history. I made some conventional arguments about the impossibility of objectivity but also espoused a methodology derived from the increasingly fashionable forms of microhistory. Both Clare and I

## THE POSTGRADUATE SEMINAR IN THEORY AND METHOD (1986–2008)  209

insisted that the pursuit of history was inseparable from politics. Maria Dowling (1955–2011: LSE PhD, 1981) did the second seminar about the practice of historical biography with reference to Anne Boleyn.[14] The paper provoked a discussion of whether biography was an appropriate pursuit for historians. At the time social historians often disdained biography because they wanted to talk about big structures. Kelly Boyd (Rutgers PhD, 1991) did the third one which looked at the history of masculinity, through her research on British boys' story papers (text-based precursors to the comic book, such as the Sexton Blake stories).[15] At the time the history of masculinity was a subject that barely existed so there was a real sense in which the Seminar broke new ground right from the start. The focus in all of these papers was on bigger methodological questions rather than detailed research, so that everyone could contribute regardless of whether they specialized in the area discussed or not. By not being tied to a particular period, we were able to take a wider view on the practice of history.

The Seminar thus proved a place where important new questions could be asked about how history should be written. The 1980s was the moment when the Marxist categories were being contested and we were asking new and difficult questions about the Left, trying to understand why it was so unsuccessful. Well before the so-called 'Red Wall' crumbled in 2019, it was clear that there was a significant working-class vote for the Conservative Party.[16] Many of us were reading *Marxism Today* (1957–1991), which had developed out of the reformist wing of the Communist Party, going to its conferences and cherry-picking parts of Gramsci's *Prison Notebooks*.[17] The key work which expressed the political dilemmas of this moment was Eric Hobsbawm's article, 'The Forward March of Labour Halted?' which first appeared in 1978 and was heavily debated over the next ten years.[18] An important moment was the appearance of *Marxism Today*'s 'New Times' analysis in 1989 with its emphasis on the way post-Fordist economic structures were changing political realities in the modern world.[19] History Workshop was still running events (including its annual conference and a London group that met every month run by Anna Davin). We subscribed to the idea, strongly influenced by E. P. Thompson (1924–93), that historical writing could make a difference to politics in the present. Coming from Sussex University (where there had been much grand talk about giving the working class back its history) I felt at home.[20] We were full of politics itself, interpreting everything in political terms.

And yet the atmosphere was not hugely ideological in the sense that protagonists were deeply immersed in theoretical debates. Marxism was being contested. Categories such as 'class' now seemed more complex, not least in the light of gender analysis. Those of us who had been reading Gareth Stedman Jones's *Languages of Class* (1983) were increasingly focused on the linguistic turn. We talked about the politics of language and the way it constituted forms of power. Thus Jonathan Fulcher (Cambridge PhD, 1993) in 1990 gave a paper on 'Language and Discourse and History', drawing on his own research about British politics in the 1820s. Increasingly, we began to identify with forms of cultural history. In 1989, for example, Marybeth Hamilton (Princeton PhD, 1991) spoke on 'Brothels, Drag Queens and Mae West in 1920s New York City'.[21] For me, one of the formative moments was when Michael Roper (Essex PhD, 1989) – now a professor in sociology at Essex University – spoke about his work on masculinity. He had developed an oral history of businessmen which showed the importance of mentors early in their careers.[22] We spent some time discussing whether women had mentors in the same way – Phyllis Deutsch (New York University PhD, 1991) insisted they didn't.[23] Roper also argued against Marxist ideas of false consciousness. This was central to our purpose as it allowed for different stories about social class to be written. Too often the Left had argued that capitalist society had prevented the workers from properly appreciating their exploitation. At worst, this led to crude and reductionist portraits of working-class life. Increasingly, we wanted a social history that thought seriously about the ways different social groups had agency and negotiated with each other (which might be thought of as the Gramsci influence). There was much talk about post-Marxism though not much agreement about what it was.[24] Looking back, many of these conversations anticipated current discussions of the importance of intersectionality. We sought analyses that highlighted the differing roles of class, race, sexuality and gender as dynamic forces in the construction of identities and social structures.

This set the stage for the defining event of the Seminar's first year. We knew John Styles (Cambridge BA, 1971) and John Seed (Hull PhD, 1981) as two historians who thought deeply about social history in different ways but were open to theory. John Styles was at the time writing about eighteenth-century crime although his work with the Royal College of Art was drawing him into design and textile history (he went on to become professor of history at the University of Hertfordshire). John Seed was teaching at Roehampton University: his exploration of the social formation of the Manchester middle class was informed by a deep grounding in critical theory that few could rival.[25] We asked them to speak at a meeting of the Seminar in the summer of 1987 about culture and politics (we did not define their brief any more than that). On the day, I recall the International Relations Room was packed out with postgraduates. Styles and Seed had very different perspectives but critiqued conventional empirical approaches to the past and discussed the complexities of using theory. Both argued for richer forms of cultural history which incorporated the material base but also the agency of representation, image and the power of design. The freedom to talk about politics and theory as well as history made the whole event quite liberating. I recall that Anna Clark (working on politics and nineteenth-century women with Judith Walkowitz) argued from the floor that many of the conventional ideas about empiricism versus theory looked tired when compared to the work coming out of feminism and women's history. Pamela Edwards (researching a thesis on the political thought of Samuel Taylor Coleridge with Fred Rosen at University College London) argued that theories about meaning and interpretation remained important and that they had not been displaced by an approach based upon gender. There was a sympathy for ideas derived from cultural anthropology although, looking back, I am surprised at how little attention was paid to the kind of perspectives coming out of literature departments, despite the fact that we were interested in language and vocabulary. In many ways, what interested us were ideas expressed in language rather than language in itself: a reinvigorated intellectual history that was a marked feature of these years. Styles spoke warmly about J. G. A. Pocock's intellectual history, sending me off to read his work on the politics of virtue, which had recently appeared.[26] In a different mode, there was also strong admiration for Roger Chartier's explorations in cultural history, using appropriation models for understanding popular culture, which allowed for a concept of people's agency (exactly what we wanted to uncover).[27]

Through the late 1980s, there was increasing interest in Michel Foucault (1926–84), not least because his work spoke to the histories of both crime and sexuality (which preoccupied many members of the Seminar). There was less interest in categories around post-modernism and history although Hilda Christensen (IHR Research Fellow, 1991–2) spoke in 1992 about 'History, Feminism and Post-Structuralism'. The latter became a marked characteristic of historical discussion in the 1990s, following a series of interventions by Patrick Joyce (b. 1945).[28] Explorations of post-modernism became much more a feature of the reading group on cultural history that Joyce and Raphael Samuel (1934–96) organized for some years in the mid-1990s at the IHR and which sought to rethink ideas about history in the wake of figures such as Hayden White.[29]

## Renewing the Seminar

In the summer of 1987 (and before I finished my thesis), I got my first job teaching part-time in the history department at the then Polytechnic of North London. Although I remained with the Seminar, I handed the running of it to Amanda Vickery who organized it for a year. It was run after that by a collective rather than a single person. Tim Hitchcock, Kelly Boyd and Tony Claydon (London PhD, 1993, and later professor of early modern history at Bangor) ran it together. They were then succeeded in the 1990s by collectives which involved, at various times, Tony Henderson (London PhD, 1992), James Ryan (London PhD, 1994), Deborah Sugg Ryan (East London PhD, 1995), Heather Shore (London PhD, 1996), Tim Meldrum (London PhD, 1996), Theresa Ploszajska (London PhD, 1996), Jonathan Nix (London PhD, 1997), Adam Sutcliffe (London PhD, 1998), Brenda Assael (Toronto PhD, 1998), Hera Cook (Sussex PhD, 1999) and Karen Harvey (London PhD, 1999). By 2000 the line-up was made up of Louise Gray (London PhD, 2001), Tanya Evans (London PhD, 2002), Hannah Greig (London PhD, 2003), Cathy McClive (Warwick PhD, 2004) and Tim Fletcher (London PhD, 2008).

In 1990–91, Tony Henderson (then researching a PhD on eighteenth-century prostitution at Royal Holloway with Penelope Corfield) was asked, on the basis of his role as a convenor of the Seminar, to take part in a working party on postgraduate training in historical research chaired by Roger Mettam. The group reviewed the issue of whether there was a need for a more professional approach to postgraduate training and to assess the question of whether a PhD should be seen as a work that can be done in three years. The working party recommended the expansion of the kind of training courses available at the IHR with increasing government funds being made available to get more postgraduates to take part. It also recommended that postgraduates receive greater opportunities to teach.[30]

Numbers at the Postgraduate Seminar could vary wildly, depending on who was speaking and what the topic was. Only a few had an embarrassingly low attendance. When Tony Claydon spoke about the origins of English nationalism, the register shows there were twenty-four people there. I was annoyed by one postgraduate who asked to speak and (as we later discovered) used the Seminar as a dress rehearsal for giving a paper at one of the other IHR seminars a few weeks later. I felt that our seminar needed to be more than just a springboard for speaking to the 'grown ups'.

The Seminar could respond to political events as they happened. When Margaret Thatcher resigned in 1990, we put on a seminar the following week, titled 'Thatcher and the Historians', where we looked at her legacy. Edmund Green (London PhD, 1992) was quite brilliant, exposing the gap between Thatcher's rhetoric and what she had actually accomplished. Changes in the political left were registered by the Seminar. Patrick Curry delivered a paper titled 'New New Left and Old New Right' on 12 February 1990 which floated arguments about post-Marxism.[31] A couple of months before this, I delivered a paper titled 'Disinventing the Radical Tradition, 1660–2000', seeking to rethink the history of the Left, moving away from a simplistic emphasis on the rise of socialism and emphasizing liberal and progressive currents of thought. In retrospect, I realize I was playing around with some of the arguments that would go into the formation of New Labour.

At the same time, the Seminar was also concerned with wider issues about how history was being taught. Peter D'Sena (now associate professor of learning and teaching at the University of Hertfordshire and a senior fellow at the IHR) spoke in 1990 about the new National Curriculum. In October 1992 there was a round-table discussion of 'Postgraduate Study in an Era of Mass Higher Education' and, the following year, a similar discussion of 'Heritage and the Preservation of History'. James Ryan (now professor of history at Portsmouth University) organized a session titled 'Politics on the Campus: Political Correctness and the Practice of History in Universities'. The Seminar also had a consultative meeting in 1993 with the History at Universities Defence Group which was responding to concerns about cuts to funding for the discipline (it later became part of History UK).

Having had a slightly unofficial quality, the Seminar was increasingly accepted as a significant part of academic life at the IHR. Towards the end of his tenure as director, Michael Thompson agreed to give a talk (in 1990). We had hoped to get him to talk about his own theory of history. Michael did not quite do this, but he did talk about the threats to the writing of history as existed at that time. There were other established historians who spoke at the Seminar. In 1995, Alun Howkins (1947–2018) from Sussex University spoke about what the Mass Observation project revealed about rural England in the Second World War.[32]

Another sign of change was when, early in the new century, Hannah Greig (now reader in early modern history at the University of York) and Tanya Evans (now associate professor in history at Macquarie University in Australia) organized what may have been the first ever postgraduate-run conference at the IHR (on 'desire in history') with graduate students delivering papers on material culture (the desire for things), the history of the emotions (desire as an experience, is desire an emotion?) and the histories of sex and sexualities.[33] The postgraduate experience at the IHR was therefore rather different from what it had been in the mid-1980s. The Seminar in the 1990s started to become a more postgraduate-only event, something it had not been before. It did, however, prove enduring and, after 2008, merged into the History Lab which became a national network for postgraduate students.

## Looking back

When I look back from 2023, it is striking how preoccupied we were with issues of gender and class and how little we had to say about race – especially given the origins of the Seminar in the Enoch Powell protest. Furthermore, the Seminar was never terribly rigorous in its discussion of theory which was meant to be its *raison d'être*. There were certainly few examples of 'high theory'. I suspect we all felt we were feeling our way. I am also struck by the way we did not talk about digital history. Mine was a cohort that commenced researching our PhDs on pads of paper and completed them on laptops. The Internet, of course, barely existed at that time. We had no inkling of how the process of historical research was going to change in some fundamental ways through the application of new technology, though Tim Hitchcock proved to be a leader in this respect.

At an intellectual level, the Postgraduate Seminar did seek to recast some of the grand narratives that we inherited, especially from Marxism. We thought about class but increasingly felt the challenge of arguments about language and about post-structuralist approaches (though it is arguable how much the latter really caught on amongst historians). If there was a hallmark of the discussions, it was a rejection of reductive explanations based on the economy. There was a strong emphasis on the fact that the coming of women's history (and the greater role of women in the academy) had to change the way we thought about the past. We also tended to see cultural history (or, at least, a blend of social and cultural history) as very much the way forward. To that extent, the Postgraduate Seminar reflected the way the discipline was changing.

Hannah Greig recollected her fondness for the Seminar: it

> was where I presented my first paper, learned how to drive forward seminar discussions, how to chair a paper, and was the centre of my PhD experience for a number of years. It gave us a sense of ownership and belonging in the IHR. It was a robust and challenging forum though.[34]

Looking over the Seminar's registers, one sees the genesis of major books and articles that were subsequently published. Many of the organizers and participants were people who went on to have major academic careers. Yet one notes wistfully the names in the registers of people who were postgraduates and who, for various reasons, were not able to get academic jobs but who were nevertheless an important part of the IHR community. As an historical source, the registers provide a useful record not only of people's affiliations but also of what they considered their research interests at the time when they signed their names. The regularity of the Seminar's meetings is worth mentioning. In the academic year 1992–3, for example, fourteen papers were delivered.[35]

The Postgraduate Seminar was an empowering space for a generation of postgraduates who would subsequently shape the writing of history in various ways from the 1990s onwards. It prefigured the networks created by the History Lab but also helped change the culture of the IHR, extending the range of topics discussed and creating a sense of welcome. I have tried here to identify some of its intellectual formation so as to explore the academic culture of the 1980s and 1990s.

## Notes

1. R. Vinen, *Thatcher's Britain: The Politics and Social Upheaval of the Thatcher Era* (London, 2010); B. Jackson and R. Saunders (ed.), *Making Thatcher's Britain* (Cambridge, 2012); and E. Evans, *Thatcher and Thatcherism* (London, 2018).

2. R. McWilliam, 'From Scholarship Boy to Social Historian: J. F. C. Harrison (1921–2018): An Appreciation', *Cultural and Social History*, xv (2018), 463–8; M. Chase, 'J. F. C. Harrison (1921–2018)', *Labour History Review*, lxxxiv (2019), 71–83. See also J. F. C. Harrison, *Scholarship Boy: A Personal History of the Twentieth Century* (London, 1995).

3. For one example, see D. J. Munro, *Writings on British History 1946–1948: A Bibliography of Books and Articles on the History of Great Britain from about 450 A.D. to 1914* (London, 1973). See also Bibliography of British and Irish History: https:// www.history.ac.uk/publications/bibliography-british-and-irish-history [accessed 26 Apr. 2023].

4. For complementary details on the Witness Seminars and the Enoch Powell affair at the IHR, see the contribution by Alice Prochaska in Chapter 11; and for selected correspondence relating Powell's visit, see Institute of Historical Research, Wohl Library: IHR/3/3/22.

5. Midgley was concerned in her research with issues around race and empire which went on to inform her subsequent work: C. Midgley, *Women Against Slavery: The British Campaigns, 1780–1870* (London, 1992); and C. Midgley, *Feminism and Empire: Women Activists in Imperial Britain, 1790–1865* (London, 2007).

6. C. L. Riley (ed.), *The Free Speech Wars: How Did We Get Here and Why Does it Matter?* (Manchester, 2020).

7. Clare Midgley (b. 1955) recently retired as professor of history at Sheffield Hallam University. She was also President of the International Federation for Research in Women's History between 2010 and 2015. Amanda Vickery (b. 1962) is professor of early modern history at Queen Mary University of London and one of the UK's most prominent public historians.

8. P. Edwards, *The Statesman's Science: History, Nature and Law in the Political Thought of Samuel Taylor Coleridge* (New York, 2014).

9. J. Wheelwright, *Amazons and Military Maids: Women Who Dressed as Men in the Pursuit of Life, Liberty and Happiness* (London, 1989). Wheelwright completed an MA at Sussex University in 1986. Following a career in journalism, she received a London University PhD in 2014 and became director of the Centre for Culture and the Creative Industries at City University.

10. IHR/3/3/50. See also IHR/3/3/52 and IHR 05/1/1 for subsequent registers.

11. M. Chase, 'Sussex University History Workshop', *History Workshop Journal*, xii (1981), 195–6; and R. Samuel, *History Workshop: A Collectanea, 1967–1991* (London, 1991).

12. Tim Hitchcock, who was then teaching at the Polytechnic of North London, went on to become professor of digital history at Sussex University. Lee Davison became the historian attached to the Federal Deposit Corporation, Washington, DC. Tim Kiern became director of liberal studies at California State University, Long Beach. Robert Shoemaker became professor of history at Sheffield University. Hitchcock and Shoemaker became pioneers of digital history, going on to collaborate with Clive Emsley (1944–2020) on The Proceedings of the Old Bailey, 1674–1913, Old Bailey Online: https://www.oldbaileyonline.org/ [accessed 20 Apr. 2023].

13. L. Davison, T. Hitchcock, T. Keirn and R. Shoemaker (ed.), *Stilling the Grumbling Hive: Response to Social and Economic Problems in England, 1689–1750*

(Stroud, 1992): the preface (p. ix) acknowledges the origins of the book in the tearoom of the IHR.

14. Maria Dowling later became a lecturer at St Mary's University College, Strawberry Hill.

15. This became her book, K. Boyd, *Manliness and the Boys' Story Paper in Britain: A Cultural History, 1855–1940* (Basingstoke, 2003). Kelly Boyd was later a lecturer in History at Middlesex University and is now a senior fellow at the IHR.

16. M. Pugh, *The Tories and the People, 1880–1935* (Oxford, 1985); and B. Campbell, *Iron Ladies: Why Do Women Vote Tory?* (London, 1987).

17. Q. Hoare and G. Nowell-Smith (ed.), *Selections from the Prison Notebooks of Antonio Gramsci* (London, 1971). See also J. Harris, 'Marxism Today: The Forgotten Visionaries Whose Ideas Could Save Labour', *Guardian*, 29 September 2015.

18. E. Hobsbawm, 'The Forward March of Labour Halted?', *Marxism Today*, xxii (1978), 279–86. For the subsequent debate, see the book that *Marxism Today* issued which reprinted the article and offered multiple responses from figures on the British left: E. Hobsbawm, *The Forward March of Labour Halted?* (London, 1981).

19. S. Hall and M. Jacques (ed.), *New Times: The Changing Face of Politics in the 1990s* (London, 1989). For the impact of this, see the following special issue: M. Hilton, C. Moores and F. Sutcliffe-Braithwaite (ed.), *'New Times* Revisited: Britain in the 1980s', *Contemporary British History*, xxxi (2017). See also C. Clarke: 'Learning the Lessons of *Marxism Today*': *Progressive Review* (20 Dec. 2011): https://www.ippr.org/juncture-item/learning-the-lessons-of-marxism-today [accessed 20 Apr. 2023].

20. F. Gray (ed.), *Making the Future: A History of the University of Sussex* (Brighton, 2011), pp. 143–52, and pp. 252–6.

21. M. Hamilton, *The Queen of Camp: Mae West, Sex and Popular Culture* (London, 1996). Marybeth Hamilton is now administrative editor of *History Workshop Journal*.

22. This later was developed into M. Roper, *Masculinity and the British Organisation Man since 1945* (Oxford, 1993).

23. Phyllis Deutsch went on to become editor-in-chief at the University Press of New England (1996–2017).

24. Some of these perspectives went on to inform my analysis in R. McWilliam, *The Tichborne Claimant: A Victorian Sensation* (London, 2007).

25. J. Styles, *The Dress of the People: Everyday Fashion in Eighteenth-Century England* (London, 2007); J. Seed, 'Unitarianism, Political Economy and the Antinomies of Liberal Culture in Manchester, 1830–1850', *Social History*, vii (1982), pp. 1–25; and J. Seed, *Marx: A Guide for the Perplexed* (London, 2010).

26. J. G. A. Pocock, *Virtue, Commerce, and History: Essays on Political Thought and History, Chiefly in the Eighteenth Century* (Cambridge, 1985).

27. R. Chartier, *The Cultural Uses of Print in Early Modern France* (Princeton, NJ, 1987). See also L. Hunt (ed.), *The New Cultural History* (Berkeley, CA, 1989).

28. P. Joyce, *Democratic Subjects: The Self and the Social in Nineteenth Century England* (Cambridge, 1994). On Joyce, see R. Colls, 'Post-Modern Pat: The Work of Patrick Joyce', and J. Vernon, 'More Secondary Modern than Post-Modern: Patrick Joyce and the Peculiarities of Liberal Modernity in Britain', *Cultural and Social History*, xiii (2016), 135–48 and 149–54.

29. On Samuel, see A. Light, *A Radical Romance: A Memoir of Love, Grief and Consolation* (London, 2019); S. Scott-Brown, *The Histories of Raphael Samuel: A Portrait of a People's Historian* (Acton, Australia, 2017). On White, see H. White, *Metahistory: The Historical Imagination in Nineteenth-Century Europe* (Baltimore, 1975).

**30.** 'Working Party of Postgraduate Training in Historical Research Report' (1991), copy in author's possession; Tony Henderson's thesis became the book, *Disorderly Women in Eighteenth-Century London: Prostitution and Control in the Metropolis, 1730–1830* (London,1999).

**31.** On post-Marxism, see P. Curry, 'Towards a Post-Marxist Social History: Thompson, Clark and Beyond', in *Rethinking Social History*, ed. A. Wilson (Manchester, 1993), pp. 158–200.

**32.** N. Verdon, 'Remembering Alun Howkins, 1947–2018', *History Workshop Journal*, lxxxviii (2019), 299–313.

**33.** Hannah Greig, email to the author, 13 Oct. 2021.

**34.** Hannah Greig, email to the author, 13 Oct. 2021.

**35.** *Institute of Historical Research: Annual Report, 1992–1993* (London, 1993), 42–3.

# References

## Archived sources

Institute of Historical Research, Wohl Library:

IHR/3/3/22.
IHR/3/3/50.
IHR/3/3/52.
IHR/05/1/1.

## Published sources

Bibliography of British and Irish History: https://www.history.ac.uk/publications/bibliography-british-and-irish-history [accessed 26 Apr. 2023].

Boyd, K., *Manliness and the Boys' Story Paper in Britain: A Cultural History, 1855–1940* (Basingstoke, 2003).

Campbell, B., *Iron Ladies: Why Do Women Vote Tory?* (London, 1987).

Chartier, R., *The Cultural Uses of Print in Early Modern France* (Princeton, NJ, 1987).

Chase, M., 'Sussex University History Workshop', *History Workshop Journal*, xii (1981), 195–6.

Chase, M., 'J. F. C. Harrison (1921–2018)', *Labour History Review*, lxxxiv (2019), 71–83.

Clarke, C., 'Learning the Lessons of *Marxism Today*', *Progressive Review* [Institute for Public Policy Research], (20 Dec. 2011): https://www.ippr.org/juncture-item/learning-the-lessons-of-marxism-today [accessed 20 Apr. 2023].

Colls, R., 'Post-Modern Pat: The Work of Patrick Joyce', *Cultural and Social History*, xiii (2016), 135–48.

Curry, P., 'Towards a Post-Marxist Social History: Thompson, Clark and Beyond', in *Rethinking Social History*, ed. A. Wilson (Manchester, 1993), pp. 158–200.

Davison, L. et al. (ed.), *Stilling the Grumbling Hive: Response to Social and Economic Problems in England, 1689–1750* (Stroud, 1992).

Edwards, P., *The Statesman's Science: History, Nature and Law in the Political Thought of Samuel Taylor Coleridge* (New York, 2014).

Evans, E., *Thatcher and Thatcherism* (London, 2018).

Gray, F. (ed.), *Making the Future: A History of the University of Sussex* (Brighton, 2011).

Hall, S., and Jacques, M. (ed.), *New Times: The Changing Face of Politics in the 1990s* (London, 1989).

Hamilton, M., *The Queen of Camp: Mae West, Sex and Popular Culture* (London, 1996).

Harris, J., 'Marxism Today: The Forgotten Visionaries Whose Ideas Could Save Labour', *Guardian*, 29 September 2015.

Harrison, J. F. C., *Scholarship Boy: A Personal History of the Twentieth Century* (London, 1995).

Henderson, T., *Disorderly Women in Eighteenth-Century London: Prostitution and Control in the Metropolis, 1730–1830* (London, 1999).

Hilton, M., Moores, C., and Sutcliffe-Braithwaite, F. (ed.), 'New Times Revisited: Britain in the 1980s', *Contemporary British History*, xxxi (2017).

Hoare, Q., and Nowell-Smith, G. (ed.), *Selections from the Prison Notebooks of Antonio Gramsci* (London, 1971).

Hobsbawm, E., 'The Forward March of Labour Halted?', *Marxism Today*, xxii (1978), 279–86.

Hobsbawm, E., *The Forward March of Labour Halted?* (London, 1981).

Hunt, L. (ed.), *The New Cultural History* (Berkeley, CA, 1989).

*Institute of Historical Research: Annual Report, 1992–1993* (London, 1993).

Jackson, B., and Saunders, R. (ed.), *Making Thatcher's Britain* (Cambridge, 2012).

Joyce, P., *Democratic Subjects: The Self and the Social in Nineteenth Century England* (Cambridge, 1994).

Light, A., *A Radical Romance: A Memoir of Love, Grief and Consolation* (London, 2019).

McWilliam, R., *The Tichborne Claimant: A Victorian Sensation* (London, 2007).

McWilliam, R., 'From Scholarship Boy to Social Historian: J. F. C. Harrison (1921–2018): An Appreciation', *Cultural and Social History*, xv (2018), 463–8.

Midgley, C., *Women Against Slavery: The British Campaigns, 1780–1870* (London, 1992).

Midgley, C., *Feminism and Empire: Women Activists in Imperial Britain, 1790–1865* (London, 2007).

Munro, D. J., *Writings on British History 1946–1948: A Bibliography of Books and Articles on the History of Great Britain from about 450 A.D. to 1914* (London, 1973).

Pocock, J. G. A., *Virtue, Commerce, and History: Essays on Political Thought and History, Chiefly in the Eighteenth Century* (Cambridge, 1985).

The Proceedings of the Old Bailey, 1674–1913: https://www.oldbailey online.org/ [20 Apr. 2023].

Pugh, M., *The Tories and the People, 1880–1935* (Oxford, 1985).

Riley, C. L. (ed.), *The Free Speech Wars: How Did We Get Here and Why Does it Matter?* (Manchester, 2020).

Roper, M., *Masculinity and the British Organisation Man since 1945* (Oxford, 1993).

Samuel, R., *History Workshop: A Collectanea, 1967–1991* (London, 1991).

Scott-Brown, S., *The Histories of Raphael Samuel: A Portrait of a People's Historian* (Acton, Australia, 2017).

Seed, J., 'Unitarianism, Political Economy and the Antinomies of Liberal Culture in Manchester, 1830–1850', *Social History*, vii (1982), pp. 1–25

Seed, J., *Marx: A Guide for the Perplexed* (London, 2010).

Styles, J., *The Dress of the People: Everyday Fashion in Eighteenth-Century England* (London, 2007).

Verdon, N., 'Remembering Alun Howkins, 1947–2018', *History Workshop Journal*, lxxxviii (2019), 299–313.

Vernon, J., 'More Secondary Modern than Post-Modern: Patrick Joyce and the Peculiarities of Liberal Modernity in Britain', *Cultural and Social History*, xiii (2016), 149–54.

Vinen, R., *Thatcher's Britain: The Politics and Social Upheaval of the Thatcher Era* (London, 2010)

Wheelwright, J., *Amazons and Military Maids: Women Who Dressed as Men in the Pursuit of Life, Liberty and Happiness* (London, 1989).

White, H., *Metahistory: The Historical Imagination in Nineteenth-Century Europe* (Baltimore, 1975).

## Unpublished sources

McWilliam, R., Miscellaneous Private Correspondence and Notes.

Chapter 10

# The Women's History Seminar

## Kelly Boyd*

In the spring of 1986, during a period of some ferment at the IHR, the Women's History Seminar was founded. At the time there were about twenty-five ongoing seminars, many of them long running, and its establishment marked an opening up of the institution to new ways of thinking about history that went beyond the geographical and the chronological and towards the theoretical and thematic. The Seminar's purpose was to interrogate the role of women in the past, but also would come to consider the question of how gender might have affected the way men interacted with the world. It was an example of the way the discipline was moving past earlier categories of exploration (political, intellectual, economic or social) to engaging with ideas about identity (race, sexuality) or a range of other areas of focus (public history, historiography). This chapter will examine the Seminar's origins, its subsequent development, its goals and its efforts to foster new ways of thinking about both women's history and historians of women – to explore the historical realities of people's lives.

## Background and founding

The year 1986 was a good time to start a seminar in women's history. It was deep into the age of Margaret Thatcher, a woman who notoriously objected to any gendered analysis of her rise to power. But Thatcher and Thatcherism were not central to the founding of the Seminar. Of greater import was the advancement of second-wave feminism, which paralleled movements for racial equality and the insights of the New Left. These general movements had seen increasing numbers of women entering the academy and more and more of them were interested in understanding both women's traditional roles in society and the ways these had been challenged. Additionally, academic research was developing that interrogated the breadth of women's work and the specific way it had been both central to the working of modern society while at the same time being diminished as important or crucial to the economic and social structures underpinning every culture. Thus, the Seminar's foundation represented an infiltration of the academy by forces that were already in evidence and gathering steam. It did not happen overnight but was the result of effective lobbying within the IHR and a recognition of the rising profile of women's history within the larger category of history.

Women's history had begun to take shape as a sub-disciplinary field of enquiry in the late 1960s and early 1970s as second-wave feminism began to forge ahead. It reflected the expansion of social history and its spotlight on non-elites as proper subjects of study. Also key was the increasing use of oral history as it systematically provided testimonies about everyday life that had not been available in the written record. This allowed access into lives back to the late nineteenth century.[1] By the 1970s there were more focused accounts of women's fight for the vote, a recognition that their role in the industrial revolution was crucial, and that the division of labour between the sexes was not fixed but was often fluid from era to era. In the Anglophone world, in particular, this meant the increasing appearance of research and analysis of women's roles throughout time and place. Sheila Rowbotham's *Hidden from History* (1973) led the way.[2] Collections of essays like *Clio's Consciousness Raised* (1974) and *Suffer and Be Still* (1972) brought together scholars from across the globe who studied periods from the ancient to the modern to offer analytical essays about women's lives in the past.[3] The London-based feminist publisher Virago (est. 1973) not only reprinted pertinent historical books from the past, it commissioned new ones, making women's history a visible topic on bookshelves.[4] As a student at a US women's liberal arts college in the mid-1970s I was lucky to be able to take a semester-long module on European women's history.[5] The course was a bit over-ambitious with a reading list that ranged from John Stuart Mill's *On the Subjection of Women* (1869), to George Bernard Shaw's *Mrs Warren's Profession* (1898), to Simone de Beauvoir's *The Second Sex* (1949). But for me the book we read that demonstrated how the history of women could be rigorously studied was Ivy Pinchbeck's *Women Workers in the Industrial Revolution*. Published in 1930 this demanding economic history was exhaustive in laying out the many forms of women's labour outside the home. It failed, in the short term, to spark studies that were female centred. However, by the 1970s women were once again on the agenda. As well as conferences where women's past was explored, there were collections of essays published, and more academic research was begrudgingly supported on an institutional level.[6] But the welcoming of women's history was only slowly accepted and often depended on individual scholars cajoling funding from their institutions to support such ventures.

Scholars themselves often worked together to offer venues to present this new research. In Britain, the History Workshop movement unwittingly propelled some feminist activity when at a 1969 gathering at Ruskin College in Oxford, the mostly male audience 'shrieked with laughter' when Sheila Rowbotham suggested the history of women was a proper topic of research.[7] Ruskin was a working-man's college (adjacent to, but not part of, Oxford University), and thus, the historical study of trade unions was its general centre of attention. History Workshop itself was initially dedicated to history from below, especially by providing studies of work across a broad spectrum – but much of its scholarship illuminated men's labour. Sally Alexander was one of two women enrolled at Ruskin at the time and she described how this spurred a group of women to organize what was to be a conference on women's history, but swiftly shifted to women's liberation when it was held in 1970.[8] History Workshop itself was soon on board with women's history, including the field in its conferences. The first volume of *History Workshop Journal* in 1976 included an editorial by Sally Alexander and Anna Davin that spelled out how central a feminist analysis would be in the publication.[9] In spring 1982 its subtitle would make it explicit as it became *A Journal of Socialist and Feminist Historians*.[10]

More focused was the Feminist History Group (FHG).[11] Founded in 1973 and mostly made up of women researchers – many of whom were doctoral students – it had no institutional base. This London group met monthly in a variety of venues: for example, the Mary Ward Centre in Queen's Square. It too produced a volume of essays: *The Sexual Dynamics of History* (1983).[12] The book's title confirms the analytical nature of the field as it sought to tease out how gender relations were constantly re-shaped – usually to female disadvantage. And there were similar groups in Birmingham, Manchester and Bradford. But these groups operated outside formal academic settings. Many early researchers in the field remember being informed that their desire to explore women's history did not fit into the structures of studying history. They were often actively discouraged from writing dissertations on the topic as undergraduates. By the 1980s there were no professors of women's history in Britain and there were no designated entry-level jobs being advertised either. Few universities offered formal training in what was soon to become a thriving field of study. If there were institutions that had appointed more than one person working on women's history topics it had been more by accident than design. If you were a budding women's historian pursuing a postgraduate degree – and understood how things worked – you applied for a place in a programme that had someone you read and admired on the faculty. On a personal level, I was lucky. As an American, I applied to Rutgers University in New Jersey to work with Judith Walkowitz (b. 1945) because I had been wowed by an essay of hers in the edited volume *Clio's Consciousness Raised* (1974). Because Rutgers at that time was made up of several different constituent colleges in and around New Brunswick, New Jersey, and was just beginning to reorganize itself into larger faculties across the university, it had at least half a dozen members of faculty working on aspects of women's history. But it was the exception, not the rule. I was also fortunate that as a doctoral candidate at Rutgers I was teaching an undergraduate module in women's history within a couple of years.

When I arrived in the UK to do my doctoral research in 1984, I had three groups my Rutgers doctoral advisor advised me to forge links with. History Workshop and the Feminist History Group were the first two. But most important was the Institute of Historical Research, as it offered a base for visiting international research students. Let me set the scene by saying a little bit about the IHR in the 1980s. The Institute was in many ways very lively back then with the Common Room a meeting place for historians at lunch, teatime before seminars, and as a spot to meet people to go for drinks. People streamed in just before 5 p.m. as that was when the backdoor to the British Museum was closed and it saved having to walk all the way around the block. It was generally hard to get a seat at teatime and the room was wreathed in cigarette and pipe smoke. The area was configured differently from how it is today, and the periodicals room always had five or six people hovering around the shelves and reading. Along the edges of the Common Room were bound issues of *Punch*. Despite always having women and men historians involved in its seminars, I think it would be fair to say that it still had a pretty masculine vibe.

I had registered at the IHR and examined the seminar lists for appropriate papers to attend. I was told it was generally best to write to a convenor of any seminar I wished to attend to introduce myself and secure permission to do so. However, no advice was given on where to send such a letter and it did not encourage me to plunge into the seminar scene.[13] For decades, IHR seminars had been a creature of the University of London history departments and perpetuated a model that mixed the training of doctoral students with opportunities to hear invited speakers share their latest research. Professors, readers and lecturers attended the seminars as well so they could hear new work, but also to meet colleagues from other institutions and, perhaps, to spot upcoming talent. The IHR offered a venue like few others in the world, gathering dozens of historians under one roof on a daily or weekly basis. Seminars themselves, however, seldom offered papers on women's history and gender history was not even thought of. The events could often be uncomfortable as some were renowned for their brutality and occasionally a speaker might be reduced to tears.

Research on the history of women could, of course, be presented elsewhere. As noted above, History Workshop welcomed the subject by the 1980s. At the Feminist History Group, discussion often turned to the topic of whether a place like the IHR might be persuaded to establish a seminar on the discipline. One of our current co-convenors, Cornelie Usborne, remembered the Feminist History Group as 'an ideal platform to air work in progress, to receive ideas, information and general encouragement' as well as the long-term friends she made.[14] Both she and Alison Oram stressed that the group's emphasis was on the word 'feminist' rather than 'history' in its name.[15] Cornelie noted the tension between 'the value of pure feminism (i.e. staying autonomous and outside universities)' and 'gaining a foothold inside academia to raise the profile of women but having to compromise ideals to fit in'.[16] She also remembered that:

> the idea to form a seminar in the IHR was, I think, aired on several occasions within the FHG. When it came to the preparatory meeting in the IHR Common Room (or was it a seminar room?) I remember quite a passionate discussion and a split between those ... who argued for the old name of 'Feminist History' Seminar [and] who were also quite sceptical of submitting to rules and customs of the establishment, i.e., the IHR, and those [who wished] to consider ... courting hostility and disapproval by insisting on this name. Well, that side won, *women's history* it was and still is today.[17]

The founding of the Seminar, however, did not emerge from the Feminist History Group, but instead was the product of lobbying by established scholars from within the University of London who were both already embedded in the seminar culture of the IHR, and indeed, well known in their respective fields. Fascinatingly, women and gender had not necessarily been at the heart of their work, although in coming years it sometimes became more central. They included Janet (Jinty) Nelson, Pat Thane and Penelope (Penny) Corfield.[18] Intriguingly, Penny remembered an initial plan to call it Seminar on the History of Women, but almost immediately people began to refer to it as the Women's History Seminar and that was the name that stuck. No one remembers the specific negotiations to allow its foundation, but Penny 'recollect[ed] that there was some hostile huffing and puffing from a few noisily conservative men at the IHR, which had the effect of rallying left/liberal support from the surprisingly large numbers of men and women who were initially sceptical'.[19] Pat Thane confirms this. It was to be a bold experiment and it took place at a moment of some contention at the IHR. The spring of 1986 had been rocky, with postgraduate complaints about the invitation to Enoch Powell to speak (see Chapter 9 by Rohan McWilliam). This resulted in a large meeting to discuss the role of institutions. The IHR was opening up to new modes of working, which was to the credit of F. M. L. Thompson and Alice Prochaska, at that time respectively the director and the librarian (that is, chief administrator). They navigated a cultural shift as many organizations began to open up.

In the spring of 1986, the Women's History Seminar had its first invited speaker, who was probably the eminent economic and social historian of agriculture Joan Thirsk (1922–2013). The first full term of the Seminar began on 6 June 1986 and Jinty's diaries indicate the first speaker was Pat, who talked about 'Ideologies of Gender'. Rohan McWilliam remembered the second seminar was given by Leonore Davidoff (1932–2014); *Family Fortunes: Men and Women of the English Middle Class, 1780–1850*, her widely influential study of separate spheres (written with our soon-to-be seminar co-convenor Catherine Hall), appeared the next year. Lyndal Roper recalled that this was the first seminar she attended. At the time, Lyndal was a junior research fellow at Merton College, Oxford, but she would soon become a co-convenor of the Seminar after she was appointed to a permanent post at Royal Holloway.

## Establishing the Seminar

Within a few years, the Seminar would be an unofficial part of the Royal Holloway MA in Women's History founded by Lyndal and Amanda Vickery – also by that time a co-convenor of the Seminar.[20] That MA was designed to be taught on Fridays during the day at Royal Holloway's Bedford Square outpost, ending with everyone trooping over to the IHR to hear the latest research on the subject. It was one of the reasons that we remained a Friday seminar and it also affected our starting time for many years. The third seminar that first term was a panel of postgraduates speaking about their current research and included medievalist Sarah Lambert, who is now at Goldsmiths, early modernist Rachel Weil, now at Cornell, and myself. Rohan McWilliam remembered that Anna Clark (now at Minnesota) chaired. What I do recall is that the crowd for that day was standing room only, and I think we were in the Common Room. Since then, we've been all around the IHR and Senate House and, of course lately, on Zoom.

What should be made clear is that in its earliest years there was a real enthusiasm to hear about research on women's lives not just in Britain, but around the world, and not just from the past few centuries but across several millennia. Seminar papers confirmed that women did have a history which varied in terms of context, class, power, sexual identity, religion and other factors too numerous to mention. The point here is that the Women's History Seminar was a huge success and quickly established itself as a key place to speak about the history of women. I would love to be able to tell you about speakers in the first couple of years, but there are no records except those that individuals have retrieved from their own diaries. My own diaries only go back as far as 1988, but from these I can tell you that in that year many of the women who spoke were relatively early in their careers and not always situated firmly in academic jobs. Many were presenting gestating research sometimes derived from doctoral studies. They also hailed from around the globe and were part of a web of relationships that echoed early suffrage networks. Many have returned to the Seminar several times since its founding.

A few examples of the first academic term for which we have complete records (autumn 1988) reveal the variety of speakers and of research interests. The Australian feminist historian Barbara Caine spoke about suffragist Millicent Garrett Fawcett (1847–1929). Co-convenor sociologist Jane Lewis explored both Beatrice Webb (1858–1943), the feminist, Fabian socialist co-founder of the London School of Economics, and Mrs Humphrey Ward (1851–1920), the anti-feminist popular novelist and social reformer. Other papers ventured beyond the British Isles. Mary Vincent investigated women in the Second Spanish Republic. (She would later co-author the Royal Historical Society's 2018 report *Promoting Gender Equality in UK History* and is now a Trustee of the IHR.) The American historian Nancy Hewitt exposed us to the lives of women in late nineteenth- and early twentieth-century Tampa, Florida. At the end of the year there was a seminar on the term's themes: women's work, Christianity and gender. Other early speakers – many sharing their doctoral research which would result in important monographs and academic jobs around the world – included Catherine Hall, Amanda Vickery, Meg Arnot, Barbara Hanawalt, Elizabeth Ward, Anna Clark, Ulinka Rublack, Marilyn Lake, Carolyn Steedman, Paola di Cori (twice), Nell Painter, Barbara Taylor, Joanna Bourke, Sylvia Walby and Marina Warner. I could go on with the list, but the thing I would like to note is that many of these speakers successfully infiltrated women's history into the academy and most of their work would illuminate and re-define aspects of both women's history and other disciplines.[21] Very few of these speakers have disappeared and many of these women have risen through the ranks to professorships at major institutions around the world. We have been privileged to be able to engage with many of the projects which set the agenda for women's history over the years and seen many of the papers we've heard become part of landmark books and articles – not to mention the occasional radio or television programme.

The Seminar has also sought to schedule regular round tables where the latest scholarship on a specific approach was discussed.[22] For example, 'Complicating Categories, Crossing Cultures: Periodization in the History of Women from Medieval to Modern' and 'Women and Material Culture in Eighteenth-Century England' were typical sessions of this type. In 2000 the question debated was 'Women's History or Gender History? A Discussion'. The Seminar began with an introduction by Penelope Corfield; formal comments were then made by Jinty Nelson, John Tosh, Seth Denbo and Hera Cook (the latter two were just finishing their doctorates at the time).[23] This session was notable as we packed out the Local History Room (then the largest room at the IHR). More recently, sparked by a recent survey, 'Women's History in the Curriculum' saw the IHR's first woman director, Jo Fox, chair a session featuring several of our co-convenors. Alana Harris (KCL), Clare Midgley (Sheffield Hallam) and Imaobong Umoren (LSE) discussed the past, present and future of women's history in the British university curriculum.[24] During the pandemic we hosted several book launches and celebrated the publication of a volume in the *Past & Present* themed supplement series that explored mothering in a variety of guises.[25] Many of these works derived from research papers presented earlier at the Seminar. And we have also joined with other IHR seminars to co-present papers over the years.

The number of seminar convenors has waxed and waned. Since its founding, several others not mentioned above have been involved including Marybeth Hamilton and Lucy Delap.[26] I am currently joined by co-convenors Anna Davin (History Workshop), Amy Erickson (Cambridge), Laura Gowing (KCL), Alana Harris (KCL), Claire Langhamer (IHR), Carmen Mangion (Birkbeck), Clare Midgley (Sheffield Hallam), Krisztina Robert (Roehampton), Laura Schwartz (Warwick) and Cornelie Usborne (Roehampton/IHR).[27] What I'd call attention to here is that no longer does the University of London dominate the list, but there are representatives from a wider range of institutions from around the UK or sometimes no institution at all. This reflects the mobility of many convenors who frequently moved to new institutions during their careers, as well as the fact that post-1992 universities were some of the earliest to offer modules in women's history. The latter were perhaps earliest to give women's history a home because they welcomed mature students and many of the earliest researchers on women only entered higher education after pursuing other types of work or raising a family. Over the years we've received much support from the IHR, and I'm happy to think that the Seminar opened up the possibility for the wide range of topics that are covered today at the IHR. Indeed, an early A4 flyer found in the IHR archive shows an expansion to about forty seminars by 1991; today there are around sixty.

## Debates and trends

The Seminar itself has engaged in debates over the years about its focus and its name. Several times there has been a discussion of whether to reshape the name to include Gender History, but at the end of each of these we've decided to retain the simple Women's History. Retention of that name is a political statement about the necessity of interrogating women's role in the past, present and future. This doesn't mean that gender history hasn't been central to the papers presented at the Seminar. From the beginning we've had speakers about masculinity and its historical meaning as well. We have also been a victim of women's history's success in permeating the mainstream. Papers on women and gender are now present in many seminars. (The email newsletter I send out each week about seminars of interest to women's and gender historians generally lists three or four most weeks.) There is also now a separate seminar at the IHR that concentrates on Gender and History in the Americas. And additional organizations have emerged, like the Women's History Network, which has a national programme. However, there remains a role for a seminar exploring the issues we find compelling. Women's lives, their activities, their subjectivities, their emotions, their work, their centrality to the running of society, all remain of interest and I'm sure we'll enjoy hearing about the new research into these topics in the future.

Changing trends in higher education have also somewhat re-shaped the terrain. In the 1980s and 1990s there was an expansion of undergraduate and postgraduate teaching of women's history. The MA at Royal Holloway was not the only one in London; there was also an MA in Women's History at Guildhall. Women's Studies degrees were offered by a range of institutions, often under the direction of sociology departments, but always with a strong historical component. But more structural changes within higher education have seen falling numbers of students for not just these focused degrees on women, but for history degrees in general. Researchers in women's history now often combine that interest with a variety of approaches too great to be enumerated here.

Although hearing about the latest research is the core function of the Seminar, it is but one aspect of what our seminar seeks to do. Perhaps more important is the long discussion that follows each paper. This is sparked by asking the speaker questions after the paper, but at its best becomes a colloquy amongst those in attendance. The group probes the conclusions, suggests other aspects that might be investigated, shares knowledge of other sources that might be explored, and offers a venue for historical problems to be interrogated. Seminar papers are expected to be works in progress that might benefit from a supportive engaged audience. The arrival of PowerPoint presentations has eased the sharing of images and data which often led to hurried trips to the photocopier in the past. In an effort to be non-hierarchical we are seated around a seminar table, which allows everyone in attendance a real as well as a metaphorical seat at the table. If there are more people in attendance than can fit around a table, the chair will strive to include them all. Two practices of the Seminar have allowed us to reinforce our role in establishing links between scholars. The first was that from its inception the Seminar has always striven to be supportive. To this end, at the beginning of each seminar we go around the room to introduce ourselves and say where we're from and what we are working on.[28] This tradition, which is not employed by many other seminars, is important. It allows us to know what others are working on, but it also permits speakers to know who is in the room. You may find someone whose work you have admired and wanted to speak to. Or come across someone who would be good to talk to about putting a panel together for a conference. Or the speaker may discover that someone heavily criticized in her paper is present and can decide whether she may try to tweak the paper on the fly. A second innovation – unfortunately no longer practised since the IHR abandoned sign-in books for sign-in sheets – added a column for 'interests' for people to add as the sign-in book went around the seminar room. The book would then be re-circulated so attendees could take down details of people they wanted to speak to. Finally, after each seminar everyone is invited to join us for a drink in the IHR Common Room.[29] In the early years we frequently went out for a meal, but the practice has been abandoned with more and more speakers and attendees having other places they need to be. The IHR Common Room offers a pleasant place for informal talk. Here discussions continue, friendships are strengthened and networks are formed.

Networking, in point of fact, is one of the crucial functions of our seminar. In its earliest days it was one of the few places where people doing women's history could casually meet others doing similar topics. Although today this objective may rely more heavily on social media, it remains to be seen if electronic networks will function as fruitfully as older ones that sprang from in-person meetings. Networking, of course, means different things at different stages of an academic career. When one is a doctoral student or an early career researcher, one connects with people who will be vying for the same jobs and trying to get published in the same journals, as well as discovering those who can be relied upon for a joint venture like a conference panel or a co-edited work. Later those people will be sitting on similar committees, searching for people to review books, to referee journal submissions, or to examine doctoral theses. Some scholars will leave academe to become book editors, to commission documentaries for radio or television, or to run institutions. Doctoral candidates from overseas in London either to study or research are welcomed, and, in the future, may offer an invitation to speak or a faculty exchange to someone they've met at the Seminar. This is not peculiar to the Women's History Seminar, but historically women have networked in this way as far back as the abolition and suffrage movements of the nineteenth century. Links are particularly strong with Canada, Australia, New Zealand, the USA, Europe and Japan. The Seminar is fortunate that most years we enjoy news of a returning member who is offering a paper for the coming year. In our first two decades, dinner after seminar meetings also strengthened these links, but the ability to have drinks in the Common Room more recently has seen that practice become rarer. All of these strands of networking become useful over the course of a career, especially in a time when fewer jobs are on offer, departments are under pressure and careers have to be constantly reinvented.

Our seminar discussions on women's history and gender history have been complemented by interrogating other related issues, particularly the pressures on women working the university sector. Most recently, on Zoom, there was a discussion of the stresses of lockdown on women scholars who were often thrust into the challenges of full-time parenting while they also had to teach online.[30] New trends in historical research have allowed the Seminar to see how both new sources and analytical frameworks are enriching the field. The ability to explore new types of evidence on the internet has facilitated a deeper understanding of women's work across the globe, and enabled comparisons across cultures. Recent panels included a comparison of businesswomen in Australia and London, a roundtable on women's history in the British higher education curriculum, a foray into the lives of Chinese women migrants in the UK, a consideration of the intersection of race, gender and patriarchy in the seventeenth-century Atlantic, and a joint seminar with History of Sexuality to consider enforced female relationships in Second World War concentration camps. Thus 'inclusion' as it is often defined today has always been part of our DNA.

The recent pandemic period has provided us with an opportunity to welcome international speakers and attendees who otherwise might not have been able to join us at the IHR. Of course, this community was built on relationships formed over the past thirty years. Since 2020, our speakers have hailed from the UK, the USA, Sweden, Germany and New Zealand, while attendees have come from these places and Australia, Canada, Japan and India as well. The challenges here have been different. Most obviously time differences make it difficult for some, but the nature of the event itself has changed. The papers remain to be of a high standard, but Zoom has not been conducive to the best of discussions. Attendance numbers may be higher, but there are many who never turn their camera on, and the format seems to be more Q&A than deep discussion amongst the attendees. The pandemic period has, however, allowed us to see how women's history has continued to thrive. Even as there is a return to in-house events it will be illuminating to see how hybrid sessions will change things. Perhaps in the best cases, the scholars we have recently met online will be able to speak in person in the future.

## Conclusion

In 2016 the Seminar celebrated its thirtieth anniversary with a party. In our earliest days we heard agenda-setting debates over the role of separate spheres articulated by Leonore Davidoff, Catherine Hall and Amanda Vickery.[31] In the late twentieth century presentations ranged over a wide variety of topics such as questions of work, feminism, sexuality, class, dress, politics, stages of life, periodization, witchcraft, education, imperial roles, wartime service and cross-dressing. All of these topics are alive today and have been joined by work on the body, subjectivities, emotions, race, single mothers, female love and friendship, and monarchy. Women in the British Empire are now examined in terms of new debates about race and class. Women's bodies are interrogated not just in terms of the history of childbearing, but in terms of, amongst other things, the treatment of menstruation. Women's labour is probed across several cultures to reveal the way gender and class may reinforce working practices. And the culture of celebrity allows the opening up of a variety of subjects beyond monarchs and suffragettes. In fact, suffragettes and the fight for women's political rights remain popular topics and today we have more papers exploring second-wave feminism – exactly the context in which the seminar was founded. After four decades, the field remains strong, and researchers continue to expand and deepen their research. From a subject that was often derided fifty years ago, it has become a central part of any discussion and has been incorporated into the work of historians of multiple approaches, eras and cultures. It will be illuminating to discover the new aspects that will be delved into in the future.

# Notes

\* This chapter began as a paper to celebrate the thirtieth anniversary of the Seminar's foundation. I would also like to thank my fellow convenors for sharing their memories with me and Rohan McWilliam for his comments on both the original paper and this version.

1. Anna Davin (b. 1940) – pioneering feminist, community historian and co-founder of the *History Workshop Journal* [uniform title] (1976), as well as a former course teacher at both Birkbeck College and the IHR – has been explicit about how oral history may be used to uncover women's lives. See Anna Davin interviewed by Michelene Wandor (n.d.), in M. Wandor (ed.), *Once a Feminist: Stories of a Generation* (London, 1990), pp. 55–70 at p. 62. This book is an excellent source for researchers looking at the way select women came to feminism and then women's history. For Davin's personal archive, see The LSE Library, Women's Library Archives: GB 106 7ADA.

2. S. Rowbotham, *Hidden from History: 300 Years of Women's Oppression and the Fight Against It* (London, 1973).

3. M. Hartman and L. Banner (ed.), *Clio's Consciousness Raised: New Perspectives on the History of Women* (New York, 1974); M. Vicinus (ed.), *Suffer and Be Still: Women in the Victorian Age* (Bloomington, IN, 1972); M. Vicinus (ed.), *A Widening Sphere: Changing Roles of Victorian Women* (Bloomington, IN, 1977); B. Carroll (ed.), *Liberating Women's History: Theoretical and Critical Essays* (Urbana, IL, 1976). See also D. Beddoe, *Discovering Women's History: A Practical Manual* (London, 1983); Interviews with Sheila Rowbotham, Natalie Zemon Davis and Linda Gordon, in H. Abelove et al. (ed.), *Visions of History*, [for MARHO The Radical Historians Organization] (Manchester, 1984), pp. 47–70, 71–96, and 97–122; and J. Hannam 'Women's History, Feminist History' (online, 2008): https://archives.history.ac.uk /makinghistory/resources/articles/womens_history.html [accessed 1 Nov. 2022].

4. Virago set out to be the first mass-market publisher dedicated to women writers and readers. Virago's commitment to reprinting works by early twentieth-century women authors was formative to teaching and learning in modern women's history. Valuable titles included: F. Bell, *At the Works: A Study of a Manufacturing Town*, new intro. A. John (London, [1907] 1985); M. Reeves, *Round About a Pound a Week*, new intro. S. Alexander (London, [1913] 1977); C. Black (ed.), *Married Women's Work*, new intro. E. F. Mappen (London, [1915] 1983); B. Drake, *Women in Trade Unions*, new intro. N. Branson (London, [1920] 1984); M. L. Davies (ed.), *Life as We Have Known It by Cooperative Working Women*, new intro. A. Davin (London, [1931] 1977); and *Ada Nield Chew: The Life and Writings of a Working Woman*, comp. and bio. by D. Chew, foreword by A. Davin (London, 1982). For further context, see C. Riley, *The Virago Story: Assessing the Impact of a Feminist Publishing Phenomenon* (New York, 2018); and D.-M. Withers, *Virago Reprints and Modern Classics: The Timely Business of Feminist Publishing* (Cambridge, 2021).

5. Mount Holyoke College (founded as Mount Holyoke Female Seminary in 1837), was one of the first institutions of higher learning for women in the USA. In the nineteenth century, it became one of the 'Seven Sisters', a group of all-female liberal arts colleges to rival the traditionally all-male Ivy League. When co-education took hold in the 1960s, 70s and 80s, Mount Holyoke remained and is still a women's college.

6. The most notable was the USA's Berkshire Conference, established in 1973 and still going strong: Berkshire Conference of Women Historians (Berks): https:// berksconference.org/ [accessed 1 Nov. 2022].

7. Sheila Rowbotham, Sally Alexander and Anna Davin each speak of this in their interviews with Michelene Wandor in the latter's *Once a Feminist*, pp. 28–42, 81–92,

55–70: Rowbotham saw the laughter as 'patronizing', p. 28; Alexander remembered the 'shrieks of laughter' (p. 81); Davin characterized it as a 'guffaw' (p. 55). For further context, see S. Rowbotham, *Daring to Hope: My Life in the 1970s* (London, 2021). Rowbotham's personal archive is at the LSE Library, Women's Library Archives: GB 106 7SHR. For more information on the History Workshop movement, see B. Taylor, 'History of the History Workshop' (22 Nov. 2012): https://www .historyworkshop.org.uk/museums-archives-heritage/the-history-of-history -workshop/ [accessed 23 Feb. 2023].

**8.** Sally Alexander's experience of the culture of traditional history departments at the time is depicted in the comedy-drama film *Misbehaviour* (2020), directed by Philippa Lowthorpe, which deals with the feminist disruption of the 1970 Miss World contest in London: Alexander is portrayed by Keira Knightley. See also Sally Alexander, 'In Conversation with Poppy Sebag-Montefiore' (11 Mar. 2020): https:// www.historyworkshop.org.uk/beyond-misbehaviour/ [accessed 20 Oct. 2022].

**9.** S. Alexander and A. Davin, 'Feminist History', *History Workshop: A Journal of Socialist Historians*, i (1976), 4–6.

**10.** This was volume xiii, the last one to sport this subtitle was volume xxxix (1994).

**11.** A. Davin, 'The London Feminist History Group', *History Workshop: A Journal of Socialist Historians*, ix (1980), 192–94.

**12.** London Feminist History Group (ed.), *The Sexual Dynamics of History: Men's Power, Women's Resistance* (London, 1983).

**13.** This system was breaking down and I quickly found that if you just arrived at a seminar, you wouldn't be turned away – although you might not be called on if you wished to pose a question. Seminar culture at the IHR, however, was beginning to change.

**14.** Cornelie Usborne (b. 1942) – professor emerita of history at the University of Roehampton and senior fellow at the IHR – is a leading historian of women in modern Germany.

**15.** Alison Oram (b. 1956) – professor emerita of social and cultural history at Leeds Beckett University, senior fellow at the IHR, and co-convenor of the IHR's History of Sexuality Seminar – has published widely on the history of sexuality, particularly lesbian and queer history.

**16.** Private correspondence with me in anticipation of the Seminar's thirtieth anniversary in 2016.

**17.** Private correspondence with me in anticipation of the Seminar's thirtieth anniversary in 2016.

**18.** None of these women were professors at the time but all were involved in convening other seminars at the IHR; their subsequent careers proved extraordinary. Janet Nelson (b. 1942) – emerita professor of medieval history at King's College London – was the first female president of the Royal Historical Society (2000–2004) and Vice-President of the British Academy (1999–2001), and she was appointed dame commander of the British Empire in 2006. Pat Thane – formerly professor of contemporary history at King's College London and currently honorary fellow at Birkbeck, University of London – was sometime chief scientific adviser to the UK Government's department for work and pensions and co-led the Equalities in Great Britain, 1946–2006 project. Penelope Corfield – professor emeritus of history at Royal Holloway, University of London, and co-convenor of the IHR's British History in the Long Eighteenth Century Seminar – served as president of the British Society for Eighteenth-Century Studies (2008–10) and also President of the International Society for Eighteenth-Century Studies (2019–23). For further insights, see J. Nelson, 'Interview with Danny Millum at the Institute of Historical Research' (30 May 2008): https://archives.history.ac.uk/makinghistory/resources/interviews/Nelson_Janet.html;

and P. Corfield, 'Interview with Danny Millum at the Institute of Historical Research' (28 Apr. 2008): https://archives.history.ac.uk/makinghistory/resources/interviews/Corfield_Penelope.html [accessed 1 Nov. 2022].

19. Private correspondence with me in anticipation of the Seminar's thirtieth anniversary in 2016.

20. Lyndal Roper is the first woman to hold the regius professorship of history at the University of Oxford (2011–present); Amanda Vickery, a PhD student of Penelope Corfield, is professor of early modern history at Queen Mary, University of London.

21. The accomplishments of these speakers are too numerous to explore here, but over the years they and our many other speakers helped to define and re-define the central questions in the field as well as to bring these questions to bear on other types of history. Gender is now explored across a historical range of topics.

22. Details here reflect the speaker's institutional affiliation at the time; many have moved to other locales in the intervening years.

23. For context, see P. Corfield, 'History and the Challenge of Gender History', *Rethinking History*, i (1997), 241–58; J. Purvis and A. Wetherill, 'Playing the Gender History Game', *Rethinking History*, iii (1999), 333–8; and, P. Corfield, 'From Women's History to Gender History: A Reply to "Playing the Gender History Game"', *Rethinking History*, iii (1999), 339–41.

24. Alana Harris – reader in modern British social, cultural and gender history at KCL – has interdisciplinary interests that stretch across religion, gender, ethnicity and sexuality in modern Britain; Clare Midgley – formerly research professor in history at Sheffield Hallam University and president of the International Federation for Research in Women's History (2010–15) – has published on women who worked to eradicate the slave trade, both in Britain and across the British Empire; and Imaobong Umoren – associate professor of international history at the LSE – works on race, gender, activism and political thought in the Caribbean.

25. S. Knott and E. Griffin (ed.), *Mothering's Many Labours* [*Past & Present* Supplement 15] (Oxford, 2020).

26. Marybeth Hamilton – formerly reader in American history at Birkbeck College, University of London – has published on twentieth-century American women, sexuality and popular culture. Lucy Delap – professor in modern British and gender history at the University of Cambridge – has published on both domestic service and sexual violence in twentieth-century Britain as well as feminisms in global contexts.

27. Amy Erickson – professor of feminist history at the University of Cambridge – centres her research on female entrepreneurs and shopkeepers during the long eighteenth century, particularly in London. Laura Gowing – professor of early modern history at KCL – focuses on women, gender and the body in early modern London, especially through the lens of crime and court proceedings. Claire Langhamer – director of the IHR and professor of modern history at the University of London – is known for her exploration of the history of everyday life and the history of feeling, especially as they relate to twentieth-century women and girls. Carmen Mangion – senior lecturer in history at Birkbeck – examines the links between gender and religion in nineteenth- and twentieth-century Britain. Krisztina Robert – honorary research fellow at the University of Roehampton – explores the founding of women in the British military during the First World War. Laura Schwartz – reader in modern British history at the University of Warwick – has published on women's education, religion and domestic labour in twentieth-century Britain. See above for information on the others.

28. In a recent email to me (28 Sept. 2022), Lyndal Roper thought the practice derived from the Oxford Women's History Group which was established by Christine Collette and Anne Gelling in the early 1980s. This group was crucial, she thinks, in

THE WOMEN'S HISTORY SEMINAR    239

the recent establishment of the Hilary Rodham Clinton chair in Women's History at Oxford, but it also was a place to hear the early work of women's historians who would find success around the world.

**29.** Who pays has changed over the years, but the seminar budget has been used for the last few years to provide a free glass of wine for all.

**30.** The seminar, which included discussants Sarah Knott (Indiana) and Margot Finn (UCL) and took place on 16 Oct. 2020, was sparked by S. Crook, 'Parenting during the Covid-19 Pandemic of 2020: Academia, Labour and Care Work', *Women's History Review*, xxix ([online publ. 10 Sept.] 2020), 1226–38; as of Jun. 2022, the online version of the article had received 7930 views.

**31.** L. Davidoff and C. Hall, *Family Fortunes; Men and Women of the English Middle Class, 1780–1850* (London, 1987); A. Vickery, 'Golden Age to Separate Spheres? A Review of the Categories and Chronology of English Women's History', *Historical Journal*, xxxvi (1993), 383–414.

# References

## Archived sources

LSE Library, Women's Library Archives:

GB 106 7ADA.
GB 106 7SHR.

## Published sources

Abelove, H. et al. (ed.), [for MARHO The Radical Historians Organization] *Visions of History* (Manchester, 1984).

*Ada Nield Chew: The Life and Writings of a Working Woman*, comp. and bio. D. Chew, foreword A. Davin (London, 1982).

Alexander, S., 'In conversation with Poppy Sebag-Montefiore' (11 Mar. 2020): https://www.historyworkshop.org.uk/beyond-misbehaviour/ [accessed 20 Oct. 2022].

Alexander, S., and Davin, A., 'Feminist History', *History Workshop: A Journal of Socialist Historians*, i (1976), 4–6.

Beddoe, D., *Discovering Women's History: A Practical Manual* (London, 1983).

Bell, F., *At the Works: A Study of a Manufacturing Town*, new intro. A. John (London, [1907] 1985).

Berkshire Conference of Women Historians (Berks): https://berksconference.org/ [accessed 1 Nov. 2022].

Black, C. (ed.), *Married Women's Work*, new intro. E. F. Mappen (London, [1915] 1983).

Carroll, B. (ed.), *Liberating Women's History: Theoretical and Critical Essays* (Urbana, IL, 1976).

Corfield, P., 'History and the Challenge of Gender History', *Rethinking History*, i (1997), 241–58.

Corfield, P., 'From Women's History to Gender History: A Reply to "Playing the Gender History Game"', *Rethinking History*, iii (1999), 339–41.

Corfield, P., 'Interview with Danny Millum at the Institute of Historical Research' (28 Apr. 2008): https://archives.history.ac.uk /makinghistory/resources/interviews/Corfield_Penelope.html [accessed 1 Nov. 2022].

Crook, S., 'Parenting during the Covid-19 Pandemic of 2020: Academia, Labour and Care Work', *Women's History Review*, xxix (2020), 1226–38.

Davidoff, L. and Hall, C., *Family Fortunes; Men and Women of the English Middle Class, 1780–1850* (London, 1987).

Davies, M. L. (ed.), *Life as We Have Known It by Cooperative Working Women*, new intro. A. Davin (London, [1931] 1977).

Davin, A., 'The London Feminist History Group', *History Workshop: A Journal of Socialist Historians*, ix (1980), 192–4.

Drake, B., *Women in Trade Unions*, new intro. N. Branson (London, [1920] 1984).

Hannam, J., 'Women's History, Feminist History' (2008): https://archives.history.ac.uk/makinghistory/resources/articles/womens_history.html [accessed 1 Nov. 2022].

Hartman, M., and Banner, L. (ed.), *Clio's Consciousness Raised: New Perspectives on the History of Women* (New York, 1974).

Knott, S., and Griffin, E. (ed.), *Mothering's Many Labours* [*Past & Present* Supplement 15] (Oxford, 2020).

London Feminist History Group (ed.), *The Sexual Dynamics of History: Men's Power, Women's Resistance* (London, 1983).

Nelson, J., 'Interview with Danny Millum at the Institute of Historical Research' (30 May 2008): https://archives.history.ac.uk/makinghistory/resources/interviews/Nelson_Janet.html [accessed 1 Nov. 2022].

Purvis, J., and Wetherill, A., 'Playing the Gender History Game', *Rethinking History*, iii (1999), 333–8.

Reeves, M., *Round About a Pound a Week*, new intro. S. Alexander (London, [1913] 1977).

Riley, C., *The Virago Story: Assessing the Impact of a Feminist Publishing Phenomenon* (New York, 2018).

Rowbotham, S., *Hidden from History: 300 Years of Women's Oppression and the Fight Against It* (London, 1973).

Rowbotham, S., *Daring to Hope: My Life in the 1970s* (London, 2021).

Taylor, B., 'History of the History Workshop' (22 Nov. 2012): https://www.historyworkshop.org.uk/museums-archives-heritage/the-history-of-history-workshop/ [accessed 23 Feb. 2023].

Vicinus, M. (ed.), *Suffer and Be Still: Women in the Victorian Age* (Bloomington, IN, 1972).

Vicinus, M. (ed.), *A Widening Sphere: Changing Roles of Victorian Women* (Bloomington, IN, 1977).

Vickery, A., 'Golden Age to Separate Spheres? A Review of the Categories and Chronology of English Women's History', *Historical Journal*, xxxvi (1993), 383–414.

Wandor, M. (ed.), *Once a Feminist: Stories of a Generation* (London, 1990).

Withers, D.-M., *Virago Reprints and Modern Classics: The Timely Business of Feminist Publishing* (Cambridge, 2021).

## Unpublished sources

Boyd, K., Miscellaneous Private Diaries, Correspondence and Notes.

Chapter 11

# The IHR's seminar culture: past, present and future – a round-table discussion

David Bates, Alice Prochaska, Tim Hitchcock, Kate Wilcox, Ellen Smith and Rachel Bynoth, and Claire Langhamer

Our final chapter brings together seven distinguished contributors with contrasting perspectives on the IHR's seminar culture: past, present and future. David Bates is emeritus professor in medieval history at the University of East Anglia and served as the director of the IHR from 2003 to 2008. Alice Prochaska is an honorary fellow and former principal of Somerville College, Oxford, and worked as secretary and librarian at the IHR from 1984 to 1992. Tim Hitchcock is professor emeritus of digital history at the University of Sussex and has been a seminar series co-convenor at the IHR since 1993. Kate Wilcox has been working at the IHR since 2004 and is library services manager at the IHR Library. Ellen Smith is a final-year PhD student in history at the University of Leicester and co-convenor of the IHR's History Lab Seminar from 2020 to 2022. Rachel Bynoth is lecturer in historical and critical studies at Bath Spa University and co-convenor of the IHR's History Lab Seminar from 2020 to 2022. Claire Langhamer is professor of modern history at the University of London and the current director of the IHR.

Each contributor was invited by the editor to respond to five stimuli questions. What is your experience of the IHR's seminars? How does the life of the IHR's seminars inform what historians do? How does the life of the IHR's seminars shape scholarly communities? How does the life of the IHR's seminars engage with and participate in broader society? Why do the IHR's seminars matter? The conversation that follows reflects the unique experiences and insights of our contributors as scholars and people.

## What is your experience of the IHR's seminars?

### David Bates

My experience of the IHR's seminars is that of someone who first came to the IHR in 1967 and who held posts at the Imperial War Museum (1969–71) and the Universities of Cardiff (1971–94) and Glasgow (1994–2003), before becoming director of the IHR (2003–8). I have remained in regular contact with the IHR since then.

As a PhD student at the University of Exeter (1966–9) and during the two years at the Imperial War Museum, London, during which time I was not certain that I would be able to have a career as a medieval historian, the IHR provided succour and a refuge which shaped my future. My experience was both social and intellectual. The seminars were places to meet with like-minded people in ways which were stimulating and, in ways I have since learnt, unique. During my Cardiff and Glasgow times, I would often try to ensure that doctoral students were invited to give a paper at the relevant IHR seminar. The way in which students and the postdocs were required to present their research to a rigorous, but usually friendly, audience helped them, and also informed my opinion of their work. This experience is just one facet of the IHR's support for historians in Wales and Scotland before and after devolution.

My years as director gave me an overview that I had not previously possessed. The sheer range of subjects covered and the way in which scholarly communities are brought together has no equivalent that I know of. The mixture of the long-established seminars and the new ones that were created demonstrated both the dynamism of the historical discipline and a role that I believe only the IHR can play. They supplied a remarkable overview of what the study of history involves. Those years also convinced me that the seminars must be as generously funded as possible.

### Alice Prochaska

I started in the 1970s as a migrant from Oxford, where I was writing a DPhil thesis on Westminster Reform 1807–1832. After the required graduate year residing in Oxford, I moved to London to use the archives at UCL and the British Library. My supervisor recommended that I join the IHR and allocated to me one of Oxford's paid-for places there. The IHR's Eighteenth-Century English History Seminar and the Common Room gave me the base I needed, both academically and socially, when I would otherwise have been quite unmoored. It was sometimes – but not always –

challenging and the best of the papers gave important insights and leads on sources. There was too much rather dry administrative and military history for my taste, but I was grateful to be introduced to an international social circle of fellow graduate students, and grateful too, for the friendship and encouragement offered by Ian Christie (1919–98) and John Dinwiddy (1939–90), the Seminar's two co-convenors.

For full disclosure: it was at the IHR and this Seminar in particular, that I met and got to know my future husband, the American historian Frank Prochaska. In the early 1970s there were many American graduate students at the IHR; they seemed extremely well informed about a wide range of world history, and they enriched the life of the Common Room, and our post-seminar visits to the pub, intellectually as well as socially. I also met people of different nationalities and generations embarking on careers in historical research. My horizons opened up in ways that would not have happened, or at least not so much, had I stayed in Oxford.

Later, working at the Public Record Office (PRO, now the National Archives), 1976 to 1984, and then as secretary and librarian at the IHR between 1984 and 1992, my research interests shifted to the twentieth century. I was commissioned to write a history of trade unions and worked as an archivist ordering and describing a broad range of modern records that were then being made available for research for the first time, under the thirty-year rule. I got involved in running the seminar on twentieth-century British history (sometimes hosted at the PRO), and the slate of co-convenors included the journalist and historian Peter Hennessy (b. 1947) and schoolteacher and historian Anthony Seldon (b. 1953) – who co-founded the Institute of Contemporary British History (ICBH) in 1986, which in turn formally joined the IHR in 1999 – as well as Ben Pimlott (1945–2004), Kathleen Burk (b. 1945) and John Turner (b. 1949).

This distinguished company really changed the nature of the contemporary historical research seminar. Our 'Witness Seminars' were the brainchild of Hennessy and Seldon at the ICBH and drew on the co-convenors' extraordinary contacts, especially in broadcasting and politics, to enable historians to benefit from the testimony of the participants and decision makers of recent past events. I can remember half the former members of the Edward Heath cabinet standing in the IHR's overcrowded Common Room sipping tea from polystyrene cups before going upstairs to the Local History Room to share their reflections. Another memorable encounter brought together people from both sides of the fascist-communist divide who had fought each other at the Battle of Cable Street in 1936. One of my co-convenors suggested we should invite Enoch Powell, who had been health secretary under Harold Macmillan, to speak about Conservative policy on the NHS, and it fell to me to issue the invitation (and selected correspondence relating to Powell's visit has been archived in the Institute's Wohl Library IHR/3/3/22). Not surprisingly, this particular event attracted protests and pickets and led to a subsequent special session to discuss, amongst much else, the nature of historical evidence in a contested contemporary context. Powell himself meticulously insisted on addressing only the topic he had been invited for and would not be drawn on his subsequent disastrous career. It was a fascinating, if nerve-shredding, episode. And here I must pay tribute to Michael Thompson (1925–2017), the wise and benign director of the IHR, who treated the considerable fuss with calmness and a great sense of proportion and presided over a special session to discuss issues of free speech and dispassionate historical enquiry.

## Tim Hitchcock

The IHR seminars, and the British History in the Long Eighteenth Century Seminar in particular, have been at the centre of my intellectual and academic life since the early 1980s. Adrift among the precariat created by Margaret Thatcher's assault on the universities, for half a decade the IHR became my intellectual sanctuary and only connection with the academy. Here a generation of scholars made connections and argued – creating a remarkable community drawn from around the world. The mid-1980s also saw the creation of the Postgraduate Seminar and the Women's History Seminar – both helping to fundamentally change how all the other seminars worked, making them more open, outward-looking and welcoming. I have had the huge privilege of co-convening the Long Eighteenth Century History Seminar since 1993.

In those almost forty years, I have attended perhaps a thousand seminars. First, there is the anticipation. Chat in the tearoom (that is, the Common Room), meeting the speaker and catching up with old friends. Anything can happen. The paper could change how you see the world, or it could leave you flat. But in those moments before sitting down to listen, no one knows which it will be. And what follows is the most intimate of conversations. Initially all the talk is one way, as the speaker guides you through their thinking and their evidence. But in my mind, it is always a dialogue, as questions rise, and judgements are made. How does this fit with the literature? Have they considered other sources? How does this change how I think about the period? After fifty minutes, or so – just enough time to present what will perhaps become a journal article, or chapter of a thesis, you may have learned something, or not, but you have followed along with someone else's thoughts on a research journey. And in the questions, the other side of that dialogue is given voice.

By the time you get to the pub, the single conversation has become many, as that last question – how does this change how I think? – is interrogated from half a dozen perspectives.

## Kate Wilcox

My experience of the seminars is varied. I have wide-ranging interests in history but no specific research area of my own, so I have been to many different seminars. It's always a lovely aspect of them that things of interest can come up in unexpected places. I have felt very welcome at most seminars I have been to; although, I've had a couple of isolated incidents of people expressing surprise that a librarian would come to a seminar.

My favourite moments have been going to papers given by people I have known, for a long time, as library readers. It is nice to see the outcome of their research. I remember especially papers by the Canadian historian Robert Tittler on the trade of painting and Tim Wales speaking on some findings of the Intoxicants and Early Modernity project based at the University of Sheffield. As a librarian at the IHR, it's always interesting to learn about how sources are used in research, and this is also very useful in developing lateral thinking when answering library enquiries.

My other experience of the seminars is from the organizational side. In the early years of the Institute there was a direct link between the teaching seminars and the editions of primary sources that were on the shelves in the room at IHR where the seminar was being held. As the seminars moved away from being teaching seminars and became pre-prepared research papers, this link has been lost. However, librarians now assist in other ways. The library team would be called to help with technological issues, and I remember having to stand on a chair in the old Wolfson Room on several occasions adjusting data projectors, with a room full of people. We'd also sometimes be asked to help photocopy handouts. I suppose that support role was a continuation of the librarians fetching books at the early seminars. The reception and other events staff have been key to the smooth running of the seminars. It has been sad to see the receptionist role eroded in recent years after their line management was separated from the IHR.

Livestreaming has of course opened up seminars to people who can't attend physically and began before the COVID-19 pandemic necessitated wider take-up. I remember watching the first IHR livestreamed seminar from the library enquiries office. When working fully and partially from home during the lockdowns I went to more seminars, it was nice to go to one at the end of the working day. Since returning to working full-time in Senate House, it has become harder to attend. The Internet connection on the train is not reliable enough to stay connected to Zoom and staying late to go to an online seminar doesn't have quite the same draw as staying late to go to an in-person one.

## Ellen Smith and Rachel Bynoth

We are seminar convenors at History Lab – a network of postgraduate students in history and related disciplines, based at the IHR. History Lab was founded in 2005, and a year later it had 500 members worldwide. The seminar series associated with History Lab was previously called the Postgraduate Seminar, the Postgraduate and Early Careers Seminar and also the Lab at Lunch Seminar. The committee finally landed on its current eponymous title the History Lab Seminar, harking back to the early twentieth-century conception of the IHR as a postgraduate research 'laboratory'. In contrast to other seminars at the IHR, which are orientated around the study of a particular theme, time period, geographical area, theory or method, the History Lab Seminar is run by postgraduates for postgraduates and is not restricted to any form of subject specialization or periodization.

The seminar series at History Lab offers postgraduate members a welcoming, collegiate space to present, often their first paper, and receive feedback to progress their theses or first publications. Through the COVID-19 pandemic, the Seminar was forced to move online, using its blog, as well as its Tweets and Zoom meetings to substitute for in-person seminars. As a result, it could afford to be less London-centric than before, incorporating committee members from all over the UK, and even giving postgraduates from across the world the opportunity to present their research in an esteemed IHR seminar online.

More generally, we have found that being part of the IHR's seminar culture means we can connect postgraduates, especially PhD students, to other seminars, scholars and opportunities, both in London and beyond.

## Claire Langhamer

I can't now remember exactly when I delivered my first IHR paper, nor can I recall the precise details of what it was about; I imagine it had something to do with women's leisure and was probably delivered to the Women's History Seminar. I know that it would have been after I started my first job at Sussex University. As a PhD student at the University of Central Lancashire, the London seminar scene seemed a long way away – geographically, and in other ways too. It was not part of my own doctoral rite of passage.

What I do remember from my first IHR seminars are the feelings they engendered: the fear of being exposed as an academic fraud, the quiet pleasure of being taken seriously and the kindness of the participants. The imposing architecture of Senate House, the proximity to historians who had shaped fields of enquiry, the easy – and not so easy – sociability afterwards, all contributed to a sense that there was a distinctive structure of seminar feeling.

More recently, my experience of the seminars has been one of unalloyed joy against a backdrop of deep uncertainty. During the 2020–22 COVID-19 lockdowns the ability to attend a range of different papers on Zoom was a lifeline like no other. The seminars offered a sense of community and purpose at a time when both felt under threat, drawing together academics from across the continents in the global experiment of pandemic seminar production. The importance of the seminar space as a place of collegiality and care, as well as challenge and debate, was never more apparent. The move to hybrid and in-person seminars later in 2022 was infused with hope that a kind of normality might indeed return. My first year as IHR Director was marked by the need to balance the enhanced accessibility of the online seminar with the desire to be back in a room with other human beings.

The seminar experience then reflects the specificities of, and relationship between, historical change and career stage. Both the academic life cycle and the shifting context of intellectual production frame the meaning of the seminar for individuals and for communities of scholars. Changes in the form and content of seminars, as well as in the identity of participants, correspond to wider historical developments, though there are also striking continuities. The contingency of the seminar seems to have become more obvious in recent years – and not only because of COVID-19. Longer term shifts within the higher education sector have changed the conditions under which academics at all career stages perform their labour, squeezing the time and resource available for acts of collegiality and community-building. The way that we do our job may be rooted in academic tradition, but it is also impacted by, and responds to, shifts in the world around us.

## How does the life of the IHR's seminars inform what historians do?

### David Bates

The seventy-fifth anniversary publication *The History Laboratory* (1996) contained a good account of the seminars' history which is thought-provoking in relation to their changing role within the academic profession and the IHR. For all that, the seminars can be said to have democratized since then. That said, the basic point made there that the seminar is a place for informed discussion and the sharing of knowledge remains as relevant as ever. The regular attendance that a programme of seminars throughout the academic year requires is a way to safeguard against excessively narrow specialization. This is of the greatest importance to teaching, as well as research. It is also important to be aware that the benefits that an individual takes away from any seminar are often intangible ones that only become clear over time.

The national role for which the IHR was founded, and for which the School of Advanced Study (SAS) has been funded since 1994, means that the seminars are institutionally neutral because they do not belong to any single higher education institution in the UK. SAS's role and that of its constituent Institutes, about which I became very well informed while I was director, are a part of national life that should be developed. All this certainly informs what historians do because they bring together people from many institutions in a way that seminars elsewhere rarely do. At the IHR's seminars, 'guests' are not just speakers, but individuals who happen to be in or near London at a particular time. Also, the consequential benefits from the core personnel of most IHR seminars being drawn from across London and its vicinities also inform what historians do because they routinely bring together the staff of many institutions. The IHR's international reputation means that scholars from abroad visiting London and the UK attend a situation that has global significance. The remarkable range of expertise that the seminars often bring together can provide opportunities for discussion and networking that are unparalleled even in leading research-led universities. This informs what historians do because it brings them together for intellectual and social exchange. The national and international contacts that are created can lead to participants in the seminars being invited to other countries and benefitting from the discussions that follow.

## THE IHR'S SEMINAR CULTURE: A ROUND-TABLE DISCUSSION    251

## Alice Prochaska

At their best, the IHR's seminars provide a testing ground for historians at all stages of their career to try out theories and learn from each other. They can also help provide information on historical resources. Quite often, discussion in the seminars will change the direction of someone's research. Sometimes, collaborative opportunities will open up. The seminars also offer opportunities for historians to compare notes on teaching and curricula. A great deal of informal mentoring goes on. And there must be untold occasions when people have been saved from error and misunderstanding.

## Tim Hitchcock

When I first started attending seminars at the IHR they were intimate drafting sessions, composed mainly of University of London PhD students (which I was not), led by a professor. But even then, they contrasted strongly with my previous experience of academic life at the Universities of California, Berkeley and Oxford. At Berkeley, public lectures by famous academics were the order of the day; while at Oxford the pressing need to rush back to college for dinner stymied post-seminar conviviality and debate. And while IHR seminars were superficially similar to their Oxford counterparts, they felt different, always more sociable, although in the early days frequently more rebarbative (particularly once you got to the pub). In the 1980s the expectation was that you would approach the convenor beforehand and ask their permission to attend. The speaker would read out the paper – perhaps a draft thesis chapter – pencil in hand, marking up typos and awkward phrases as they went. At the end of six or seven thousand words, the professor would critique, while others chipped in with points of clarification or minor correction. It was a system designed to work at the pace of the printing press – a brief stopping point between drafts and a viva, on the way towards an article or a book, with its peer reviews and revisions, galleys, first and second proofs. Seminars were an all-important part of a machine for the management of academic production. No article saw the light of day without first gaining the approval of a seminar audience. But even in that more cloistered age, IHR seminars then led to the pub and dinner, and an evening of debate.

Since the 1980s their role has changed. As typewriters and linotype have given way to word processors, PowerPoint and the Internet; as the universities expanded and international travel grew; as the costs of publication plummeted and publishers were turned from gatekeepers to touts in search of ever more content, seminars evolved dramatically. Perhaps most obviously, they changed from drafting sessions to a species of public performance. Backed by the ubiquitous, gaudy PowerPoint, the speaker now stands at a podium rather than sitting at a table, their eyes challenging the audience to engage. For many postgraduates, it is their first introduction to the queasy feeling that accompanies giving a large undergraduate lecture. But it is also a form of public outreach. Each new book needs to be promoted, and each funded project needs to demonstrate its 'impact'. The intimate conversation remains, but the place of the seminar in the machinery of the academy has changed. From a kitchen-table conversation among colleagues, it is now a shout from the rooftops. In the process historians have become much better performers, to the detriment, perhaps, of a quieter culture of scholarship.

## Kate Wilcox

In the past, especially when the library was more fully staffed, some librarians were research-active and engaged with particular seminars as researchers in the field, including as seminar convenors. None of the current library staff holds an academic post, although we do engage with the seminars and feel that they are an important part of the life of the Institute.

From the seminars I have attended, I have seen that the informal format leads to feedback, discussion and increased knowledge of sources. The themes in the seminars come directly from things historians are researching and interested in, and this in turn develops new ideas.

With many seminars being held online now, we miss the buzzy atmosphere in the building when people are gathering for the seminars to start. It's nice that some are starting to return to in-person meetings. In the library, we could always tell when a particular seminar was on because there'd be an increase of people using the relevant library collection that afternoon. Our recent library survey results have shown that some people have not been using the library as much recently because they have not been in the building for seminars.

## Ellen Smith and Rachel Bynoth

The History Lab has the funding and resources to deliver a regular seminar every two weeks during term time. This provides postgraduates with a space for discussion that generates scholarly networks, ideas and critiques which in turn inform projects such as theses and articles, often in the absence of established postgraduate seminar groups at their home universities.

Speakers are confined to forty minutes in which to present their paper, generally aided with a visual presentation on PowerPoint. Speakers have the opportunity to shape and sharpen their arguments through formulating their ideas for a general, non-specialist audience and through rigorous comments and debate. Audience members collect theoretical and methodological insights from the papers, which we know has helped them develop their own research ideas. The post-paper question and answer segments of the seminar can be challenging for speakers, but they enable ideas to be reaffirmed and refined. As a postgraduate-tailored seminar space, History Lab is less hierarchical than other seminars, encouraging livelier, more dynamic conversations between speaker and audience, and facilitating easier dialogue and collaboration between scholars, often across disciplinary boundaries. We tend to get audiences of around twenty people with a variety of research interests. From time to time, we welcome senior scholars to our seminars, interested in the papers of our postgraduate speakers, which enables postgraduates to connect with these more established historians in a casual setting. As convenors, we often prefer smaller, more intimate gatherings at seminars, finding they are conducive to motivating attendees to reflect deeply and critically about the paper with comments and questions, and to build relationships with the speaker and other listeners. Those who attend History Lab regularly become part of an intellectual culture which approaches the past beyond, irrespective of specializations, in a supportive environment, enabling postgraduates to become more confident, well-rounded and receptive historians.

## Claire Langhamer

History-making is always a collaborative process, even if the single-authored monograph continues to flourish within the discipline. Historical research develops in dialogue with students, with supervisors, with colleagues, with archivists and librarians, with referees and reviewers, and with those closest to us. When we co-author work, that dialogue is more immediately manifest, but when we publish alone the texture of collaboration is necessarily flattened into the gratitude that underpins acknowledgements and the formality of academic references.

The seminar is a place where we perform the collaborative dynamic together, rather than through the to-and-fro of written comment and response. It is a place where we can think collectively and where we can build on other questions and contributions in the quest for new understandings. It is a place where production and reception are evenly balanced. Whilst the formal presentation of single-authored papers still tends to dominate, the point of a seminar is less about performance and more about exchange. The very best seminars leave the presenter with a sense that their work has in some way been transformed by the act of being discussed; and they leave other participants feeling that they too think differently, because of what they have heard.

Seminars are made up of engaged commentators and critical friends, willing to offer their thoughts on whatever is being presented. The seminar experience can thus have a fundamental impact on the development of a particular project, a wider approach or even a career. Many seminar series sit right at the heart of their sub-field, some persisting over many decades, others newly emerging to reflect disciplinary shifts. They generate intellectual energy and can exert profound and lasting influence.

Seminars inform what historians do, and they surface how we work. They also model a commitment to the future of the discipline – most notably in their support for early career scholars – and show that the history community coheres across institutional, career stage and geographical boundaries.

## How does the life of the IHR's seminars shape scholarly communities?

### David Bates

The diversification of the discipline since the 1960s has produced a huge increase in the number of IHR seminars and reflects scholarly communities as they are now defined. The result of the sheer range of subjects is that it keeps their subjects up-to-date historiographically and enables scholarly communities to examine the themes that have brought them into existence. This also shapes scholarly communities by conferring an identity requiring them to look to the future.

In thinking about how the seminars shape scholarly communities, the definition of 'scholarly community' should be as broad as possible. For this reason, it is best that the seminars be as open as possible and that they welcome, not just those who are manifestly specialists in the field, but all with a general interest in the topic of any specific seminar. The scholarly community should not consist only of individuals who work in higher education institutions, but all who have a serious interest in the subject.

As someone much of whose life has been spent at a distance from London, I would warn against the danger of becoming too London-centric in defining the scholarly communities for which the seminars cater. Scholarly communities comprise all with an interest in a particular field, something that is reflected in the national role for which the IHR and SAS are funded. This means that seminar convenors should watch out for scholars from the rest of the UK and abroad visiting London and invite them to attend seminars, sometimes to give papers, but also for social as well as intellectual reasons.

The integration of the holders of IHR fellowships and bursaries into seminars in recent decades is a good and positive development because it contributes to shaping scholarly communities for the future. It is of crucial importance for the discipline and for the IHR's role that this integration be further reinforced. There are reasons why the use of Zoom and Teams during the COVID-19 pandemic ought to be continued because it can allow international participation in ways that previously took place only intermittently. However, almost everyone I talk to argues, as I do, that face-to-face discussion is preferable and socializing after a seminar is a foundation for robust and new networks. Future strategy must balance the pros and cons, and give thought to hybrid seminars, but it must not lose sight of the immense profits that have followed for scholarly communities from a century of IHR seminars.

In a lot of ways, this question can be answered along lines similar to the previous one. The emphasis on the social alongside the intellectual is of the greatest importance.

## Alice Prochaska

Of the two seminars that I was involved in, the eighteenth-century one followed a more usual path, creating a network of people with research interests in the period. Many friendships were formed, and some have lasted for decades, leading to academic engagement far beyond the IHR itself (for example, invitations to speak in North America, joint research projects, special teaching initiatives, references to publishers, and much more).

The seminar on twentieth-century Britain helped shape a community of academic interest in the subject that went far beyond scholarly historians as conventionally understood. There was a fluid interchange between historians, politicians, policy makers, journalists and broadcasters. It was possible, for example, to see how the seminar allowed political practitioners to try out their ideas whilst also learning from others about particular aspects of policy. Similar work is now carried out by History & Policy

256  DAVID BATES ET AL.

(est. 2002), which under the directorship of Philip Murphy has just moved back to its original home at the IHR.

## Tim Hitchcock

Generations of scholarship, and links between generations, are made by seminars. In part, it is a simple matter of perhaps a few dozen people coming together every two weeks in term time – exchanging pleasantries and relieving the isolation that frequently comes with historical research. But seminars also create wider 'virtual' communities, that in their turn underpin imagined ones. Over the decades, most historians of eighteenth-century Britain, for instance, have attended the Long Eighteenth Century History Seminar. Hundreds of researchers have come along for perhaps five or six occasions while doing the research for a doctorate in London's archives, or on research leave later in their career. The field is small enough that few universities have more than one or two specialists in eighteenth-century history, or more than one or two postgraduates in the area at a time. As a result, this virtual community is spread across space and time; from Japan to India, to North America and back to Europe and across generations from the 1970s to the 2020s. But it is in the Seminar that this virtual community conducts its debates and acknowledges its ever-changing collection of sub-disciplines, from histories of space and place, gender, sexuality, disability and emotion – to whatever comes next.

During the COVID-19 pandemic, as the Seminar went online, the virtual community that the seminar had always enabled came together in remarkable ways. With an audience (and speakers) Zooming in from around the world, the breadth and shape of the seminar's scholarly community was both revealed and expanded. It has made the easy conversation about a paper much more difficult to conduct. There were no more quiet discussions on the way to the pub, pointing out a paper's strengths (or flaws). But it has also allowed old friends of the seminar to be reincorporated into the formal online event, and for many new colleagues to join. For the Long Eighteenth Century Seminar, the future is hybrid. The sociability and the debate in the pub and over dinner remain all important, but the inclusive global audience also needs to be maintained.

## Kate Wilcox

The seminars enable relationship building and collaborations through the seminars themselves but also through the informal conversations that happen before and after the seminar. Some seminars bring together people from different fields.

The online seminars have perhaps reshaped these communities by enabling access for people who wouldn't normally be able to attend. It's clear that new connections and discoveries are being made both through discussions but also through comments made through text-chat functions on platforms like Zoom or on social media.

## Ellen Smith and Rachel Bynoth

Since COVID-19, History Lab has changed dramatically, allowing the committee to provide a meaningful and wide-reaching forum for the postgraduate community to gather online and mitigate the isolation of PhD life. Zoom and hybrid seminar environments have lessened travel and financial barriers which affected past attendance figures, attracting participants beyond London-based researchers. Now speakers and audience members come together not only from across the UK, but also the world, and develop, deepen and refine their ongoing research, from home and office environments, following up conversations and contacts through social media, email and our recently developed blog.

Comments from seminar speakers indicate that they often leave the seminar having met and gained positive feedback from their peers, and occasionally from members of the public or leading scholars in their field, inspired to follow new avenues of research, and armed with contacts from, and introductions to, various institutions and researchers. History Lab always sets the expectation for seminars to provide a safe, inclusive and welcoming atmosphere for speakers to receive constructive criticism.

## Claire Langhamer

Like a good conference or workshop, a seminar is capable of producing something that goes well beyond the sum of its parts – a feeling that the terrain has shifted as the result of thinking together. A seminar series – framed thematically or chronologically – can advance agendas, whilst also shaping disciplinary and sub-disciplinary memory: it is, of course, always important to know where we have come from as well as where we might be going.

The deceptively simple act of coming together – of being bodies in a room, virtual or otherwise – is itself an act of community development and maintenance, notably so in an academic environment where time for open intellectual discussion is often in short supply. Seminars shape scholarly communities through this everyday practice and through being open and welcoming to all. Some have more defined constituencies: the History Lab Seminar offers both an intellectual and social forum for PhD students, whilst History Lab Plus offers a space for early career historians and independent researchers. The IHR's seminars play a distinctive role in transcending university affiliations and helping to generate a critical mass that might not be available in single institutions. They are explicitly open to all who are history-curious wherever they are located.

And yet the seminars do far more than act as a location for discussion. They also provide a space to create new communities of scholarship or to bring together those working on the most dynamic parts of the discipline in new formations. Sometimes this happens organically as seminars develop or emerge over time; sometimes it is actively encouraged. In its centenary year, the IHR initiated ten Partnership Seminars to address new areas of research and approaches to the past. These had a particular emphasis on collaboration and interdisciplinarity and a commitment to cross-sectional and global approaches. They included the interactive series Historians across Boundaries: Collaborative Historical Research, which was explicitly designed to 'promote awareness of existing research in different fields and explore how we can embed collaboration into our future research'.

## How does the life of the IHR's seminars engage with and participate in broader society?

### David Bates

To an extent, this depends on the subject of the particular seminar. In some cases, the nature and ethos of the topic requires it. Manifestly the diversification of the historical discipline since the 1960s has produced a much greater interdisciplinarity. This on its own can require engagement with broader societies outside the historical community that is composed of members of a higher education school or department of history and of major research projects. As to the place of the seminars within both the University of London and wider publics, local, national and international, the seminars should surely be as open as possible. As someone much of whose life has been spent at a distance from London, I would again warn against the danger of becoming too London-centric. The national role must always be emphasized. I also think that seminars could become a vehicle for discussion between academics and public figures, including politicians, museum staff, journalists, etc. This is already the case, but in the future more could and should be done. Through its conferences, the IHR has a long and praiseworthy tradition of engaging with the place of the historical discipline in broader society. While the autonomy of each seminar series must continue to be respected, a case exists for encouraging seminars to pick up themes that any conference has identified as particularly stimulating and worthy of further exploration.

## Alice Prochaska

My experience is not current but let me give a few examples. First of all, the seminars have provided a recruiting ground for talks to the Historical Association and the Association for Local History, as well as membership of other societies. I joined the Council of the Royal Historical Society as Vice President. I also joined the committee of the History at the Universities Defence Group (HUDG) and I believe it was they who nominated me to the 1989–90 History Working Group on the National Curriculum, set up by Kenneth Baker at the Department of Education and Science, as it then was. There followed an intensive couple of years working with the other members of the group to design the first national curriculum in history, and testing it out in the media, and at public meetings and group seminars around the country. And, in May 2022, Philip Murphy organized a 'Witness Seminar' on that experience.

## Tim Hitchcock

History is at the heart of how every society understands itself. In a constant dialogue between the past and the present, each new problem is interrogated via a distant mirror. In the case of the Long Eighteenth Century Seminar, this works on a number of different levels. First and foremost, this is a global conversation. We actively seek to engage with scholars everywhere the topic is discussed. And since Britain's place in a global history of the eighteenth century is important (however problematic), the Seminar responds to developments in public discourse, in India and North America, the Caribbean and Australia. But as importantly, the period is part of Britain's national discussion. In a narrower sense, the Seminar is also in dialogue with its immediate community, with London. There has been a remarkable flourishing of independent London history groups in the last two decades, and we seek to maintain strong links to them, providing an important venue for London's history. And whether this is focused on economics, race, poverty or politics, the seminar responds, seeking out papers and speakers.

Historians are fundamentally engaged in the present. For myself, history is quite simply a way of thinking more clearly about the present. The seminar provides a supportive environment for historians to engage with history, and by doing so, engage in a debate.

And as the IHR seminars evolved from the late twentieth century, they have become ever more open to public participation. Each session remains an 'academic' event, but increasingly the audience includes independent scholars, making the seminars themselves feel ever more amphibious: an academic discussion, held in an increasingly public space.

## Kate Wilcox

Membership of the IHR library is open to everyone. The library runs inductions and tours for new students and other researchers. Although they are overtly introductions to the library they also serve as an introduction to the Institute's other activities including the seminars. New library users are always impressed and excited by the range of seminars. New readers from outside academia are sometimes surprised that they are open to everyone.

Some seminars are clearly making a conscious effort to reach new public audiences by introducing new topics and different types of speakers, including practitioners working in galleries, libraries, archives and museums. With the introduction of the new IHR Partnership Seminars, the IHR has sought to do this in a more formalized way.

The online format has made casual participation in the seminars easier. People who are unable or may feel intimidated by going to an in-person session in Senate House find it easier to drop in anonymously online.

## Ellen Smith and Rachel Bynoth

The History Lab Seminar responds to and engages with social shifts and trends in a number of ways. They support, represent and remain attentive to the needs of postgraduates, from master's students to doctoral researchers. The seminars are an excellent space to make current day connections and figure out the relevance of research to today's societies and cultures. This not only helps postgraduates with the 'so what' question but it also encourages further ideas on how this work can benefit societies post submission and with next steps. This fits in with a large part of History Lab's agenda to assist postgraduates as they learn about themselves during their PhDs, find their place in the world and work towards building and shaping their careers.

To further this agenda, our tenure as seminar co-convenors saw us spearhead a popular series of special events catering to history postgraduates as they prepare for their future. Whilst some of these events have been academic in nature, others have been designed to mitigate the emotional and practical difficulties of finding gainful employment outside the university sector.

The History Lab seminars naturally reflect the wider ethos and mission of the History Lab, which continues to develop in response to the challenges of diversity, equality and inclusion. The spring of 2021 saw the launch of the Olivette Otele prize to be awarded annually for the best paper submitted to the History Lab Seminar by a Black PhD research student in the UK. We hope that this prize gestures towards the need for similar schemes for other marginalized groups as well as wider social action.

Public history and outreach are also gaining significance as areas of historical enquiry and practice, encouraging researchers to access new and wider audiences for their publications and to think about the contemporary social, cultural and political resonances of their work. The seminars we have hosted as seminar convenors have asked pertinent questions of the past that also interrogate and invite modern-day issues, highlighting the significance of the historian's craft to areas of policy-making, current international affairs, political discourse and navigating cultural and social life.

## Claire Langhamer

History has never been more popular within broader society. From high-profile works of historical fiction, and the transformative work of community historians, to the boom in genealogical research and economic importance of the heritage sector, people continue to find meaning – and pleasure – in understanding the lives of people in the past. The COVID-19 pandemic encouraged even more people to think historically, and to record their own experiences for the benefit of future historians. Individuals are interested in their own family histories and the history of their own communities. They are also interested in people, places and times that have no immediate personal resonance. This is partly because these things are intrinsically interesting, but it is also because understanding lives that are strikingly different and strangely familiar helps us place ourselves and others in context. The past can provoke strong feelings; it can spark political action; and it can encourage new solutions. Thinking historically encourages us to think critically about the present and to plan for the future.

The IHR seminars have long welcomed those with an interest in the past but no formal academic affiliation. Increasingly the seminars model the impact that history as a discipline can have. They build partnerships across different sectors and constituencies, bridging the gap between university-life and historical practice beyond the academy. The Black British History Seminar, for example, brings together scholars, activists, artists and heritage practitioners. Others take contemporary challenges as their starting point covering themes such as 'Archives and Truth', 'Risk and Uncertainty' and 'Spaces of Sickness and Wellbeing'. Seminars change their remit over time and according to wider context, reflecting historiographical developments rooted in a wider political culture. The Britain at Home and Abroad Seminar was formed from a merger of the Modern British History Seminar and the seminar entitled Reconfiguring the British: Nation, Empire, World 1600–1900; new seminars reflect societal change. The Women's History Seminar was established in 1986 to provide a forum for work on women and gender, whilst the emergence of the Digital History Seminar in 2012 reflected the growing importance of digital practice within the discipline.

## Why do the IHR's seminars matter?

### David Bates

For obvious reasons (i.e., age!), I am no longer involved in debates about seminars and pedagogy. I would nonetheless say that, however they are conducted, seminars matter because they produce intellectual and social exchange in ways that are unique. This will always be the case, no matter how practice changes. In saying this, I immediately think of the need to distinguish between a seminar and a workshop, with the latter usually having an intended specific outcome. The unpredictability of the seminar actually matters a great deal. Without naming any names, all of us will remember a poor paper that produced a lively and enlightening discussion that benefitted the speaker and the participants. And indeed, a magisterial and brilliant one that did not.

As long as the argument that seminars matter is accepted, the case for an exchange of ideas about the present and the future involving the seminar convenors and IHR management might be a persuasive one. The historical ambience that the IHR provides is also a stimulus. We have come a long way from the days when it was normal practice for seminars to take books from the shelves to consult them, but the setting remains important in ways which I have already set out. When it comes to demographics, attention must be given to ensuring that programmes do include scholars at all stages of their professional careers and, where desirable, figures from public life.

## Alice Prochaska

They matter to different people for all sorts of different reasons. They are a training ground for research historians – often including people in middle age who find themselves irresistibly drawn back to research into a subject that fascinates them; and in this respect the fact that the IHR is based in central London has made it a mecca for such people, as it now remains through its website. For all graduate students in history, they form an important part of the experience of doing a PhD. They form social networks around the intellectual pursuit of history. They can and do introduce new research techniques, as well as new insights based on people's research. They can challenge conventional assumptions. Above all, the IHR seminars are part of the lifeblood of the discipline and practice of history. The discipline is constantly changing and being renewed and challenged. Without the exchange of ideas and knowledge that happens at these seminars, historical research nationally and internationally would be very much the poorer.

## Tim Hitchcock

The seminars have three basic functions. First, they form a space in which a serious, long-form conversation about the past can take place, leading to the creation of a shared body of knowledge and a point of reference. Second, they both make generations of historical scholarship, and build bridges across generations. They are where postgraduate students have conversations with senior scholars and where they themselves hold the conversations that will shape the field for decades to come. And finally, they are an all-important social space that makes the quotidian job of historical research possible.

On the best of days, after long hours working through manuscripts in the archives, or struggling to turn evidence into argument on paper, that late afternoon journey to the IHR for a cup of tea and a seminar is what makes sense of it all. The beauty and the art of history lies in the depth of the historian's engagement with a single topic. Days, weeks, months and years are spent becoming ever more immersed. The seminars provide the context that makes sense of that journey. They allow micro-histories and meta-histories to confront one another; they encourage the political historian to listen to the cultural historian; and for them both to listen to the historians of race, emotions and the economy.

The IHR seminar programme is unique. There is no equivalent anywhere else in the world; and they are a prime factor in explaining why the historical profession in Britain is so dynamic, so productive and so important.

## Kate Wilcox

They're a central place for people from different departments, disciplines and sectors to come together to share ideas. They're important for the IHR as a showcase for the Institute across London, the UK and the world. They complement the library and other Institute functions. They are clearly valued by the people who attend them. They give an opportunity for people to make connections and be inspired by each other's research and feedback. Comments in the recent library survey showed a mixture of views: some people keen for the online format to continue and others desperate for them to return to in-person, either due to technological preferences or because they felt that the online format is lacking certain essential elements of a seminar. Making the seminars work for a hybrid audience will be important to meet both these needs.

## Ellen Smith and Rachel Bynoth

Seminars provide a forum for the development of academic relationships, fostering a sense of collegiality that was shown to be fragile during the recent COVID-19 crisis. Seminars form important steps in the research process, facilitating debate and critique. They reflect the spirit of research at particular moments in time and foreground new and ground-breaking projects. History Lab also pays acute attention to the needs of the postgraduate community, an especially vulnerable group as regards economic and social precarity. In this way, History Lab performs a vital function for aiding the collective wellbeing of those who participate, allowing them to navigate the isolation of PhD research.

Through the careful and considered curation of seminar programmes, convenors can spotlight particular voices or underrepresented scholars, and raise the profile of certain historiographical trends. Seminars do not simply reflect or respond to social or academic currents, rather, seminar committees, convenors, speakers and audiences can effect change and impact or shape the pathways of research and the ways this research is conducted through the seminars they hold.

Seminars require the time, effort and enthusiasm of individuals, generally PhD students. A collective sense of purpose is evident as post-graduates work for each other.

## Claire Langhamer

In an increasingly personalized world, the collectivist nature of the seminar matters. The seminar draws attention to the collaborative nature of historical practice and models a collegiality rooted in professional expertise. To be sure, seminars provide a vital space for the presentation of individual research as it is developing, and occasionally they might fail to engage or even descend into bickering. But their primary purpose is dialogue. A presentation is the starting point for discussion, not its conclusion; questions beget further questions; conversation spills out into the social spaces that follow. Writing and archival research can be solitary experiences framed by anxiety as well as delight; once research is published it has a life of its own. The seminar offers a space in between – a space where we can show our workings, try things out and, crucially, make mistakes. It allows us to engage with ideas as they are forming and to help push them forward. Seminars allow us to watch ideas in motion and communities in action; they matter because history is as much about dialogue as it is about findings.

# Afterword

## Natalie Thomlinson

I write this piece sitting in the IHR Common Room, empty apart from me but filled with the presence of all the historians past who have sat in this space, reading, thinking, talking; often enough, waiting for the appointed hour when the seminar that they have come to the Institute for will begin. It's a different place now even from when I first came to the IHR in 2009 as a postgraduate student on the now-defunct MA in Contemporary British History. I certainly miss the canteen, and the large presence of retired historians to be reliably found here, even if I cannot say that I always agreed with the political views I overheard; reading the essays in this collection has made me realize both how much the Institute and its seminar series have changed since they began in 1921, but also what has persisted.

Before I began reading, I had no idea that the seminars were first set up as a space for postgraduate education; of just how long some seminar series had been going on for; or for just how long in some of them what one might politely call the 'traditional' way of conducting affairs had persisted. (That said, some legends do get handed down; I had heard from my colleagues in the Modern British History Seminar all about F. M. L. Thompson's habit of ordering food for the entire table – it probably wouldn't go down so well today.) Some things have come full circle. The original function of the IHR as a place of postgraduate education has again been placed centre-stage with the development of the Postgraduate History Seminar and the History Lab Seminar (as detailed by Rohan McWilliam, and Ellen Smith and Rachel Bynoth respectively); many seminars also make an effort to have a termly slot in which postgraduate work can be showcased. Likewise, the key role that women played in the setting-up of the IHR was not evident from the way that the seminars came to operate by the mid-century. And yet, the thriving of the Women's History Seminar, and the fact that the last two directors of the Institute have been women, have placed women at the centre of things again – as the staircase at the IHR, now wonderfully decorated with photographs of London's female historians over the last century, serves to underline.

My own first encounter with IHR seminars came in 2009 at the Contemporary British History series held late on Wednesday afternoon, which those of us on the MA programme were encouraged to attend. I had a distinct sense of joining the grown-ups, of not being an undergraduate anymore (I seem to remember that the free wine was also something of a draw). I experienced the intellectual exchange of seminar culture for the first time, the vibrant trading of views noted by all the contributors to this book. An encounter at the Women's History Seminar later that year fundamentally changed the course of my proposed PhD; several years later, I was to give my first IHR seminar paper at the same series on my doctoral research on the Women's Liberation Movement. As I moved back to London after gaining an academic post at the University of Reading, I became involved in convening the Modern British History Seminar, as it then was; the attendance of myself and several other convenors at the Reconfiguring the British: Nation, Empire, World 1600–1990 Seminar led to the merging of those two series, headed by a notably younger group of convenors, part of the process of change and evolution illuminated by this volume. I found myself nodding with familiarity at comments about the different atmospheres of the different seminar series, though it must be said that I have never found any seminar to be anything other than friendly and supportive – perhaps illustrating the shift away from the more combative atmosphere of the past described by some of the contributors here. The traditions of conviviality at the pub have just about survived the COVID-19 pandemic; and it is perhaps that tradition of dinner and drinks afterwards, of discussing the paper and the ideas – and often enough, the state of higher education – that is the thing that all the seminar series have in common. Hopefully those last few seminars that have yet to come back in person after COVID-19 will be able to do so in some form soon. After all, our labours must have some reward!

A number of these essays – particularly Kelly Boyd's and Rohan McWilliam's – make clear that much has changed for the better in terms of the opening up of IHR seminars to both a wider range of topics and a wider audience. Indeed, the pioneering nature of particularly the Women's History and the Postgraduate History seminars in this respect can hardly be understated. I was struck by a sense of how much we owe these groups of historians and the work they undertook in opening up the discipline. Without wishing to indulge *too* much in whiggish notions of historical progress, it seems inevitable that the direction of travel for the IHR will be for it to continue opening up its seminars in different directions. As Ulrich Tiedau, Claire Langhamer and Kate Wilcox have all noted, the increasing emphasis on public outreach has led to a greater desire to engage with a wider range of historical practitioners, to think more broadly about who gets to be called an historian. Such moves are partly, but not wholly, the result of the Research Excellence Framework (REF) and its requirements to show the 'impact' of our research; we should note that the work of the History Workshop movement in bringing a much wider range of people into dialogue with professional academics considerably predated the advent of REF, and is surely an equally important part of this impulse to democratize the practice of the past.

As all the contributors have made clear, huge strides have been made in issues of gender representation in the Institute, but perhaps issues of race and ethnicity have somewhat lagged behind in terms of the consideration that has been given to them by convenors. The Black British History Seminar was instituted only in 2020, and the IHR is still a notably white space in what is one of the most ethnically diverse cities on earth. Like academia in general, seminar series also remain notably middle-class. We should not underestimate the very real structural barriers to participation in events such as IHR seminar series, though I don't doubt the commitment of many in the Institute to trying to overcome them (whether they can be overcome fully without profound changes in wider social structures seems doubtful). Online and hybrid seminars seem here to stay, despite the occasional faff of setting them up; the desire to be 'back in the room' and the recognition of the wider audience that a hybrid format enables sometimes rub up against each other, but the authors here all seem to recognize this as the future. Such a model also allows for a truly global range of speakers, in a way that surely could not have been predicted in Pollard's time; one of the highlights of the Britain at Home and Abroad seminar in 2022 was Chris Hilliard (University of Sydney) 'zooming' in at 4 a.m. from his home in Australia to deliver a truly excellent paper. That he wanted to do so despite being unable to partake in the usual post-seminar reward of dinner and drinks speaks to the still vastly important function of the seminar as a space to try out ideas and gain rigorous feedback. Now the Institute comes to people, as well as people to the Institute, and this shift will surely only increase the global reach of the IHR.

Inevitably, the Institute will keep changing, shifting, evolving in ways that we both can and can't foresee. The impact of COVID-19 in hastening the move to online and hybrid formats certainly couldn't have been predicted, and yet has had a profound impact on the way that the Institute operates. Who knows what will be around the corner next? (Not another pandemic, one hopes.) The wider trends of academic life, of higher education policy and the demands of REF, will undoubtedly shape the future of the Institute, as will broader social shifts. The strength of the IHR over the past hundred years has resided in its flexibility, and its ability to shape itself to the needs of the day; if the Institute is to continue for another hundred years, it is clearly these qualities that it must retain – aided by the presence of a committed staff and the wider support of its users and the historical profession at large. The IHR, is, after all, nothing without the people who make it; witness the outpouring of grief for Glen Jacques, the much-loved receptionist who died in 2022, and who did so much to make the Institute a friendly and welcoming place.

It is difficult to imagine history in the UK – and particularly in London – without the IHR and its seminars series. It's a place many of us have spent so much time, somewhere that's always there. Sometimes, perhaps, we take the place for granted – but how much poorer life would be without it! We can only hope that in another hundred years' time, another volume will be prepared to celebrate two hundred years of seminars, another century's worth of talk to be recorded, discussed, probed. Of course, none of us will be there to see it. But here's to the future – long live the IHR! And long live the seminar!

# Index

**A**

administration, of history departments, 12, 31, 45, 49–50, 64, 75–6, 102, 135–7, 139, 147, 159, 161, 182, 202, 237n8, 258

amateurism, of historians, 28, 94.
*See also* public history

**B**

British Broadcasting Corporation (BBC), 15, 45, 139, 141

British Library, Euston Rd, 106, 166

British Library, Great Russell St, 7, 99, 106, 166, 202, 244

British Museum, Great Russell St, 136, 202, 226

**C**

civil honours, of historians, 5, 21, 24–5, 163–5, 178, 237n18

civil servant, 18, 162, 204

Christianity, 15, 18–19, 49, 50, 80, 94, 184, 190, 229

colonialism, 15, 20, 45, 167, 176–86
decolonization, 176, 181, 183, 192

Communism, 26, 158, 160, 164, 186, 209–10, 214, 245
anticommunism, 26, 160, 203

convenors, of seminars,
Assael, Brenda, 212
Bauer, Stefan, 44
Beer, Esmond de, 93, 137
Bellot, Hugh, 118, 121, 128n5–6, 136, 33n10
Bindoff, Stanley, 101, 109n3, 138, 140, 150n14, 161
Bivar, Venus, 167
Boyd, Kelly, 6, 203, 209, 212, 217n15, 223–42
Broch, Ludivine, 167
Brown, Alison, 45, 49, 52, 59n4, n12
Burns, Arthur, 124, 193n*
Bynoth, Rachel, 6, 243–65
Carrol, Alison, 167
Carus-Wilson, Eleanora, 64
Champion, Justin, 36n67, 73, 94, 101, 104, 109n11
Christie, Ian, 118, 121–3, 245
Clarke, Georgia, 49
Claydon, Tony, 212
Cobban, Alfred, 158–64
Colley, Linda, 191
Connolly, James, 167

Cook, Hera, 212, 230

Corfield, Penelope, 2, 6, 65–6, 75, 115–33, 212, 227, 230, 237n18, 238n20, n23

Cozens, Joe, 124

D'Amico, Geraldine, 165, 167, 171n34

Davin, Anna, 205, 209, 225, 230, 236n1

Davis, Eliza, 21–2, 35n37

Dean, Trevor, 4, 43–61

Delap, Lucy, 230, 238n26

Dickens, Arthur, 34n29, 98, 109n3, 110n17. *See also* IHR, director

Dinwiddy, John, 123–4, 129n25, 245

Dodwell, Henry, 21

Drayton, Richard, 80, 84n50, 85n57, 188, 191, 193n2

Duke, Alastair, 146–7, 151n17, 152n53

Earle, Peter, 65–7, 82n15

Epstein, Stefan ('Larry'), 49, 66, 77

Erickson, Amy, 33n6, 230, 238n27

Esser, Raingard, 147

Evans, Tanya, 212–13

Faucher, Charlotte, 167, 169n2

Ferente, Serena, 44, 49, 56

Finn, Margot, 124, 239n30

Fisher, Jack, 63–6, 68, 74–5, 185

Fletcher, Tim, 212

Gerson, Renée, 146–7

Geyl, Pieter, 135–9, 141, 143, 145

Gibbs, Graham, 144, 147

Gilbert, Lesley, 147

Goldgar, Anne 128n4, 147

Goodrich, Amanda, 124

Gowing, Laura, 230, 238n27

Graham, Gerald (Gerry), 180–88

Gray, Louise, 212

Green, Toby, 192

Greig, Hannah, 212, 213–14

Gretton, Tom, 165

Hall, Catherine, 190, 228–9, 234, 239n31

Hamilton, Marybeth, 210, 217n21, 230, 238n26

Harcourt, Freda, 188–9

Harding, Vanessa, 65–6, 73, 77, 83n35

Harlow, Vincent, 178–81

Harris, Alana, 230, 238n24

Harte, Negley, 65–6, 74

Harvey, Karen, 117, 128n3, 212

Hatton, Ragnhild, 140, 142–4, 151n26–8

Henderson, Tony, 212, 218n30

Hitchcock, Tim, 6, 124, 129n9, 208, 212, 214, 216n12–13, 243–65

271

272 INDEX

convenors, of seminars, (*continued*)
Hobsbawm, Eric, 26–7, 36n53–6, 209, 217n18
Holloway, Sally, 124
Hoppit, Julian, 66, 69, 71, 83n25, n32, 124
Hurstfield, Joel, 92, 109n3
Irigoin, Alejandra, 66, 72, 80
Israel, Jonathan, 146–8
Jackson, Julian, 167
James, Leslie, 191
Jennings, Jeremy, 167
Johnson, Douglas, 163–4, 166
Johnstone, Hilda, 21, 35n37
Jones, Colin, 167
Kaplan, Benjamin, 147, 152n48
Keen, Catherine, 44
Kelly, Debra, 167
Killingray, David, 188–9
Knowles, Lilian, 13, 21
Kossmann, Ernst, 143–6, 150n15
Langhamer, Claire, 6, 230, 238n27, 243–65. *See also* IHR, director
Lantschner, Patrick, 44
Latham, Robert, 93, 96, 97–8, 104, 109n8, 185
Latham, Simon, 191
Lee, Daniel, 167
Leuchter, Tyson, 167
Lloyd, Sarah, 124
Lockyer, Roger, 93–4, 97, 104, 109n9
Lowe, Kate, 4, 43–61
Mangion, Carmen, 230, 238n27
Marshall, Peter James, 187–90, 192
Martin, Eveline, 176–7, 179–80
McClive, Cathy, 212
McGregor, Oliver, 26
McWilliam, Rohan, 201–21, 228
Meldrum, Tim, 212
Metcalf, George, 180, 188
Mettam, Roger, 3, 162, 165–6, 205, 212
Midgley, Clare, 204–5, 208, 216n5, n7, 230, 238n24
Miller, John, 94–6, 101, 104, 109n10
Moore, Stuart, 147
Motadel, David, 191
Murphy, Anne, 72
Murphy, Philip, 259
Namier, Lewis, 24, 26–7, 36n52, 121–2, 125, 128n11, n14–15, 129n18, 141–2
Neale, John, 19, 23–5, 28, 92
Nelson, Janet (Jinty), 166, 205, 227, 230, 237n18
Newton, Arthur, 137, 176–8, 182, 184, 194n16
Nicholls, Julia, 167
Nix, Jonathan, 212

Oliver, Roland, 185–6, 195n64–5, 196n67–8
Ormrod, David, 6, 63–90
Parsloe, Guy, 9n2, 121, 128n7–8
Peacey, Jason, 6, 91–113
Penson, Lillian, 5, 21, 177, 184, 193n12
Pilbeam, Pamela, 6, 157–74
Ploszajska, Theresa, 212
Pollard, Albert, 8, 9n6, 14–15, 19–20, 22, 33n11, 34n13, n27, 63, 92, 136, 149, 150n9 177, 269. *See also* IHR, director
Pollmann, Judith, 147
Porter, Andrew, 188–9
Powell, I. G., 93
Power, Eileen, 13, 23, 28, 33n8, 35n46, 63–4, 81
Priest, Robert, 167
Prochaska, Alice, 6, 122, 129n19–20, 203, 228, 243–65
Quinault, Roland, 204
Ranke, Leopold von, 12
Rebecchini, Guido, 44
Reese, Trevor, 188
Renier, Gustaaf, 137, 139–44
Robbins, Caroline, 22, 35n43
Robert, Krisztina, 230, 238n27
Roseveare, Henry, 93–5, 104
Roy, Ian, 93–7, 99, 101, 104, 107
Rubinstein, Nicolai, 6, 43–61
Ruddock, Alwyn, 64
Russell, Conrad, 27–8, 36n57–8, n62, 92, 96
Ryan, Deborah, 212
Ryan, James, 212–13
Schwartz, Laura, 230, 238n27
Shore, Heather, 212
Smith, Andrew, 167
Smith, Ellen, 6, 243–65
Sood, Gavin, 191
Spang, Rebecca, 165, 167
Stephenson, Judy, 66, 74
Stockwell, Sarah, 6, 175–200
Sturgis, Jim, 188–9
Sutcliffe, Adam, 212
Sutherland, Nicola, 162, 165, 171n32
Swart, Koen, 145–7, 149
Sykes, Norman, 93, 109n6
Tawney, Richard, 63–4, 67–8, 75, 81, 82n1, n16, 84n55, 157
Thane, Pat, 204, 207–8, 237n18
Thomlinson, Natalie, 6, 267–70
Thompson, Michael, 19, 34n29, 150n5, 203–5, 213, 228, 246, 267. *See also* IHR, director
Thomson, Mark, 118, 121, 128n9
Tiedau, Ulrich, 6, 135–56, 168

INDEX 273

Tout, Thomas, 13–14, 21, 33n9
Toynbee, Arnold, 20–21, 139, 141, 151n18
Tunçer, Coşkun, 66, 72
Usborne, Cornelie, 227, 230, 237n14
Vaucher, Paul, 157–8, 161, 169n4
Vickery, Amanda, 205, 211, 216n7, 228–9, 234, 238n20, 239n31
Wagner, Kim, 191
Wallis, Patrick, 66, 74, 77
Warde, Paul, 66, 69–70, 77, 83n27
Williams, Glyndwr, 180–81, 188–9, 192, 194n26, n29
Williamson, Gillian, 124
Wilson, Jon, 191
Wright, Alison, 49, 53, 57
Zahedieh, Nuala, 66, 71–2, 83n30–31
Zeitlin, Jonathan, 204
Coronavirus (COVID-19), 2, 105, 135, 147, 167, 239n30, 247–9, 255–7, 261, 264, 268–9

**D**

death, of historians, 2–3, 52, 54, 59n15, 63, 109n8–9, n11, 110n14–15, n20, 124, 129n22, 145, 169n1, 193n*, 270
dinner and drink, 7, 18, 22–3, 28, 57, 65, 81, 82n9, 96, 109n13, 116, 120, 146, 160, 165, 188–9, 204, 208, 226, 232–3, 239n29, 251, 256, 160, 189, 267–9. *See also* pubs and restaurants
coffee and/or tea, 4, 74, 202, 208, 263. *See also* IHR common room

**E**

employment, of historians,14, 20–22, 30–31, 54, 76, 118, 122, 139, 157, 160, 163, 170n23, 201–2, 206–8, 211, 214, 225–6, 229, 233, 249
ethnicity, of historians, 20–21, 23–4, 26, 44, 46, 49, 56, 66, 71, 99, 100–11, 127, 135–46, 157–8, 160–67, 170n23, 178–90, 208, 226, 229, 234, 244–5, 247, 256

**F**

Fabian Society, 26, 157–8, 229
feminism, 6, 22, 28, 116–17, 211, 216n5, 223–7, 229, 234, 236n1–7, 237n7–12, 238n23–7
antifeminism, 22, 229
First World War, 135, 139, 157, 177
friendship, amongst historians, 6, 28, 51–2, 54, 57, 100–101, 105, 107, 109n13, 118, 142, 148, 160–64, 188, 208, 227, 232, 244–6, 254, 255–6, 268, 270

**G**

genealogy, of historians, 27, 46, 65, 103, 160–61, 180, 182–3, 202, 208, 238n20

**H**

historiography
cultural history, 7, 48, 50–51, 74–6, 79, 104, 124–6, 145, 148, 179, 201, 210–14, 261, 264
digital history, 4, 76, 125, 129n29, 150n7, 148, 214, 216n12, 262
gender history, 33n6–8, 35n35, 75, 104, 126, 148, 190, 206, 209–11, 214, 223–42, 256, 262
*Promoting Gender Equality in UK History* (2018), 229
global history, 6, 20, 71–2, 76–7, 80–81, 127, 140, 142–3, 176, 190–91, 245, 258–9
history of sexuality, 51, 206, 210–11, 223, 233–4, 237n15, 238n24, n26, 256
political history, 12–13, 19, 23–9, 32, 44–50, 63, 71, 93–4, 97–8, 104, 118, 121–4, 148, 158, 160–61, 168, 204, 209, 211–13, 223, 231, 234, 255–6, 261–2, 264
public history, 9n5, 32, 35n35, 36n63, n67, 109n11, 166, 193n2, 213, 223, 251, 261
religious history, 15, 18–19, 48–50, 94, 98, 145, 184, 190, 192, 229
social and economic history, 6, 21, 27, 48–50, 63–90, 94, 104, 121, 124–6, 139, 145, 148, 157–8, 160, 163, 179, 191, 201, 209–14, 223–6, 228–9, 261. *See also* Communism

**I**

Institut Français du Royaume-Uni (IFRU), Queensberry Pl., 157, 164–7
Institute of Commonwealth Studies, 186, 188
Institute of Historical Research (IHR)
common room, 4–5, 187, 202, 204, 207–8, 226–8, 232–3, 244–6, 267
director, 8, 19, 33n1, 34n29, 75–6, 84n45, 98, 142, 150n12, 203, 213, 228, 230, 238n27, 243–4, 246, 248–50, 257–9, 261–3, 265, 267
librarian, 23, 118, 122, 138, 181, 203, 228, 243, 245, 247, 252
receptionist, 247, 270
secretary, 118, 122, 128n8, 203, 243, 245
temporary building, Malet St, 16–17, 136
witness seminars, 204–5, 216n4, 245, 259

274   INDEX

internationalism, 6–7, 15, 19–21, 23, 26,
  57–8, 103, 107, 127, 140, 142–3, 145–6,
  157, 165–7, 178–9, 181–2, 186, 216n7,
  226, 234, 237n18, 245, 250–51, 255,
  258, 263. *See also* universities

## J

journalism, 18, 139, 151n19, 163, 216n9,
  245, 255, 259
Judaism, 23–4, 26, 49, 143, 151n32, 164
  antisemitism, 24

## L

learned societies, 13–15, 19, 26, 65–6,
  72–3, 75–6, 118, 127, 159–60, 178, 183,
  186, 206, 209, 213, 225–7, 229, 237n7,
  n11–12, n18, 238n28, 259, 268–9
lectures, 14, 23, 27, 31, 36n63, 64, 84n55,
  119, 121, 135, 158, 166, 171n37, 190,
  193n2, 251–2

## M

marriage, of historians, 28, 44, 46, 49, 57,
  123, 142–3, 160–61, 163, 169n6, 185,
  188, 236n4, 245
  'Miss', 22, 25, 93, 96–7
  'Mrs', 97, 101, 224, 229
  same-sex marriage, 109n9
memories, of historians, 1–3, 6–7, 23, 43,
  47, 52–8, 77, 92, 101, 117, 126, 141, 144
  161, 166, 184, 186, 189, 193n*, 201,
  214, 236n*, 245, 257

## N

nationalism, 14–15, 138–9, 145, 181–4,
  192, 250
nationality, of historians. *See ethnicity*
networking, 7, 52, 106, 116, 118, 127, 148,
  168, 182, 186, 190, 207, 213, 215, 229,
  231–3, 248, 250, 252, 255, 263

## P

parenting, by historians, 191, 208,
  230–31, 233–4, 238n25, 239n30
politicians, 15, 24, 97, 122, 144, 163, 201–2,
  204–5, 212, 214, 216n4, 223, 228,
  245–6, 259
politics, of historians, 11–12, 19, 22–31,
  97, 121, 125, 139, 144, 158, 160, 163–6,
  169n9, 186, 201–6, 212–13, 216n1, 223,
  227–8, 267. *See also* Communism and
  feminism
postgraduate, 3–4, 6, 13–15, 18–23, 26–30,
  44–8, 53–5, 64–5, 91, 93–4, 96–103,
  106–7, 116–20, 122–4, 136–7, 139–40,
  143–5, 158, 160–63, 176–80, 182, 184,

187, 189, 201–18, 226, 228, 230–31,
  243–4, 246, 248–9, 251–3, 256–8,
  260–61, 263–5, 267–8
professoriate, 12–15, 20–21, 23–8, 45–6,
  48, 51, 53, 93, 97, 99, 116–17, 122–3,
  135–8, 141–3, 147–8, 157–9, 161–3,
  165–6, 175, 178–9, 180, 183, 188–9,
  210, 212–13, 225–6, 230, 237n14, n18,
  238n20, n24, n26–7, 234, 251
pubs and restaurants
  Dee's, off Boswell St, 208
  Garibaldi's, off Farringdon Rd, 26
  [Giardinetto?], Charlotte St, 96
  Kwai's, Tottenham Court Rd, 159
  Museum Tavern, Great Russell St, 57
  Neel Kamal, Charlotte St, 82n9
  Olivelli's, Store St, 188
  Pizza Express, Wardour St, 57
  Royal Academy of Dramatic Art
    (RADA), Malet St, 57
  Schmidt's, Charlotte St, 159, 170n17
  Skinners' Arms, Judd St, 96, 109n3
  Spaghetti House, Goodge St, 159
  Students' Union Bar, Birkbeck, 188
  Students' Union Bar, SOAS, 208
  The Jack Horner [aka the Fuller's pub],
    Tottenham Court Rd, 96
  The Life Goddess, Store St, 57
  Trattoria Mondello, Goodge St, 96
  University Tavern [now the College
    Arms], Store St, 57, 65
Public Record Office (PRO), Chancery
  Lane, 99, 181, 245
public service, by historians, 7, 11–12, 15,
  20, 45, 118, 127, 141, 145, 157, 178, 180,
  202. *See also* learned societies and
  employment

## R

religion, of historians. *See* Christianity
  and/or Judaism

## S

Second World War, 26, 45, 93, 118, 139,
  141–3, 175, 178, 213, 233–4
  Nazi concentration camps, 136, 143,
    234
  Nuremberg Trials, 145
seminar
  conventions, 31, 47, 50, 53, 56, 116,
    119–20, 180, 226, 232, 252, 165
  convenors. *See* convenors, of
    seminars
  culture, beyond the IHR, 12–15, 18,
    21–2, 24, 26, 28, 44, 53, 54, 118, 122,
    138–9, 178–9, 181, 189, 225, 238n28,
    245, 251

INDEX   275

experiences, 28, 56, 95–6, 102, 116, 122, 140, 146, 180–81, 187, 243–65
online. *See* webinar
papers, 4, 22, 29, 31, 43, 45–51, 54–7, 66, 68–75, 77–8, 80, 92, 94, 96, 101–7 115–17, 119–20, 122–3, 126–7, 140, 147–8, 159, 164–8, 181, 184, 190–91, 193n*, 202, 205–6, 208–10, 212–15, 226–34, 244–9, 251, 253–6, 260–63, 265, 268–9
questions, 4, 22, 31, 50, 53–4, 102, 115–17, 119–20, 140, 181, 190, 203, 232, 237n13, 246–7, 253–4, 260–61, 265
rooms, 16–17, 23, 25, 31, 56, 136–7, 150n7, 159, 164, 180, 202, 205, 210, 230, 245, 247
Senate House, University of London, Malet St, 24, 203, 229, 248
sociability, of historians. *See* dinner anddrink, friendship, pubs and restaurants
smoking, 7, 26–7, 119, 140, 180, 226
social media, 119, 169n8, 232, 235, 248, 257

**T**

teaching, 1–2, 4, 7, 11–41, 45–6, 48, 55, 64–5, 76, 94, 98–100, 103–4, 106–7, 117, 136–9, 142, 145, 147, 157–62, 163, 176–9, 180, 182–6, 189, 191, 192, 202, 206–8, 210–213, 226, 231, 236n4, 244, 247, 250–51, 253, 255
technology, in seminars, 31, 121, 140, 148, 232, 247, 251–3. *See also* webinars

**U**

undergraduate, 3, 12–14, 23, 26, 29–31, 64, 76, 98–9, 137, 143, 158–9, 162, 170n17, 225–6, 231, 252, 267
third-year special subject, 12–13, 30, 64, 159, 162
universities, other than London
Adelaide, Australia, 160
British Columbia, Canada, 161
Bureau of Empire, 178
Cambridge, UK, 12–13, 21, 26, 28–9, 44, 46, 48, 54, 66, 68–9, 72–3, 93–4, 98, 102–3, 122, 146, 148, 158, 160, 162, 175–6, 180, 182, 187, 189, 191, 210, 230
California, USA, 46, 93, 99, 189, 251
Cardiff, UK 98, 244
Calcutta, India, 178
Chicago, USA, 158
Concordia, Canada, 160
Dalhousie, Canada, 182

East Anglia, UK 66, 243
Edinburgh, UK 66, 137
Friedrich-Wilhelms / Humboldt, Germany, 53
Ghana, Ghana, 183
Glasgow, UK, 244
Harvard, USA, 13, 99, 147, 163, 180, 183, 208
Hertfordshire, UK, 66, 124, 210, 213
Ibadan, Nigeria, 177, 182–4
Ife [Obafemi Awolowo], Nigeria, 183
Khartoum, Sudan, 183
Königsberg [defunct], formerly Germany, 12
La Trobe, Australia, 46, 100
Lausanne, Switzerland, 121
Leicester, UK, 68, 243
Leiden, Netherlands, 143
Manchester, UK, 12, 21, 24, 30, 98–9, 118
Massey, New Zealand, 107
Makerere, Uganda, 183, 185
Melbourne, Australia, 99, 100
New Brunswick, Canada, 182
Oxford, UK, 12–14, 21–4, 27, 29, 44–6, 48, 54, 66, 68, 93–4, 98, 102, 122, 137, 144, 146–8, 159–60, 163, 175, 177–9, 181–2, 184, 189, 191, 208, 228, 243–5, 251
Paris, France, 27, 163, 166–7
Princeton, USA, 46, 100, 147
Punjab, India, 178
Queen's, Belfast, UK, 158
Queen's, Ontario, Canada, 180
Rochester, USA, 178
Rutgers, USA, 208–9, 226
Sheffield, UK, 102, 129n29, 216n12, 247
Sheffield Hallem, UK, 216n7, 230, 238
Trinity College, Dublin, Ireland, 21
Southampton, UK, 99, 144, 147, 178
Sussex, UK, 124, 129n29, 164, 202, 209, 213, 243, 249
Sydney, Australia, 269
Toronto, Canada, 93, 103, 162
Yale, USA, 98–100, 129n24
York, Toronto, Canada, 107, 162

**W**

webinars, 31, 81, 105, 115, 120, 129, 135, 147, 167, 233–5, 248–9, 252, 255–7, 260, 264, 269
women historians, 21–3, 28, 35n35, 47, 52, 65–6, 76, 84n42, 143–4, 162–3, 177, 192, 202–3, 208, 210, 223–39, 267

Printed in the USA
CPSIA information can be obtained
at www.ICGtesting.com
CBHW051305231024
16204CB00028B/10